THE CHURCH AT PRAYER

THE CHURCH AT PRAYER
Introduction to the Liturgy
New Edition

THE CHURCH AT PRAYER

An Introduction to the Liturgy

New Edition

Edited by Aimé Georges Martimort
with the Collaboration of R. Cabié, I. H. Dalmais,
J. Evenou, P. M. Gy, P. Jounel, A. Nocent, and D. Sicard

Volume IV

THE LITURGY AND TIME

by

Irénée Henri Dalmais, Pierre Jounel,
and Aimé Georges Martimort

Translated by Matthew J. O'Connell

THE LITURGICAL PRESS
Collegeville, Minnesota

Cover design by Donald A. Molloy

THE CHURCH AT PRAYER—VOLUME IV: THE LITURGY AND TIME is the author-
ized English translation of *L'Eglise en Prière: La Liturgie et le Temps,* published by Desclée,
Paris-Tournai, 1983.

Nihil obstat: Rev. Robert C. Harren, J.C.L., *Censor deputatus.*

Imprimatur: +George H. Speltz, D.D., Bishop of St. Cloud. November 21, 1985.

Excerpts from the English translation of *The Roman Missal* © 1973, 1985, International
Committee on English in the Liturgy, Inc. (ICEL); excerpts from the English translation of
The Liturgy of the Hours © 1974, ICEL; excerpts from the English translation of General
Norms for the Liturgical Year and the Calendar (1969), the General Instruction of the Liturgy of the Hours (1974), and the General Instruction of the Roman Missal (1975) from *Documents on the Liturgy 1963–1979: Curial, Papal, and Conciliar Texts* © 1982, ICEL. All rights
reserved.

Library of Congress Cataloging-in-Publication Data

Eglise en prière. English.

    The Church at prayer.

    Translation of: L'Eglise en prière.

    Includes bibliographies and index.

    Contents: —v. 4. Liturgy and time.

    1. Catholic Church—Liturgy—Collected works.

I. Martimort, Aimé Georges. II. Title.

BX1970.E313   1985   264'.02   85-24174

ISBN 0-8146-1366-7 (v. 4)

Contents

Contributors to Volume IV

Irénée Henri Dalmais, O.P., *Professor of the Institut Supérieur de Liturgie in Paris*

Pierre Jounel, *Honorary Professor in the Institut Catholique of Paris, Consultor of the Congregation for Divine Worship*

Aimé Georges Martimort, *Honorary Dean of the Faculty of Theology in Toulouse, Consultor of the Congregation for Divine Worship*

Preface

The third French edition of the present work was published in 1965, less than two years after the promulgation of the Constitution on the Liturgy of Vatican II. It was clear, of course, that this solemn document was but the starting point of a work of restoration and reform which could be carried out only gradually.

Now, twenty years after the Constitution *Sacrosanctum Concilium*, the reform of the liturgy is virtually complete. A task of immense scope, unparalleled in the history of the Church, brought bishops and liturgists together from all over the world, first in the Council for the Implementation of the Constitution on the Sacred Liturgy (1964–69) and then in the Congregation for Divine Worship (1969–75). The problems which the contemporary world and its culture (or, rather, its varied cultures) raise for the prayer of the Church were pointed out with great clarity by the Council, which also enunciated the principles to be followed in solving them. The application of these principles, however, led to a revision of perspectives and to decisions that we could not have clearly anticipated in 1965.

The new liturgical books take, in fact, a new approach to the act of celebrating: they always begin with instructions or introductions which are quite different in character from the rubrics of old, since they include doctrinal and spiritual guidelines, the pastoral aspect, and possible ways of adapting the rites in question.

This bold new approach would not have been possible without the work done, especially in the twentieth century, by the historians of liturgy and the theologians. *The Church at Prayer* was an attempt at a summary assessment of all that labor. But, far from putting an end to research, the liturgical reform gave it a new stimulus, because it raised new problems or called for a more profound and scholarly grasp of the tradition. Moreover, it was no longer only isolated pioneers, as in the days of Duchesne and Batiffol, Baumstark and Andrieu, who ventured into this field. On the contrary, teams now meet periodically, as at the Semaines de Saint-Serge, and liturgical schools train students (the Liturgical Institutes of Paris and of San Anselmo in Rome have celebrated the twentieth anniversary of their foundation).

Scholars have been devoting their efforts especially to the prehistory of the Christian liturgy: to its beginnings and its relation to Jewish prayer. In addition, the comparative method initially developed by Baumstark has given a splendid impulse to the study of the Eastern and Western liturgies. It is no longer possible to reconstruct the history of the Roman liturgy without locating it in this broader framework. That same larger perspective is indispensable especially for answering doctrinal questions about the sacraments and for resolving the sensitive problem of adaptation to local Churches, as well as for inspiring the creative responses which adaptation calls for. The controversies to which the liturgical reform has given rise in various places are to be explained by an ignorance of the tradition and of the diversity it allows.

For all these reasons it has not been possible simply to correct and reprint *The Church at Prayer*. An entirely new edition is called for that will, on the one hand, highlight the spiritual and pastoral directions taken in the liturgical reform with which the name of Pope Paul VI will be permanently linked, and that will, on the other, set forth more fully than in earlier editions what we know of the varied expressions which the Church has given to its prayer according to historical and geographical circumstances.

Several of the men and women who contributed to earlier editions have since departed for the heavenly liturgy: Dom Bernard Capelle (1961), Noële Maurice Denis-Boulet (1969), Dom Bernard Botte (1980), Mgr. Pierre Salmon (1982). Others have had to resign from the work because of other commitments or for reasons of health. Madame Boulet has been replaced by Robert Cabié, my successor as professor of liturgy on the Faculty of Theology in Toulouse. Two other new contributors will likewise add their talents to the team: Canon Damien Sicard, Secretary of the Provence-Méditerranée Apostolic Region and author of an important study of the liturgy of death; and Jean Evenou, of the diocese of Vannes, editor of *La Maison-Dieu*.

In keeping with the procedure adopted earlier for *L'Introduction à la Bible*, we shall publish separately each of the four parts of this new edition of *The Church at Prayer*. For pragmatic reasons we begin the publication with Volume IV, *The Liturgy and Time*. Fr. Irénée Henri Dalmais expands the introductory essay on "Time in the Liturgy" which he contributed to the previous editions. Mgr. Pierre Jounel, in addition to the chapters for which he had previously been responsible, has here taken over those which in past editions were written by Canon Antoine Chavasse and Dom Bernard Capelle. Finally, the reader will not be surprised that since I myself was in charge, in the days of the *Consilium*, of the various task forces responsible for the reform of the Breviary, I have here taken the place of the late lamented Mgr. Salmon for the section on the Liturgy of the Hours.

Finally, let me mention once again the limits of this work; they are the same as those mentioned in 1961 in the very first French edition of the work. Readers will not find here a complete exposition that includes the entire content of the instructions and introductions to the new liturgical books, any more than they would have found in earlier editions of *The Church at Prayer* a complete course in rubrics. For that kind of information they must seek out the practical instruction that is given to students in institutions of priestly formation.

In addition, the contributors always suppose that their readers have at hand at least the main liturgical texts now in use. We urge them to be constantly rereading these texts and, even more, to discover the meaning of the rites by participating in them. It is by meditating on the texts, those now in use and those of the past, and by participating as fervently as possible in the liturgical celebration, that we will be able to enter with understanding into the mysteries of the praying Church, in which Christ himself is present and active.

Aimé Georges Martimort

Abbreviations

Gen	Genesis	Dan	Daniel
Exod	Exodus	Ezra	Ezra
Lev	Leviticus	Neh	Nehemiah
Num	Numbers	1-2 Chr	1-2 Chronicles
Deut	Deuteronomy	Bar	Baruch
Josh	Joshua	Jdt	Judith
Judg	Judges	1-2 Mac	1-2 Maccabees
1-2 Sam	1 and 2 Samuel	Sir	Sirach
1-2 Kgs	1 and 2 Kings	Tob	Tobit
Isa	Isaiah	Wis	Wisdom
Jer	Jeremiah	Matt	Matthew
Ezek	Ezekiel	Mark	Mark
Hos	Hosea	Luke	Luke
Joel	Joel	John	John
Amos	Amos	Acts	Acts of the Apostles
Obad	Obadiah	Rom	Romans
Jonah	Jonah	1-2 Cor	1-2 Corinthians
Mic	Micah	Gal	Galatians
Nah	Nahum	Eph	Ephesians
Hab	Habakkuk	Phil	Philippians
Zeph	Zephaniah	Col	Colossians
Hag	Haggai	1-2 Thess	1-2 Thessalonians
Zech	Zechariah	1-2 Tim	1-2 Timothy
Mal	Malachi	Titus	Titus
Ps (Pss)	Psalm(s)	Phlm	Philemon
Job	Job	Heb	Hebrews
Prov	Proverbs	Jas	James
Ruth	Ruth	1-2 Pet	1-2 Peter
Cant	Canticle of Canticles	1-3 John	1-3 John
Eccl	Ecclesiastes	Jude	Jude
Lam	Lamentations	Rev	Revelation
Esth	Esther		

WORKS MOST FREQUENTLY CITED

AAS	*Acta Apostolicae Sedis* (Rome, then Vatican City, 1909ff.)
Acta sanctorum	*Acta sanctorum collecta . . . a Sociis Bollandianis* (3rd ed.; Paris: Palmé, 1861ff.; then Brussels: Bollandistes).
ALW	*Archiv für Liturgiewissenschaft* (Regensburg: F. Pustet, 1950ff.).
Andrieu, OR	M. Andrieu, *Les Ordines Romani du haut moyen âge* (5 vols. Spicilegium Sacrum Lovaniense 11, 23, 24, 28, 29; Louvain: Spicilegium, 1931ff.) A sixth volume is in preparation.
Andrieu, PR	M. Andrieu, *Le pontifical romain au moyen âge* (4 vols. Studi e Testi 86, 87, 88, 99; Vatican City, 1938–41).
Brightman	F. E. Brightman, *Liturgies Eastern and Western* I. *Eastern Liturgies* (Oxford: Clarendon Press, 1896). Only Volume I was published.
CCL	Corpus Christianorum collectum a monachis O.S.B. abbatiae S. Petri in Steenbrugge, Series Latina (Turnhout: Brepols, 1954ff.).
CECSL	Consilium ad exsequendam Constitutionem de sacra Liturgia (Council for the Implementation of the Constitution on the Sacred Liturgy).
CSCO	Corpus scriptorum christianorum orientalium editum consilio Universitatis Catholicae Americae et Universitatis Catholicae Lovaniensis (Louvain, 1903ff.).
CSEL	Corpus scriptorum ecclesiasticorum Latinorum editum consilio et impensis Academiae litterarum . . . Vindobonensis (Vienna: Tempsky, 1866ff.).
DACL	*Dictionnaire d'archéologie chrétienne et de liturgie*, edited by F. Cabrol, H. Leclercq [and H. Marrou] (Paris: Letouzey et Ané, 1907–53).
DBS	Dictionnaire de la Bible: Supplement (Paris, 1928ff.).
Denz	H. Denzinger, *Ritus orientalium . . . in administrandis sacramentis . . .* (2 vols. Würzburg: Stahel, 1863; repr., Graz: Akademische Druck, 1961).
DS	*Enchiridion symbolorum, definitionum et declarationum de rebus fidei et morum*, edited by H. Denzinger. 32nd ed. by A. Schönmetzer (Barcelona: Herder, 1963).
EDIL	*Enchiridion documentorum instaurationis liturgicae* I. *1963–1973* (Turin: Marietti, 1976).
EL	*Ephemerides liturgicae* (Rome: Edizioni liturgiche, 1887ff.). For years with two series the references are to the series *Analecta ascetico-historicae*, without this being expressly stated.
Fabre-Duchesne	P. Fabre and L. Duchesne, *Le Liber censuum de l'Eglise romaine* (3 vols. Fontemoing: E. de Boccard, 1910–52).
GCS	Die griechischen christlichen Schriftsteller der ersten Jahrhunderte, edited by the German Academy of Sciences in Berlin (Berlin: Akademie Verlag, 1897ff.).

Ge	Old Gelasian Sacramentary = Ms. Reginen. Lat. 316 in the Vatican Library, ed. L. K. Mohlberg, P. Siffrin, and L. Eizenhöfer, *Liber sacramentorum Romanae aeclesiae ordinis anni circuli* (REDMF 4; Rome: Herder, 1960).
Gell	Sacramentaire de Gellone, Paris, Bibl. Nat., ms. lat. 12048. —Ed. A. Dumas (CCL 159; Turnhout: Brepols, 1981).
GILH	*General Instruction of the Liturgy of the Hours*, trans. in *Documents on the Liturgy 1963-1979: Conciliar, Papal, and Curial Texts* (Collegeville, Minn.: The Liturgical Press, 1982).
GIRM	*General Instruction of the Roman Missal*, trans. in *Documents on the Liturgy 1963-1979: Conciliar, Papal, and Curial Texts* (Collegeville, Minn.: The Liturgical Press, 1982).
GNLYC	*General Norms for the Liturgical Year and the Calendar*, trans. in *Documents on the Liturgy 1963-1979: Conciliar, Papal, and Curial Texts* (Collegeville, Minn.: The Liturgical Press, 1982).
Gr	Gregorian Sacramentary, ed. J. Deshusses (Spicilegium Friburgense 16; Freiburg: Universitätsverlag, 1971).
Hänggi-Pahl	A. Hänggi and I. Pahl, *Prex eucharistica. Textus e variis liturgiis antiquioribus selecti* (Spicilegium Friburgense 12; Freiburg: Universitätsverlag, 1968).
HBS	Henry Bradshaw Society for Editing Rare Liturgical Texts. London, 1891ff.
JLW	*Jahrbuch für Liturgiewissenschaft*, ed. O. Casel (Münster: Aschendorff, 1921-41).
JTS	*Journal of Theological Studies* (London: Macmillan, and then Oxford: Clarendon Press, 1900ff.).
Le	The sacramentary formerly known as the Leonine Sacramentary. Manuscript of Verona, Bibl. Capitolare, LXXXV [80]. —Ed. L. K. Mohlberg, L. Eizenhöfer, and P. Siffrin, *Sacramentarium Veronense* (REDMF 1; Rome: Herder, 1955-56).
LMD	*La Maison-Dieu. Revue de pastorale liturgique* (Paris: Cerf, 1945ff.).
LO	*Lex orandi* (Paris: Cerf, 1944-70).
LQF	Liturgiegeschichtliche (later Liturgiewissenschaftliche) Quellen und Forschungen (Münster: Aschendorff, 1919ff.).
LXX	The Septuagint. —Ed. A. Rahlfs, *Septuaginta id est Vetus Testamentum graece iuxta LXX interpretes* (3rd ed.; Stuttgart: Württembergische Bibelanstalt, 1935).
Mansi	J. D. Mansi, *Sacrorum conciliorum nova et amplissima collectio* (31 vols.; Florence-Venice, 1757-98. Reprint and continuation, vols. 1-53; Paris, Leipzig, and Arnheim, 1901-27).
Martène	E. Martène, *De antiquis Ecclesiae ritibus*. (References to the various editions are given in A. G. Martimort, *La docu-*

	mentation liturgique de dom Edmond Martène [ST 279; Vatican City, 1978].)
MGH	Monumenta Germaniae historica (Hannover: Hahn, and Berlin: Weidmann, 1826ff.).
MTZ	*Münchener theologische Zeitschrift* (Munich, 1950ff.).
OC	*Oriens christianus. Halbjahrshefte für die Kunde des christlichen Orients*, 1901ff.
OCA	Orientalia christiana analecta (Rome: Pontificio Istituto Orientale).
OCP	*Orientalia christiana periodica* (Rome: Pontificio Istituto Orientale, 1935ff.).
OR 23, 34 . . .	*Ordo Romanus.* Unless the contrary is indicated the number accompanying this abbreviation is that given in Andrieu, *OR.*
OR Mab	*Ordo Romanus* according to the numbering in J. Mabillon, *Musaei Italici* II (Paris, 1969) = PL 78:851-1372
OS	*L'Orient syrien* (Paris: 1956–67).
PG	J. P. Migne, Patrologiae cursus completus, Series graeca (Paris-Montrouge, 1857–66). 161 volumes.
PL	J. P. Migne, Patrologiae cursus completus, Series latina (Paris-Montrouge, 1844–64). 221 volumes.
PLS	A. Hamman, *Supplementum Patrologiae Latinae* (Turnhout: Brepols, 1958–74). 5 volumes.
PO	Patrologia orientalis. First editors: R. Graffin and F. Nau (Paris: Firmin-Didot; then Turnhout: Brepols, 1903ff.).
POC	*Proche-Orient chrétien* (Jerusalem, 1951ff.).
PR	Pontificale Romanum (Roman Pontifical).
PRG	C. Vogel and R. Elze, *Le Pontifical romano-germanique du xe siècle* (ST 226, 227, 269; Vatican City, 1963–72). 3 volumes.
QL	*Questions liturgiques et paroissiales,* then simply *Questions liturgiques* (Louvain: Abbaye du Mont César, 1910ff.).
RAC	*Reallexikon für Antike und Christentum,* ed. T. Klauser (Stuttgart: Hiersemann, 1950ff.).
RBen	*Revue bénédictine* (Abbaye de Maredsous, 1884ff.).
RechSR	*Recherches de science religieuse* (Paris, 1910ff.).
REDMF	Rerum ecclesiasticarum documenta, Series maior: Fontes (Rome: Herder, 1955ff.).
Renaudot	E. Renaudot, *Liturgiarum orientalium collectio* (Paris, 1716. More accurate 2nd ed.: Frankfurt: E. Baer, 1847, in 2 volumes).
RevSR	*Revue des sciences religieuses* (Strasbourg: Palais Universitaire, 1921ff.).
RHE	*Revue d'histoire ecclésiastique* (Louvain, 1900ff.).
ROC	*Revue de l'Orient chrétien* (Paris: Leroux, then Paris: Picard, 1896).
RR	Rituale Romanum

RTAM	*Revue de théologie ancienne et médiévale* (Louvain: Abbaye du Mont César, 1929ff.).
SC	Sources chrétiennes. Collection ed. by H. de Lubac and J. Daniélou (later: C. Mondésert) (Paris: Cerf, 1942ff.).
SCDW	Sacred Congregation for Divine Worship (May 8, 1969, to July 11, 1975).
SCR	Sacred Congregation of Rites. When this abbreviation is followed by a number, the reference is to *Decreta authentica Congregationis sacrorum rituum* (Rome, 1898–1927). 7 volumes or, more accurately, 5 volumes and 2 of appendixes.
SCSDW	Sacred Congregation for the Sacraments and Divine Worship (from July 11, 1975, to April 5, 1984).
SE	*Sacris erudiri. Jaarboek voor Godsdienstwetenschappen* (Steenbrugge: St.-Pietersabdij, 1948ff.).
ST	Studi e testi (Rome, then Vatican City, 1900ff.).
TA	Texte und Arbeiten, published by the Archabbey of Beuron, 1917ff. (Unless there is an indication to the contrary, the references are to the first section of this series.)
TS	Texts and Studies. Contributions to Biblical and Patristic Literature (Cambridge: Cambridge University Press, 1882ff.).
TU	Texte und Untersuchungen zur Geschichte der altchristlichen Literatur (Leipzig, then Berlin: Akademie Verlag, 1882ff.).
VSC	Vatican Council II, Constitution *Sacrosanctum Concilium* on the Sacred Liturgy. Latin text: *AAS* 56 (1964) 97–138. Unless some other indication is given, the translation of this and the other conciliar documents is taken from *Vatican II. The Conciliar and Postconciliar Documents*, ed. A. Flannery (Collegeville: The Liturgical Press, 1975).
ZKT	*Zeitschrift für katholische Theologie* (Innsbruck, 1877ff.).

Time in the Liturgy

I. H. Dalmais

BIBLIOGRAPHY

O. Casel, *The Mystery of Christian Worship* (Westminster, Md.: Newman, 1960), 63–93.

_____, *Das christliche Festmysterium* (Paderborn: Bonifacius-Druckerei, 1941).

T. G. Chifflot, "Le Christ et le temps," *LMD* no. 13 (1948) 26–49.

LMD no. 30 (1952): "L'économie du salut et le cycle liturgique."

M. B. de Soos, *Le mystère liturgique d'après saint Léon le Grand* (LQF 34; Münster: Aschendorff, 1958).

J. Hennig, "Zur Theologie des Kirchenjahres," *ALW* 9 (1966) 437–43.

A. J. Chupungco, *The Cosmic Elements of Christian Passover* (Studia Anselmiana 72: Analecta Liturgica 3; Rome: Herder, 1977).

M. Gimenez, "La liturgie et le temps," *Irénikon* 53 (1980) 468–500.

LMD nos. 147 and 148 (1981): "Temps et liturgie."

I. H. Dalmais, "At One Time and in One Place: Local Calendars and Their Promotion," *Concilium* no. 142 (Feb., 1981), 31–36.

Liturgical Time. Papers Read at the Congress of Societas Liturgica, ed. W. Vos and G. Wainwright (Rotterdam: Liturgical Ecumenical Center, 1982).

I. LITURGY AND THE RHYTHMS OF THE COSMOS

Any organization of the liturgy must inevitably be related in complex ways to the various cosmic cycles that determine the rhythm of existence in time. This necessary relationship arises in part because of the significance attached to the flow of time and to those "opportune moments" (*kairoi*) in it that are regarded as especially important; in other words, there is a theology of time, which has been discussed elsewhere in these volumes

1

(Vol. I). At a more pragmatic level it is also necessary to take into account the complex relations that exist between the annual rhythm of the seasons (regulated by the seeming course of the sun), the cycle of lunations (with their characteristic phases that have almost universally been accorded a special importance), and the daily alternation of day and night (with their salient moments: evening, morning, midday and, sometimes, midnight).

When a given religious universe is primarily of the cosmic type or when it assigns importance only to commemorations, it is rather easy to organize its celebrations. The various Christian traditions, on the other hand, find it especially difficult to establish liturgical cycles. The reason is that as a result of their biblical origin they have what they usually regard as a fundamental obligation to accept the religious conception of the cosmos and its rhythms that is reflected in the first chapter of Genesis and in the seasonal feasts (especially Passover) of the Mosaic tradition. In addition, the incarnation and human life of Jesus have sealed God's involvement in human history and thus given a new dimension to the theology of history. For, while this theology is already characteristic of the biblical tradition, the glorification of Jesus as the Christ and the gift of the Spirit open up for it new eschatological perspectives which are an essential element in every liturgy of the new and definitive covenant.

These are the basic points ratified in the conciliar constitution of Vatican II on the liturgy, especially in chapter V, "The Liturgical Year":

> Holy Mother Church believes that it is for her to celebrate the saving work of her divine Spouse in a sacred commemoration on certain days throughout the course of the year. Once each week, on the day which she has called the Lord's Day, she keeps the memory of the Lord's resurrection. She also celebrates it once every year, together with his blessed passion, at Easter, that most solemn of all feasts.
>
> In the course of the year, moreover, she unfolds the whole mystery of Christ from the incarnation and nativity to the ascension, to Pentecost and the expectation of the blessed hope of the coming of the Lord.
>
> Thus recalling the mysteries of the redemption, she opens up to the faithful the riches of her Lord's powers and merits, so that these are in some way made present for all time; the faithful lay hold of them and are filled with saving grace (no. 102).

It must be admitted, however, that this neat arrangement has not always found smooth and undistorted expression in all the liturgical traditions. Today, moreover, the spread of the Christian faith throughout the entire world is setting new problems for which no completely satisfactory solution can be expected. These problems arise because local Churches are concerned to harmonize their liturgical celebrations with local cultural and climatic conditions while at the same time making clear, at least on the most important feasts, their communion in faith with the rest of the Church by celebrating these feasts at the same time of the year.

Ultimately the problem is to take into account the two great cosmic cycles, the solar and the lunar, which in varying ways have served as the basis for calendars. The biblical traditions show that from a very early period there was a concern to harmonize the two cycles. Thus we are told in the great liturgical poem on creation that is placed "at the head" (*beresit*) of Genesis: "God said, 'Let there be lights in the vault of heaven to divide day from night, and let them indicate festivals, days and years. Let there be lights in the vault of heaven to shine on the earth.' And so it was. God made the two great lights: the greater light to govern the day, the smaller light to govern the night, and the stars" (Gen 1:14-16 JB).

II. THE WEEKLY CYCLE

Pastoral peoples have always given priority to the moon, and the Arabs, in fidelity to this usage, have made it the law for Islam. Among the Jews, as a result perhaps of the amalgamation of pastoral and farming groups into a single nation, the annual cycle of the sun and the seasons cuts across the cycle of the lunar phases which sets the rhythm for the succession of weeks from sabbath to sabbath. Doubtless due to the influence of the astral religions this arrangement gradually made its way throughout the Roman Empire and had gained predominance by about the end of the third century.

It is impossible to exaggerate the importance of these facts. The earliest witnesses already show the week to be the axial element in Christian liturgical time. The resurrection of Christ on the first day of the Jewish week, the day after the sabbath, turned it into the "Lord's Day" (*Kyriakē* in Greek, *Dominica* [*dies*] in Latin, with the Romance language names for Sunday—*dimanche, domenica, domingo*—being derived from *dominica*). The rhythm of the week and the celebration of this day that was both the first and the eighth were always considered to be the fundamental points of reference in relation to which time was organized within Christianity.

The *Declaration of the Second Vatican Ecumenical Council on Revision of the Calendar*, which appears as an appendix to the *Constitution on the Liturgy*, makes all this explicitly clear. After saying that the Council "is not opposed to assigning the feast of Easter to a fixed Sunday in the Gregorian Calendar" nor to the establishment of a perpetual calendar, the conciliar document continues:

> But among the various systems that are being devised with a view to establishing a perpetual calendar and introducing it into civil life, those and

only those are unopposed by the Church which retain and safeguard a seven-day week, with Sunday, without the introduction of any days outside the week, so that the succession of weeks may be left intact, unless in the judgment of the Apostolic See there are extremely weighty reasons to the contrary.

It is worth noting, moreover, that in the astral calendar, which was coming into widespread use in the Greco-Roman world during the third century, the first day of the week was placed under the sign of the sun. Even after the empire had become officially Christian, the languages of Germanic origin would keep that designation (*Sonntag, Sunday*, etc.) because it seemed a suitable vehicle of Christian symbolism, as we shall see subsequently. On the other hand, some of these same languages, German among them, used for the name of the seventh day one or another derivative of "sabbath," probably in a form originally adopted in the Balkan region. The very complexity marking these derivations highlights the complexity of the relations that obtained between, on the one hand, the Christian conception of time and, on the other, cosmic rhythms and cultural environments.

The cycle of weeks thus provided Christian communities deeply rooted in a Semitic cultural universe with a framework for the entire liturgical year. This was the case with the Churches in the Syrian tradition and especially those that developed their organization in Mesopotamia. Astral cults were so strongly entrenched, especially in northern Mesopotamia, that they could not fail to exercise a profound influence, more so than anywhere else. Moreover, the Jewish communities of Babylon, within which the Christian communities had their origin to a much greater extent than elsewhere, likewise played their part. Tradition attributes the definitive organization of this system to the Nestorian patriarch or catholicos Isho'yab III at the time when the Arab conquest was giving new vitality to Semitic ways.

The Mesopotamian Church nonetheless was an exception, even if it affected to some extent the organization of the Armenian liturgical calendar. We do, however, find almost universally a sort of germ of a similar system in the establishment of a paschal or Easter cycle made up of a "week of weeks" and culminating in a "fiftieth day" (Pentecost).

III. THE ANNUAL EASTER CYCLE

From at least the middle of the second century we find that the Christian conception of time was extended to include not only the annual celebration of Easter but the entire year. There were at that time two opposing traditions on the date of Easter. The primary concern of one tradition, known for this reason as the "Quartodeciman" tradition, was to maintain continuity with the Mosaic Passover on "the fourteenth day of Nisan," that is, on the first day of the full moon that followed upon the spring equinox. The other tradition was concerned primarily to preserve the weekly rhythm that determined the celebration of the "Lord's Day."

This second tradition won the day after a long crisis that all but led to a break in ecclesial communion, so important to both sides did this matter of dating seem. Moreover, the painful crisis has recurred, for various reasons, down to our own time, with no solution yet in sight. It raises new questions for the Churches of the Southern Hemisphere by reason of the rich symbolic values associated with the revival of life in the spring; it is a symbolism that is at the very source of every Easter celebration and that the liturgies have delighted to emphasize. It is even more important, however, that there should be a clear continuity between the Christian Easter as a celebration of the saving passion (according to a conception of Easter that seems to have been the earliest held) and the "passage" of Christ from death to life, taking with him to the Father those who place their trust in him.

Easter is "the solemnity of solemnities" and was for a long time the only feast celebrated by Christians; it is a feast in which the "Day"—"the day that the Lord has made"—is prolonged for an entire week and renewed throughout a week of weeks. As such, Easter is the center and summit of Christian time. There is question here of something quite different from a mere commemoration. St. Augustine, in his *Letter to Januarius*, rightly regards it as being, in a privileged though not exclusive way, a *sacramentum* which brings the faithful into contact with an invisible reality that directly involves them. Easter is not simply a *festivitas* or feast like others; it is a *sollemnitas* or solemnity in the full sense of a term which indicates that it is a celebration unparalleled in the annual cycle.

In all the liturgical traditions, therefore, Easter became the pivot of a cycle. This had as its starting point and center the *triduum sacrum* or sacred triduum (into which the celebration of Easter had been expanded from as early as the fourth century) and the week that prolonged it. The cycle developed to include, on the one hand, the Pentecostal "week of weeks" and, on the other, a period of preparation which in some cases extended even beyond the time of the Lenten fast.

The explicit moments in this Easter cycle differed somewhat in the various liturgical traditions. The cycle found its most fully developed form in the Byzantine liturgy with the composition, probably within the ambit of the monastery of Studios and in the eighth century, of two liturgical books, the Triodion and the Pentekostarion. These contain the offices for each day of, respectively, the ten weeks of preparation for Easter and the seven weeks of Easter. The entire remainder of the year is covered by the Paraklitikē, but this provides only a cycle of eight weeks, which corresponds, in a rather arbitrary way, to the eight tones used in psalmody.

This latter type of organization, which bears no relation to an annual cycle in the proper sense, has been adopted in the renewed Roman liturgy for the period now designated as "Ordinary Time."

As a matter of fact, only the Roman liturgy—and the liturgies closely related to it—ever attempted to organize an annual *temporale* or seasonal cycle. Since, however, the date of Easter varied in function of the lunar cycle, a complex system of computation had to be developed which for centuries remained the basis for the teaching of astronomical mathematics. The same problem did not arise to an equal force for liturgies that resolutely distinguished between the Easter cycle and commemorations on fixed days. Some of these liturgies did, however, create other difficulties for themselves by reserving set days of the week for these commemorations. The Armenians, for example, transferred all feasts of the Lord to Sunday, and the Assyro-Chaldeans assigned most commemorations of the saints (not very numerous in any case) to Friday.

IV. ANNIVERSARIES

If we examine closely the way in which the various liturgical calendars were established, we find several concerns simultaneously at work. On the one hand, there were anniversaries that more or less faithfully commemorated the *natale* ("birthday") of a saint (or else the translation of his or her relics, or the anniversary of the dedication of a church of which the saint was patron). On the other, there were commemorations recalling a historical event, and still others assigned to a date that may seem arbitrary—unless, as seems to have been rather often the case, the intention was to Christianize a festival that could not have been eliminated without great difficulty.

This last seems to have been the case with feasts celebrating either the birth of Christ or his "manifestations" (epiphanies), which gradually formed, at least in the West, the nucleus of a cycle comparable to the Easter cycle. At Rome, the celebration of the presentation and the meeting *(Hypapantē)* in the temple forty days after the birth was transformed into a feast of the "Purification of the Virgin Mary" to replace the rites of purification at the beginning of February. Likewise, again at Rome, the annual commemoration of the ancestors toward the end of February seems to have been at the origin of the celebration of the *Cathedra Petri* (Chair of Peter), the patronal feast of the Christian community of Rome.

These few examples show how complex the relations are between liturgy and time. There may be question of cosmic time with its various cycles and the many traditional computations to which these have given rise. There may be references to historical time; these are especially important for the Christian faith, which is concerned to make clear the divine "deeds" in human history. Or finally there may be contingent cultural applications, with regard to which discernment is difficult, but which in many cases bear witness to the desire to locate the proclamation of the gospel solidly in the setting of the traditions to which each human group has been long attached.

Every liturgical calendar is linked to situations of time and place, whether or not those who follow these calendars recognize the fact. In the new "General Calendar" for the Churches that follow Roman liturgical usage, an attempt has been made to be attentive to the complexity of situations as well as to that of a long history and of customs now become traditional. But for these very reasons is not the calendar a somewhat artificial construction that will have to be adapted, perhaps to a greater extent than now anticipated, to the variety of times and places?

SUNDAY AND THE WEEK

P. Jounel

Sunday and the Week

§1. Sunday

Vatican Council II describes Sunday as follows:

> By a tradition handed down from the apostles, which took its origin from the very day of Christ's resurrection, the Church celebrates the paschal mystery every seventh day, which day is appropriately called the Lord's Day or Sunday. For on this day Christ's faithful are bound to come together into one place. They should listen to the word of God and take part in the Eucharist, thus calling to mind the passion, resurrection, and glory of the Lord Jesus, and giving thanks to God who "has begotten them again, through the resurrection of Christ from the dead, unto a living hope" (1 Pet 1:3). The Lord's Day is the original feast day, and it should be proposed to the faithful and taught to them so that it may in fact become a day of joy and of freedom from work.[1]

As a quasi-commentary on this passage, I shall discuss in succession the history, the theology, and the celebration of Sunday, and then the organization of the Sundays *per annum* ("through the year" = Ordinary Time) in the Roman liturgy.

I. HISTORY OF SUNDAY

BIBLIOGRAPHY

J. Gaillard, "Dimanche," *Dictionnaire de spiritualité* 3 (1957), col. 948–82.

---

1. *VSC* 106.

P. Grelot, "Du sabbat juif au dimanche chrétien," *LMD* no. 123 (1975) 79–107; no. 124 (1975) 15–54.

C. S. Mosna, *Storia della domenica dalle origini fino agli inizi del V secolo* (Analecta Gregoriana 170; Rome: Gregorian University Press, 1969).

W. Rordorf, *Sabbat et dimanche dans l'Eglise ancienne* (Traditio christiana 2; Neuchâtel: Delachaux et Niestlé, 1972).

_____, "Origine et signification de la célébration du dimanche dans le christianisme primitif. Etat actuel de la recherche," *LMD* no. 148 (1981) 103–12.

The history of Sunday begins with the resurrection of Christ, and it may be asserted that the Christian Sunday acquired its definitive form well before the Council of Nicaea (325).

1. *The Easter Event*

It was on the morning of "the first day of the week" (Matt 28:1; Mark 16:9; Luke 24:1; John 20:1) that the Lord Jesus rose from the dead and showed himself to his disciples. After appearing to the holy women and then to Peter, he showed himself "that very day" to the two disciples at Emmaus and made himself "known to them in the breaking of the bread" (Luke 24:35). He then presented himself in the midst of his assembled apostles, ate with them (Luke 24:41-43), and told them: "As the Father has sent me, even so I send you." After this, he breathed on them and said: "Receive the Holy Spirit. If you forgive the sins of any, they are forgiven" (John 20:21-23).

The resurrection of Christ from the dead, his appearance in the assembly of his disciples, the messianic meal he took with them, the gift of the Spirit, and the missionary mandate to the Church: all these comprise the Christian Passover in its full form. Such is the central event of salvation history, and it has left its mark for good on *the first day of the week*. The entire mystery which Sunday celebrates was already present on Easter day; Sunday is simply the weekly celebration of the paschal mystery.

2. *The First Day of the Week*

The Christian celebration of the first day began as early as the week following on the resurrection of Christ: "Eight days later, his disciples were again in the house . . . . Jesus came and stood among them, and said, 'Peace be with you.' Then he said to Thomas, 'Put your finger here, and see my hands; and put out your hand, and place it in my side; do not be faithless, but believing'" (John 20:26-27).

Jesus here adds nothing to the mystery of his presence among his disciples, for this presence was already fully manifested on Easter evening. He does, however, draw their attention to two points: by showing them his glorious wounds he places the cross at the center of the Christian ritual assembly, and by calling for faith from Thomas he requires that this assembly be a gathering of believers, of "faithful."

The apostolic generation immediately grasped the importance of the first day, connected as it was with the memory and presence of the crucified and risen Jesus.[2] In the First Letter to the Corinthians (around Easter, 57), St. Paul links the collection for the brethren in Jerusalem with the weekly reunion: "On the first day of every week, each of you is to put something aside and store it up, as he may prosper" (1 Cor 16:2). The Acts of the Apostles gives us a description of the assembly at Troas in which Paul was the central figure: "On the first day of the week . . . we were gathered together to break bread" (Acts 20:7-12). The gathering took place at night, on the third story of a Christian's home; it included a lengthy sermon by Paul and the breaking of bread.

3. *The Lord's Day*

Up to this point there had been question only of "the first day of the week" (according to the Jewish method of counting); this is the only designation to be kept in the Syriac-speaking Churches. With the Apocalypse (ca. 95) a new name for this day made its appearance: "I was in the Spirit on the Lord's day *(en tē kyriakē hēmera)*, and I heard behind me a loud voice" (Rev 1:10). "The Lord's Day" was the name that would spread throughout the Greek-speaking Churches and then, in its Latin form *(dominicus dies[3])*, in the Churches of the West. The noun soon disappeared, leaving only the adjective, which in turn, however, became a noun: *kyriakē, dominica*, and, in the Romance languages, *dimanche, domenica, domingo*.

4. *Sunday in the Church of the First Three Centuries*

Sunday was so important in the life of the Church that testimonies to its celebration have survived in abundance. It is very likely, of course, that the Jerusalem community had to be satisfied with adding the Sunday Eucharistic assembly to the sabbath observance.[4] But by about the end of the first century the separation of the two was complete, and St. Ig-

---

2. To the commemoration of the resurrection was later added that of Pentecost, because the resurrection, the ascension, and the outpouring of the Spirit are but three aspects of a single mystery; see H. Dumaine, "Dimanche" *DACL* 4 (1920), col. 896–97. Later on there was added to these commemorations a series of "blessings" of Sunday as supposedly the day on which many other saving events took place; *ibid.*, col. 985–90.

3. Tertullian, *De corona* 3, 4 (CCL 2:1043); 11, 3 (CCL 2:1056); *De idololatria* 14, 7 (CCL 2:1115); *De jejunio* 15, 2 (CCL 2:1273).

4. For the discussions of the relation between sabbath and Sunday see H. Dumaine, *ibid.*, col. 900–5.

natius of Antioch (ca. 107) would soon be able to make the observance of Sunday the sign *par excellence* of a Christian: "Those who used to live according to the old order of things have attained to a new hope and they observe no longer the sabbath but Sunday, the day on which Christ and his death raised up our life."[5]

A document contemporary with Ignatius and perhaps even with the Apocalypse gives us some insight into the ethos of a Christian assembly of that age: "Come together on the Lord's day, break bread and give thanks, having first confessed your sin so that your sacrifice may be pure. Anyone who has a quarrel with a fellow Christian should not gather with you until the two are reconciled, lest your sacrifice be profaned."[6]

A pagan witness adds a detail to this brief description. In a letter to Trajan (112) Pliny the Younger, then governor of Bithynia, says that the Christians he had arrested "claimed that their entire fault or error was to have gathered regularly before dawn on a set day in order to join in singing a hymn to the Christ as to a god."[7]

There can be no doubt that the "set day" of which Pliny speaks was Sunday. We also learn from Pliny that the Christian assembly took place before dawn, included a hymn to Christ (was this the Eucharistic Prayer?), and, as the part of the passage not quoted here makes clear, was now separate from the evening agape.

Fifty years later, St. Justin († 165) provides us with the first description of the Sunday assembly:

> On the day named after the sun, all who live in city or countryside assemble in the same place, and the memoirs of the apostles or the writings of the prophets are read . . . . The reason why we all assemble on Sunday is that it is the first day: the day on which God transformed darkness and matter and created the world, and the day on which Jesus Christ our Savior rose from the dead.[8]

It is clear that in an age when Sunday was not yet a holiday all the faithful of Christ nonetheless gathered on that day. We can understand the intensity of feeling with which the *Teaching of the Apostles* (middle of the third century) says:

---

5. St. Ignatius of Antioch, *Ad Magnesios* 9, ed. P. Th. Camelot (SC 10; 2nd ed., Paris: Cerf, 1951) 102–3.

6. *Didache* 14, ed. W. Rordorf and T. Tuilier (SC 248; Paris: Cerf, 1978) 193; commentary, 63–71. The translation, slightly modified, is from Johannes H. Emminghaus, *The Eucharist: Essence, Form, Celebration*, trans. Matthew J. O'Connell (Collegeville, Minn.: The Liturgical Press, 1978) 27.

7. Pliny the Younger, *Epistolarum lib.* 10, 96; cited in W. Rordorf, *Sabbat et Dimanche* 79.

8. St. Justin, *Apologia I* 67, 3 and 7, ed. L. Pautigny (Textes et Documents; Paris: Picard, 1904) 143. Text also in Hänggi-Pahl 72; translation from Emminghaus, *ibid.*, 36.

> Make not your worldly affairs of more account than the word of God;
> but on the Lord's day leave everything and run eagerly to your Church;
> for she is your glory. Otherwise, what excuse have they before God who
> do not assemble on the Lord's day to hear the word of life and be nourished
> with the divine food which abides for ever?[9]

What echo did the prescriptions of the ecclesiastical lawgiver awaken
in the minds of the faithful? The testimony of Pliny and that of Justin,
a Christian layman, suggest the answer. More moving, undoubtedly, is
the testimony of the martyrs of Abitina (near Medjez el-Bab in Tunisia),
who might well be called "martyrs for Sunday." Thirty-one men and
eighteen women arrested for illegal assembly appeared before Proconsul
Anulinus in Carthage on February 12, 304. When the official accused them
of disobeying the imperial edicts, Saturninus, a priest, answered: "We must
celebrate the Lord's Day. It is a law for us." Emeritus, a lector, in whose
home the community had assembled, spoke to the same effect: "Yes, it was
in my house that we celebrated the Lord's Day. We cannot live without
celebrating the Lord's Day." And Victoria, a virgin, proudly declared: "I
attended the meeting because I am a Christian."[10]

5. *Sunday after the Peace of Constantine (313)*

The Acts of the Martyrs of Abitina show that when the period of
persecution was ending the Church had already fully grasped the sacramental reality of Sunday, a day which brought intense joy to the Christian
people even in the midst of the most severe trials.[11] The advent of peace
now meant that even the laws of the empire paid homage to Sunday.
Faithful to his intention of promoting simultaneously the cult of the sun
and the cult of Christ, Constantine was glad to honor both the sun-god
and Christ by making a holiday of the day that was at once the day of
the sun and the day of Kyrios Christ.[12]

A first law (March 321) ordained that no work be done on "the
venerable day of the sun": "All judges and the people of the towns and
all craftsmen are to remain at rest on the venerable day of the sun."[13] Only
agricultural work might be done in order to take advantage of the weather.
A second law (July 321) added that just as it was unbecoming to fill the
day of the sun, "renowned for the worship paid to him," with trials and

---

9. *Didascalia Apostolorum* 23, trans. R. Hugh Connolly, *Didascalia Apostolorum* (Oxford: Clarendon Press, 1929) 124.

10. *Bibliographia hagiographica Latina*, no. 7492; text cited in Rordorf, *ibid.*, 109.

11. See the passage in the *Didascalia Apostolorum* that is cited further on at n. 40.

12. On Constantine's syncretism see H. Stern, *Le calendrier de 354* (Institut Français
de Beyrouth, Bibliothèque archéologique et historique 55; Paris: Geuthner, 1953).

13. *Codex Justinianus* lib. 3, tit. 12, 2; ed. Krüger (Berlin: Weidmann, 1877 [1926]) 127.
— Eusebius, *Vita Constantini* 4, 18 (PG 20:1165), cited in Rordorf, *ibid.*, 111–13.

disputes, so on the contrary it was fitting to make this a day for manumitting and emancipating slaves.[14]

On the eve of the Council of Nicaea, then, the Christian Sunday was a day of liturgical assembly at which the Word of God was proclaimed and the Eucharist was celebrated; it was a day of festivity that was to find expression in the laying aside of everyday tasks. The councils of subsequent centuries would pass laws regarding the extent of the Sunday rest and remind the faithful of the obligation to participate in the Christian assembly.[15] They would, however, add nothing to the special character of this Christian day of days, "the day of light and joy and resurrection from the dead,"[16] the day that "does not belong to everyone but only to those who have died to sin and now live for God."[17]

II. THEOLOGY OF SUNDAY

BIBLIOGRAPHY

Le Jour du Seigneur (Congrès du Centre de Pastorale Liturgique, Lyon, 17–22 septembre 1947; Paris: Robert Laffont, 1948).

J. Hild, *Dimanche et vie pascale* (Exsultet 1; Turnhout: Brepols, 1949).

J. Daniélou, *The Bible and the Liturgy* (Notre Dame: University of Notre Dame Press, 1956).

J. Tillard, "Le dimanche, jour d'Alliance," *Sciences ecclésiastiques* 16 (1964) 225–50.

J. Gaillard, "Où en est la théologie du dimanche?" *LMD* no. 83 (1965) 7–33.

B. Botte, Mgr. Cassien, *et al.*, *Le Dimanche* (9ᵉ *Semaine d'études liturgiques de l'Institut Saint-Serge*) (Lex orandi 39; Paris: Cerf, 1965).

In the early centuries Christians experienced Sunday in an intense way because they had a profound grasp of the mystery it contained. Those centuries bore witness not only to the outward celebration of the Lord's Day but also to the faith with which the Church celebrated it. This faith found expression both in an awareness of the radical newness of the Lord's Day and in the reflection of the Fathers on the names chosen to convey this new reality.

---

14. J. Gaudemet, "La législation religieuse de Constantin," *Revue d'histoire de l'Eglise en France* 33 (1947) 43–47.

15. E.g., the Councils of Agde (506), can. 47, ed. C. Munier (CCL 148:212), and Orleans (511), can. 26, ed. C. de Clercq (CCL 148A:11).

16. Abu'l Barakat, *La lampe des ténèbres*, in W. Riedel, *Die Kirchenrechtsquellen des Patriarchats Alexandrien* (Leipzig: A. Deichert, 1900) 44.

17. St. Athanasius, *De sabbato et circumcisione* 5 (PG 28:140).

1. *The Newness of Sunday*

The newness was affirmed above all in relation to the Jewish sabbath. This is not to say that the Church failed to recognize the close continuity between the two covenants. In fact, the Fathers occasionally speak of Sunday as the new and perfect sabbath, as Eusebius does in the following passage:

> Once the Jews had proved faithless, the Word transferred the sabbath feast to the dawn and gave us, as an image of true rest, the saving, first, Lord's day of light. This is the day on which the Savior of the world, having accomplished all his works among us and having overcome death, entered the gates of heaven. He thus passed beyond the creation that was made in six days, and received the blessed sabbath and its beatific rest.[18]

But, as is clear, Eusebius connects Sunday with the Jewish sabbath only via the "blessed sabbath," which suggests the typology of the eighth day. The Church's basic attitude to the sabbath was expressed by St. Ignatius of Antioch: "Those who have attained to the new hope observe no longer the sabbath but Sunday."[19] There is in fact no continuity between sabbath and Sunday as institutions. The former consisted essentially in a cessation of work and acquired a religious value only because it was given a meaning in relation to the Mosaic covenant. Sunday, on the other hand, consists essentially in the present commemoration of the Lord's resurrection by his assembled disciples and in their expectation of his return.[20]

2. *The Names for Sunday*

The Lord's Day—This is the basic name for the Christian day of worship. It first appeared, as we saw, in the Apocalypse (1:10); beginning in the fifth century it was to replace *dies solis* (sun-day) in the list of legal names for the days of the week.[21] It subsequently entered the Romance languages (*dimanche, domenica, domingo*), whereas the Germanic languages kept the name taken from the sun (Sunday, *Sonntag, Zondag, Sönntag*).

But what precisely does the name "Lord's Day" say and imply? To begin with, the name refers to Kyrios Christ and not to God the creator. Sunday is the day of Christ, because it is the day of his resurrection. We must not forget, however, that the day of the Lord's resurrection was also the day on which he presented himself in the midst of his disciples and

---

18. Eusebius, *Commentarius in Ps. 91* (PG 23:1169).

19. See above at n. 5.

20. See H. Féret, "Les sources bibliques" and J. Daniélou, "La doctrine patristique du dimanche" in *Le Jour du Seigneur* 92–94 and 113–19.

21. H. Dumaine, "Dimanche," col. 870–79.

drank with them the new wine of the kingdom (Luke 22:18). Finally, if Jesus manifested himself once again—this time to the entire apostolic college—on the eighth day after his resurrection, it was probably because the disciples had gathered to wait for him.

Thus the name "Lord's Day" already suggests the three main aspects which other names for the day will particularize: it is the memorial day of the resurrection, which we celebrate in faith; it is a day of expectation of the Lord's return, which we celebrate in hope; and, because Christians come together on this day and the Word of God is proclaimed and the Eucharistic sacrifice is offered, it is a day of actual presence of the Lord among his followers, and we commune with him there in love.[22]

The day of the resurrection—This name, to which the Byzantine Church is especially attached, has the advantage of recalling explicitly the connection of Sunday with the passover or passage of the Lord. The name is perhaps to some extent responsible for the fact that the Byzantine liturgy gives each of its Sundays a more explicitly paschal character than other liturgies do.[23]

The first and eighth day—The first day of the week is the day of creation: it is, says St. Justin, "the day on which God transformed darkness and matter and created the world."[24] Thus in the Office of Readings for Sundays we sing the hymn *Primo dierum omnium, quo mundus exstat conditus* ("On the first of all days, when the world was created"). Ps.-Eusebius of Alexandria (fifth century) comments: "It was on this day that the Lord began the first fruits of creation, and it was on this same day that he gave the world the first fruits of the resurrection."[25] The connection between resurrection and creation is forcefully stated in the Easter Vigil service.

But the first day of the week is also the one that comes after the seventh: it is the eighth day. St. Justin already saw this fact as containing "a mystery."[26] St. Augustine writes: "The eighth [day] will be like the first, so that the first life will be restored, but now as unending."[27] Inasmuch as Sunday is an eighth day, it is the sign of eternal life. It commemorates the resurrection of Christ and thereby anticipates his return; we celebrate it "until he comes." On this day we already share in advance in the great and definitive sabbath.

---

22. Ps.-Eusebius of Alexandria calls the Lord's Day "the lord of days" (Daniélou, *ibid.*, 122).

23. I. H. Dalmais, "Le dimanche dans la liturgie byzantine," *LMD* no. 46 (1956) 60–66.

24. St. Justin, *Apologia I* 67, 3; see above, n. 8.

25. Above, n. 22.

26. St. Justin, *Dialogus cum Tryphone* 24, 1, ed. G. Archambault, vol. 1 (Textes et Documents 8; Paris: Picard, 1909) 108.

27. St. Augustine, *Ep.* 55, 17, ed. A. Goldbacher (CSEL 33/2:188).

[In this passage the Lord means:] It is not the sabbaths now celebrated that please me, but the sabbath which I made and on which, after bringing all things to their rest, I will begin an eighth day, that is, a new world. That is why we celebrate as a joyous feast the eighth day on which Jesus rose from the dead and, after appearing to his disciples, ascended into heaven.[28]

We may sum up this theology of the names for Sunday by saying that the name "day of the resurrection" stresses more the commemorative aspect, the name "eighth day" the prophetic aspect, and the name "Lord's Day" the mysterious presence of the risen Lord in his Church. As memorial, prophecy, and presence, "our Lord's Day is truly the coming of the new creation and the breakthrough of the life from above."[29]

III. CELEBRATION OF SUNDAY

BIBLIOGRAPHY

H. Dumaine, "Dimanche," *DACL* 4 (1920), col. 956–90.
J. Hild, *Dimanche et vie pascale*, Part 4: "La célébration du dimanche," 349–462.
I. H. Dalmais, "Le dimanche dans la liturgie byzantine," *LMD* no. 46 (1956) 60–67.
Le Dimanche, LMD no. 83 (1965) 33–147.
Recherches actuelles sur le Dimanche, LMD no. 124 (1975).

The Lord's Day is also the day of the Church, the day, that is, on which the people of God, with all its constituent parts, gathers locally to listen together to the Word of God, celebrate the Eucharist, and share as brothers and sisters in the joy of the risen Christ.

Sunday begins at sunset on Saturday evening, in accordance with the custom of the Christian communities that originated in Judaism. The Fathers of the Church—St. Augustine and St. Leo the Great, for example—emphasize this point in dealing with the faithful of Africa and Rome, because these were accustomed to a different way of calculating the successive days. When authorization was given to celebrate Sunday Mass on Saturday evening for pastoral reasons, this was consonant with the practice of the early Christian generations.

1. *The Eucharistic Assembly*

The Eucharistic assembly is the specific characteristic of Sunday, according to the overwhelming testimony of the tradition and the teaching of Vatican II. In the Western Church, all of the faithful are obliged to

---

28. *Epistula Barnabae* 15, 8–9, trans. P. Prigent (SC 171; Paris: Cerf, 1971) 187–89.
29. St. Gregory of Nazianzus, *De nov. Dom.* 5 (PG 36:612).

take part in the Sunday Eucharist.[30] They have a duty to attend the entire celebration,[31] and they are urged to receive Communion during it.[32]

The main lines of the Sunday liturgy were already determined in the second century, as St. Justin shows in his testimony:

> On the day named after the sun, all [of our people] who live in city or countryside assemble in the same place, and the memoirs of the apostles or the writings of the prophets are read for as long as time allows. When the lector has finished, the president addresses us, admonishing us and exhorting us to imitate the splendid things we have heard. Then we all stand and pray, and, as we said earlier, when we have finished praying, bread, wine, and water are brought up. The president offers prayers of thanksgiving, according to his ability, and the people give their assent with an "Amen!"
>
> Next, the gifts over which the thanksgiving has been spoken are distributed, and each one shares in them, while they are also sent via the deacons to the absent brethren.
>
> The wealthy who are willing make contributions, each as he or she pleases, and the collection is deposited with the president, who aids orphans and widows, those who are in want because of sickness or other cause, those in prison, and visiting strangers; in short, he takes care of all in need.[33]

The passage displays the pattern followed in the Sunday celebration of the Eucharist right down to our own day. Like every Mass, Sunday Mass contains a Penitential Rite, the Liturgy of the Word, and the Eucharistic Liturgy. On Sunday, however, the Penitential Rite (recommended as early as the *Didache*) may take the form of a sprinkling with blessed water, which reminds those present of their baptism and serves as an allusion to the Easter Vigil. The Word of God is proclaimed more extensively on Sunday, since there are three readings; a homily and the prayer of the faithful are obligatory. The offering of the bread and wine is accompanied by a collection for the needs of the community or of Christians scattered throughout the world. The Eucharistic Prayer regularly reminds us that Sunday is the day of Christ's resurrection and of the Church's sharing in his paschal mystery.

In many areas the lack of priests makes it impossible to celebrate the Eucharist every week. This has always been the situation in the young Churches of Africa and Asia and in Latin America; it is now becoming

---

30. A. Villien, *Histoire des commandements de l'Eglise* (Paris: Gabalda, 1936) 21–58.

31. *VSC* 56: "The two parts which in a sense go to make up the Mass, viz. the liturgy of the word and the eucharistic liturgy, are so closely connected with each other that they form but one single act of worship. Accordingly this sacred Synod strongly urges pastors of souls that, when instructing the faithful, they insistently teach them to take their part in the entire Mass, especially on Sundays and holidays of obligation."

32. See H. Dumaine, "Dimanche," col. 965–68.

33. St. Justin, *Apologia I* 67, 3–6. See above, n. 8.

increasingly the situation in the old Christian countries. The faithful in these regions need nonetheless to come together on the Lord's Day, in order to celebrate the Liturgy of the Word and, if possible, to receive the Body of Christ, whether this be reserved at the place of assembly or brought by one of the faithful from a neighboring town where Mass is being celebrated on that Sunday.

2. *The Sunday Vigil*

Apart from the celebration of the Eucharist, the oldest of the Sunday services is the vigil. This assembly for prayer during the final hours of Saturday night is attested in the East, and especially in Jerusalem, in the fourth century; the Frankish councils of the sixth to the ninth centuries make frequent reference to it, but Rome was never to have it. On the other hand, at Rome the two sacred vigils for Easter Sunday and Pentecost Sunday and the vigils for the Ember Days used to begin on Saturday evening and continue to morning.

The Liturgy of the Hours suggests a more developed form of the Office of Readings for those who would like to celebrate this Sunday vigil after a fashion. In this *vigilia protracta* (extended vigil) the Office of Readings is supplemented by the singing of three canticles from the Old Testament and, before the *Te Deum*, the reading of the gospel of the resurrection. The singing of the canticles is taken over from the third nocturn of the Benedictine Office. The proclamation of the resurrection at this point is already attested in Jerusalem at the end of the fourth century and has been continued in the Byzantine liturgy.

In the East, the Sunday vigil (which is anticipated on Saturday evening) has retained "a vitality which it has doubtless never known in the West. Many of the faithful, especially among the Russians, consider this lengthy vigil, which creates an Easter atmosphere in the church every Saturday evening, to be almost as important as the Eucharistic celebration itself."[34] As everyone knows, First Vespers for Sunday has never had this popular character among us, although in the ninth century Theodulphus of Orleans prescribed in his capitulary that "on Saturday every Christian must come to the church carrying a candle."[35] Perhaps we should see in this prescription a distant memory of the *lucernarium* (service of light) which used to be celebrated in antiquity and of which the Milanese office of Vespers still shows traces.

---

34. I. H. Dalmais, "Le dimanche dans la liturgie byzantine," 61. See H. Dumaine, "Dimanche," col. 968–71. Egeria (ch. 24) gives a description of this Sunday vigil at Jerusalem: *Egeria's Travels*, trans. John Wilkinson (London: SPCK, 1971) 123.

35. Theodulphus of Orléans, *Capitula*, c. 24 (PL 105:198).

3. *The Celebration of the Sacraments*

The sacraments came into existence with the blood and water that flowed from the open side of Christ. While the Sunday Eucharist actualizes, or renders present, the passage of the Lord, baptism means death and resurrection in Christ. For this reason Sunday was, at a very early date, assigned as the day for its celebration. The Easter Vigil is to be the normal context for the baptism of adults, after the Lenten ascent through the catechumenate. Sunday is the appropriate day for infant baptism,[36] which may be celebrated during the parish Mass or immediately after it in the presence of some members of the Christian community.

Sunday is also the preferred day for the first Communion of children and for the renewal by adolescents of their profession of faith (confirmation). Ordinations of bishops, priests, and deacons should likewise in principle be celebrated on a Sunday. Such was already the practice in the early centuries, as St. Leo the Great reminds a correspondent. It was (he says) on Easter evening and on Pentecost that the Lord poured out his Spirit on the apostles; consequently "the blessing of those to be consecrated should never be imparted except on the day of the resurrection," for Sunday is the day "on which all the gifts of grace were bestowed."[37]

4. *Sunday Evening Services*

Medieval conciliar legislation said nothing about any Sunday evening services, because in the view of the day Sunday ended at sunset. Only at the beginning of the modern age did fervent Christians begin to participate on Sunday evening either in Vespers, which was part of the Church's daily prayer, or in new forms of devotion such as Benediction, which was known as the *funzione* ("ceremony") in Counter-Reformation countries and as the *salut* ("salutation") in France.[38] The Second Vatican Council calls upon pastors to see to it "that the principal hours, especially Vespers, are celebrated in common in church on Sundays and on the more solemn feasts," but the Council equally favors Bible services on these occasions.[39]

---

36. *Rite of Baptism for Children* 9.
37. St. Leo the Great, *Ep. 9 ad Dioscorum Alexandrinum* 1 (PL 54:625-26). — Hippolytus, *Traditio Apostolica* 2, ed. B. Botte, *La Tradition apostolique de saint Hippolyte* (LQF 39; Münster: Aschendorff, 1963) 4, already has Sunday as the day for the consecration of a bishop.
38. A. G. Martimort, "Les offices du dimanche soir," in *Le Jour du Seigneur* 250. — Nor should we forget the time given to adult catechesis on Sunday afternoons down to the beginning of this century.
39. *VSC* 100; 35, 4. — See SCR, Instruction *Inter oecumenici* of September 26, 1964, no. 38.

Despite the urging of the Council, Sunday evening services are hardly celebrated any more except in some cathedrals and in monasteries and convents, where a few of the faithful gather to join in the prayer of the community. The conditions of present-day life, in which Sunday afternoons are a time for leisure activities, while in some places there is an evening Mass, prevent regular evening services in parishes.

5. *The Joy of Sunday*

The third-century *Teaching of the Apostles* tells Christians: "On the first day of the week make good cheer at all times; for he is guilty of sin, whoever afflicts his soul on the first of the week."[40] It is a weekly day of festival, says Tertullian,[41] while St. Ephraem compares the joy of this day with that which the apostles felt when the risen Lord showed himself to them. This is a joy that must be sustained by contemplation (Sunday is a day for *lectio divina*—the reading of God's Word) and find an outlet in fraternal charity; it should be reflected in the life of family and city. But early Christians saw this joy as having two privileged forms of expression: no Christian anywhere fasts on Sunday,[42] and on Sunday Christians pray standing: "Because we are risen with Christ and must seek the things above, on the day of the resurrection we remain standing as a sign that we recall the grace bestowed on us."[43]

[handwritten margin note: Stand to pray on Sun]

IV. THE SUNDAYS OF ORDINARY TIME

BIBLIOGRAPHY

L. Brou, "Etude historique sur les oraisons des dimanches après la Pentecôte," *SE* 2 (1949) 123–224.

A. Dumas, "Les sources du nouveau Missel romain," *Notitiae* 7 (1941) 37–42, 94–95.

Il Messale Romano del Vaticano II, Orazionale e Lezionario (Turin-Leumann: ElleDiCi, 1981).

Ordo lectionum Missae, editio typica altera (Città del Vaticano: Libreria Editrice Vaticana, 1981), *Praenotanda* xiii–liii.

The thirty-four Sundays *per annum* or of Ordinary Time represent the ideal Christian Sunday, without any further specification. That is, each of them is the Lord's Day in its pure state as presented to us in the Church's tradition. Each is an Easter, each a feast. In the Tridentine Missal they

---

40. *Didascalia Apostolorum* 21, trans. R. Hugh Connolly, 192.
41. Texts cited in H. Dumaine, "Dimanche," col. 958.
42. *Ibid.*, col. 957–59.
43. St. Basil, *De Sancto Spiritu* 27, ed. B. Pruche (SC 17), 236.

were divided into Sundays after Epiphany and Sundays after Pentecost, but they had no special connection with either feast.

The paschal character of the Sundays of Ordinary Time finds expression both in the Liturgy of the Hours and in the Mass.

1. *The Liturgy of the Hours*

Each Sunday, the celebration of the Hours includes the singing of the psalms most evocative of the paschal mystery. Ps 118 (v. 24: "This is the day which the Lord has made") is sung at Morning Prayer (second and fourth weeks) or at Daytime Prayer (first and third weeks). Pss 110 ("The Lord says to my lord") and 114 ("When Israel went forth from Egypt") are sung at Vespers.

2. *The Celebration of the Eucharist*

Among the formularies of the Mass, special attention must be given to the readings, the prayers, and the songs, although it is not possible to subsume all under a single theme on each Sunday of Ordinary Time. The readings from the Old Testament, the apostles, and the gospel are spread out over three years; the cycle receives its impress from the continuous reading of the gospel: a year for Matthew (A), a year for Mark and John (B), and a year for Luke (C). The letters of St. Paul are likewise read in a continuing manner over the three years. The reading from the Old Testament, on the other hand, has usually been chosen in function of the gospel of the day; the Old Testament reading prepares the way for the good news proclaimed that day. The responsorial psalm is geared to the Old Testament reading, the material of which it turns into prayer. Thus from Sunday to Sunday, Christians gathered to celebrate the Eucharist are given a condensed version of the preaching of the apostles.

The opening prayers and the prayers over the gifts and after Communion are taken, for the most part, from the Tridentine Missal (twenty-five collects out of thirty-four); the ancient sacramentaries supply the remainder. It is to be regretted that these prayers, though of great doctrinal richness, never refer explicitly to the mystery of the risen Christ.

The paschal character of these Sundays is, however, given vivid expression in the eight prefaces for the Sundays of Ordinary Time. Some recall the unfolding of the saving mystery (2, 4, 6), others the "mighty works" which Christ has accomplished through the mystery of his Pasch (1): he has restored their original greatness to human beings (3, 7) and gathered around him the new People of God (1), a people called "to praise your wisdom in all your works" and to be "the body of Christ and the dwelling-place of the Holy Spirit" (8). The ensuing Eucharistic Prayer contains, in the French and German Missals, an insertion reminding the congregation that "on this first day of the week we celebrate the day on which Christ was raised from the dead."

The songs are taken from the Roman antiphonary of the high Middle Ages, but it is impossible to discover the idea which determined the choice made. At most we can call attention to a set of sixteen entrance songs taken from a semi-continuous series of psalms (seventh to twenty-second Sundays); the set seems to have been part of an early collection (fifth century).

We may note, finally, that Sunday is not only a feast, but "the original feast day." This is why "other celebrations, unless they be truly of the greatest importance, shall not have precedence over Sunday, which is the foundation and kernel of the whole liturgical year."[44] Only in exceptional circumstances, therefore, should a Sunday of Ordinary Time yield place to the solemnity of a saint.

§2. The Week

BIBLIOGRAPHY

F. Cabrol, "Fêtes chrétiennes," *DACL* 5 (1922) col. 1403–12.

M. Righetti, *Manuale di storia liturgica* 2 (2nd ed.; Milan: Edizioni Ancora, 1955) 27–32.

M. Andrieu, *OR* IV (1956) 213-31 and 258-63.

V. Grumel, *Traité d'études byzantines* I. *La Chronologie* (Paris: Presses Universitaires de France, 1958) 165–66 and 228–32.

J. Janini, *S. Siricio y las cuatro Temporas* (Valencia: Seminario Metropolitano, 1958).

From the outset the weekly celebration of the Lord's Day imposed the rhythm of the Hebrew week on Christian life. Christians named the days of the week in the Jewish manner by using the ordinal numbers. Meanwhile, however, many regions of the empire had already adopted the week, but had placed each of its days under the patronage of a planetary deity. The followers of Christ used these other names only with reluctance. Thus from the very beginnings of Christian Latin literature we see each day of the week being called *feria* (weekday) with a number indicating its place in the succession of days. The Fathers of the fifth and sixth centuries tried to have people substitute these Christian designations for the pagan names, but they were unsuccessful. The old names, cleansed now by usage of their pagan overtones, continued to be used by the people, while *feria* remained an exclusively liturgical term, except in Portuguese.

---

44. *VSC* 106.

I. WEDNESDAY, FRIDAY, AND SATURDAY

In the liturgical organization of the week three days were very soon given a privileged place: Wednesday, Friday, and Saturday.

As early as the end of the first century, the *Didache* speaks of Wednesday and Friday as fast days. In the next century, the *Shepherd* of Hermas, Clement of Alexandria, and Tertullian speak of them as "stational" days, that is, days of fasting and penitential prayer.

All of Christian antiquity, without exception, observed the Wednesday and Friday fasts. Rome added Saturday. In the West we find the discipline being softened between the sixth and tenth centuries: first, the Wednesday observance was reduced to one of abstinence, then the Wednesday abstinence disappeared, as did the Friday fast. Only Ember Wednesdays, Fridays, and Saturdays remained as witnesses to the ancient discipline down to the Second World War.

Prayer on Wednesdays and Fridays became progressively communal instead of private, but the assembly held on these two days varied in form according to period and place. At Alexandria, in the middle of the fifth century, there was still an aliturgical assembly, that is, an assembly without any Eucharist. "The scriptures are read, and teachers interpret them; everything is done except the offering." The historian Socrates, who attests this usage, adds that in the preceding century Origen had written a number of his commentaries for use at the Wednesday and Friday gatherings.[45] It seems that in the time of St. Leo the Great Rome, too, had the custom of aliturgical stations on Wednesdays and Fridays.

On the other hand, the Churches of Africa, like those of Jerusalem and Cappadocia, used to celebrate the Eucharist on Wednesdays and Fridays. When, beginning in the sixth century, the West too began to celebrate Mass on these days, we see the lectionaries providing special epistles and gospels for these two ferial Masses, and this usage was to continue in France until the twelfth century.[46]

It is easy to see why Friday was given a special place, but why did the Church decide to honor Wednesday, too, in a special way? St. Epiphanius († 413), echoing the *Teaching of the Apostles* of the third century, says: "Wednesday and Friday are spent fasting until the ninth hour, because when Wednesday was beginning the Lord was arrested, and on Friday he was crucified."[47]

---

45. Socrates, *Historia Ecclesiastica* 5, 22 (PG 67:636–37).

46. For the gospels see T. Klauser, *Das römische Capitulare Evangeliorum* (LQF 28; Münster: Aschendorff, 1935); for the epistles, A. Wilmart, "Le lectionnaire d'Alcuin," *EL* 51 (1937) 165–68, 195–97.

47. St. Epiphanius, *De fide* 22, ed. K. Holl (GCS 37), 522; see A. Jaubert, *La date de la cène* (Etudes bibliques; Paris: Gabalda, 1957) 88.

The Christian Saturday replaced the sabbath but kept its name (Latin: *sabbatum*). This connection explains the very different attitudes the Church adopted in regard to Saturday. Some, in their concern not to judaize, refused to mark it by any special religious practices. Others, such as the Churches of Rome and Alexandria, made it a fast day beginning in the third century; the fast was meant as a weekly recall of the great paschal or Lenten fast.[48] In the East, on the other hand, Saturday was drawn into the orbit of Sunday and became a feast day. Thus the Saturdays of Lent were assimilated to the Sundays: there was no fast, the Eucharist was celebrated (whereas all the other weekdays were aliturgical), and the *natalitia* ("birthdays") of the saints were commemorated.

Beginning in the tenth century the custom spread in the West of honoring the Blessed Virgin in a special way on Saturdays. The Mass *de Sancta Maria in Sabbato* (of Our Lady on Saturday), which Alcuin had inserted into his votive sacramentary,[49] had by the twelfth century been given a place in the Lateran Missal.[50] The Roman Missal of Pius V put its seal of approval on this devotion.

II. THE DEVELOPMENT OF THE WEEKS

Readings—weekdays

The weeks unfold under the influence of the Sundays that begin them. They belong either to a particular liturgical season or to the thirty-four weeks of Ordinary Time.

The lectionary for Mass provides texts proper to each day of the year. The first readings, which are taken from either the Old Testament or the writings of the apostles, form a two-year cycle. The same holds for the psalms which follow the first reading. The gospels, on the other hand, are read in the course of a single year. Since the reading of John is assigned to the end of Lent and the Easter season, Mark is read from the first to the ninth weeks (inclusive) of Ordinary Time, Matthew from the tenth to the twenty-first weeks, and Luke from the twenty-second to the thirty-fourth.

---

48. Innocent I, *Ep. 25 ad Decentium Eugubinum*, ed. R. Cabié, *La lettre du pape Innocent Ier à Decentius de Gubbio* (Bibliothèque de la RHE 58; Louvain: Publications Universitaires, 1973) 24.

49. Alcuin, *Liber sacramentorum* (PL 101:455); J. Deshusses, *Le sacramentaire grégorien* 2 (Spicilegium Friburgense 24; Fribourg, 1979) 45.

50. Missale Romanum scriptum saec. XII = Fondo della Scala santa, no 997, in the Archivio di Stato Italiano, Rome. — See L. Gougaud, *Devotional and Ascetical Practices in the Middle Ages* (London: Burns, Oates, and Washbourne, 1927) 66–74: "Why Was Saturday Dedicated to Our Lady?"

As far as the presidential prayers are concerned, the weekdays of the end of Advent, Lent, and the final week of the Easter season all have complete formularies of their own. The weekdays of the Christmas and Easter seasons have several weekly series of prayers. The weekdays of Ordinary Time draw from the formularies for the Sundays, but they have six proper prefaces.

Outside of Lent, the weekdays are often days of the feasts or memorials of the saints. Within prescribed limits, Masses for various intentions may also be celebrated.

III. THE START OF THE SEASONS

At Rome, where the ancestral religion had had a strongly agrarian character, the Church decided, beginning in the fourth or fifth century, to mark the beginning of each season of the year with a week of more solemn fast and prayer. The beginnings of summer, fall, and winter coincided with the three main harvests in the Mediterranean countries: the grain harvest, the grape harvest, and the olive harvest. The Christians of the Apostolic City began by solemnizing the "three seasons" of June, September, and December. They subsequently added the celebration of the beginning of spring, thus keeping alive the memory of the time when the month of March was the first of the year. These four were the *Quatuor tempora* (four seasons), known in the English-speaking countries as the Ember Days. They may go back to Pope Siricius, at the end of the fourth century. St. Leo the Great already regarded them as traditional.[51]

An Ember week included not only fasting but stational liturgical assemblies on Wednesday and Friday and again during the night between Saturday and Sunday. These assemblies were held successively at the churches of St. Mary Major and of the Holy Apostles and the Basilica

---

51. St. Leo (440–61), *Sermones* 12–20 and 75–81. *Sermo* 19, 2: "[Fasts] are distributed throughout the entire year so that the law of abstinence may have a place in every season. Thus we celebrate the spring fast during Lent, the summer fast at Pentecost, the fall fast in the seventh month, and the winter fast in the tenth month" (CCL 138:77). Gelasius (493–96): "They are to know that they are likewise to ordain priests and deacons only at certain times and on certain days, namely, during the fasts of the fourth, seventh, and tenth months, as well as the fasts at the beginning and middle of Lent; the ordinations are to be celebrated during the Saturday fast, in the evening" (ed. A. Thiel, *Epist. Rom. Pontif.* I [Braunsberg: Peter, 1868] 368). *LP* I, 63: "He decreed a Saturday fast three times in the year, at the times of grain, wine, and oil (see Joel 2:19), in accordance with the prophecy concerning the fourth, seventh, and tenth months (see Zech 8:19)." *Ge* I, 82: "Announcement of the fasts for the fourth, seventh, and tenth months"; III, 16: "After this the people are to be advised of the times for the fasts of the fourth, seventh, and tenth months."

of St. Peter. Ordinations soon came to be connected with the three stations: the names of the candidates were announced on Wednesday; the men themselves were presented to the people on Friday; and they were ordained during the Saturday night vigil.

As use of the Roman liturgy spread, the Ember Days came to be celebrated throughout the West (Naples, seventh century; England, seventh–eighth; Gaul, eighth; Spain, eleventh; Milan, twelfth). They were never received in the Eastern Churches. Until 1969, the five Old Testament readings that preceded the epistle and gospel on Ember Saturday kept alive in the Missal the memory of the old Sunday vigil.

When, beginning in the sixteenth century, the missionary movement led to the Church being introduced into all parts of the world, the seasonal character of the Ember Days became difficult to grasp outside the Northern Hemisphere. Vatican Council II therefore decided to make the practice more flexible. The special formularies disappeared from the 1970 Missal. The General Norms for the Liturgical Year place under one heading the Ember Days and the Rogations, or prayers for the blessings of the earth, that had hitherto been offered on the three days before the Ascension. The Norms then speak as follows:

> On rogation and ember days the practice of the Church is to offer prayers to the Lord for the needs of all people, especially for the productivity of the earth and for human labor, and to give him public thanks.
>
> In order to adapt the rogation and ember days to various regions and the different needs of the people, the conferences of bishops should arrange the time and plan of their celebration.
>
> Consequently, the competent authority should lay down norms, in view of local conditions, on extending such celebrations over one or several days and on repeating them during the year.
>
> On each day of these celebrations the Mass should be one of the votive Masses for various needs and occasions that is best suited to the intentions of the petitioners.[52]

---

52. *General Norms for the Liturgical Year and the Calendar* 45–47.

THE YEAR

P. Jounel

The Easter Cycle

BIBLIOGRAPHY

B. Botte, "La question pascale, Pâque du vendredi ou Pâque du dimanche?" *LMD* no. 41 (1955) 84–95.

B. Botte, "Pascha," *OS* 8 (1963) 213–26.

R. Cantalamessa, *La Paque dans l'Eglise ancienne* (Traditio Christiana 4; Bern: Peter Lang, 1980).

O. Casel, *La fête de Pâques dans l'Eglise des Pères* (Lex orandi 37; Paris: Cerf, 1951).

J. Daniélou, *The Bible and the Liturgy* (Notre Dame: University of Notre Dame Press, 1956).

P. Duployé, "Pâque la sainte," *LMD* no. 6 (1946) 12–30.

C. Mohrmann, "*Pascha, Passio, Transitus*," in *Etudes sur le latin des chrétiens* I (Rome: Edizioni di storia e letteratura, 1958) 205–22.

J. van Goudoever, *Fêtes et calendriers bibliques* (Théologie historique 7; Paris: Beauchesne, 1967).

From the time of the apostles on, the Christians who commemorated the Lord's resurrection every Sunday could not fail to project the light of their faith on the annual celebration of the Jewish Passover as well. Thus St. Paul wrote to the faithful at Corinth: "Christ, our paschal lamb, has been sacrificed. Let us, therefore, celebrate the festival, not with the old leaven, the leaven of malice and evil, but with the unleavened bread of sincerity and truth" (1 Cor 5:7-8). Nonetheless it was not until the early years of the second century that there was any thought of celebrating a specifically Christian feast of Easter,[1] and even then the Church of Rome waited until the second half of the century before accepting it.

---

1. M. Richard, "La question pascale au IIe siècle," *OS* 6 (1961) 179-212. A complete dossier on the Easter question may be found in R. Cantalamessa, *La Pâque dans l'Eglise ancienne* xx, 18-29, 86-89.

Moreover, until Pope Victor intervened (ca. 189-98), two ways of calculating the date for Easter were in use. The Churches of Asia Minor were bent on Christianizing the day of the Jewish Passover, the fourteenth of Nisan, and so they stopped their fast on that day. The other Churches celebrated their paschal feast on the following Sunday, the "first day of the week." The Roman Church in particular followed this second way, and it became the rule for all from the beginning of the third century. Even then, however, differences arose in calculating the day when the fourteenth of the lunar month of Nisan fell in a solar calendar. In 325 the Council of Nicaea urged all the Churches to accept the Alexandrian computation of the date, and Easter was henceforth celebrated on the Sunday that followed the first full moon after the spring equinox (therefore between March 22 and April 25).[2]

From at least the beginning of the third century, the celebration of the resurrection was continued for a period of fifty days *(Pentekostē)*, but only from the fourth century on was the fiftieth day itself marked by special observances. At this same period the "sacred triduum of Christ crucified, buried, and risen" made its appearance, to be followed a little later by the celebration of Holy Week as a whole. The celebration of Easter had also been accompanied, from an early date, by a fast on the days commemorating Christ's suffering and death; this fast was rather quickly extended until it lasted for the forty days of Lent, and became a time of preparation for Easter.

§1. The Easter Vigil

BIBLIOGRAPHY

G. Bertonière, *The Historical Development of the Easter Vigil and Related Services in the Greek Church* (OCA 193; Rome: Pontificio Istituto Orientale, 1972).

B. Capelle, "La procession du Lumen Christi au samedi soir," in *Travaux liturgiques* 3 (Louvain: Mont César, 1967) 221-35.

B. Capelle, "Le rite des cinq grains d'encens," *ibid.* 236-41.

F. Dell'Oro, "La solenne veglia pasquale," *Rivista Liturgica* 40 (1953) 1-93.

P. Jounel, "La liturgie du Mystère pascal: La nuit pascale," *LMD* no. 67 (1961) 123-44.

R. Le Déaut, *La nuit pascale* (Analecta Biblica 22; Rome: Pontificio Istituto Biblico, 1963).

---

2. Although the Council of Nicaea had required that "all, with one heart and one mind, offer their prayers on the same day, the most holy day of Easter" (Cantalamessa, *ibid.*, 89), the discrepancy, beginning in 1583, between the old Julian calendar and the reformed calendar of Pope Gregory XIII was to mean a different date for the Easter celebration in the Churches that accepted the reform and those who decided to remain with the Julian calendar. The difference could be more than a month (e.g., April 4 and May 8 in 1983).

J. Pinell, "La benedicció del ciri pasqual i els seus textos," in *Liturgica* 2 (Montserrat: Abadía de Montserrat, 1958) 1–119.

I. ORIGIN AND EVOLUTION

1. *The Early Celebration of Easter*

In the earliest documents the celebration of Easter takes the form essentially of a strict fast lasting one, two, or more days[3] and followed by a nocturnal assembly for prayer, which closes with the Eucharist. The obligation of taking part in this nocturnal assembly was so fundamental that Tertullian saw it as an obstacle to a Christian woman marrying a nonbeliever: Would her husband allow her to go out at night for the Easter Vigil?[4] The fast itself was complete and no less binding. The *Apostolic Tradition* (third century) states: "No one is to take anything at Easter until the sacrifice has been offered; anyone acting differently will not be considered to have fasted."[5]

At that time, then, the Christian Easter consisted in a fast, a feast, and a transition from the one to the other during a holy night in which the hours of fasting were completed by prayer and in which the feast day was opened by the Eucharist. The two components of this celebration were inseparable. The fast as such was simply a preparation and a purification. This Easter fast, which according to Tertullian paid homage to the days when the bridegroom was taken away from the Church,[6] was the first phase of Easter or the Christian Passover, that is, of the *passage* of the whole Christ, head and body, from death to life, from tears to joy.

The *Teaching of the Apostles*, a Syrian work of the third century, provides us with our earliest description of the Easter celebration:

> On the Friday and on the Sabbath fast wholly, and taste nothing. You shall come together and watch and keep vigil all the night with prayers and intercessions, and with reading of the Prophets, and with the Gospel and with Psalms . . . until the third hour in the night after the Sabbath; and then break your fasts. . . . And then offer your oblations; and thereafter eat and make good cheer, and rejoice and be glad, because the earnest of

---

3. Eusebius of Caesarea, *Historia Ecclesiastica* V, 24, 2, ed. G. Bardy (SC 45; Paris: Cerf, 1955) 70 (witness of St. Irenaeus). See P. Jounel, "Le jeune pascal" *LMD* no. 45 (1956) 87–92.

4. Tertullian, *Ad uxorem* II, 4 (CCL 1:388). Cited by Cantalamessa, *ibid.*, 144–46.

5. Hippolytus, *Traditio Apostolica* 33, ed. B. Botte, *La Tradition apostolique de saint Hippolyte* (LQF 39; Münster: Aschendorff, 1963) 78–79.

6. Tertullian, *De ieiunio* 2 and 14 (CCL 1:1258 and 1271). Cited by Cantalamessa, *ibid.* 148–49.

our resurrection, Christ, is risen. And this shall be a law to you for ever, unto the end of the world.[7]

Here we have all the basic elements of the Easter Vigil: fasting, assembly of the community of believers, prayer vigil, readings from the Old and New Testaments, celebration of the Eucharist, fraternal agapes in the joy of the risen Christ.

2. *Expansions of the Roman Easter Vigil*

a) *The celebration of baptism*—According to the teaching of St. Paul, in baptism Christians are immersed in the death of Christ and buried with him, in order that they may share in the new life of the risen Lord (Rom 6:3-5). The early Church was most attentive to the relation between baptism and the pasch or passage of Christ. For this reason it made Sunday the preferred day for administering the sacrament.[8] Once the Peace of Constantine (313) made mass conversions possible, the Easter Vigil became the supreme baptismal night of the year, coming as it did at the end of Lent and the final stages of the catechumenate.

This was the golden age of the catechesis which prepared candidates for Christian initiation and of mystagogical catechesis as well. We need think only of such names as Ambrose, Cyril of Jerusalem, John Chrysostom, Theodore of Mopsuestia, Augustine, and Chromatius of Aquileia. It was also the period that saw the development of the baptismal rites for the Easter Vigil and the Easter octave and of their formularies: the procession to the font, the prayer for the consecration of the water, the removal of garments by the candidates for baptism, the triple immersion accompanied by the triple profession of faith, the anointing with chrism, and the donning of the white garment; then confirmation by the bishop, and the return to the basilica for the celebration of the Eucharist, with the neophytes sharing for the first time in the Easter banquet of the faithful.

Only adult candidates could fully appreciate the expressive power of such a liturgy. Once adult baptism became the exception, the popes tried in vain to preserve the exclusive right of the Easter and Pentecost Vigils as the occasions for baptism. The Church did nonetheless continue to bless

---

7. Ch. 21. Text in *Didascalia et Constitutiones Apostolorum*, ed. F. X. Funk, I (Paderborn: Schöningh, 1905) 288; trans. R. Hugh Connolly, *Didascalia Apostolorum* (Oxford: Clarendon Press, 1929) 189.

8. Tertullian, *De baptismo* 19, 1-3 (CCL 1:293-94; SC 35:93-95). See Cantalamessa, *ibid.* 144-45.

the baptismal water during the Easter Vigil; and the formularies for the octave, with their frequent mentions of the neophytes, remained unchanged. In the East any echo of Christian initiation disappeared from the Easter liturgy from the eleventh century on.[9]

b) *The lighting of the Easter candle*—The second expansion of the Easter Vigil in the West consisted of a *lucernarium*, or lighting of the Easter candle, that was introduced as an opening rite for the service.

In an age when there were no electric lights, the lighting of lamps at nightfall was a daily family ritual; it brought joy and ensured security. The ritual had its place especially at the start of a banquet of friends and, among the Jews, at the start of the Friday evening meal that marked the beginning of the sabbath. Christians liked to think of this evening light as an image of Christ the Light of the world. Thus, beginning in the fourth century, the lighting of the lamp at the beginning of community meals was accompanied by a hymn to Christ as "joyous light of the Father's eternal glory."[10]

The holiest night of the year could not be allowed to begin without a solemn celebration of light. In the time of Jerome and Augustine, this ritual was part of the vigil in Africa and Northern Italy, and probably in Spain and Gaul as well. The offering to God of the light that would illumine the nocturnal vigil was accompanied by a proclamation of paschal joy; the proclamation was sung by a deacon in the form of a lengthy thanksgiving. That is how the *Exsultet* was born.

The version of the *Exsultet* that was sung in certain churches of Rome in the seventh century and became part of the papal liturgy in the eleventh century is only the best-known formulary, and doubtless the most beautiful as well, from an abundant literature of which only a few texts have survived.[11] The people, gathered around the ambo (a raised platform), followed the Easter proclamation with such joyful attention that in many areas the scroll which the deacon unrolled as he sang was illuminated for their benefit.

The *Exsultet* is an important witness to the theological content of the Easter Vigil, as we shall see a little further on. We find an early form of

9. *Le Typicon de la Grande Eglise* (tenth century) still makes reference to it; ed. J. Mateos (OCA 166; Rome: Pontificio Istituto Orientale, 1966) 2:84-91.

10. F. J. Dölger, *Lumen Christi*, trans. from the German (Paris: Cerf, 1958) 35-42.

11. J. M. Pinell, "La benedicció del ciri pasqual i els seus textos," in *Liturgica* 2 (Montserrat: Abadía de Montserrat, 1958) 1-119; see also H. Schmidt, *Hebdomada Sancta* (Rome: Herder, 1956) 627-50 and 814; P. Verbraken, "Une Laus cerei africaine," *RBén* 70 (1960) 301-12.

12. L. Grodecki and F. Mutherich, *Le siècle de l'an mil* (L'univers des formes; Paris: Gallimard, 1973) 221-25. In addition to *Exsultet* rolls, there were also rolls for the blessing of the font: *DACL* 13 (1938) col. 1559-66.

it in the oldest Easter homilies, such as those of Pseudo-Hippolytus, Asterius the Sophist, and St. Ephraem.[13]

c) *The blessing of the new fire and the procession with the Easter candle*—The practice of striking new fire at Easter was made necessary by the custom of extinguishing all the lamps on Holy Thursday evening. A new flame had therefore to be struck if the minimum illumination needed for the nocturnal office were to be available, and this not only in preparation for the Easter Vigil but also on Good Friday.[14] The Roman Pontifical of the twelfth century is the first document to provide prayers for the blessing of fire on Holy Saturday and a description of the *Lumen Christi* procession.[15] In the thirteenth century, perhaps under the influence of the Jerusalem liturgy, a three-branched candle was introduced which was lit at the new fire and then used to light the Easter candle in turn. It disappeared in 1951, when the Easter Vigil was restored.

3. *The Mystery Content of the Easter Vigil*

a) *Transition between the mystery of the death and the mystery of the resurrection*—This night, with its "exceptional solemnity" that marks it as the high point of the liturgical year, belongs still to the period when we celebrate the death of Christ, but in addition "it already belongs to the beginning of Sunday, which the Lord has hallowed by his glorious resurrection."[16] This night is therefore located at the pivot of the mystery of salvation. As a result Easter Sunday is counted in two ways. It is the third day of the paschal or Easter triduum and the first day of the ensuing fifty-day period. Nor may it be divided to satisfy both requirements; rather, in its unity it looks back to Good Friday and the time of preparation for Easter, but also forward to the fifty-day period that will be an unbroken celebration of the risen Lord's victory.

b) *Mystery of Christ the Savior and of the Christian who is saved*— When the Church celebrates the death and resurrection of Christ, it does not simply recall a past historical event. Rather, it celebrates the mystery of salvation "sacramentally,"[17] and in calling to mind the death and resurrection of Christ it actualizes or renders present their mysterious efficacy.[18] The mystery of Easter is therefore at once the mystery of Christ the head and the mystery of the Church as Body of Christ. In the Easter Vigil Christ

---

13. R. Cantalamessa, *ibid.* 47–55, 102–3, 140–43. For Pseudo-Hippolytus: P. Nautin, *Homélies pascales* I (SC 27; Paris: Cerf, 1950) 117–23.

14. *OR* 23, Andrieu, *OR* 3:272.

15. Andrieu, *PR* 1:241.

16. St. Augustine, *Sermo* 220 and 221 (PL 38:1089 and 1090).

17. St. Leo the Great, *Tractatus* 47, 1 (CCL 138A:274).

18. St. Leo the Great, *Tractatus* 72, 1 (CCL 138A:441).

applies the saving power of his death and resurrection to the Church in a privileged way, and the means by which he does this is the very celebration of that death and resurrection by the Church.

c) *"The mother of all holy vigils"*—It is not irrelevant that the Christian assembly celebrates the paschal mystery in the context of a prayer vigil and while listening to the Word of God and celebrating various sacraments. St. Augustine calls the Easter Vigil "the mother of all holy vigils."[19] The Missal of 1970 sums up the meaning of the Vigil as follows: "In accord with ancient tradition, this night is one of vigil for the Lord (Exod 12:42). The Gospel of Luke (12:35ff.) is a reminder to the faithful to have their lamps burning ready, to be like men awaiting their master's return so that when he arrives he will find them wide awake and will seat them at his table."

In its content, then, the Easter Vigil is a commemoration of the exodus of the Old Testament people, as well as of the death and resurrection of the Lord; it brings the presence of the risen Christ in the assembly of the people of the new covenant through the sacraments of Christian initiation; and it is a time of waiting for his return, which, it was long thought, would occur precisely during an Easter Vigil. The *Exsultet* brings out all these aspects in turn:

> . . . This is our passover feast, when Christ, the true Lamb, is slain, whose blood consecrates the homes of all believers.
>
> This is the night when first you saved our fathers: you freed the people of Israel from their slavery and led them dry-shod through the sea.
>
> This is the night when the pillar of fire destroyed the darkness of sin!
>
> This is the night when Christians everywhere, washed clean of sin and freed from all defilement, are restored to grace and grow together in holiness.
>
> This is the night when Jesus Christ broke the chains of death and rose triumphant from the grave.
>
> . . . Night truly blessed when heaven is wedded to earth and man is reconciled with God!
>
> Therefore, heavenly Father, in the joy of this night, receive our evening sacrifice of praise, your Church's solemn offering.
>
> Accept this Easter candle . . . Let it mingle with the lights of heaven and continue bravely burning to dispel the darkness of this night!
>
> May the Morning Star which never sets find this flame still burning: Christ, that Morning Star, who came back from the dead, and shed his peaceful light on all mankind. . . .

4. Decline and Rebirth of the Easter Vigil

a) *Decline (seventh–seventeenth centuries)*—The rites of the Easter Vigil, which were inherited from the Roman Sacramentaries of the seventh

---

19. St. Augustine, *Sermo* 219 (PL 38:1088).

century by way of the Frankish Sacramentaries of the eighth and ninth centuries (with twelve readings), had acquired their definitive form by the time of Innocent III († 1216). The final innovation had been the insertion into the Easter candle of five grains of incense, embedded there in the form of a cross; the purpose was to give a more concrete form to the blessing it had received and to fix the memory of this blessing in the minds of viewers.[20]

Meanwhile, however, the celebration of the holy night had for a long time been in a gradual decline as a result of its being anticipated at an increasingly early hour on Saturday. From the seventh century on there was no longer any question of devoting the entire night to the vigil. The ceremony now began at two in the afternoon, although the celebrants did wait for the first star to appear before beginning the Mass.[21] Soon the blessing of the new fire was beginning at midday. There was now a contradiction between the spring sun that was filling the church with its light and the singing of the *Exsultet* with its praise of a "night truly blessed." The entire symbolism of the vigil had now been falsified. Nor were the people deceived: they absented themselves in growing numbers from the celebration and instead came on Sunday morning to take part in the office of Matins, which in many places was climaxed by a performance representing the visit of the holy women to the tomb.

St. Pius V dealt the Easter Vigil a new blow when he forbade the celebration of Mass after midday (1556). Finally, in 1642 Urban VIII removed the days of Holy Week from the list of feast days of obligation.

b) *Rebirth (1951)*—The fourteen years preceding the Second Vatican Council were marked by a biblical, patristic, liturgical, and theological renewal from which the Council derived its substance. The convergent approaches of these various disciplines to the mystery of redemption served to highlight the importance of Christ's Pasch and of the sacred vigil which celebrated it. Dom Odo Casel's study of the feast of Easter in the Church of the Fathers (German original, 1934; French translation, 1963) made a decisive contribution to the discovery of the holy night as the high point of the Christian year. Pius XII was responding to a fervent desire of the liturgical movement, already solidly established in a number of countries, when in 1951 he authorized the nocturnal celebration of the Easter Vigil and, four years later (1955), made it obligatory.

The Ordo of 1951 once more located the vigil in the depths of the night, since Mass was now not to begin before midnight. The Ordo did, however, give permission to move the ceremonies back to the early evening hours.

---

20. Bernhard, *Ordo officiorum ecclesiae Lateranensis*, ed. L. Fischer (Historische Forschungen und Quellen, Heft 2–3; Munich: Datterer, 1916) 61.

21. *Ge*, no. 443.

The rites were simplified and organized with a view to eliciting the participation of the people. Thus the blessing of the new fire was normally to take place outside the church and in the midst of the faithful, who would then enter the building in procession behind the Easter candle, each of them holding a lighted candle, as had been done in Jerusalem in the fifth century.[22] The number of readings was reduced from twelve to four, as in the Gregorian Sacramentary. After the blessing of the water and the celebration of any baptisms, the congregation was urged to renew its baptismal profession of faith.

In the Missal of 1970, the Ordo for the Easter Vigil reflects a further stage in the adaptation begun in 1951. The timetable for the ceremonies is made more flexible. In the Liturgy of the Word, the discontinuity that formerly existed between the Old Testament and New Testament readings is eliminated, since the baptismal liturgy now begins only after the proclamation of the Lord's resurrection and the homily. Finally, without returning to the twelve Old Testament readings of the Tridentine Missal, seven are suggested. The innovations of 1951 in regard to the entrance procession and the renewal of baptismal promises are retained.

II. THE CELEBRATION OF THE HOLY NIGHT

The Easter Vigil is essentially a nocturnal celebration. It can begin as soon as night has fallen and must end before sunrise. The majority of Christian communities celebrate it in the early part of the night, but in some regions that are accustomed to early rising, the service is held toward the end of the night.

It is appropriate that all the faithful of a given area gather to celebrate a single vigil as an expression of their one faith, even though ordinarily they would gather separately in smaller groups. It is also appropriate that the vigil include baptisms. If there are no adults to be baptized, it would be well to baptize some infants.

1. *The Beginning of the Vigil: The New Fire and the Easter Candle*

The people gather outside the church around a fire. After greeting the assembly, the priest explains briefly the meaning of this vigil and blesses the fire. He then prepares the Easter candle, using a stylus to cut a cross in it and trace the number of the current year. He then lights the candle with a flame taken from the new fire, referring, as he does so, to "the light of Christ, rising in glory."

22. A. Renoux, *Le Codex arménien Jérusalem 121* (PO 36; Turnhout: Brepols, 1971) 297.

The deacon or, if there be no deacon, the priest takes the candle and, holding it aloft toward the people, sings: "Christ our light." The congregation then enters the church, which is completely dark. After the acclamation has been sung a second time, the priest (unless he is carrying the Easter candle) and then the faithful light their own candles from the Easter candle. Finally, the acclamation is sung a third time. This procession suggests the journey of the Israelites through the wilderness following the pillar of fire. Even more, however, it reminds us of the words of Jesus: "I am the light of the world; he who follows me will not walk in darkness" (John 8:12).

After the Easter candle has been placed on a candlestick near the ambo, where it will remain throughout the Easter season, the deacon sings the *Exsultet*. This is both a prayer, in which the candle is offered to God, and a proclamation of Easter. It takes the form of a joyful act of thanksgiving whose lyrical quality is exceeded only by its depth of thought.

2. *The Liturgy of the Word*

One of the vigil prayers says: "Father, you teach us in both the Old and the New Testament to celebrate this passover mystery." If the lesson is to be learned, the Liturgy of the Word will have to be somewhat lengthy. Again, this is the time beyond all others when the assembled people keep watch and pray together for the coming of their Lord. While no more than two Old Testament readings are obligatory, one of which must be the story of the crossing of the Red Sea (third reading), only a complete reading of the seven suggested texts, together with the intervening psalms or biblical canticles and prayers, will yield what may properly be called a "vigil."

a) *The choice of readings*—Six of the seven readings from the Old Testament are taken from the twelve in use prior to 1951; the seventh replaces Ezek 37, used in the evening Mass of Pentecost, with Ezek 36, which the Fathers interpreted as a prophecy of baptism. Several of these passages are also read on the same day in the Eastern Churches. We are therefore dealing here with a catechetical resource that is in universal use.

Nor is the choice a fortuitous one. It has its basis in the Jewish tradition, since, according to the Palestinian Talmud, during the night of Passover the Jews commemorated "Four Nights": those of the creation of the world, the sacrifice of Abraham, the Exodus, and the coming of the Messiah.[23] But the seven Old Testament readings of the Christian Easter Vigil begin precisely with the stories of creation, the sacrifice of Abraham, and the crossing of the Red Sea, followed by an eschatological passage from Isaiah (54:5-14). Next come three other readings that look forward more directly to the celebration of baptism; the reading from the Apostle

---

23. R. Le Déaut, *La Nuit pascale* (Analecta Biblica 22; Rome: Pontificio Istituto Biblico, 1963) 73–129.

is also concerned with baptism (Rom 6:3-11). The final reading is the account of how the spice-bearing women found the tomb empty and were told by the angel: "He is risen."

Each Old Testament reading is followed by a psalm or canticle, which echoes it, and by a prayer which serves as a conclusion. The transition from the Old Testament to the New is effected by the singing of the *Glory to God in the Highest* while the church bells are rung. The *Glory to God* is the Christian Easter song par excellence. In the West it was for a long time sung only during this holy night, whereas the Eastern Churches have made it their daily morning hymn. After listening to the passage from St. Paul, the congregation sings the Alleluia which the priest first intones. According to the Apocalypse (Rev 19:1-16) Alleluia is the song sung in heaven. But it is also the pilgrim song of Christians on earth, who are sure that in Jesus Christ they have already won the victory over the powers of evil. St. Augustine speaks as follows of the Easter Alleluia:

> And now we sing Alleluia! How sweet, how joyous a song it is! How overflowing with tender charm! If we were to repeat it constantly we would grow weary of it, but when it returns after absence, what festivity!
>
> Our joy, my brothers and sisters, is the joy of being together, the joy of singing psalms and hymns, the joy of remembering the passion and resurrection of Christ, the joy of hoping for eternal life. And if the simple hope fills us with such lively joy, what will our joy be when the hope is fulfilled? Yes, during these days when the Alleluia echoes our souls are no longer the same. Do we not almost smell the fragrance of the heavenly city? . . . In that place where the saints are reunited, they will meet those they never saw on earth. In that place those who know one another will meet again, and there their union will be complete.[24]

b) *The prayers*—The prayers which conclude each of the Old Testament readings are all from the Gelasian Sacramentary (seventh century). Each refers more or less explicitly to the reading just heard. One of these prayers, *Deus incommutabilis virtus* ("God of unchanging power"—after the seventh reading) develops what would one day be the main theme of the conciliar Constitution *Lumen gentium* on the Church: the Church is a mystery, a *mirabile sacramentum* (wonderful sacrament), that is, the principal sign of God's intervention throughout history for the salvation of humanity. It is the sign that creation has been entirely renewed, that what had fallen into ruins is now restored, that the human person is completely rejuvenated in Jesus Christ, who is the source of all reality. It would be difficult to find a more profound theological reflection on the paschal mystery as mystery of salvation.

---

24. St. Augustine, *Enarr. in Ps. 118* (PL 37:1463).

3. *The Baptismal Liturgy*

The baptismal liturgy has as its first main part the blessing of the water to be used in the celebration of baptism throughout the Easter season. The blessing is introduced by the singing of a litany, which may be omitted if there is to be no baptism at the Easter Vigil itself. Then comes the prayer for the blessing of the water. It is the old Roman prayer, although now altered somewhat in order to give more emphasis to the New Testament figures of baptism in addition to those from the Old Testament. The blessing refers successively to the primeval waters, the deluge, the crossing of the Red Sea, then the baptism of Jesus by John, the water which flowed from the open side of Jesus on the cross, and the mission which the risen Lord gave to his apostles: "Go therefore and make disciples of all nations, baptizing them in the name of the Father and of the Son and of the Holy Spirit." While calling upon the Holy Spirit to sanctify the water by his power, the celebrant may lower the Easter candle into the water in a symbolic gesture.

After the blessing of the water, each of the catechumens—first adults, then children--is baptized according to the usual ritual: renunciation of Satan and profession of faith (uttered by the parents and godparents for infants), then total or partial immersion in the water or a triple pouring of water on the head of the candidate. In the case of little children, who will be confirmed only later on, the baptism is followed by an anointing with chrism. For adults this anointing is omitted, since they will proceed directly to confirmation. Finally, the candidates don a white garment and are given a candle lit from the Easter candle.

If the bishop is present, he administers confirmation; otherwise the priest who has just baptized also confirms. The usual ritual is followed.

Baptism is followed by a congregational renewal of baptismal promises. If there is no font in the church and therefore no blessing of the baptismal water, the priest begins this ceremony by blessing the water for the sprinkling. The prayer is a new one. It first recalls the natural and biblical symbolism of water; it then calls to mind the baptism formerly received by each person present and associates it with the joy of those throughout the world who are receiving baptism on this occasion.

The dialogue between priest and faithful in the renunciation of Satan and the profession of faith is the same as the one used in baptism, in accordance with the Ordo of 1951. The priest then proceeds through the church sprinkling the congregation with baptismal water or with the water he has just blessed.

4. *The Eucharistic Liturgy*

The Eucharistic liturgy is as usual. The preface in its Latin original recalls the cosmic extent of the paschal mystery. This mystery is truly a feast for the world, since it inaugurates the new heavens and the new earth. Therefore *totus in orbe terrarum mundus exsultat*—the entire world rejoices. As they receive Communion for the first time with their brothers and sisters, the newly baptized complete their Christian initiation. In order that on this holy night the sign of participation in the Lord's table may be as complete as possible, it is fitting that all should receive from the cup after receiving the bread of life.

To the repeated singing of the Alleluia the priest dismisses the congregation in peace and the congregation cries out its joyful thanksgiving.

5. *The Easter Vigil in the Byzantine Rite*

In the Churches of the Byzantine rite, no less than in the Churches of the West, the Easter Vigil came to be anticipated on Saturday, and for the same reason: the absence of adult baptisms. But whereas the Roman liturgy had only an exceptionally short office of Matins and Lauds for the final hours of the night, at Byzantium the daily monastic vigil was enriched on this occasion with rites and songs that turned it into the most popular and beautiful of the entire year.[25]

a) *The anticipated vigil*—The ancient vigil, celebrated on Saturday morning, begins with a *lucernarium* or service of light. At Jerusalem the patriarch strikes the new fire inside the Holy Sepulcher and from it lights the candles of clergy and faithful. Popular devotion regards this fire as miraculous in origin; it is fire that has "descended from heaven." Next come fifteen readings from the Old Testament[26] and the reading (Rom 8:6, 3-11) from St. Paul. The priest then dons white vestments in order to read the gospel of the resurrection. Finally, the Eucharist is celebrated according to the Liturgy of St. Basil.

b) *The nocturnal vigil*—The medieval office of the holy night begins with the lighting of candles and with a procession outside the church that ends with the reading of the gospel of the resurrection. This is followed by the usual vigil office and morning office, at the end of which those present kiss the book of the gospels and exchange the kiss of peace: "Christ is risen!—Yes, he is truly risen!" After this a sermon attributed to St. John Chrysostom is read:

> Let none bemoan their poverty for our common kingdom has appeared. Let none lament their sins, for now forgiveness has gushed from the tomb. . . . Christ is risen and the demons are laid low. Christ is risen and the angels are rejoicing. Christ is risen and life is in command. Christ is risen

25. G. Bertonière, *The Historical Development of the Easter Vigil and Related Services in the Greek Church* (OCA 193; Rome: Pontificio Istituto Orientale, 1972).

26. E. Mercenier and F. Paris, *La prière des Eglises de rite byzantin* II/2 (Chevetogne, 1948) 260-61. See also N. Edelby, *Liturgicon* (Beirut: Editions du Renouveau, 1960) 148.

and there is no longer a dead man in the tomb. For Christ, risen from the dead, is the first fruits of those who have died.[27]

The concluding prayer of the morning office is followed by the Eucharist according to the Liturgy of St. John Chrysostom.

The texts are inseparable from the rites and from the ambiance created by the lights, the incense, and the melodies. Nonetheless they themselves have an unmatched depth and lyricism. Over and over the Easter troparion is heard: "Christ is risen from the dead! By his death he has destroyed death! He gives life to those in the grave!"

There is an echo of this in the canon by St. John Damascene that has been adopted as an Easter hymn in the French edition of the Liturgy of the Hours.

§2. The Easter Triduum

BIBLIOGRAPHY

P. F. Beatrice, *La lavanda dei piedi. Contributo a la storia delle antiche liturgie cristiane* (Bibliotheca EL, Subsidia 28; Rome: Edizioni liturgiche, 1982).

B. Capelle, "Problèmes de pastorale liturgique: Le vendredi saint," *QL* 34 (1953) 251–74.

A. Chavasse, "A Rome, le jeudi saint, au VIIe siècle, d'après un ancien Ordo," *RHE* 50 (1955) 61–80.

R. H. Connolly, "Liturgical Prayers of Intercession. I. The Good Friday *Orationes sollemnes*," *JTS* 21 (1920) 219–32.

P. Jounel, "La liturgie du Mystère pascal: Le vendredi saint," *LMD* no. 67 (1961) 199–214; "Le jeudi saint," *LMD* no. 68 (1961) 13–29.

E. Moeller, "L'antiquité de la double messe de Pâques et de Pentecôte," *QL* 26 (1942) 26–49.

V. Raffa, "Afania ed epifania della luce nel Triduo sacro," in *Miscellanea liturgica . . . Giacomo Lercaro* I (Rome: Desclée, 1966) 559–95.

G. Ropa, "Il preludio medioevale all'adorazione della croce nel venerdì santo," in *ibid.* 609–59.

O. Rousseau, "La descente aux enfers dans le cadre des liturgies chrétiennes," *LMD* no. 43 (1955) 104–23.

The term "Easter triduum" (or "paschal triduum") became common only in the thirties.[28] It was to receive official approval in 1969 in the renewed norms for the liturgical year. But as early as the end of the fourth century Ambrose was speaking of the "sacred triduum" (*triduum sacrum*) in which Christ "suffered and rested and rose" (*et passus est, et requievit,*

---

27. Mercenier-Paris, *ibid.* 280–81.

28. It occurs in Cardinal I. Schuster, *The Sacramentary (Liber Sacramentorum)* 3, trans. A. Levelis-Marke (New York: Benziger, 1925) 13–29.

et resurrexit).[29] A short time later Augustine was referring to "the most holy triduum of the crucified, buried, and risen Lord" (*sacratissimum triduum crucifixi, sepulti et ressuscitati)*.[30] Ambrose saw parallel between the day of the passion and the day of the resurrection: the first a day of bitterness, the second a day of jubilation.[31] Although St. Leo the Great continues to speak during the holy night of the *paschalis festivitas* and the *sacramentum paschale*, what we are seeing is a break-up, a fragmentation, of the celebration of the Easter mystery.

True enough, the celebration of Good Friday did not introduce a major liturgical innovation, since every Friday, like every Wednesday, was already marked by a liturgical assembly, with or without the Eucharist. It was quite natural, therefore, that on the Friday in the week of the Easter fast the readings should be organized around the passion of the Lord. Soon, however, the Thursday evening Mass *in Coena Domini* made its appearance, as did the second Mass on Easter Sunday, along with Easter Vespers as the close of the triduum.

I. ORIGIN AND EVOLUTION OF THE EASTER TRIDUUM

The Easter triduum had its roots in the liturgy of the Church of Jerusalem. It was to be expected that, living as they did in the very place of the passion, people there would want to relive each event of the gospel at the time and on the spot where it had occurred. That is precisely what we are told of the Jerusalem Church by Egeria, whose travels took her there in 381–84.[32] That kind of traveling celebration did not, of course, claim to replace the sacramental celebration of the passion-resurrection during the holy night; indeed, the *Catecheses* of Cyril and the *Mystagogical Catecheses* from Jerusalem paint a vivid picture of the vigil. Nor should we underestimate the influence of the anti-Arian reaction on the origin of the liturgical celebration of the Easter triduum, for that reaction intensified the devotion of the faithful to the person of Jesus, Son of God and Son of Mary.[33]

1. Holy Thursday

Holy Thursday belongs to two different liturgical periods: until the hour of Vespers it is the final day of Lent, while the evening Mass *in Coena*

---

29. St. Ambrose, *Ep.* 23, 13 (PL 16:1030).

30. St. Augustine, *Ep.* 54, 14 (PL 33:215). Cited in Cantalamessa, *ibid.* 192.

31. St. Ambrose, *Ep.* 23, 12 (PL 16:1030).

32. *Egeria's Travels*, trans. John Wilkinson (London: SPCK, 1971) 125ff. and passim. Cited by Cantalamessa, *ibid.*, 170–77.

33. R. Taft, "Historicisme: Une conception à revoir," *LMD* no. 147 (1981) 73–75.

Domini (commemorating the Last Supper) opens the Easter triduum. For this reason I shall discuss the consecration of the holy oils in the context of Lent.

a) *In the beginning*—The evening Mass *in Coena Domini* is attested for Jerusalem in the time of Egeria. On this Thursday, she says, two Masses were celebrated: one at mid-afternoon in the Basilica of the Martyrium, and the other immediately after on Calvary, at which "everyone receives Communion."[34] The first was the Lenten Mass for the end of the fast; the second, celebrated by exception at the foot of the cross, commemorated the institution of the Eucharistic sacrifice.

At the end of the fourth century many Western Churches had this double Eucharist on Holy Thursday; the hours for the Masses varied according to traditions. According to St. Augustine, some in Africa celebrated Mass on Thursday morning in order to allow those who wished to do so to break their fast after taking their Easter bath; others celebrated it in the afternoon at the usual hour for the days of Lent; still others, finally, celebrated it after supper in order to imitate more closely the original Lord's Supper. Augustine was unwilling to condemn any of these practices, even though he personally regarded himself as having no authority to infringe the law of Eucharistic fasting.[35]

b) *At Rome in the seventh century*—In fourth-century Rome Holy Thursday was above all the day for the reconciliation of penitents, as we are told by St. Jerome.[36] There was no question of any Mass *in Coena Domini*. In the middle of the fifth century St. Leo still makes no reference to it.

In the seventh century the situation changed. In churches served by presbyters there were two Masses: a morning Mass marking the end of the Lenten fast and an evening Mass commemorating the Supper. At the Lateran, however, the pope celebrated a midday Mass *in Coena Domini*, during which he consecrated the chrism and blessed the oil of the sick and the oil of exorcism. This Mass commemorating the Supper, like the one which priests celebrated in the evening, contained no Liturgy of the Word, but began with the offertory.

The Gelasian Sacramentary was to combine the two traditions, the papal and the presbyteral, and end with three Masses on Holy Thursday: one for the reconciliation of penitents, another for the consecration of chrism, and a third in commemoration of the Supper. This last still began

---

34. *Egeria's Travels* 134–35. Cited in Cantalamessa, *ibid.* 170–71.

35. St. Augustine, *Ep.* 54, 5 (PL 33:202). The Council of Carthage in 397 had authorized the celebration of the Eucharist after the evening meal "on the anniversary day on which the Supper of the Lord is celebrated."

36. St. Jerome, *Ep.* 77. ed. Labourt (Collection Budé) 4:43.

with the prayer over the gifts. We may add that on this day the pope washed the feet of his household and that each cleric did the same in his own home.[37] Finally, as in preceding centuries, the reconciliation of penitents was still celebrated.

c) *Later development*—In Gaul, from the fifth century on, a morning Mass was celebrated on Holy Thursday and another in the evening, this last known as *Natale Calicis* ("Birthday of the cup").[38] When the Roman liturgy replaced local usages at the end of the seventh century, the single Mass of the papal sacramentary became the custom, although this had in the meantime been given an opening prayer and the two readings which were to continue in use down to our time. In cathedrals the consecration of chrism and the blessing of the oils took place during this Mass.

The hour for the celebration of this single Mass would vary over the centuries between the third hour and the ninth hour, until St. Pius V's prohibition against celebrating Mass after midday made morning celebration obligatory. Henceforth the whole of Holy Thursday was part of the Easter triduum; the result was that, contrary to the theological and liturgical tradition of the early Church, Easter day itself ceased to be part of the triduum.

2. Good Friday

a) *In the beginning*—The first testimony to the liturgical celebration of Good Friday comes from Jerusalem at the end of the fourth century. According to Egeria's very lively account, this was a day given over entirely to itinerant prayer that took the faithful on Thursday evening from the Mount of Olives to Gethsemane and then, on Friday, from the cenacle or upper room (where they venerated the pillar of the scourging) to Golgotha. On Golgotha the bishop presented the wood of the cross to the faithful for their veneration. Each station included a reading of passion prophecies and of the gospel, along with the singing of psalms and prayers.[39]

b) *At Rome in the seventh century*—The earliest witnesses to the liturgy of Good Friday at Rome are the Gregorian Sacramentary and the evangeliary from the middle of the seventh century. The evangeliary assigns the reading of the passion according to St. John, and the Sacramentary gives the text of the prayer of the faithful that was offered in the Basilica of the Holy-Cross-in-Jerusalem.[40] It seems that at that time the

---

37. A. Chavasse, "A Rome, le jeudi saint, au VIIᵉ siècle, d'après un vieil Ordo," *RHE* 50 (1955) 24–28.

38. Calendar of Polemius Silvius (448), in *Corpus inscriptionum latinarum* I (Berlin, 1863) 337. Other references in *LMD* no. 68 (1961) 20, n. 30.

39. *Egeria's Travels* 135–38.

40. *Gr*, p. 630.

papal liturgy consisted solely of biblical readings followed by the prayer
of the faithful.

At this same period the sacramentary for the presbyteral churches
presented a more popular kind of service. It began with the displaying
of the cross on the altar; then came the Liturgy of the Word, which was
identical with that of the papal liturgy. When this had been completed,
the deacons went to bring the Body and Blood of Christ from the sac-
risty, where they had been placed after the Mass of Thursday. The priest
then went before the altar to venerate and kiss the cross. Finally, after
the recitation of the Our Father, all venerated the cross and received Communion.[41] We do not know what songs accompanied the veneration of
the cross, but the presence in the later antiphonaries of the Trisagion and
the antiphon *Crucem tuam* (translated from the Greek) undoubtedly
demonstrates a Byzantine influence, as does the reception of Communion
on this day of complete fasting.

c) *Later development*—In the eighth century the veneration of the cross
had become part of the papal liturgy. Andrieu's Ordo 23 describes the
procession from the Lateran to Holy Cross; in this the pope walked, censer
in hand, before the relic of the cross that was carried by a deacon, in accordance with a practice more Eastern than Roman. On arrival at the
Sessorian Basilica, the participants began the veneration of the wood of
the cross; this was followed by the Liturgy of the Word.[42] There was no
Communion.

In the Frankish lands the order followed in the presbyteral churches
of Rome was to prevail: Liturgy of the Word before a reading of the passion and the prayer of the faithful; adoration of the cross; Communion
of the congregation in the Body and Blood of Christ. In the middle of
the tenth century the Pontifical of St. Alban's at Mainz gives a detailed
description of the ritual.[43] The thirteenth century brought an important
change: henceforth only the celebrating priest receives Communion, after
placing a bit of the host in a cup of unconsecrated wine (a relic of the
ancient belief in "consecration by contact,"[44] which Innocent had rejected).
Such would be the practice until 1955. Throughout the Middle Ages the
celebration was anticipated at an increasingly early hour, until finally it
was set for the morning in the sixteenth century.

3. Holy Saturday

Holy Saturday, or Great Saturday as it is called in the East, honors

---

41. *Ge*, pp. 64–67.
42. *OR 23*, in Andrieu, *OR* 2:270-72.
43. *PRG* 2:86-93.
44. M. Andrieu, *Immixtio et consecratio. La consécration par contact dans les documents liturgiques du moyen âge* (Paris: Picard, 1924) 15–16.

the repose of Jesus in the tomb, but also his descent into hell and his mysterious encounter there with all those who were waiting for him to open the gate of heaven, as Peter the Apostle teaches (1 Pet 3:19-20; 4:6). It is a day for recollection and peaceful expectation. In the early centuries the main characteristic of this day was the complete fast which constituted the first phase of the Easter celebration. Later on, the catechumens assembled in the morning in order to "give back the creed" (*redditio symboli*) which had been entrusted to them during Lent; in other words, they made a public profession of their faith before the congregation of believers. St. Augustine has left us a vivid description of the occasion.[45]

Apart from the ordinary morning and evening offices, the Church never sought to organize a celebration aimed specifically at honoring the stay of Christ in the tomb. Unfortunately, however, the progressive anticipation of the Easter Vigil was increasingly to fill this eloquent void. Consequently, when the Easter Vigil came to be celebrated in the morning from the sixteenth century on, people heard the bells of Easter ringing out on Saturday morning, and this day was wholly stripped of its original meaning. One of the benefits of the restoration of the Vigil to Saturday night has been to give Holy Saturday its primitive meaning once again.

4. *Resurrection Sunday*

In the very beginning, the Easter solemnity consisted of the holy vigil, which ended just before dawn.[46] Very soon, however, there was a desire to prolong the festivity through Sunday, a day so filled with memories— from the message of the angel to the spice-bearing women, to the manifestation of the risen Lord to his disciples at nightfall. Not surprisingly, this extended celebration of Easter Sunday began in Jerusalem, as Egeria tells us.[47] It will be helpful to separate out the various elements.

a) *The Mass*—The second Easter Mass, celebrated in the daylight hours, is already attested for Africa in the time of St. Augustine, who does not fail to preach despite the fatiguing night he has had.[48] This second Mass is also attested by Hesychius of Jerusalem and Basil of Seleucia,[49] but it does not seem to have been accepted as soon at Rome. St. Leo the Great was satisfied to preach during the vigil. In the seventh century, on the other hand, the sacramentary and the evangeliary provide texts for this Mass.

---

45. St. Augustine, *Conf.* VIII, 2, 5, ed. P. Labriolle (Collection Budé; Paris: Belles Lettres, 1941) 1:180.

46. Paulinus, *Vita s. Ambrosii* 10, 48 (PL 14:43).

47. *Egeria's Travels* 139.

48. St. Augustine, *Sermons pour la Pâque*, ed. S. Poque (SC 116; Paris: Cerf, 1966) 78–81.

49. *Homélies pascales*, ed. M. Aubineau (SC 187; Paris: Cerf, 1972) 58 and 201.

b) *Mystagogical catechesis*—Easter Sunday is the first day of the Easter octave, which was devoted to mystagogical catechesis not only of the newly baptized but of the people as a whole, as we see from Egeria and St. Augustine.

c) *Easter Vespers at Rome*—In the fourth century, Jerusalem had a celebration in mid-afternoon. In the seventh century, Easter Vespers make their appearance at Rome.[50] The Gregorian Sacramentary gives the prayers for it,[51] but a complete description comes from Ordo 27 (eighth century).[52]

The newly baptized, along with the rest of the faithful, were summoned to the Lateran Basilica in mid-afternoon. Vespers began with an entrance procession of the clergy to the singing of the *Kyrie eleison*. Pss 109 and 110 were then sung, followed by responsorial Ps 92 and Ps 111; the whole was interspersed with numerous alleluias. The entire assembly then went in procession to the baptistery to the singing of Ps 112, which was followed once more by responsorial Ps 92, but sung this time in Greek. In the baptistery Ps 113 and the *Magnificat* were sung. The procession then made its way to the chapel of the Holy Cross, while singing the *Vidi aquam* ("I saw water . . . ."); it was in this chapel that the pope had administered confirmation during the vigil.

The celebration ended for the clergy in the portico of the chapel, where three kinds of wine were served to them. The twelfth-century Ordo adds that the choir sang, in Greek, an Easter troparion which concluded with a prayer for the pope.[53] The priests then went to their respective churches in order to sing Vespers there once again and to distribute wine.

As the papal liturgy spread, the "glorious office" of Easter Vespers, which won the admiration of Amalarius in the ninth century,[54] likewise spread throughout the entire West. It disappeared from Rome in the thirteenth century along with the stational liturgy, but it has continued down to our own day in many churches of France and the Germanic countries.

d) *Medieval developments*—In the Middle Ages numerous practices lent a special character to Easter morning. In the ninth century, all who took part in the office at the end of the night "greeted one another with mutual love, saying, 'The Lord is truly risen.' "[55] Between the vigil and Lauds the cross was carried in a procession, or else the reserved Blessed Sacrament was carried from the "tomb," where it had been placed on Good

50. P. Jounel, "Les Vêpres de Pâques," *LMD* 49 (1957) 96–111.

51. *Gr*, p. 193.

52. *OR* 27, in Andrieu, *OR* 3:343–72.

53. Cencio Savelli, *Romanus ordo de consuetudinibus et observantiis* 36, ed. in P. Fabre and L. Duchesne, *Le Liber censuum de l'Eglise romaine* I (Fontemoing, 1910) 290.

54. Amalarius, *Liber de ordine antiphonarii* 52, ed. J. M. Hanssens, *Amalarii opera liturgica omnia* 3 (ST 140; Vatican City: 1950) 83–85.

55. *OR* 31, 124, in Andrieu, *OR* 3:508.

Friday, to the main altar. At this time, too, the *Officium sepulchri* (office of the tomb), depicting the meeting of the angels and the women at the empty tomb, was celebrated in many cathedral or monastic churches of France, England, Germany, and Spain.[56]

In the twelfth century the pope went early in the morning to the oratory of the *Sancta Sanctorum* (Holy of Holies) near his apartment in the Lateran. There he venerated the icon of Christ the Savior and proclaimed to the members of his household: "The Lord is risen from the tomb." Everyone followed him in venerating the holy image, and then the papal cortege left for St. Mary Major, where Mass was celebrated.[57]

Another element in the Easter Sunday liturgy was the blessing of the Easter lamb, which is attested for Frankish territory in the eighth century[58] and for Italy in the ninth. It took place before the *Per quem haec omnia* prayer at the end of the Canon. Various foods were likewise blessed in accordance with local usage.

The refreshments distributed at the end of Vespers in the Lateran were not neglected by the canons of the transalpine lands. The rejoicing even found expression in dancing, in which the canons participated in the early Middle Ages and, here and there in some countries, down to the eighteenth century.[59]

II. CELEBRATION OF THE EASTER TRIDUUM

1. *Holy Thursday*

The Ordo of 1955 profoundly altered the shape of Holy Thursday as this had been established by post-Tridentine piety. In the past Mass had been celebrated in the morning, with the result that the rest of the day was devoted to adoration of the Eucharist. The transfer of the Body of Christ to the place of its reservation till the morrow had been a secondary rite but had acquired a disproportionate prominence. The altar of reservation had become the "repository" which the Baroque age had delighted in decorating with a profusion of lights and flowers. "Visits to the repositories" in the various churches of the city had become a tradition for devout persons and children.

---

56. B. D. Berger, *Le drame liturgique de Pâques* (Théologie historique 37; Paris: Beauchesne, 1976).

57. Benedict, *Liber politicus* . . . 49, in P. Fabre and L. Duchesne, *Le Liber censuum* . . . 2 (Fontemoing, 1910) 154.

58. *Sacramentaire d'Angoulême*, ed. P. Cagin (Angoulême: Société historique et archéologique, 1919) 59.

59. William Durandus, *Rationale divinorum officiorum* lib. VI, 85, 10; French trans. by Ch. Barthelemy (Paris, 1854) 4:204 and note 8: "Sur deux anciennes danses ecclésiastiques" (447–59).

a) *The Ordo of 1955*—In 1955 the Mass commemorating the Supper was restored to its original time, Holy Thursday evening. Henceforth, outside of cathedrals, the daytime no longer had any special rites apart from the choral office with its reading of the Lamentations attributed to the prophet Jeremiah. In cathedrals, on the other hand, the bishop, surrounded by his priests, celebrated the chrismal Mass in the morning; the formularies for this had been taken from the Gelasian Sacramentary.[60]

In order to emphasize the connection made by the Lord himself between the institution of the Eucharist and the commandment of fraternal service, the new Ordo proposed that the washing of feet follow upon the Liturgy of the Word at the evening Mass. The place where the Eucharist was to be reserved should be decorated in an unobtrusive manner; the faithful could prolong their adoration until midnight.

b) *The Ordo of 1970*—The Missal of 1970 kept all the innovations of 1955. Its own contribution to renewal was in the area of the texts, which had not been touched fifteen years earlier. The two readings, from St. Paul and the Gospel of John, are now preceded by the account of the eating of the lamb on the evening of the Jewish Passover (Exod 12:1-14). This passage from the Old Testament had an important place in the Easter catechesis of the Fathers in the very early centuries; henceforth it serves as the prologue to the biblical readings of the "most holy triduum." Among the prayers, the collect or opening prayer is new, while the others are taken from older sources: the prayer over the gifts is from the former Missal (ninth Sunday after Pentecost), and the prayer after Communion is Gallican.[61] The preface, from the Paris Missal of 1738, had itself been based on Gallican Missals of the eighth century.[62]

In addition to new texts there are two rites which, though not peculiar to Holy Thursday, have the power to modify the Holy Thursday celebration in a profound way. The two rites are concelebration by all the priests of the parish and the opportunity given the faithful of receiving Communion from the Lord's cup, as the apostles did.

Until Vespers the Liturgy of the Hours is that of a Thursday of Lent and has no distinguishing mark except the reading of a passage from the Easter homily in which Melito of Sardis speaks lyrically of the sacrifice of the perfect and spotless Lamb.

2. Good Friday

Before 1955 the Good Friday service took place in the morning, while the afternoon was devoted to the Way of the Cross and the evening to

---

60. *Ge*, nos. 375–90.

61. *Missale Gothicum*, ed. L. C. Mohlberg (REDMF 5; Rome: Herder, 1961) no. 214.

62. P. Jounel, "Le nouveau Propre de France," *LMD* no. 72 (1962) 156–59.

a sermon on the passion. The Ordo of 1955 assigned the service of "the passion and death of the Lord" to the afternoon or evening hours and allowed the faithful to share in the Eucharist, while at the same time it simplified the rite of Communion.

In the Ordo of 1970, Good Friday received back its ancient title *In Passione Domini* (Celebration of the Lord's Passion).[63] As in the case of Holy Thursday, the new changes concerned chiefly the texts. The two readings before the reading of the passion according to John had been a prophecy of Hosea (6:1-6) and the account of the eating of the Passover lamb (Exod 12:1-11). The first referred to the Lord's death and resurrection only when reread by Christian eyes, and the second had now been transferred to the Mass *in Coena Domini*. The two were therefore replaced by one of the Suffering Servant songs (Isa 52:13–53:12) and a passage from the Letter to the Hebrews on the saving character of the death of Jesus (4:14-16; 5:7-9).

The various intentions of the old Prayer of the Faithful[64] were redistributed in accordance with the order proposed for the modern prayer of the faithful; in addition, some of the prayers (for Christian unity, for the Jews, for unbelievers) were modified in the spirit of Vatican II. With the Muslims especially in mind, an intention was added for those who believe in God without believing in Christ. The Liturgy of the Hours contains no ceremonial modifications for Good Friday and Holy Saturday.

3. Holy Saturday

There is no liturgical assembly on Holy Saturday apart from the daily celebration of the Hours. The psalms and antiphons of the latter are from the old office. The spiritual meaning of "the holy and great sabbath," of Christ's repose in death, and of the proclamation of the glory soon to be manifested to the children of Adam, is highlighted in the patristic reading. In this homily, attributed to St. Epiphanius of Salamis (fifth century?), the theology of the descent of Christ among the dead is conveyed in the dramatic form peculiar to the Eastern liturgies. The theme reappears, but expressed with greater sobriety, in the prayer of the day, which is new.

4. Easter Sunday

The liturgy of Easter Sunday had not been affected by the reform of Holy Week, except to the extent that Matins and Lauds were suppressed: in 1951 they were completely replaced by the Easter Vigil; in 1952 a short form of Lauds was introduced at the end of the Vigil.

---

63. *Ge*, no. 395.

64. P. de Clerck, *La "prière universelle" dans les liturgies latines anciennes* (LQF 62; Münster: Aschendorff, 1977) 125-44.

The Liturgy of the Hours that was promulgated in 1970 restored Easter Lauds in the form of morning praise after the rest which followed upon the holy vigil. The vigil service is the only service for the night; thus Easter Sunday is unique in being the only day of the year without a reading from the Fathers.

The story of Peter and John finding the tomb empty (John 20:1-9) is read at the daytime Mass. It fits in harmoniously between the angel's announcement of the resurrection to the women in the gospel of the vigil and the manifestation of Jesus to the disciples at Emmaus, which is proposed for an evening Mass, should there be one. The Liturgy of the Word begins with the Easter message of Peter (Acts 10:34-43). This reading marks the beginning of the reading of Acts, which will continue until Pentecost. For the second reading there is a choice: either the passage in which St. Paul connects the Pasch of Christ with the Jewish Passover (1 Cor 5:6-8) or the one in which he reminds Christians that they must live as people who have been raised from the dead (Col 3:1-4). These two readings had previously been the epistles for Easter Sunday and the Vigil.

The prayers of this Mass have all been altered. The opening prayer and the preface have been restored to their original form (but with a slight modification for the former).[65] The prayer over the gifts had formerly been that of Easter Wednesday. The prayer after Communion, which in the past was a repetition of the prayer in the Vigil Mass, is from the Ambrosian liturgy.[66]

§3. The Easter Season

BIBLIOGRAPHY

R. Cabié, *La Pentecôte* (Bibliothèque liturgique; Paris: Desclée, 1965).

J. Gibert, *Festum Resurrectionis* (Bibliotheca EL, Subsidia 10; Rome: Edizioni liturgiche, 1977).

P. Jounel, "La liturgie du Mystère pascal: Le temps pascal," *LMD* no. 67 (1961) 163–82.

H. Leclercq, "Pentecôte," *DACL* 14 (1939) col. 259–74.

S. Poque, *Augustin d'Hippone. Sermons pour la Pâque* (SC 116; Paris: Cerf, 1966).

The Sunday of the resurrection begins a period of fifty days that were known originally as Pentecost and then, once the name "Pentecost" was reserved to the fiftieth day, as the Easter season.[67]

---

65. *Ge*, nos. 463 and 458.

66. *Sacramentarium Bergomense*, ed. A. Paredi (Monumenta Bergomensia 6; Bergamo, 1962) no. 564.

67. The basic resource for studying the evolution of the fifty-day Easter period in the first five centuries is R. Cabié, *La Pentecôte* (Tournai: Desclée, 1965).

I. ORIGIN AND EVOLUTION OF THE FIFTY-DAY EASTER PERIOD

1. A Fifty-Day Period of Rejoicing

Almost as soon as the Christian Easter made its appearance in history, it presented itself as a feast that went on for fifty days. All the days of this fifty-day period were to be celebrated "with great joy"; according to Tertullian,[68] they comprise a single feast day, and according to Saint Irenaeus it is a feast day "with the same import as Sunday."[69]

Whereas the Jewish Pentecost was a harvest feast and one commemorating the covenant and was assigned to the fiftieth day after Passover, the Christian Pentecost was originally a period of fifty days during which each day had the same value and function. The mystery of the resurrection was here celebrated in all its aspects and implications. It is worth noting that while the Greek text of Acts speaks of the day of Pentecost in the singular (Acts 2:1), the Latin text, which reflects ecclesial usage of the fourth century, puts the word in the plural: *Dum complerentur dies Pentecostes*, "When the fifty days were completed."

The privileges attaching to the Lord's Day were extended to the fifty-day period of Easter: during this time people prayed standing, and fasting was prohibited. So too the entire period was "the most felicitous time" for administering baptism.[70] Somewhat as Sunday was the first and the eighth day, so the "great Sunday"[71] constituted by the fifty days of Pentecost opened with the day of the resurrection and continued through eight Sundays. It was therefore an octave of Sundays and "a week of weeks."[72] The emphasis on the octave of Sundays underscores the eschatological character of the fifty-day Easter period. St. Basil writes: "All of Pentecost reminds us of the resurrection which we await in the other world."[73]

The Fathers of the Church still continued to use the same kind of language in the fifth century. By this time, however, the celebration of the entire paschal mystery as an indivisible unity was already being set aside to some extent as the Church responded to the psychological need which the Christian people felt of honoring successively, in the course of these weeks, first the resurrection of the Lord, then his ascension, and

---

68. Tertullian, *De ieiunio* 14, 2 (CCL 2:1273); R. Cabié 39.
69. Cited in *Quaestiones et Responsiones ad orthodoxos*, a text presented in R. Cabié 37.
70. Tertullian, *De baptismo* 19, 2 (CCL 1:293; SC 35:94-95).
71. St. Athanasius, *Epistulae festivae* 1 (PG 26:1366); Cabié 64.
72. St. Hilary of Poitiers, *Instructio psalmorum* (CSEL 22:11); Cabié 50.
73. St. Basil, *De Sancto Spiritu* 27, 66 (PG 32:192; SC 17:237); Cabié 51.

finally the sending of the Spirit on the apostles. In other words, the liturgy gradually conformed to the chronology in the Book of Acts.

2. *The Organization of the Easter Season*

The Easter season begins with the Sunday of the resurrection, which is also the third day of the sacred triduum and the first of the baptismal octave. The season ends on a Sunday that marks the close of the fifty-day period. In several regions this closing Sunday used to celebrate both the sending of the Holy Spirit and the ascension of the Lord. But Pentecost soon came to be dedicated exclusively to the coming of the Spirit on the apostles, while the ascension came to be celebrated on the fortieth day after Easter.

a) *The Easter octave*—The Easter octave, or week *in albis* (in white garments) as it is called in Rome, owes its fourth-century origin to the concern of pastors that the newly baptized receive a postbaptismal, mystagogical catechesis on the mysteries in which they had now participated. If we may judge by the experience of Hippo, the catechesis in fact attracted the entire Christian people. Some of Augustine's sermons for the Easter octave are meant for the *infantes* (the newly baptized, who are "infants" or "children" in the Lord), but others are addressed to the people generally. In the former the bishop speaks of the mysteries; in the latter he comments tirelessly on all the gospel passages which relate to the Lord's resurrection. Augustine has these passages read daily at Mass and often comes back to the resurrection of the body, which he says is peculiar to the Christian faith.[74]

At Milan, in Spain, and in Gaul there were two different daily Masses, a "Mass for the baptized" and a "Mass of the octave." Daily participation of the people in the celebration was facilitated by the fact that from 389 on civil law made the Easter octave a week of complete holiday.

After resurrection Sunday itself the most solemn day of the Easter octave was the eighth day, the Sunday that ended the octave. On this day the newly baptized put aside their white garments and took their places in the congregation. The sermons of the Fathers for this Sunday speak of the mystery of the "eighth day," which is an anticipation of eternal life. They are also filled, however, with the final pieces of advice which the pastor gives both to the newly baptized, who must live their baptismal faith in the midst of the world, and to the faithful who have come into the city for the feasts and will now be returning to their everyday occupations.[75]

---

74. St. Augustine, *Serm.* 241, 1 (PL 38:1135).
75. R. Cabié 240–47; see also P. Jounel, "Le temps pascal," *LMD* no. 67 (1961) 165–67.

The Introit for the Mass of the Sunday *in albis:* "Like newborn children . . . ," and all the references to baptism in the Masses of the octave show that in its practice the Church of Rome did not differ from the other Churches. Unfortunately, there is no trace of any Roman baptismal catechesis. The homilies of Gregory the Great for the Easter octave make no reference to the newly baptized. In the homily he delivered on the Gospel of John in the Lateran on the octave Sunday he addresses his recommendations to the people alone: "We are ending the Easter festival, but we must live in such a way as to reach the eternal festival."[76] By calling the octave Sunday *die dominico post albas* (the Sunday after the white garments), the Gregorian Sacramentary stresses the fact that the newly baptized had put off their white garments on Saturday. That Sunday remained nonetheless the octave day, as the Gelasian Sacramentary and the evangeliary from the mid-seventh century make clear.[77]

b) *The closing feast of the fifty-day Easter period*—It was natural that the ending of the fifty-day Easter period should be solemnized by a feast that, like the Jewish feast, was called Pentecost. The end of the third century was doubtless the time when people began to celebrate the fiftieth day of Easter festivity in this way; the day, of course, necessarily fell on a Sunday. In about 300 the Council of Elvira prescribed "that we all celebrate the day of Pentecost."[78] Some years later, shortly after 332, Eusebius of Caesarea linked the commemoration of the ascension with this day.[79] We might think this an aberration, were it not confirmed by several other writers, such as St. Maximus of Turin in the mid-fifth century[80] and, especially, Egeria.

Egeria tells us that at Jerusalem the people gathered in the basilica on holy Sion at the third hour on the morning of the fiftieth day. It was the place of "the descent of the Spirit," where "all the languages spoken were understood." There the passage from Acts that reports the event was read. In the afternoon everyone went to the top of Mount Olivet, to the Imbomon, that is, "the place from which the Lord ascended into heaven." There the story of the ascension was read from the Acts of the Apostles and the gospel.[81]

---

76. St. Gregory the Great, *Homilia 26 habita ad populum in basilica beati Iohannis, quae dicitur Constantiniana, in octava paschae* 10 (PL 76:1202).

77. T. Klauser, *Das römische Capitulare Evangeliorum* (LQF 28; Münster: Aschendorff, 1935) 25; *Ge*, no 499; *Gr*, no. 435.

78. H. T. Bruns, *Canones Apostolorum et Conciliorum* (Berlin: Reimer, 1839) 2:7.

79. Eusebius of Caesarea, *De sollemnitate paschali* 3 (PG 25:697).

80. St. Maximus of Turin, *Homiliae* 40, 44, and 56 (CCL 22:161-226). See R. Cabié 138–42.

81. *Egeria's Travels* 141.

c) *The two feasts of the Ascension and Pentecost*—At the time when the Church of Jerusalem was still celebrating the ascension of the Lord and the sending of the Spirit on the final day of the fifty-day Easter period, most of the Churches were honoring the two mysteries separately and on the days suggested by the Acts of the Apostles.

St. John Chrysostom already regarded the ascension as an ancient and universal feast.[82] According to St. Augustine, it was celebrated throughout the world and, like the feasts of Easter and Pentecost, originated with the apostles.[83] The feast was in fact of more recent origin than either of these Fathers realized and must have become widespread only in the last quarter of the fourth century. St. Gregory of Nyssa may have been influential in its spread.[84] In any case, it was accepted in Jerusalem ca. 420–430, as the Armenian lectionary shows,[85] while at Rome St. Leo the Great presents the theology of the ascension in the two sermons he preached about it: *Christi ascensio nostra provectio est* ("The ascension of Christ advances us").[86] It was even necessary to make sure that the people did not make the ascension the final day of Easter joy; thus Cassian says: "The ten days between the ascension and Pentecost must be celebrated with the same solemnity and joy as the forty days that precede them."[87]

A full description of Pentecost as the feast of the coming of the Holy Spirit on the apostles and of the missionary origin of the Church is to be found in the sermons of St. Augustine and St. Leo the Great in the West and in those of St. Gregory of Nyssa and St. John Chrysostom in the East.[88]

While continuing to commemorate a particular event, Pentecost became toward the end of the fourth century, at least in the West, a kind of repetition of Easter, inasmuch as it became the time for the Christian initiation of those who could not be baptized during the holy night of the Easter Vigil. St. Leo the Great attests this development at Rome, both in his preaching and in a letter he wrote to the bishops of Sicily.[89] For this reason Pentecost was given a nocturnal vigil modeled on that of Easter. In the sixth century it already had a preparatory fast on Saturday.[90] Such

---

82. St. John Chrysostom, *Sermo in ascensionem* (PG 50:441-52).

83. St. Augustine, *Serm.* 262, 3 (PL 38:1208).

84. J. Daniélou, "Grégoire de Nysse et les origines de la fête de l'Ascension," in *Kyriakon. Festschrift Johannes Quasten* (Münster: Aschendorff, 1970) 2:663-66.

85. A. Renoux, *ibid.* 336-39.

86. St. Leo the Great, *Tractatus* 73, 4 (CCL 138A:453).

87. John Cassian, *Conlationes* 21, 19-20, ed. E. Pichery (SC 64; Paris: Cerf, 1959) 94-95.

88. St. John Chrysostom, *Sermo in ascensionem* 1 (PG 50:441).

89. St. Leo the Great, *Epistola 16 ad universos episcopos per Siciliam constitutos* 3 (PL 54:699).

90. *Le*, nos. 192-93.

a fast was contrary, of course, to the conception of the fifty-day period as one of festivity, and many churches stayed with the older usage and refused for a long time to observe the fast.

Another result of Pentecost becoming an occasion for baptisms was that it acquired an octave during which the newly baptized might receive a mystagogical catechesis. This octave is already attested in the Roman epistolary from the beginning of the seventh century.[91] The octave coincided, however, with the week in which fasting, in abeyance since Easter, was resumed in the fast of the fourth month (June); it was difficult to bring octave and fasting into harmony. The introduction in Gaul of three days of penance or Rogations before ascension (end of the fifth century) represented the final breakup of the unity of the fifty-day period of rejoicing, during which people prayed standing and did not fast; the Rogations were accepted into the Roman liturgy at the beginning of the ninth century.

II. THE CELEBRATION OF THE EASTER SEASON

The norms for the liturgical year that were promulgated in 1969 highlight once again the unity of the fifty-day Easter period. They do so first of all by eliminating the Pentecost octave, thus emphasizing the point that God willed *paschale sacramentum quinquaginta dierum mysterio contineri* ("that the paschal mystery be contained within the symbolic period of fifty days").[92] Furthermore, each of the Sundays that precede Pentecost is regarded as a "Sunday of Easter" and not a "Sunday after Easter." The Sunday after the ascension is the seventh Sunday of Easter, showing that the ascension does not introduce a break into the fifty-day period. Finally, these Sundays take precedence over every solemnity of the Lord or the saints. The Rogation Days, which introduced a penitential note into the Easter season, may be celebrated in some other season of the year. It is now possible to say once again, in the language of the Fathers, that "the fifty days from Easter Sunday to Pentecost are celebrated in joyful exultation as one feast day, or better as one 'great Sunday.' "[93]

Such is the framework within which the celebration of the Easter season unfolds. Before discussing other details, we should note the festive setting: the white vestments of priests and ministers, which recall those of the angels on Easter morning and at the ascension; the alleluia, which is

---

91. G. Morin, "Le plus ancien Comes ou Lectionnaire de l'Eglise romaine," *RBén* 27 (1910) 57–58.

92. Opening Prayer of the Mass for the Vigil of Pentecost in the *Missale Romanum*. It is taken from *Le*, no. 191.

93. *General Norms for the Liturgical Year and the Calendar* 22–26 and 45–46.

the song of those redeemed by the blood of the Lamb; the Easter candle, symbol of the risen Christ who "shed his peaceful light on all mankind" (*Exsultet*).

1. *The Celebration of the Eucharist*

a) *The readings*—In the Liturgy of the Word two books dominate: the Acts of the Apostles and the Gospel according to St. John. The Book of Acts is read every day (Sunday and weekdays), the Gospel of John every weekday and every Sunday except the third in A and B years.

The reading of Acts was already traditional in the time of Augustine, and we find it in almost all the rites (Ambrosian, Spanish, Gallican, Byzantine, Armenian)[94]; it replaces the reading from the Old Testament. It brings out the continuity of the history of salvation by recounting the origin of the new people of God under the action of the risen Jesus. The reading of the Gospel of John, begun in the Roman liturgy in the fourth week of Lent, likewise continues throughout the Easter season; the same is true of the Ambrosian and Byzantine rites. In the Byzantine rite the complete reading of John is begun on Easter day itself with the proclamation of the Prologue in various languages.

In the Easter season, as in the remainder of the year, the Sunday readings form a three-year cycle. On the eight Sundays of Easter, they are unified by the message they proclaim: Jesus Christ, the Lord, died and rose to save the world. As such, they may be said to expound the essential substance of the Christian faith.

The second reading is taken, depending on the year, from the First Letter of St. Peter (A), the First Letter of St. John (B), or the Apocalypse (C). The paschal nature of the Letter of Peter is immediately evident. The passages chosen all refer explicitly to the death and resurrection of Christ. The extracts from the Letter of St. John convey the essentials of the great Johannine themes: faith in Jesus, salvation through his blood, the law of love. The passages from the Apocalypse speak either of the risen Christ or of the heavenly Jerusalem, of which his resurrection is our pledge.

b) *Prayers and prefaces*—Before 1970 the Missal had special Easter season formularies only for the Sundays and for the octaves of Easter and Pentecost. Now, in addition to Masses for the Sundays, the Easter octave, and the week preceding Pentecost, it has an opening prayer for each weekday. All of these opening prayers have been taken from the old

---

94. There is a table of the readings for the Masses of the Easter season according to the Ambrosian, Spanish, Byzantine, and old Roman rites in P. Jounel, "Le temps pascal," *LMD* no. 67 (1961) 178–79. The reader will also see there that in the Spanish and Byzantine rites the Sundays are designated as "Sundays of Easter" and not "Sundays after Easter."

Roman, Ambrosian, or Gallican Sacramentaries.[95] The Sunday prayers in the old Missal did not have a specifically paschal character and could without difficulty have been moved to the Sundays of Ordinary Time. The new Sunday prayers, on the other hand, all refer to the paschal mystery.

Among the most important prayers are the five prefaces. These have been composed according to an identical pattern. The first part, "It is right to give him thanks and praise," and the last part, "The joy of resurrection . . . ," are the same in all the formularies. The middle section highlights an aspect of the mystery of Christ's death and resurrection that is summed up in the title. Like the presidential prayers, the prefaces are taken from ancient sources.[96]

c) *The songs*—In the Latin text all the songs have been taken from the *Graduale Romanum* of 1907. But the entrance antiphons and Communion antiphons, which may be substituted for these songs, are distributed according to a scheme which brings out certain basic themes of the Easter celebration. In the entrance antiphons, after the Easter octave, the same theme is repeated on the same day of each week: Christ is risen (Monday), the triumph of the risen Lord at the end of time (Tuesday), the psalmody of the redeemed (Wednesday), the new Exodus (Thursday), salvation through the Blood of the risen Christ (Friday), and new life in Jesus Christ (Saturday). The Communion antiphons are not arranged according to as rigorous a pattern, but every Friday they do recall the sacrifice of Christ. During the week preceding Pentecost the Communion antiphons contain sayings of Jesus in which he promises to send the Spirit.

2. The Liturgy of the Hours

The hymns, responses, and prayers of praise and intercession that are used during the Easter season are worth attention. It is, nonetheless, the biblical and patristic readings that constitute the most outstanding body of texts.

If a one-year cycle is being followed in the Office of Readings, the First Letter of St. Peter is read during Easter week. The Apocalypse is read during the next four weeks, and the Letters of St. John during the final two. If a two-year cycle is being followed, in the second year there is a semi-continuous reading of the Acts of the Apostles throughout the fifty days of the Easter season. The daytime Hours have five short readings for each day of the week. Thus those celebrating the Liturgy of the Hours have thirty-five readings proposed each week for their meditation.

---

95. A. Dumas, "Les sources du Missel romain," *Notitiae* 7 (1971) 74–76.
96. *Ibid.* 76.

The forty-nine patristic readings provide an exceptional selection of passages dealing with the paschal mystery and its celebration. The sources range from the earliest documents (Justin, Melito of Sardis, Irenaeus) down to the most recent (Vatican II). But, except for Vatican II, only a single text dates from after the ninth century: the one from Isaac of Stella (twelfth century). The forty-nine readings are from fifteen Fathers who wrote in Greek (or Syriac) and eleven who wrote in Latin. St. Augustine and St. Cyril of Alexandria lead the list with six passages each.

3. *Ascension and Pentecost*

a) *Ascension*—Of the three presidential prayers of the Mass, the opening prayer is a new composition based on a sermon of St. Leo the Great; the other two are from the Gelasian and Leonine Sacramentaries. They emphasize the point that the Lord's ascension is our own as well. The same is to be said of the two prefaces, the second of which is from the old Missal. While the account in the Acts of the Apostles is read every year, the other two readings follow a three-year cycle.

The same theme—the correlation between the ascension of Christ and that of the human race—is developed in the Liturgy of the Hours by St. Augustine and, on the following day, by St. Leo the Great. The reading from St. Leo contains the well-known words: *Quod Redemptoris nostri conspicuum fuit, in sacramenta transivit,* "What was visible in the person of our redeemer is now represented in the mysteries."

b) *Pentecost*—Pentecost Sunday has two Masses, one for the vigil on Saturday evening and one for the day itself.

The first of these two Masses offers a choice of four Old Testament readings. These complement one another, and the four together help us grasp the various aspects of the mystery of the Spirit's coming on the apostles at Pentecost. That coming turns the Church into an anti-Babel, an assembly of formerly divided human beings (first reading); Pentecost is the feast of the promulgation of the new law that is written by the Spirit in the hearts of human beings (second reading); the gift of the Spirit has caused a new people of God to rise from the dead (third reading); finally, the prophecy of Joel is the passage which St. Peter quotes when he addresses the crowd on Pentecost (fourth reading). At the beginning of the Mass on Pentecost day itself, we relive the Pentecost event (Acts of the Apostles). The passages that are read from the Gospel and the Apostle in these two Masses recall the promise Jesus had made of sending the Spirit and the action of the Spirit in the Christian community and in each Christian. The various orations turn all this teaching into prayer.

In the Liturgy of the Hours for Saturday, an African homily reminds us that though the Church throughout the world speaks all languages it is yet one. On the day itself, St. Irenaeus in turn says that in descending on the apostles "the Spirit brought all the estranged races into unity and offered to the Father the first fruits of all the peoples."

§4. The Preparation for Easter

BIBLIOGRAPHY

A. Chavasse, "Le carême romain et les scrutins prebaptismaux avant la IXe siècle," *RechSR* 35 (1948) 325–81.

_____, "La préparation de la Pâque à Rome avant le Ve siècle, jeûne et organisation religieuse," in *Mémorial J. Chaine* (Bibliothèque de la Faculté de Théologie de Lyon 5; Lyons, 1950) 61–80.

_____, "Temps de préparation à la Pâque d'après quelques livres liturgiques romains," *RechSR* 37 (1950) 125–45.

_____, "La structure du carême et les lectures des messes quadragésimales dans la liturgie romaine," *LMD* no. 31 (1952) 76–120.

_____, "La discipline romaine des sept scrutins prébaptismaux," *RechSR* 48 (1960) 227–40.

_____, "Les féries du carême celebrées au temps de saint Léon le Grand (440–461)," in *Miscellanea liturgica . . . Giacomo Lercaro* 1 (Rome: Desclée, 1966) 551–57.

_____, "L'organisation stationnale du carême romain avant le VIIIe siècle, une organisation 'pastorale,' " *RevSR* 56 (1982) 17–32.

B. Fischer, "The Patristic Interpretation of the Three Great Lenten Baptismal Pericopes," in *I Simboli dell'iniziazione cristiana* (Studia Anselmiana 87, Analecta liturgica 7; Rome, 1983).

J. Froger, "Les anticipations du jeûne quadragésimal," *Mélanges de science religieuse* 3 (1946) 204–34.

H. J. Gräf, *Palmenweihe und Palmenprozession in der lateinischen Liturgie* (Veröffentlichungen des Missionspriesterseminar St. Augustin, Siegburg, 5; Kaldenkirchen: Steyler Verlag, 1959).

P. Jounel, "La liturgie du mystère pascal: Le dimanche des Rameaux," *LMD* no. 68 (1961) 45–64.

J. Mateos, "Les 'semaines des mystères' du carême chaldéen," *OS* 4 (1949) 449–58.

V. Peri, "La durata e la struttura della quaresima nell'antico uso ecclesiastico gerosolomitano," *Aevum* 37 (1963) 31–62.

_____, "La cronologia delle lettere festali di sant'Atanasio e la quaresima," *Aevum* 35 (1961) 28–86.

J. W. Tyrer, *Historical Survey of Holy Week, Its Services and Ceremonial* (Alcuin Club Collections 29; London: Oxford University Press, 1932).

The absolute fast of one or two days that ended with the Eucharist of the Easter Vigil came to be preceded at an early date by a less strict fast during the first part of the week. The *Teaching of the Apostles* (third century) attests this development for an Eastern area: "You shall fast in the days of the Pascha from the tenth, which is the second day of the week;

and you shall sustain yourselves with bread and salt and water only, at the ninth hour, until the fifth day of the week."[97]

In the fourth century this purificatory fast in preparation for the Pasch of Christ was to spread throughout the entire Church and was to be observed for forty days (*Quadragesima*; Lent).

I. ORIGIN AND EVOLUTION OF LENT

1. *The Origin and Content of Lent*

A forty-day fast that was independent of the Easter fast appeared in Egypt at the end of the third century or the beginning of the fourth. Its purpose seems to have been less to prepare for Easter than to celebrate the Lord's fast in the desert during the weeks after his baptism.[98] Soon, however, it took the form of a penitential preparation for celebrating the death and resurrection of the Lord. (St. Paul had written in 1 Cor 5:8, "Let us celebrate the festival, not with the old leaven . . . .") The fast observed during these days was simply an extension to Mondays, Tuesdays, and Thursdays of the fast observed throughout the year, apart from the Easter season, on Wednesdays and Fridays (and, at Rome, on Saturdays as well).

In his teaching the Lord never separated fasting from almsgiving and prayer (Matt 6:1-18). The Fathers of the Church were persistently to remind the faithful of this each year; the sermons of St. Leo the Great in particular are a good example.[99] The fast was therefore always accompanied by meetings for prayer and for listening to the Word of God.

Once the catechumenate had been well organized in the fourth century, Lent offered an appropriate framework in which to conduct the final preparation of the catechumens for their baptism during the Easter Vigil. Furthermore, since God had reconciled human beings to himself through the death and resurrection of his Son, the vigil inevitably seemed the right occasion for readmitting to communion those sinners who had completed their period of penance; Lent thus became a time of preparation for this reconciliation. At Rome, of course, the reconciliation took place on Holy Thursday.

As a result, from the time of Augustine and Chrysostom Lent had the characteristics that it was to retain thenceforth: a period of fasting, shar-

---

97. *Didascalia Apostolorum* 21, trans. R. H. Connolly 189.

98. R. G. Coquin, "Les origines de l'Epiphanie en Egypte," in B. Botte and E. Melia, *Noel, Epiphanie, Retour du Christ* (Lex orandi 40; Paris: Cerf, 1967) 139–70.

99. A. Guillaume, *Jeûne et charité dans l'Eglise latine des origines au XIIe siècle, en particulier chez S. Léon le Grand* (Paris: Ed. SOS, 1958).

ing, and prayer for the whole Christian people; a period of preparation of catechumens for baptism; a period of preparation of penitents for their reconciliation.

2. The Evolution of Lent at Rome

a) *The stages*—At Rome, the period of preparation for Easter seems to have consisted at first in a week of fasting before the holy night.[100] The week began on Sunday with a reading of the passion. The Wednesday liturgical assembly, like that on Good Friday, did not include the Eucharist. Apart from Good Friday, this Wednesday was the day on which the prayer of the faithful continued to be said longest.

During the fourth century a three-week period of preparation for Easter made its appearance. The three weeks were counted back from Easter Sunday and thus began on Laetare Sunday. Vestiges of this three-week preparation can be seen in: the procession which the pope was later on to lead on Laetare Sunday from the Lateran to the Basilica of Holy-Cross-in-Jerusalem; the name "Middle Sunday" (*dominica in mediana*)[101] which the following Sunday was to have for a long time; and the fact that this intermediate Sunday was a day for ordinations as being the Sunday that ended the Ember Days fast. It should perhaps be mentioned that this period was coextensive with the reading of the Gospel according to St. John.

The fast of forty days must have made its appearance in Rome between 354 and 384. The first Sunday of Lent, which began the six weeks of fasting, fell on exactly the fortieth day before the sacred triduum. The Lenten fast was thus clearly distinct from the Easter fast. But, although fasting was observed every day from Monday to Saturday, official assemblies were still held only on Wednesdays and Fridays in the time of St. Leo the Great, and the Eucharist was not celebrated on these days. At the beginning of the sixth century, Mondays, Tuesdays, and Saturdays (except for Saturday of the fifth week) had also become days of assembly, and the assembly now included the Eucharist.

At this period a fast on the Wednesday and Friday preceding the opening Sunday of Lent was added so as to ensure forty days of actual fasting, including the Easter fast, since Sundays had always been excluded in the most explicit possible way from any fasting. Only in the eighth century, under Pope Gregory II (715–31), did the Thursdays of Lent receive liturgical formularies.

b) *The organization*—In the time of St. Leo the first Sunday of Lent began the preparation for the celebration of the *paschale sacramentum*

---

100. A. Chavasse, "La structure du carême et les lectures des Messes quadragesimales dans la liturgie romaine," *LMD* 31 (1952) 76–119.

101. On this strictly Roman designation see Andrieu, *OR* 3:311-12.

(paschal mystery). On that day the summons of St. Paul was read: "Now is the acceptable time," as was the account of the tempting of Jesus in the wilderness. The bishop urged the faithful to a more fervent service of the Lord. He pointed out that "all around the world thousands upon thousands of people are preparing for their rebirth in Christ." At the same time, Satan "sees those who had fallen washing themselves in the tears of repentance and being admitted to the healing of reconciliation as the Apostle's key opens the door of forgiveness to them." On the second Sunday of Lent St. Leo comments on the transfiguration of Jesus which brings on the scene the three chief representatives of a forty-day fast: Christ, Moses, and Elijah.[102] These sermons do not, however, supply any information on how the scrutinies were celebrated.

c) *The three Sunday scrutinies*—Fifty years after St. Leo the Great, a Roman deacon named John provided a lengthy explanation of the catechumenate in response to a letter from a high official at the court of Ravenna. The latter asked John, among other things, why there were three scrutinies.[103] These were celebrated on the third, fourth, and fifth Sundays of Lent, as the Gelasian Sacramentary shows.[104] It is probable that on these three days the gospels of the Samaritan woman, the man born blind, and Lazarus were read, in keeping with the practice in the other Churches of the West.

d) *The seven scrutinies celebrated during the week*—In the second half of the sixth century, the scrutinies were transferred to weekdays, and their number was increased to seven. The reason for the transfer was certainly the fact that infant baptism had replaced adult baptism during the Easter Vigil. The shift of the scrutinies to weekdays entailed the transfer of the three gospels mentioned above, along with the corresponding readings. This practice prevailed until 1969.

e) *The Lenten fast moved forward: Ash Wednesday*—At the beginning of the sixth century, out of a desire to have forty days of actual fasting (Sundays being non-fast days), the fast was begun on the preceding Wednesday; henceforth this Wednesday marked the start of Lent.[105] Ordo 22 (from the end of the eighth century) contains a description of this day.[106] The entire community assembled at St. Anastasia, at the foot of the Palatine. The pope began the ceremony and then everyone climbed

---

102. St. Leo the Great, *Tractatus* 47, 1 (CCL 138A:274); 40, 1, 3 (CCL 138A:223ff.); 49, 3 (CCL 138A:288); 51, 4 (CCL 138A:299-300).

103. *Iohannis diaconi Epistola ad Senarium* 2, ed. A. Wilmart, *Analecta Reginensia* (ST 59; Vatican City, 1933) 171.

104. *Ge*, nos. 195, 225, 283.

105. *Ge*, no. 89.

106. *OR* 22, Andrieu, *OR* 3:251-62; translation in P. Jounel, "La pénitence quadragésimale dans le Missel romain," *LMD* no. 56 (1958) 33-34.

the Aventine in procession in order to celebrate the first Lenten Mass at St. Sabina.

During the procession the people sang the antiphon *Immutemur habitu in cinere et cilicio* (Let us don sackcloth and ashes). At Rome this passage was given a spiritual meaning, but in the Rhenish countries there was a desire to give the liturgical text a corresponding visible expression and so the rite of the imposition of ashes was instituted. The practice of covering oneself with ashes as a sign of repentance and mourning is abundantly attested in the Old Testament (Josh 7:6; 1 Sam 13:19; Ezek 27:30; Job 2:12; 42:6; Jonah 3:6; Esth 4:3), and Christians in the early centuries often followed the same practice in private. It became a way for sinners to give a public sign of their repentance, but it had no liturgical connotation. In the tenth and eleventh centuries the Rhenish practice made its way into Italy. A Council of Benevento in 1091 decreed that "on Ash Wednesday everyone, clergy and laity, men and women, will receive ashes."[107] The Rhenish ritual[108] became part of the Roman Pontifical in the twelfth century. At this period, however, the rite was still not part of the papal liturgy proper. Only in the thirteenth century did the pope submit himself to this symbolic penitential act.[109]

f) *The Septuagesima season*—The advancing of the Lenten fast was not something peculiar to Rome. It was found in the East as well as in the various regions of the West, from Italy and Provence to Spain, from Frankish Gaul to England and Ireland.[110] The practice originated in monastic asceticism but spread rapidly among the people. It is not possible, however, to say what form it took apart from the liturgical celebration. Quinquagesima, Sexagesima, and Septuagesima Sundays made their appearance in succession.

Quinquagesima is attested at Rome ca. 520. That was the period when it also appeared in Provence and at Turin. Shortly afterward, the Council of Orléans (541) mentioned Sexagesima, which is also attested in Provence and at Milan at about the same time. We may suppose that it existed in Rome at this same period, since Septuagesima was soon to appear there (end of the sixth or beginning of the seventh century). But Septuagesima was limited to Rome throughout the seventh century. The set of three weeks preparatory to Lent was adopted by the entire West once the Roman liturgical books came into wide use during the eighth century.

---

107. C. de Clercq, *Concilia Galliae a. 511—a. 695* (CCL 148A:132).

108. *PRG* 2:21-23.

109. S. J. P. Van Dijk, *The Ordinal of the Papal Court from Innocent III to Boniface VIII* (Spicilegium Friburgense 22; Freiburg, Sch.: Universitätsverlag, 1975) 181.

110. J. Froger, "Les anticipations du jeûne quadragésimal," *Mélanges de science religieuse* 3 (1946) 207-34.

3. The Final Week of Lent: Holy Week

a) *Passion Sunday—Palm Sunday*—In Jerusalem, at the beginning of the sixth century, on "the next day, Sunday, [which is] the beginning of the Easter week or, as they call it here, 'The Great Week,' "[111] the triumphal entry of Jesus into the holy city was celebrated by retracing the way which he and his disciples had followed. In mid-afternoon the community assembled with the bishop in the Eleona basilica on Mount Olivet and then climbed up to the Imbomon. At about five in the evening the gospel story was read, and then the congregation descended the hill and entered the city. The procession made its way to the Anastasis, where the *lucernarium*, or lamp-lighting service, was celebrated.[112] From Jerusalem this kind of procession spread throughout the East, where the Sunday marking the beginning of the Great Week became Palm Sunday.[113]

At Rome, on the other hand, in the time of St. Leo the Great the sixth Sunday of Lent was Passion Sunday. On this day the passion according to St. Matthew was read. The pope then commented on the first half of the account, postponing his explanation of the second half to the following Wednesday.

In Spain and Gaul this same Sunday was the one on which the creed was given to the catechumens soon to be baptized (*Traditio symboli*); this action was accompanied by the *ephphatha* or anointing of the ears. At this ceremony the gospel pericope read was John 12:1-25, which tells of the anointing at Bethany and the entrance of Jesus into Jerusalem. In the seventh and eighth centuries popular piety was attracted more to the second half of the story than to the first. People came to church with palms and branches which they waved while shouting Hosannahs. The Roman authorities unobtrusively echoed this acclamation by entitling the Sunday *Dominica in palmas de passione Domini* (Gelasian Sacramentary, no. 329) or even *Die dominico ad palmas* (Gregorian Sacramentary, no. 281).

Not until the ninth century, however, are there sure attestations in the West to a procession with palms. Theodulphus, bishop of Orléans († 821) composed a hymn, *Gloria laus* (Glory, praise . . .) for the occasion. Amalarius of Metz († 853) refers to the custom in his region, which was to carry palms *per ecclesias* while shouting Hosannahs.[114] When did the procession become part of the papal liturgy? Perhaps Pope Stephen V was alluding to such a ceremony when he sent Emperor Charles the Fat "palm branches, symbols of victory, along with the Apostolic Blessing."[115]

---

111. *Egeria's Travels* 132.
112. *Ibid.* 132-33.
113. P. Jounel, "Le dimanche des Rameaux," *LMD* no. 68 (1961) 45-48.
114. J. M. Hanssens, *Amalarii episcopi opera liturgica omnia* (ST 139) 2:58.
115. P. Jaffé, *Regesta Pontificum Romanorum* (2nd ed.; Leipzig: Veit, 1885) no. 3427.

There is a sure reference to the procession in the Orational of St. Peter's from the end of the eleventh century.[116]

b) *The procession with palms*—From the time it was adopted by the various Churches of the West, the procession with palms had a triumphal character. It was a real feast of Christ the King.[117] From the tenth and eleventh centuries on, the Ordinaries of cathedrals and the Customaries of monasteries felt obliged to give it a privileged place in their descriptions of the liturgical year.

The people gathered outside the town for the blessing of the palms. After the gospel had been read, they set out in procession for a place where a cross had been set up. School children and choristers spread their cloaks before the cross; others then threw palms and branches on the cloaks; finally, various groups came forward and prostrated themselves as the antiphon *Ave, Rex noster* (Hail, our King) was sung. The procession then made its way back to the gate of the town, often carrying in triumph the book of the gospels or even the Blessed Sacrament. It was usually at the gate of the town that children perching on the wall sang the *Gloria laus* and then the response *Ingrediente Domino* (As the Lord entered). In several areas, when the bishop entered the town on this occasion, he had the privilege of freeing some prisoners. When everyone had entered the church, the Mass of the Passion was begun.[118]

In Rome the procession with palms underwent the same kind of popular development in various churches of the city, but the papal liturgy never gave it any great attention. The pope was satisfied to distribute blessed palms in a chapel of the Lateran palace, after which the procession descended to the basilica by the shortest way. The only respect in which this entrance procession for Mass differed from others was that everyone carried palms and that they accompanied the antiphons of the day with the *Gloria laus*.[119]

c) *The morning of Holy Thursday: The reconciliation of penitents*—The reconciliation of penitents, which in Rome had been assigned to Holy Thursday by the end of the fourth century, is described at length in the Gelasian Sacramentary (seventh century). The Sacramentary in fact con-

---

116. Archivio di San Pietro, F 12; P. Salmon, *Les manuscrits liturgiques de la Bibliothèque Vaticane* 2 (ST 253; Vatican City, 1969) 4.

117. H. J. Gräf, *Palmenweihe und Palmenprozession in der lateinischen Liturgie* (Veröffentlichungen des Missionspriesterseminars St. Augustin, Siegburg 5; Kaldenkirchen: Steyler Verlag, 1959) 143–48.

118. This description draws especially on the one in *PRG* 2:40-54. On French customs see P. Jounel, "La semaine sainte en France aux XVIIᵉ–XVIIIᵉ siècles," *LMD* no. 41 (1955) 133–38.

119. Andrieu, *PR* 1:210-14.

tains two distinct rituals "for reconciling penitents."[120] In the first, which belongs to the papal liturgy, a deacon addresses a lengthy petition to the bishop: *Adest, o venerabilis Pontifex* ("The acceptable time is at hand, esteemed bishop"), in which he urgently requests him to admit penitent sinners to reconciliation during these days when the Church is about to beget numerous children through baptism. Is not reconciliation a new baptism? *Lavant aquae, lavant lacrimae* ("The waters wash, but tears wash as well"). The bishop then says a prayer in which he asks God to restore the penitent to the communion of the Church.[121]

The rite for the reconciliation of penitents on Holy Thursday continued well after the ancient form of penance had disappeared. In some regions it left traces right down to the middle of the ninth century in the form of the "absolution" given on Holy Thursday after the recitation of the penitential psalms. The faithful were told, however, that they must regard this absolution not as sacramental but simply as "a prayer and a very salutary blessing which the pastor gives to his people." Holy Thursday was therefore known as "absolution Thursday."[122]

d) *The consecration of chrism and the blessing of the oils*—According to the First Council of Toledo (400) a bishop could consecrate chrism at any time.[123] The practice nonetheless arose of doing it on Holy Thursday during the final Mass to be celebrated before the sacred vigil, when the chrism would be required for the post-baptismal anointing and for confirmation. In a homily St. Eligius, bishop of Noyen († 660), says that "on this day [Holy Thursday] chrism is consecrated all over the world."[124] At Rome the pope consecrated it during the one Mass he celebrated on Holy Thursday, the Mass commemorating the Supper. In the morning the priests attached to the titular churches celebrated a special Mass for blessing the oils of catechumens and of the sick. When the Gelasian Sacramentary entered the Frankish world (eighth century), a compiler introduced into the text of this presbyteral Mass the text for the consecration of chrism. The result was a chrismal Mass.[125] Rome adopted it only in 1955.

II. THE CELEBRATION OF LENT

1. *The Beginning of Lent*

In keeping with its origins the rite of the blessing and distribution of

---

120. *Ge*, nos. 352–59, 360–63.

121. A. Chavasse, *Le Sacramentaire gélasien* (Bibliothèque de théologie; Tournai: Desclée, 1958) 141–55.

122. P. Jounel, "La semaine sainte en France . . ." 138–40.

123. H. T. Bruns, *Canones Apostolorum et Conciliorum* 207.

124. St. Eligius, *Homilia 10 in Cena Domini* (PL 87:629).

125. *Ge*, nos. 375–90; A. Chavasse, *Le Sacramentaire gélasien* 133–39.

ashes took place, until 1970, before the beginning of Mass. In the new Missal it is determined that it should follow upon a Liturgy of the Word, whether or not this is to be followed in turn by the Eucharist. The rite is therefore a penitential celebration.

In the readings the summons of Joel to communal penance (Joel 2:12-18) is followed by St. Paul's appeal to Christians to be reconciled with God (2 Cor 5:20–6:2). In the third reading Jesus teaches his disciples the manner in which they are to give alms, pray, and fast (Matt 6:1-18).

Since its first introduction the imposition of ashes was accompanied by a formula from Genesis: "Remember, man, you are dust and to dust you will return" (Gen 3:19). Now the minister may use instead the Lord's words: "Turn away from sin and be faithful to the gospel" (Mark 1:15). Here the call to conversion, already sounded by Joel, replaces the consideration of human mortality.

2. The Mass Readings of Lent

a) *Sunday readings*—The Sunday readings have the Old Testament and the gospel for the main foci, with the second reading shedding light now on the one, now on the other (usually on the gospel).

Each year the Old Testament readings of the first five Sundays recall the great stages in the ascent of the race toward the Pasch of Christ. There are, in order, the Sunday of the original covenants (the fall; the covenant with Noah; the profession of faith by the chosen people), the Sunday of Abraham (his call; the sacrifice of Isaac; God's covenant with Abraham), the Sunday of Moses (Moses strikes the rock; the Law given to Moses; God reveals his name to Moses), the Sunday of the people of the living God in the promised land (David; the exile and return; Passover in the promised land), and finally the Sunday of the prophets (Ezekiel; Jeremiah; Isaiah).

On the first and second Sundays the stories of the temptation and of the transfiguration are read, each year from a different synoptic gospel. On the next three Sundays of year A the principal gospels of the baptismal catechesis are read: the revelation of Christ to the Samaritan woman, the cure of the man born blind, and the raising of Lazarus. These may also be read in years B and C, but two other series of gospels are also available for these years. The one series (in year B) proclaims the exaltation of Christ through his being raised on the cross; the other (year C) urges conversion by revealing the Lord's mercy.

During Lent the apostolic letters are no longer read in a semi-continuous manner. Instead, they are chosen each Sunday as a help in linking the Old Testament reading and the gospel or else as a preparation for listening to the gospel.

b) *The weekday readings*—The new lectionary has retained the fundamental characteristics of the old one: the first reading is always from the Old Testament; the reading of the Gospel of John is begun in the fourth week; finally, most of the traditional pericopes have been kept. Nonetheless the lectionary has undergone a profound remodeling. This was necessary, first of all, because the most important pericopes, formerly read during the week, have been transferred to Sunday; for example, the gospels of the Samaritan woman, the man born blind, Lazarus, and the Prodigal Son, together with the Old Testament readings that used to accompany these gospels. The disappearance of the readings that used to be attached to the spring Ember Days likewise necessitated a new distribution that affected the entire season. Finally, the reading of the Gospel of John that begins in the fourth week is now done in a more orderly way: starting with John 4:43 there is now a semi-continuous reading of chapters 5, 7, 8, 10 (31-42), 11 (45-56), 12 (1-11), and 13 (21-36).

3. *The Mass Prayers of Lent*

During Lent the Eucharistic Prayer has been enriched by a dozen prefaces. Six of these for specific Sundays (temptation, transfiguration, Samaritan woman, man born blind, Lazarus, palms). Six others are general Lenten prefaces or prefaces of the passion (these last two are for the fifth and sixth weeks). All come from ancient sources or have been composed on the basis of ancient sources such as the sermons of St. Leo the Great.[126]

The same holds for the presidential prayers. Of the opening prayers for Sundays, only one from the old Missal has been kept: the one for Passion Sunday. The opening prayer of the first Sunday, from the Gelasian Sacramentary,[127] expounds the purpose of Lent by asking that the Father would "help us to understand the meaning of your Son's death and resurrection and teach us to reflect it in our lives." The opening prayer of the second Sunday is concerned with the transfiguration of Jesus, and that of the third Sunday reminds us that we must overcome our sins "by prayer, fasting and works of mercy." On the fourth Sunday, which is Laetare Sunday, the prayer speaks of Easter as approaching, while on the fifth it refers to Christ "who loved the world and died for our salvation."

For the weekday Masses of Lent, a larger number of prayers coming from the Gregorian Sacramentary via the Tridentine Missal have been kept: there are twenty-three opening prayers from this source, against fourteen from other sources. Care has been taken, in particular, to make part of

---

126. A. Dumas, "Les sources du Missel romain" 39-40.
127. *Ge*, no. 104.

Lent a number of former Sunday collects that refer to human weakness and the omnipotence of grace.

4. *Passion Sunday—Palm Sunday*

The new Holy Week ordo of 1955 gave the procession with palms an amplitude it had never previously had in the Roman Missal. This represented a return to the medieval traditions described earlier.

Before 1955 the procession took place inside the church during a Liturgy of the Word which contained two readings (one of them being the story of Jesus' entry into Jerusalem) and nine prayers, as well as a preface climaxed by the Sanctus. The clergy alone left the church for the procession, while the congregation awaited their return.

The ordo of 1955 prescribed that the people should take part in the procession and that this procession should not be scanted. It required that, if possible, the faithful assemble, and the palms be blessed, outside the church, so that the procession might recover its original purpose, which was to be a passage from one place to another. The blessing of the palms was reduced to a single prayer, which was to be followed by the gospel account of the triumphal entry of Jesus into the holy city. While retaining the traditional songs, among them the *Gloria laus*, the new ordo enriched the repertory with ancient antiphons, among them *Ave, Rex noster* (Hail, our King), which had been a favorite in the lands of the Franks.

The 1970 Missal made its own the regulations set down in 1955. Meanwhile, however, living conditions had changed and some adaptation was necessary. In the cities it is nowadays often impossible to have "the solemn procession in honor of Christ the King," which the 1955 ordo had desired. Sometimes political or social conditions are unfavorable. Consequently, the regulations have been made more flexible, while retaining the essentials of the liturgy of this day. Thus, if an outdoor procession is not feasible, the people may gather at the door of the church for the blessing of the palms and the reading of the gospel and then enter the building in procession. In case of necessity, there may be even an entrance only of the priest and ministers, while the faithful hold their palms.

At Mass the passion is read from whichever of the Synoptics is providing the basic framework for the reading of the gospel in the particular year of the cycle.

5. *Holy Week*

Holy Week, which opens with Passion Sunday, includes both the final days of Lent (until Thursday evening) and the first two days of the Easter triduum. It does not, therefore, possess a real liturgical unity.

a) *Monday, Tuesday, and Wednesday*—Before 1970 the four gospels of the passion were read annually during Holy Week: Matthew on Palm

Sunday, Mark on Tuesday, Luke on Wednesday, and John on Friday. Since the Synoptics are now read on Sundays in a three-year cycle, the reading of the passion on Tuesday and Wednesday has been replaced by the prediction of Judas' betrayal and Peter's denial (John 13:13, 21-38) on Tuesday and by the account of the preparations for Passover (Matt 26:14-25) on Wednesday.

b) *Holy Thursday: The chrismal Mass*—On Holy Thursday morning the priests of the city and delegates from the parishes of the diocese gather to concelebrate the chrismal Mass. The people are invited to participate in the celebration in large numbers. This celebration may, however, be moved forward several days if this will enable more priests to take part. For it was Pope Paul VI's wish that the chrismal Mass be a feast of the priesthood in which priests might, in the presence of their bishop, renew the commitments they undertook at their ordination "out of love for the Lord Jesus and his Church."

The rites for the consecration of chrism and blessing of oils will be studied in connection with the sacraments. The readings for this Mass emphasize the priestly character of the people of God: "You shall be called the priests of the Lord" (first reading, Isa 61:1-9); Christ has made us "a kingdom, priests to his God and Father" (second reading, Rev 1:5-8). The preface of the Eucharistic Prayer is a new and finely constructed prayer which develops the theology of Christian priesthood: Christ, "High Priest of the new and eternal covenant," has given "the dignity of a royal priesthood to the people he has made his own," and from these he has chosen others "to share his sacred ministry by the laying on of hands."

Chapter II

The Christmas Season

§1. The Feasts of Christmas and Epiphany

BIBLIOGRAPHY

B. Botte, *Les origines de la Noël et de l'Epiphanie* (Louvain: Mont César, 1932).

J. Leclercq, "Aux origines du cycle de Noël," *EL* 60 (1946) 7-26.

O. Cullmann, *Noël dans l'Eglise ancienne* (Cahiers théologiques de l'actualité protestante; Neuchâtel: Delachaux et Niestlé, 1949).

J. Lemarié, *La Manifestation du Seigneur* (Lex orandi 23; Paris: Cerf, 1957). Book 1 of this work is a careful synthesis of the history of the feasts of Manifestation (21-64); the following books bring out the fundamental themes of each feast (Christmas, Epiphany, Meeting) and illustrate them with a wealth of citations from the liturgy and the Fathers.

C. Mohrmann, *Epiphania* (Nijmegen: Dekker and Van de Vegt, 1953). French translation in idem, *Etudes sur le latin des chrétiens* (Rome: Edizioni di Storia e Letteratura, 1958) 245-75.

A. J. Vermeulen, *Le développement sémasiologique d'Epiphaneia et la fête de l'Epiphanie* (Graecitas et latinitas christianorum primaeva, Supplementa, Fasc. 1; Nijmegen: Dekker and Van de Vegt, 1964).

J. Mossay, *Les fêtes de Noël et d'Epiphanie d'après les sources littéraires cappadociennes du IVe siècle* (Textes et études liturgiques 3; Louvain: Mont César, 1965).

B. Botte and E. Melia, *Noel, Epiphanie, Retour du Christ* (Lex orandi 40; Paris: Cerf, 1967).

F. Nikolasch, "Zum Ursprung des Epiphaniefestes," *EL* 82 (1968) 393-439.

T. J. Talley, "Le temps liturgique dans l'Eglise ancienne: Etat de la recherche," *LMD* no. 147 (1981) 39-48.

I. THE ORIGINS OF CHRISTMAS AND EPIPHANY

The early Church had but one feast: the day of Kyrios Christ, the weekly and annual Pasch. Only in the course of the fourth century did the solemnity of the Lord's coming among us make its appearance. Initially, moreover, the aim was less to commemorate an anniversary in the strict sense than to provide a counterbalance to the pagan feasts of the winter solstice, which were celebrated at Rome on December 25 and in Egypt on January 6. The feast of the *Natale* (birthday) of the Christ the Sun, that is, of his epiphany, was all the more fervently received by the Church because it was a way of proclaiming the dogma of Nicaea in opposition to the Arian heresy.

1. *The Two Christian Feasts at the Winter Solstice*

The feast of Christmas is mentioned for the first time by the Chronographer of 354.[1] In his civil calendar the compiler notes at December 25, *N(atalis) Invicti* ("Birthday of the Unconquered [Sun]"); then at the beginning of the list of martyrs' anniversaries (*Depositio martyrum*) he announces: *VIII Kal. Ianuarii natus Christus in Bethleem Iudeae* ("December 25: Christ was born in Bethlehem of Judea").[2] Since the list of martyrs' anniversaries must have been drawn up in 336, the celebration of Christmas at Rome goes back to about 330. In origin, then, the feast was contemporary with the construction of Constantine's Basilica of St. Peter, and it seems initially to have been localized on the Vatican; its purpose was to direct to Christ the homage which the Roman people used to offer on that same hill to Eastern divinities.[3]

The place and date chosen, as well as the explicit allusions of the Fathers to the symbolism of Christ as Sun of Justice (Mal 4:2) and Light of the world (John 8:12), make clear beyond any doubt the Church's intention of establishing a Christian feast in opposition to the feast of the Unconquered Sun, which was the symbol of paganism's last resistance to Christianity.[4] In addition, the institution of a feast celebrating Christ's birth on the very Birthday of the Unconquered Sun fit Constantine's great syncretist vision. An emperor who in 321 had decreed a holiday for the first day of the week (day of the Sun and day of the Lord) could only approve

---

1. See p. 119.
2. *LP* 1:11.
3. N. M. Denis-Boulet, "A propos des fouilles de Saint-Pierre," *RechSR* 34 (1947) 385–406. The oldest Christian mosaic in Rome, the one in the mausoleum of the Julii (M) in the cemetery on the Vatican, shows Christ the Sun in his triumphal chariot (middle of the third century).
4. B. Botte, *Les origines de la Noël et de l'Epiphanie* (Louvain: Mont César, 1932) 50–67.

of the followers of the two cults being brought together for an annual celebration of the same day.[5]

The feast of the Epiphany, which was of Eastern origin as the very name shows, reflected the same intention on the part of the Church. In Egypt and Arabia January 6 was the day for feasts of the winter solstice. Here the homage paid to the triumphant Sun was accompanied by mythological reminiscences of great antiquity.[6] Sometime around 120–140 one of the gnostic sects tried to Christianize these beliefs, as Clement of Alexandria tells us: "The followers of Basilides also celebrate the day of the baptism of Jesus and spend the entire preceding night in reading. According to them the baptism took place in the fifteenth year of the reign of Tiberius and on the fifteenth—or, according to others, the eleventh—day of the month Tubi [= January 10 or 6]."[7]

The reason why the followers of Basilides celebrated the mystery of the baptism was that in their view the incarnation of the Word in the humanity of Jesus took place at the baptism in the Jordan. In any case, the date chosen was rich in symbolism. But the Catholic Church was to wait until the fourth century before celebrating the Epiphany of the Lord. Moreover, though the feast originated in the East (and, in all likelihood, in Egypt) the first attestation of it comes from Gaul. Epiphany was already a major feast in Gaul by 361, since according to the testimony of Ammianus Marcellinus, Emperor Julian, though interiorly converted to paganism, still made outward profession of Christianity by going to church "on the day in January which Christians celebrate as 'Epiphany.' "[8] If the Eastern Epiphany was traditional in Gaul by 360, it must have been almost contemporary in origin with the Roman Christmas. If Epiphany is to be regarded as earlier than Christmas, it cannot in any case have originated much before the Council of Nicaea (325).

2. *The Content of Christmas and Epiphany*

The names *Natale* and *Epiphaneia* already give some indication of the respective contents of the Christian solemnities on December 25 and January 6. *Natale* means "anniversary of birth" and was a term in current use in the fourth century. But the etiquette of the imperial court had broadened the meaning of the word and had applied it to days of great exaltation for the emperor, as for example the day of his accession to the purple and the day of his apotheosis.[9] This, then, was the full meaning

---

5. O. Cullmann, *Noël dans l'Eglise ancienne* (Cahiers théologiques de l'actualité protestante; Neuchâtel: Delachaux et Niestlé, 1949) 26–28.

6. B. Botte, *ibid.* 68–76.

7. *Stromata* I, 21, 146, ed. M. Caster (SC 30) 150.

8. *Rerum gestarum* XXI, 2, 5, cited in B. Botte, *ibid.* 46.

9. H. Stern, *Le Calendrier de 354* (Paris: Geuthner, 1953) 76–79.

of *Natalis Invicti*: feast of the Sun's rebirth and its divinity. Christians in the early centuries had used "birthday" for the day of a Christian's true birth, namely, the day of his or her earthly death and entrance into the promised land. But it was clearly with the pagan meaning in mind that they now applied it also to Christ, the *Sol oriens* ("Rising Sun"). As a result, the Latin *Natale* was not too different in its substantive meaning from the eastern *Epiphaneia*.

The earliest Latin translations of the Greek word bring out all its rich content: *manifestatio, apparitio, adventus* (lit.: manifestation, appearance, coming). In the Greco-Roman world the word *epiphaneia*[10] was used both of the appearance or manifestation of a divinity coming to the aid of human beings and of the festive arrivals of a sovereign (accession to the throne, triumphal entrance into a city). Paul seems to have this second context in mind when he says: "The grace of God has appeared *(apparuit, epephanē)* for the salvation of all men" (Tit 2:11), and connects this appearance with the "appearing *(epiphaneia;* Latin: *adventus,* 'coming') of the glory of our great God and Savior Jesus Christ" (Tit 2:13). In Latin, the *apparitio* used for the first coming and the *adventus* used for the second translate the same Greek word, *epiphaneia*. Moreover, the Roman liturgy has this passage from Titus in its nocturnal Mass for Christmas, while the Ambrosian liturgy uses it on January 6. This simple fact reveals the complementarity and close connection between the two feasts. There is all the more reason, then, for us to ask what aspects of the coming of God's Son among us each feast is intended to highlight.

In addition, the content of the two solemnities developed further due to the fact that as early as the end of the fourth century both feasts had been accepted by the majority of the Churches.

No one can doubt that the Roman Christmas originally honored the birth of Jesus at Bethlehem; the words of the Chronographer are too explicit on this point. But to the homage being paid to the Word made flesh and to his mother there was added mention of the events accompanying the birth of Jesus; the adoration of the shepherds and the wise men, and Herod's slaughter of the children. That, at least, is how Africa, which always stayed close to Roman usage, was celebrating Christmas around 360, according to Optatus of Milevis.[11]

When Rome began to celebrate January 6 in the second half of the fourth century, it shifted to this date the remembrance of the adoration

---

10. C. Mohrmann, *Epiphania* (Nijmegen: Dekker and Van de Vegt, 1953); French translation in *Etudes sur le latin des chrétiens* (Rome: Edizioni di Storia e Letteratura, 1958) 245–75. The study is summarized in J. Lemarié, *La Manifestation du Seigneur* (Lex orandi 23; Paris: Cerf, 1957) 44–45.

11. A. Wilmart, "Un sermon de saint Optat pour la fête de Noël," *RevSR* 2 (1922) 282.

of the wise men; this became the main theme of its Epiphany, while December 25 remained the day for celebrating the birth of Jesus and the adoration of the shepherds. On the other hand, when the feast of Christmas was taken over in the East (between 370 and 378 in Cappadocia, in 386 at Antioch, ca. 430 in Egypt, and in the next century in Palestine), it kept its original form. Even today the Byzantine Church sings at Vespers for December 24: "Lord, every creature you have made brings you its testimony of gratitude: the angels bring their song, the heavens its star, the magi their gifts, the shepherds their wonder, the earth its cave, the wilderness its manger, and we bring a Virgin Mother."[12]

Epiphany underwent a more complex evolution, as a result both of its passage from East to West and of the acceptance of Christmas in the East. All historians of liturgy are in agreement on this evolution. They disagree, however, on the original content of the Eastern feast of Epiphany. The Church of Jerusalem celebrated on January 6 only the mystery of the birth (which included the adoration of the shepherds and the wise men); Egypt added the baptism of the Savior; and St. Epiphanius of Salamis speaks, in relation to this day, of the birth, the adoration of the wise men, and the wedding feast at Cana. Was the commemoration of the birth, baptism, and first miracle of Jesus associated with the feast in the beginning, or was it the result of a fusion of several different traditions? B. Botte thinks the second hypothesis more probable, whereas C. Mohrmann regards the original Epiphany as a "typical feast of ideas" that had a number of objects and, specifically, as "the feast of the opening phases of the work of redemption."[13]

Be that as it may, in the East, Epiphany is now the feast of the Lord's baptism, and all other aspects of the mystery of the incarnation are excluded. Only the Armenian Monophysite Church, which has never accepted Christmas, celebrates on January 6 the three mysteries of the birth, the adoration of the Magi, and the baptism. The Roman liturgy sees Epiphany as primarily the day of Christ's revelation of himself to the pagans, but it nonetheless mentions the baptism of Jesus and the miracle at Cana in the antiphons of Lauds and Vespers for January 6, while celebrating the Lord's baptism in a distinct feast on the following Sunday.[14] Using the theme of the marriage of Christ and his Church, the

---

12. E. Mercenier and F. Paris, *La prière des Eglises de rite byzantin* II/1 (Amay, 1939) 113.
13. B. Botte, *ibid.* 77–88; C. Mohrmann, *ibid.* 10–11.
14. The Roman Antiphonary of the Middle Ages had inherited from Byzantium a number of magnificent antiphons for the office of January 13. Some of them are now in the Liturgy of the Hours for the feast of the Baptism of the Lord. J. Lemarié has published a critical edition of them in *EL* 72 (1958) 3–38. These antiphons, which have left no trace in the Byzantine liturgy, have been preserved, at least in part, in the Armenian rite: J. Lemarié, *La Manifestation du Seigneur* 520 (*Office de la nuit,* stanzas 4, 6, 7, 8, and 9).

liturgical formularies bring out in a very felicitous way the link between
the three mysteries that make up Epiphany: "Today the Bridegroom claims
his bride, the Church, since Christ has washed her sins away in Jordan's
waters; the Magi hasten with their gifts to the royal wedding; and the wedding guests rejoice, for Christ has changed water into wine, alleluia" (antiphon for the *Benedictus*, January 6).

3. *The Liturgical Theology of Christmas*

In its liturgy the Church celebrates but a single mystery, the paschal
mystery. Consequently, when it instituted the feast of Christmas, it
celebrated this at first as a simple anniversary, a *natale* that was placed
at the head of the *Depositiones martyrum* or anniversaries of the martyrs. December 25 soon came to be regarded as in the proper sense the
anniversary date of Christ's birth. St. Augustine was convinced of this
when, in about 400, he asserted the non-sacramental character of
Christmas: whereas Easter annually effects our passage from death to life
in the passion and resurrection of the Lord, Christmas, being a simple
anniversary, is not celebrated *in sacramento* (as a "sacrament," that is,
a rite which makes the mystery of salvation effectively present).[15]

Fifty years later, the sermons of St. Leo the Great show an important
deepening of the liturgical theology of Christmas. From that time forward
the formularies of the festal liturgy would reflect this new understanding:
Christmas is a mystery. But it is not a separate mystery, distinct and independent of the paschal mystery. Rather it links us to the beginnings of
the paschal mystery; it contains the beginning of the mystery of salvation, since Christ began to merit in our behalf from the first moment of
his human existence. Christmas thus prepares us to understand Easter better
by showing the Redeemer to be the very Son of God made man. In addition, Christmas helps us to live the paschal mystery, inasmuch as the
human birth of the Son of God puts at our disposal, so to speak, the
transcendent model of our own supernatural sonship or daughterhood.
This is why we sing in the liturgy: "Today a new day dawns, the day
of our redemption, prepared by God from ages past, the beginning of our
never ending gladness" (second responsory in the Office of Readings).

II. THE CELEBRATION OF CHRISTMAS

In the West the feast of Christmas is set apart by the fact that it has

15. I am here summing up, and even using at times the very formulations of, J. Gaillard's
study, "Noël: Memoria ou mystère?" *LMD* no. 59 (1959) 37–59. St. Augustine's thought
is studied in G. Hudon, "Le mystère de Noël dans le temps de l'Eglise d'après saint Augustin,"
ibid. 60–85.

four Masses. In addition, the liturgy has for its framework a set of popular traditions, of which the veneration paid to the crèche is the most striking.

1. *The Christmas Masses*

St. Gregory the Great († 604) begins his homily on the Nativity by saying: "The Lord in his generosity allows us to celebrate Mass three times on this day."[16] This is the earliest witness to the three Masses which remain to this day one of the peculiarities of the Christmas liturgy: Mass in the night, Mass at dawn, and Mass during the day. The three are themselves preceded by the vigil Mass on the evening of December 24. The three Masses of Christmas were originally peculiar to the papal liturgy, itself connected with local worship at various sanctuaries in Rome.

In the beginning the only Christmas Mass was the one during the day, which was celebrated at St. Peter's. This was still the case in the time of St. Leo the Great († 461). Now, shortly after the Council of Ephesus (431), which had acknowledged Mary's title as Mother of God, a basilica, St. Mary Major, was built in her honor on the Esquiline. In the next century there was a desire to have a replica of the crèche of Bethlehem at Rome, and an oratory of the Crèche was constructed near the basilica. This quickly led in turn to the desire that a nocturnal liturgy like the one at Bethlehem be celebrated in the new oratory. Such was the origin of the Mass at night. It should be noted that the Latin liturgical books have never spoken of a "Midnight Mass" but only of Mass at night.

On December 25 the anniversary of St. Anastasia was also celebrated at Rome in her basilica at the foot of the Palatine. This was a feast day for the Byzantine authorities who lived in the old imperial palaces near this basilica. In order to honor them the pope went to celebrate Mass at St. Anastasia before going on to St. Peter's to celebrate the Mass of Christmas day. After some time, the pope continued to celebrate in the Palatine basilica but he now used formularies relating to the birth of Jesus and simply commemorated the titular saint. This explains why the liturgical books used to announce an assembly, or station, at St. Mary Major on the evening of December 24, a station at the Crèche of St. Mary Major during the night, a station at St. Anastasia at dawn, and a final station at St. Peter during the day.[17] In the eleventh century this final station was replaced by a new one at St. Mary Major, which thus became to the full extent the Christmas basilica.

When the books for the papal liturgy made their way throughout Italy and beyond the Alps and, above all, when Charlemagne imposed this Roman usage on his empire, the three Christmas Masses were accepted

---

16. St. Gregory the Great, *Homilia 8 in Evangelia* 1 (PL 76:1103).
17. *Gr*, p. 609.

by the entire West. It should be noted, however, that they were to be celebrated at the hours prescribed. It was by an abuse that the modern age introduced the continuous celebration of three Masses.

2. *The Liturgical Formularies*

The high point of the Christmas liturgy is the reading of the Prologue of St. John in the daytime Mass: "And the Word became flesh and dwelt among us . . .; we have beheld his glory" (John 1:14). All the other readings lead up to this one or echo it. The same is true of the prayers of the Mass and Hours. In accordance with their varied literary genres, all of them proclaim the dogmas of Nicaea, Ephesus, and Chalcedon, in the light of which the feast was born and developed.

God became a human being in order that human beings might share in his divine life. Such is the teaching of St. Leo the Great in the Office of Readings for Christmas and of the antiphon *O admirabile commercium* ("O marvelous exchange!") for the octave day. It is also the theme of the prayer of the day for Christmas: "Lord God, we praise you for creating man, and still more for restoring him in Christ. Your Son shared our weakness: may we share his glory."

3. *The Octave of Christmas*

Until the seventh century Easter alone had the privilege of being celebrated for eight days. At that time Pentecost acquired a similar octave in order that the catechesis of the newly baptized might be continued. Christmas could not claim such an honor. This feast did, however, receive an octave day. Initially it was a day for honoring the divine motherhood of Mary; later the circumcision of the Lord was celebrated on this day.[18] The Marian feast on January 1 was the oldest of all the Marian feasts celebrated in Rome.

The three days following Christmas were popular ones, because they were the feasts respectively of St. Stephen, St. John, and the Holy Innocents. Churches and monasteries during these three days were full of festivities in honor of deacons (St. Stephen), priests (St. John), and students or young clerics (Holy Innocents). In the Middle Ages the famous "feast of fools" was celebrated on December 28.[19]

---

18. The Roman sacramentaries and lectionaries have the heading *In octavas Domini* (*Gr*, p. 612). The antiphonary has the title *Natale sanctae Mariae* (R. J. Hesbert, *Antiphonale missarum sextuplex* [Brussels: Vromant, 1935] 22), and the Gallican books have *In circumcisione Domini* (*Missale Gothicum*, ed. L. C. Mohlberg [REDMF 5; Rome: Herder, 1961] no. 51). This last title is also the one in the Tridentine Missal; in 1960 it was replaced by "Octave of Christmas," while in 1969 January 1 became once again the Solemnity of Mary, Mother of God.

19. E. Martène, *De antiquis Ecclesiae ritibus* IV, 13, 11, in the "Antwerp" edition, 3 (1737), col. 114–15.

On the Sunday after Christmas (or on December 30 if Christmas falls on a Sunday) the Holy Family of Jesus, Mary, and Joseph is celebrated as the model for Christian family life. The feast was established in 1921.[20] In 1969 it was linked with the Christmas octave and provided with a three-year cycle of readings, in which the gospels are of the flight into Egypt (A), the presentation in the temple (B), and the discovery of Jesus in the temple by Mary and Joseph (C).

4. *The Crèche*

The crèche—a term that includes both the cave and the manger where Jesus was born—is the most notable characteristic of the feast of Christmas in the West.

The earliest crèche was, of course, the one at Bethlehem. The first generations of Christians did not forget its location. Origen tells us (in 248) that "at Bethlehem they point out the cave in which Jesus was born and, in the cave, the manger in which he lay swaddled."[21] St. Helen, mother of Emperor Constantine, transformed the grotto and enclosed it in a basilica which, after undergoing some renovations in the sixth century, still exists today. In a Christmas homily St. Jerome tells us that in his day they had replaced the manger of clay with one of silver: "It is far less precious to me than the one they removed; I do not condemn those who thought to pay homage in this manner, but my wonder is at the Lord, the creator of the world, who willed to be born not in silver or gold but in clay."[22]

After the crèche at Bethlehem came the one at St. Mary Major in Rome, which dates from the sixth century. From the twelfth century on, the pieces of wood from a manger that were deposited here were regarded as being from the very manger in which Jesus lay. They are kept beneath the main altar of the basilica.[23]

The crèches in our churches originated in the liturgical plays performed in abbeys and cathedrals in order to lend a more popular note to the nocturnal liturgy of Christmas. The plays postdate the *Office of the Tomb*

---

20. *AAS* 13 (1921) 543.

21. Origen, *Contra Celsum* I, 51, ed. M. Borret, vol. 1 (SC 132; Paris: Cerf, 1967) 214–15 and Note 3 on 215–18.

22. St. Jerome, *Homilia de Nativitate Domini* (PLS 2:183); see D. Baldi, *Enchiridion locorum sanctorum* (Jerusalem, 1955) 84.

23. A distinction must be made between the bits of wood kept in a reliquary under the main altar and the ancient oratory of the Crèche, which was moved (not without damage) by Fontana in 1585 into the chapel erected by Pope Sixtus V, and was placed under the altar of the Blessed Sacrament. See J. Delumeau, *Vie economique et sociale à Rome dans la seconde moitié du XVIᵉ siècle* (Bibliothèque des Ecoles françaises d'Athènes et de Rome 184; Paris: E. de Bocard, 1957), Plate XI, p. 272.

at Easter and display a great deal of ingenuity and spontaneity. The *Office of the Shepherds*, the *Procession of the Prophets* or *Feast of the Ass* (Balaam's), the *Office of the Star*, the *Visit of the Shepherds and Wise Men* became more and more elaborate from the eleventh to the fourteenth century. All involved the construction of a kind of kiosk to which the personages involved made their way in order to adore the new-born Christ. Christ must have been represented by a wooden statue.[24]

Francis of Assisi wanted something better for Christmas, 1223, at Greccio. He set up a manger filled with straw, and stationed an ox and an ass close by it. With the permission of the pope, he placed an altar over the manger, and a priest celebrated Mass there. Francis, who was a deacon, sang the gospel and preached a sermon which touched the hearts of all the folk who had come from the surrounding area.[25] The Franciscans thus became promoters of devotion to the crèche, just as they were of the Stations of the Cross. Intended originally as humble reminders of the cave of Bethlehem, in the Baroque period the crèches became the opulent creations we see in pictures of the Nativity that were painted at that time. The *santons* (ornamental figures at a crèche) of Provence are the heirs of that tradition.

III. THE CELEBRATION OF EPIPHANY

On Christmas the Churches of the East and the West celebrate basically the same event: the birth of the Lord. On Epiphany, however, the two groups manifest an originality of their own.

1. *Epiphany in the West*

Two themes—the adoration of the wise men and the baptism of the Lord—are the objects of two distinct feasts: Epiphany proper and the Baptism of the Lord.

a) *Epiphany*—The Solemnity of the Epiphany is celebrated on January 6 in areas where it is a holiday; otherwise it falls on the Sunday after January 1. It does not have any special rites of its own. In recalling the coming of the wise men to Bethlehem, it celebrates the call of God to the pagan nation; thus the doxology of the Latin hymns says: *Iesu, tibi sit gloria, qui apparuisti gentibus* ("Jesus, glory be to you who revealed yourself to the Gentiles").

---

24. K. Young, *The Drama of the Medieval Church* (Oxford: Clarendon Press, 1933) 2:3-29.

25. Thomas of Celano, *First Life of St. Francis* 30, trans. Placid Hermann, in *St. Francis of Assisi: Writings and Early Biographies*, ed. Marion A. Habig (Chicago: Franciscan Herald Press, 1973) 299-302.

The reading of the gospel story is preceded at Mass by a passage from the Book of the Consolation of Israel in which the prophet foresees the gathering of all peoples around Jerusalem (Isa 60:1-6). In the Liturgy of the Hours, there is a lengthier reading from this same chapter of the prophet (Isa 60:1-22); the evangelist seems to allude explicitly to one verse in this passage: "All from Sheba shall come bearing gold and frankincense." Once the event had taken place, St. Paul could bring to light the meaning of the mystery present in it: through the preaching of the gospel the pagans have been given a share, in Christ, in the promise made to the Jews (Eph 3:2-6).

In the Office of Readings, St. Leo the Great develops the same theme: "In the person of the Magi let all people adore the Creator of the universe." So do the various prayers; thus the preface says: "Today you revealed in Christ your eternal plan of salvation and showed him as the light of all peoples."

b) *The Baptism of the Lord*—When Epiphany, like Christmas, was given an octave in various places (starting at the end of the eighth century) the account of the Lord's baptism was assigned as the gospel reading for the octave day. A number of medieval missals would add a special reading from the prophets.[26] The Byzantine antiphons *Veterem hominem*, which Charlemagne had had translated into Latin after hearing them sung by Greek monks, were used in the Office.[27] In the French liturgies of the eighteenth century, the octave day of Epiphany became the feast of the Baptism of the Lord, and a set of proper formularies was composed for it. This feast became part of the Roman Calendar in 1960.[28] In 1969 it was assigned to the Sunday after January 6 or to the following day when this Sunday is Epiphany Sunday.

The Mass has three sets of readings for the three-year cycle. The preface, opening prayer, and prayer after Communion are new compositions. The Liturgy of the Hours once again has the *Veterem hominem* antiphons (First Vespers, Office of Readings, Morning Prayer); "Christ is baptized, the world is made holy," says the antiphon for the *Benedictus*, which thus summarizes the sermon of St. Gregory the Great for the Feast of Lights that is read on this day.

2. *Epiphany in the East*

Throughout the Christian East, from Ethiopia to Russia, the rite

---

26. J. Lemarié, "Le Baptême du Seigneur dans le Jourdain d'après les textes scripturaires en usage dans les Eglises d'Orient et d'Occident," *LMD* no. 59 (1959) 96-98.

27. J. Lemarié, "Les antiennes 'Veterem hominem' du jour octave de l'Epiphanie," *EL* 72 (1958) 3-38.

28. *Rubricae Breviarii et Missalis Romani* (Vatican City, 1960) 98.

characteristic of Epiphany is the blessing of water on the evening of January 5 in memory of the Lord's baptism. At the beginning of the fifth century, Constantinople still preserved the tradition of baptizing catechumens during the holy night of Easter, thus signifying that to be baptized is to be immersed in the death and resurrection of Christ (Rom 6). Soon, however, the administration of baptism was transferred from Easter to Epiphany, on the grounds that when he went down into the Jordan Christ sanctified water and made it the source of eternal life. Later on, adult baptisms became infrequent and children were baptized at home, but the Church continued to bless the water for baptism at Epiphany.

In the Byzantine rite for the blessing, three passages from Isaiah are read (35:1-9; 55:1-3; 12:3-6), then some verses from the First Letter to the Corinthians (10:1-4), and finally the story of the baptism of Jesus as told by Mark (1:9-11). The readings are followed by a diaconal litany and a lengthy priestly prayer attributed to St. Sophronius of Jerusalem. The priest then dips the cross into the water three times before setting it on a platform that is adorned with flowers. Each person present approaches, kisses the cross, is sprinkled with the holy water, and takes a sip of it. After the service each may draw some water from the container and keep it at home.[29]

In Ethiopia Epiphany brings thousands of pilgrims to Aksum. The priest blesses the water in the great reservoir that supplies the city, and then everyone bathes in it in order to honor the baptism of Christ.[30]

IV. THE PRESENTATION OF THE LORD

Forty days after the Birth of the Lord, the feast of his Presentation in the Temple brings an end to the festivities of Christmas and Epiphany.

1. *Origins and Evolution of the Feast*

The fortieth day after Christmas-Epiphany (*Quadragesima de Epiphania*) was celebrated in Jerusalem ca. 386, as Egeria attests.[31] The procession with candles was added around 450.[32] In the sixth century the feast made its way into Syria and was then accepted at Constantinople under the name of *Hypapantē* or Meeting: it celebrated "the Meeting of our great God and Savior Jesus Christ with Simeon the Just when the lat-

---

29. E. Mercenier and F. Paris, *ibid.* II/1, 169–78.

30. J. Leroy, *L'Ethiopie, archéologie et culture* (Paris: Desclée de Brouwer, 1973) 25.

31. *Egeria's Travels* 128.

32. Cyril of Scythopolis, *Vita Theodosii*, edit. A.-J. Festugière in *Les moines d'Orient* III/3 (Paris: Cerf, 1963) 58.

ter took him in his arms."[33] In the beginning the feast of the Meeting also included the procession.[34]

Rome accepted this feast in the second half of the seventh century. The Gregorian Sacramentary has it under the title *Ypapanti*. The *Liber Pontificalis* speaks of *Dies S. Simeonis, quod Ypapanti Graeci appellant* ("Day of St. Simeon, which the Greeks call *Hypapantē*").[35] But in the middle of the eighth century, a new name for the feast appeared in the Frankish world: the Purification of the Blessed Virgin Mary.[36] For two centuries the two names were in competition, often within the same region, but finally the second prevailed. The French liturgies of the eighteenth century then replaced it with the title "Presentation of the Lord," which the Roman Calendar adopted in 1969.

At the end of the seventh century, Pope Sergius I (687–701) introduced into Rome the custom of having before Mass on February 2, March 25, August 15, and September 8 a procession that started at the Forum and ended at St. Mary Major.[37] The procession on February 2 took place at dawn. Everyone in the procession carried a candle, but the ceremony nonetheless had something of a penitential character. This found expression not in the songs but in the black vestments worn by the pope and his deacons.[38] The same was true of the procession at Constantinople, where the emperor walked in it barefooted.[39]

Did this penitential aspect indicate the intention of making reparation for the licentious parades held in February in ancient Rome, or was it possibly a holdover from a supplicatory ritual in a time of past disaster? It is difficult to say. In any case, down to 1970 the priest and ministers wore violet vestments for the procession, which was known as the "Candlemas" procession because of the candles which were carried in it. The blessing of candles made its appearance only in the tenth century, in the Germanic world,[40] and it is not documented for Rome before the twelfth century.[41] For the procession the antiphonary of the Mass had Byzantine chants which in the eighth and ninth centuries were still being

33. *Le Typicon de la Grande Eglise*, ed. J. Mateos 1 (OCA 165; Rome: Pontificio Istituto Orientale, 1962) 220–21.

34. *Ibid.* 222–23. The Typicon—Sainte-Croix ms 40—is a witness to the liturgical practice of the tenth century.

35. *LP* 1:376.

36. P. Jounel, *Le culte des saints dans les basiliques du Latran et du Vatican au douzième siècle* (Collection de l'Ecole Française de Rome 26; Rome: Ecole Française de Rome, 1977) 222.

37. *OR* 22, Andrieu *OR* 3:235-36.

38. *Ibid.*

39. M. Higgins, "Note on the Purification . . . in Constantinople," *ALW* 2 (1952) 81.

40. *PRG* 2:6-9.

41. Bernhard, *Ordo officiorum ecclesiae Lateranensis*, ed. L. Fischer (Historische Forschungen und Quellen, Heft. 2-3; Munich: Datterer, 1916) 128.

sung in Greek in Frankish territory, although they were also translated into Latin: *Ave gratia plena* ("Hail, full of grace"), *Adorna* ("Adorn . . .").[42]

2. *The Celebration of the Presentation*

The celebration of the Presentation of the Lord is still marked by a procession with candles and a preceding blessing of these. The service begins with an exhortation emphasizing the commemorative character of this procession to the house of the Lord: It calls to mind the meeting of Jesus and Simeon and leads to the meeting of the Christian assembly with its Lord in the breaking of the bread, which in turn is an anticipation of the definitive meeting in glory. The procession takes place to the singing of the *Nunc dimittis*. The response *Adorna* has unfortunately vanished from the Missal, but it is still in the *Graduale Romanum* and, in a shortened form, in the Liturgy of the Hours. Three of the Latin hymns amount to a paraphrase of it.

Whereas the formularies of the Missal had always celebrated the Presentation of the Lord, those of the Breviary used to honor, until very recently, the Purification of the Blessed Virgin Mary. Since 1970, however, they too concern themselves with the Presentation. The Liturgy of the Hours contains, among other things, a sermon which St. Sophronius of Jerusalem preached on the procession of candles: "Let us all hasten to meet Christ," and a paraphrase of the response *Adorna* in the form of a hymn of Peter Abelard which is sung in Morning Prayer: *Adorna, Sion, thalamum* (in the Latin Liturgy of the Hours).

§2. Advent

BIBLIOGRAPHY

F. Nogues, "Où en est la question des origines de l'Avent?" *QL* 16 (1935) 221–32, 257–67.

_____, "Avent et avènement d'après les anciens sacramentaires," *QL* 18 (1937) 233–44, 279–97.

W. Croce, "Die Adventmessen des römischen Missale in ihrer geschichtlichen Entwicklung," *ZKT* 74 (1952) 277–317.

A. Chavasse, "L'Avent romain du VIe au VIIIe siècle," *EL* 67 (1953) 297–308; see *EL* 69 (1955) 21–23.

M. Righetti, *Manuale di storia liturgica* 2 (2nd ed.; Milan: Ancora, 1955) 37–52: "Il ciclo liturgico natalizio."

A. Chavasse, *Le sacramentaire gélasien* (Tournai: Desclée, 1958) 412–26.

---

42. R. J. Hesbert, *Antiphonarium missarum sextuplex* lxxxviii–lxxxix.

I. H. Dalmais, "Le temps de préparation à Noël dans les liturgies syrienne et byzantine," *LMD* no. 59 (1959) 25–37.

J. Hild, "L'Avent," *LMD* no. 59 (1959) 10–25. A valuable study, with a bibliography.

F. Sottocornola, *L'anno liturgico nei sermoni di Pietro Crisologo* (Studia Ravennatensia 1; Cesena: Centro studi e ricerche, 1973).

Like the Greek word *Epiphaneia* which it sometimes translates, the term *Adventus (Parousia)* is a Christian word that had a pagan origin. In its cultic use it signified the annual coming of divinities into their temples in order to visit their devotees: the god or goddess, whose statue was offered for veneration, was thought to dwell in the midst of the devotees as long as the ceremony lasted. The etiquette of the imperial court used the same term for the first official visit of an important personage at the time of his accession or entrance upon his office. Thus there are Corinthian coins commemorating the *Adventus Augusti* ("The coming of Augustus," i.e., Nero), while the Chronographer of 354 designates the day of Constantine's accession as *Adventus Divi* ("Coming of the godlike one").

In Christian writings of the early centuries and especially in the Vulgate, *Adventus* became the classical term for the coming of Christ among us: both his coming in the flesh, which inaugurated the messianic age, and his coming in glory, which will crown the work of redemption at the end of time. *Adventus, Natale,* and *Epiphania* thus express the same basic reality. How did the term *Adventus* come to be used for the liturgical period of preparation for Christmas? History alone can supply the answer.

I. THE ORIGINS OF THE LITURGICAL ADVENT

1. *Preparation for Christmas in the West*

The history of Advent in Rome begins in the sixth century, but Advent had already existed in Gaul and Spain. By the end of the fourth century and during the fifth, the people of those regions seem to have felt the need of an ascetical preparation for the feasts of Christmas and Epiphany. This preparation, lasting three weeks, was doubtless connected originally with the preparation for baptism on Epiphany. It is not possible to rely on a passage attributed to St. Hilary as being the oldest witness to a "pre-Christmas Lent."[43] As early as 380, however, the Council of Saragossa did prescribe that the faithful be zealous in attending church from December 17 to Epiphany.[44] Asceticism, prayer, more frequent

---

43. Despite the authority of A. Wilmart, "Le prétendu *Liber officiorum* de saint Hilaire et l'Avent liturgique," *RBén* 27 (1910) 500–13, scholars are generally very reserved regarding the authenticity of this document; see J. P. Brisson, *Hilaire de Poitiers. Traité des mystères* (SC 19; Paris: Cerf, 1947) 64–68 and 164; E. Dekkers, *Clavis Patrum*, no. 427.

44. H. Bruns, *Canones apostolorum et conciliorum* (Berlin: Reimer, 1839) 2:13-14.

assemblies: these are the original characteristics of the time of preparation for Christmas. This discipline was to take a more specific form in
Gaul during the sixth century where we see Perpetuus of Tours († 490)
establishing a fast of three days a week from the feast of St. Martin to
Christmas.[45]

Advent makes its appearance at Rome only in the second half of the
sixth century in the sacramentaries and lectionaries that have preserved
the liturgical formularies for it. It is important to note that at Rome "Advent was from the outset a liturgical institution, whereas everywhere else
ascetical considerations had served as the point of departure and provided
the criteria for the evolution of the season."[46] Only with some difficulty,
however, did the formularies for six and then four weeks of preparation
for Christmas[47] find their place in the annual cycle: in the old Gelasian
Sacramentary the *Orationes de Adventu Domini* ("Prayers for the Coming of the Lord") are found after the Common of the Saints, at the end
of Book II which bears the title *De nataliciis sanctorum* ("For the Anniversaries of the Saints").[48] It is also at the end of the sanctoral that the
Gregorian Sacramentary places the *Orationes de Adventu*, and the lectionary of Alcuin the readings for the days *ante natale Domini*. Not until
the graduals and antiphonaries of the eighth and ninth centuries do we
find the Masses for Advent placed at the beginning of the cycle.

The Constitution on the Liturgy of Vatican II seems to make Advent
the end of the cycle of Sundays, for it says that "in the course of the year"
the Church "unfolds the whole mystery of Christ from the incarnation
and nativity to the ascension, to Pentecost and the expectation of the
blessed hope of the coming of the Lord."[49]

2. The Meaning of the Roman Advent

A study of the formularies for the Mass and Office enables us to grasp
the precise meaning which the popes of the sixth and seventh centuries
intended the Advent season to have. In keeping with the original conception of it among the Gauls, the season was first of all a time of preparation for the solemnity of the Coming of the Lord: "that this divine aid

45. Gregory of Tours, *Historia Francorum* X, 6, ed. B. Krusch and W. Levison (Han-
nover: Hahn, 1951) 529 (= PL 71:566).

46. J. Hild, "L'Avent," *LMD* no. 59 (1959) 25.

47. A. Chavasse, *Le sacramentaire gélasien* (Tournai: Desclée, 1958) 413–14.

48. *Ge* nos. 1120–77. In any study of the liturgical formularies for Advent it is appropriate
to include with the Roman sacramentaries the forty prayers in the well-known *Rotulus* of
Ravenna. They can be found in an appendix to Mohlberg's edition of the *Sacramentarium
Veronense* 173–78.

49. *VSC* no. 102.

. . . may prepare us for the coming feast."[50] But, as the feast of Christmas became increasingly important in the High Middle Ages, Advent also came to be a time of expectation: It fostered a joyful expectation of the feast of the Nativity but with a view to directing the thoughts of Christians above all to the glorious return of the Lord at the end of time.

The best symbol of Advent as celebrated in this perspective is the *Etimasia* or empty throne of the Pantocrator, which is so often shown in the mosaics of Rome and Ravenna.[51] From that point on the old pagan term *Adventus* was understood in the biblical and eschatological sense of "Parousia." Christian expectation found spontaneous expression in the prophetic texts that had been inspired by expectation of the Messiah. Isaiah and John the Baptist became the two major voices in the Roman liturgy of Advent.

3. *Preparation for Christmas in the East*

"No Eastern liturgy has established an Advent cycle comparable to that of the Roman liturgy, that is, one that embraces the messianic expectation in its full extent and openendedness."[52] It is possible to speak of a preparation for Christmas in the East only in the same sense in which it was practiced in fifth-century Gaul. Two rites, the Byzantine and the Syrian, lay greater emphasis on this preparation.

In the Byzantine liturgy we may note in particular the commemoration, on the Sunday before Christmas, of "all the Fathers who down the centuries have been pleasing to God, from Adam to Joseph, husband of the Most Holy Mother of God." All the saints of the old covenant are urged to "lead the dance for the Birth of the Savior."

In the Syrian rite the weeks before Christmas are called the "Weeks of Annunciations." There are five such weeks among the Western Syrians and four among the Eastern. They recall in succession the annunciation to Zechariah, the annunciation to Mary, followed by the Visitation, the Birth of John the Baptist, and the annunciation to Joseph.[53]

II. THE CELEBRATION OF ADVENT

The four weeks of Advent are in two stages: the first runs from

---

50. Prayer after communion for the third Sunday of Advent in the old Roman Missal. I am here summarizing J. Hild, *ibid.* 17–24.

51. M. Van Berghem and E. Clouzot, *Mosaïques chretiénnes du IVe au IXe siècle* (Geneva, 1924) xxxvii–xxxix.

52. See I. H. Dalmais, "Le temps de préparation à Noël dans les liturgies syrienne et byzantine," *LMD* no. 59 (1959) 25–37.

53. *Ibid.* 30, n. 5, the reader will find the list of the Scripture readings for the four Annunciation Sundays in the Chaldean liturgy.

December 1 to December 16; the second runs from the seventeenth to the twenty-fourth and is more directly oriented to the Christmas feasts. Each of the two prefaces for Advent sums up one of the stages. The first recalls the two comings of Christ; the second celebrates him "whose future coming was foretold by all the prophets. The virgin mother bore him in her womb with love beyond all telling. John the Baptist was his herald and made him known when at last he came."

In the Missal each day has an opening prayer of its own, taken from the old sacramentaries.[54] The Liturgy of the Hours contains not only its own proper antiphons but a collection of patristic passages that provide a fine introduction to the spirituality of Advent.

1. *The Celebration of the Eucharist*

The first thing to be pointed out in the celebration of the Eucharist during Advent is the way in which the Sunday readings are organized.

a) *The Sunday readings*—The first reading throughout the three-year cycle presents the principal messianic prophecies: the oracles of Isaiah and the additions made to these in the period of the Exile, and the oracles of Baruch and Zephaniah. Of all these prophecies the most important are the ones read on the fourth Sunday. They foretell that a woman will give birth to a descendant of David and that this child will be Emmanuel, "God with us" (Isaiah, Micah, Nathan).

The gospels for each year focus on the same theme. The first Sunday is one that looks forward to the coming of the Lord: Jesus tells us, "Watch!" The second and third Sundays are Sundays of John the Baptist. The fourth is given over to the annunciation to Mary (A), the annunciation to Joseph (B), and the Visitation (C).

The readings from the Apostle show how the prophecies have been fulfilled in Jesus. They in turn point forward to the coming of the Lord, which will be a day of salvation for all peoples and a day of joy for those who have awaited his coming with love.

b) *The prayers*—Two themes—the celebration of the Lord's coming in the flesh, and his return in glory—are intermingled in the prayers. The opening prayer of the first Monday says: "Lord our God, help us to prepare for the coming of Christ your Son. May he find us waiting, eager in joyful prayer." Throughout the final week frequent mention is made of the Virgin Mary. Thus the opening prayer for December 19 says: "Father, you show the world the splendor of your glory in the coming of Christ, born of the Virgin." On the fourth Sunday, which is one of annunciations (gospel), the prayer over the gifts asks: "Lord, may the power of the Spirit, which

---

54. A. Dumas, "Les sources du Missel romain," *Notitiae* 7 (1971) 409.

sanctified Mary the mother of your Son, make holy the gifts which we place upon this altar."

2. *The Liturgy of the Hours*

In the biblical reading Isaiah has a dominant place, and his prophecies are prolonged, both in the annual cycle and in the two-year cycle, by passages from the Book of the Consolation of Israel.

Although the East did not celebrate Advent, the compilers of the new liturgy have drawn extensively on the Greek Fathers for the patristic passages in the Office of Readings. Nonetheless the Western Fathers are the main contributors, from St. Cyprian, via the *Imitation*, to St. John of the Cross. As is only fitting, the classical texts are used, such as St. Irenaeus' parallel between Eve and Mary and St. Bernard's commentary on *Missus est* ("The angel Gabriel was sent"). The readings are followed by traditional responsories, as, for example, on the first Sunday the responsory *Aspiciens a longe* ("Watching from afar"), the dramatic structure of which was pointed out by P. Batiffol years ago.[55]

Pride of place among the antiphons belongs to the "Great O Antiphons" for the *Magnificat* from December 17 to December 23. These antiphons, which the Roman Church was singing as long ago as the time of Charlemagne,[56] not only synthesize the messianism of the Old Testament in its purest form. Using ancient biblical images, they also present the divine titles of the incarnate Word, while their *Veni* ("Come!") is freighted with all the present hopes of the Church. In them the Advent liturgy reaches its culmination.

III. THE ANNUNCIATION OF THE LORD

The Annunciation of the Lord is celebrated twice: once in Advent and once on March 25.[57]

1. *The Annunciation in Advent*

The Western liturgies all celebrate the Annunciation of the Lord during Advent. In 656 a Council of Toledo decided to attach this feast to December 18, "as is customary."[58] The Ambrosian liturgy celebrates it

---

55. P. Batiffol, *History of the Roman Breviary*, trans. A. M. Y. Baylay (London: Longmans, Green, 1912) 87–88.

56. Amalarius, *Liber de ordine antiphonarii*, in *Opera liturgica omnia*, ed. J. M. Hanssens 3 (ST 140; Vatican City, 1950) 44–49.

57. A complete dossier on the feast of the Annunciation is contained in *DACL* 1 (1907) col. 2241–45.

58. *Ibid.* col. 2244.

on the last Sunday of Advent. Until 1970, the gospel *Missus est* was read in the Roman liturgy on Ember Wednesday in December, while the gospel of the Visitation was read on Friday. Now, however, the annunciation is the subject of the fourth Sunday, as it is at Milan, and of the readings of December 18, 20, and 21, as well as of several prayers in the last days before Christmas.

2. *The Solemnity on March 25*

The Solemnity of the Annunciation on March 25 made its appearance at Rome in the second half of the seventh century under the title of *Annuntiatio Domini* ("Annunciation of the Lord").[59] Marian devotion would subsequently change the title to *Annuntiatio beatae Mariae Virginis* ("Annunciation of the Blessed Virgin Mary"), until the feast regained its original name in 1969. Although the Byzantine tradition admits of no feast during Lent, except on Saturdays, the Trullan Synod (692) made an exception for the Annunciation, which is commemorated even if it occurs during the Easter triduum.[60]

The texts for the Mass and the Liturgy of the Hours celebrate the mystery of the incarnation of the Word of God in Mary. Verse 7 of Ps 40, "Then I said, 'Lo, I come,'" provides the leitmotiv (entrance antiphon, psalm, second reading). The passage from the letter of St. Leo the Great to Flavian, patriarch of Constantinople, expounds the theology of the incarnation which the Council of Chalcedon would shortly turn into dogma: "As God does not change by his condescension, so man is not swallowed up by being exalted." But, while contemplating the Word made flesh, the celebrating congregation does not forget her "who conceived by the power of the Spirit and bore your Son in purest love" (Preface).

---

59. P. Jounel, *Le culte des saints* 229.

60. Mercenier and Paris, *ibid.* 231–32, give the quite complicated rules governing the conjunction of two Offices in Holy Week.

Chapter III

The Feasts of the Lord in Ordinary Time

Seven feasts of the Lord are celebrated in Ordinary Time. Three of them are common to all the liturgical families: the Transfiguration of the Lord, the Triumph of the Cross, and the Feast of Dedication. Four are peculiar to the West: the Trinity, Corpus Christi, the Sacred Heart of Jesus, and Christ the King.

§1. The Universal Feasts

I. THE TRANSFIGURATION OF THE LORD

BIBLIOGRAPHY

J. B. Ferreres, "La Transfiguration de Notre Seigneur. Histoire de sa fête et de sa Messe," *Ephemerides theologicae Lovanienses* 5 (1928) 632ff.

P. Jounel, *Le culte des saints dans les basiliques du Latran et du Vatican au douzième siècle* (Collection de l'Ecole Française de Rome 26; Rome: Ecole Française de Rome, 1977) 184–85 and 268–69.

J. Leclercq, *Pierre le Vénérable* (Saint-Wandrille, 1946) 382–90.

a) *Origin and evolution of the feast*—The feast of the Transfiguration commemorates, in all likelihood, the dedication of the basilicas on Mount Tabor. It was received by the Nestorian Church at the end of the fifth century or beginning of the sixth and by the western Syrian Church in the seventh.[1] It is later than the feast of the Triumph (formerly: Exaltation) of the Cross, on which it depends for the determination of its date.

---

1. E. Mercenier and F. Paris, *La prière des Eglise de rite byzantin* II/1 (Chevetogne, 1939) 259.

According to one tradition, the transfiguration of Jesus took place forty days before his crucifixion. The feast was therefore assigned to August 6, which is forty days before the feast of the Triumph (September 14).[2] The Byzantine Church underscores the connection between the two feasts by having the *katabasia* of the cross sung from Transfiguration on.[3]

The feast appeared in the West in the middle of the ninth century at Naples and in the Germanic lands, as well as in Spain. It was celebrated in France in the tenth century. The eleventh and twelfth centuries brought a more rapid spread, and the feast was then celebrated in the Vatican Basilica. Peter the Venerable was a fervent advocate of the feast and composed an office for it; with the aid of Cluny the celebration spread far and wide.[4] It was finally inscribed in the Roman Calendar by Pope Callistus III (1457) in gratitude for the victory which John Hunyadi and St. John of Capistrano had won over the Turks near Belgrade on August 6, 1456.

b) *Celebration*—In the East "the Transfiguration *(Hē Metamorphōsis)* of our great God and Savior Jesus Christ" is celebrated as one of the most important feasts of the year. In it the entire theology of human divinization finds expression: "On Tabor Christ today transformed the nature which had been darkened by Adam; having covered it with his radiance, he divinized it"[5]; "O Christ, God and friend of humankind, shed upon us the light of your inaccessible glory."[6]

Although the Roman liturgy celebrates the feast in a less solemn way, it retains echos of the East in the Office of Readings, in which Anastasius of Sinai speaks in a homily of "the heavenly vision that will renew our spiritual nature and transform us in his own likeness." At Mass, along with the story of the transfiguration of Jesus according to one or other of the Synoptics, there is also read the vision of Daniel, which the gospel writer certainly had in mind, as well as a passage from the letter attributed to Peter (2 Pet). We can understand the importance which the testimony of Peter to the transfiguration would have had for the faith of the first generation of Christians.

---

2. J. Van Goudoever, *Fêtes et calendriers bibliques* (Theologie historique 7; Paris: Beauchesne, 1967) 276–77.

3. Mercenier and Paris, *ibid.* 272.

4. P. Jounel, *Le culte des saints dans les basiliques du Latran et du Vatican au douzième siècle* (Collection de l'Ecole Française de Rome 26; Rome: Ecole Française de Rome, 1977) 268–69. The office composed by Peter the Venerable is reprinted in J. Leclercq, *Pierre le Vénérable* (Saint-Wandrille, 1946) 383–90.

5. Mercenier and Paris, *ibid.* 262.

6. *Ibid.* 266.

II. THE TRIUMPH OF THE CROSS

Sept 14

BIBLIOGRAPHY

A. Frolow, *La Relique de la Vraie Croix. Recherches sur le développement d'un culte* (Archives de l'Orient chrétien 7; Paris: Institut Français d'Etudes Byzantines, 1961).
P. Jounel, "Le culte de la Croix dans la liturgie romaine," *LMD* no. 75 (1963) 68–91.

a) *Origin and Evolution of the Feast*—The feast of the Exaltation (currently: the Triumph) of the Holy Cross came into existence in Jerusalem. In the fifth century the Church of Jerusalem celebrated on September 13 the anniversary of the dedication of the Constantinian basilicas on Golgotha. According to Egeria, this date was chosen in 335 because it was the one on which, a few years before, the cross had been discovered.[7] The Armenian Lectionary of Jerusalem for the twenties of the fifth century states that on the second day of the octave "the venerable cross is shown to the entire congregation."[8] This feast spread very rapidly throughout the East.

As early as the beginning of the sixth century, Rome used to celebrate a feast of the discovery of the holy cross on May 3. Only in the middle of the seventh century, however, did the Church begin to present the wood of the cross to the people for their veneration on September 14 in the Vatican Basilica.[9] Pope Sergius (687–701) transferred another fragment of the cross from the Vatican to the Lateran: "From that time on," says the *Liber Pontificalis*, "it was kissed and venerated by all of the Christian people on the day of the Exaltation of the Holy Cross."[10]

The veneration was all the more fervent at this period because in 614 the Persians had sacked Jerusalem, slaughtered its inhabitants, destroyed the various basilicas, and carried the cross away with them. It was recovered by Heraclius in 630 and safeguarded at Constantinople. It was not by chance, therefore, that the liturgical books began to mention the feast of September 14 in the middle of the seventh century. Beginning in the eighth century, the feast spread through the West, but it was for a long time matched in solemnity by the feast of May 3. The latter was suppressed in 1960 as being a doublet.

b) *Celebration*—In the East "the universal exaltation of the precious and life-giving cross" is celebrated on a par with Easter. The word "exalta-

---

7. *Egeria's Travels*, trans. John Wilkinson (London: SPCK, 1971) 146.
8. A. Renoux, *Le Codex arménien Jérusalem 121* II. Edition . . . (PO 36; Turnhout: Brepols, 1971) 363.
9. P. Jounel, "Le culte de la Croix dans la liturgie romaine," *LMD* no. 75 (1963) 75–82 and 87–91.
10. *LP* 1:374.

tion" (lifting up), which is taken from the gospel (John 3:14), is a strictly suitable name for the rite as practiced among the Byzantines. The priest elevates the sacred wood above his head; then, turning to the four cardinal points of the compass, he blesses the people with it while the choir sings the *Kyrie eleison* a hundred times at each point. The faithful then come forward to venerate the cross and receive one of the blossoms from the platform on which it stands.[11]

At Rome, one element in the celebration of the feast of September 14 was for a long time a procession which started at St. Mary Major and made its way to the Lateran in order to venerate the cross there before the beginning of Mass.[12] Most Churches of the West had the same practice. In some Churches the veneration took place at the Offertory, in others after the Our Father. At Rouen, where it took place during the procession, the faithful made a stop in the nave so that the cross might be washed before it was presented first to the sick, then to the clergy, and finally to the people.[13]

The liturgical formularies praise the glorious cross, which the preface compares to the tree of life in the earthly paradise. Both the gospel (John 3:13-17) and the reading from Paul (Phil 2:6-11) emphasize the lifting up of Christ first on the cross and then into glory, a double lifting up which was symbolically prefigured by the brazen serpent (first reading, Num 21:4-9). "When I am lifted up from the earth, I will draw all men to myself, says the Lord" (Communion antiphon, John 12:32). The Latin Liturgy of the Hours has the hymns which Fortunatus, later bishop of Poitiers, composed ca. 568-69: *Pange lingua* ("Sing, my tongue") and *Vexilla regis* ("The banners of the king"), including the stanza *O Crux ave* ("O Cross of Christ"), which was added to it in the tenth century. In the Office of Readings a homily of St. Andrew of Crete is read in which we are reminded that "the cross is . . . both the sign of God's suffering and the trophy of his victory."

III. THE FEAST OF DEDICATION

BIBLIOGRAPHY

    M. Black, "The Festival of *Encaenia Ecclesiae,*" *Journal of Ecclesiastical History* 5 (1954) 78-85.

---

11. Mercenier and Paris, *ibid.* 53-55.

12. John the Deacon, *Descriptio ecclesiae Lateranensis*, in R. Valentini-Zucchetti, *Codice topografico della Città di Roma* 3 (Rome, 1946) 356.

13. E. Martène, *De antiquis Ecclesiae ritibus* IV, 34, in the Venice edition of 1764, 3:213.

B. Botte, "Les dimanches de la dédicace dans les Eglises syriennes," *OS* 2 (1957) 65–70.

P. Jounel, *Le culte des saints* . . . 305–7 and 380–81 (Dedication of the Lateran).

a) *Origin of the feast*—Each year the Jews celebrated the feast of Hanukkah or Dedication (John 10:22) in remembrance of the purification and reconsecration of the temple after the victory of the Maccabees over the Syrians in 165 b.c.[14] The Church of Jerusalem was therefore adopting a now ancient tradition when it commemorated on September 13 the dedication of two basilicas, the Martyrium and the Anastasis (335).

The Hieronymian Martyrology records the dates of the dedication of basilicas built in Rome during the fifth century: St. Mary Major (August 5), St. Peter in Chains (August 1), St. Michael (September 29), St. Lawrence outside the Walls (November 2). Not until the eleventh century, however, do we find mention of the dedication of the Lateran (November 9) and of the basilicas of the Apostles Peter and Paul (November 18). While ever since the seventh century the liturgical books have had a special Mass, *Terribilis est*, which was composed for the dedication of the Pantheon (ca. 610), it was not the mystery of the Church but the titular saint that was celebrated on the anniversary of dedication, as can be seen today in the new Roman Missal for August 5 and November 18. Even at the Lateran the celebration began with an office of Christ the Savior.[15]

b) *Celebration*—In accordance with liturgical law, all churches of the Roman rite celebrate each year the dedication of the Lateran Basilica, which is the oldest church of the West and the first in dignity. Each diocese also celebrates the dedication of its cathedral, while each church commemorates the anniversary of its own dedication.

The feast of Dedication is the feast of the Church. If the edifice built by hands is called an *ecclesia*, that is, an "assembly," this is because it houses the Sunday assembly of the people of God (opening prayer). "Here you build your temple of living stones, and bring the Church to its full stature" (preface). "You are the temple of God" and "like living stones let yourselves be built" say the Communion antiphons, echoing the readings from Paul (1 Cor 3:16) and Peter (1 Pet 2:5). The various homilies from the Fathers that are proposed for the feast give the same teaching, as do the hymns *Angularis fundamentum* ("The Church's one foundation") and (in the Latin text) *Urbs Jerusalem beata* ("Jerusalem the blest").

---

14. In Jerusalem a feast of the dedication of "all altars built" was celebrated for a time on the same date; see A. Renoux, *ibid.* 229, and vol. I (PO 35; Turnhout: Brepols, 1969) 196–97. B. Botte regards this feast as the origin of the Dedication Sundays celebrated in the fall by the Syrian churches; see B. Botte, "Les Dimanches de la Dédicace dans les Eglises syriennes," *OS* 2 (1957) 65–70.

15. P. Jounel, *Le culte des saints* 307.

§2. The Western Feasts

I. THE MOST HOLY TRINITY

BIBLIOGRAPHY

F. Cabrol, "Le culte de la Trinité dans la liturgie et l'institution de la fête de la Trinité," *EL* 5 (1931) 270–78.

a) *Origin of the feast*—For the Sunday after Pentecost the Gelasian Sacramentary (seventh century) has the preface *Qui cum unigenito Filio tuo* ("Who with your only-begotten Son"), which expounds the theology of the mystery of the Blessed Trinity, laying the emphasis on the trinity of the persons and the unity of their nature.[16] This is the earliest specific mention of the mystery of the Trinity on this day.

In about 800 Alcuin composed a set of Masses for each day of the week, beginning the series with a *Missa de sancta Trinitate* (Mass of the Holy Trinity).[17] This book became very popular, especially in churches which did not have a complete sacramentary of their own. The Mass of the Holy Trinity was soon separated from the rest of votive Masses and given a place in the sacramentaries, at either the beginning or the end of the series of Sundays after Pentecost.[18] At the beginning of the tenth century Stephen, bishop of Liège, composed an Office to go with the Mass. All the required elements were now at hand for the celebration of a feast of the Holy Trinity.

Despite the diffusion of these formularies, Pope Alexander II († 1073) stated: "It is not the custom in Rome to set aside a special day for honoring the Most Holy Trinity, since, properly speaking, it is honored daily in psalmody by the singing of the 'Glory be to the Father.' "[19] A century later Pope Alexander III († 1181) spoke in identical terms.[20] The reserve shown by the Apostolic See did not, however, prevent the feast from gaining ground, especially in monasteries; it was celebrated at Cluny in 1030, and Cîteaux instituted it in 1271. There was as yet no uniformity in the date; some churches celebrated it on the octave of Pentecost, others on the Sunday before Advent. In 1334 Pope John XXII made the celebration

---

16. *Ge*, no. 680.

17. J. Deshusses, *Le sacramentaire grégorien* 2 (Spicilegium Friburgense 24; Freiburg: Universitätsverlag, 1979) nos. 1806–10.

18. For example, the *Vetus Missale romanum monasticum Lateranense* (central Italy, thirteenth century), edited by Azevedo (Rome, 1752) gives the formulary for Trinity Sunday after that of the Twenty-fourth Sunday (156).

19. Bernold of Constance, *Micrologus* 60 (PL 151:1019).

20. Letter cited in M. Righetti, *Manuale di storia liturgica* 2 (2nd ed.; Milan: Ancora, 1955) 247–48.

obligatory for the entire West and assigned it to the Sunday after Pentecost. The Tridentine Missal retained Alcuin's Mass, but the Office composed by Stephen of Liège was recast.

The Eastern Churches do not have a feast of the Holy Trinity, but they do devote most of the chants on Pentecost Sunday to a contemplation of this mystery and put off until the following day the commemoration of the sending of the Holy Spirit on the apostles.[21]

b) *Celebration*—The central formulary of the Mass of the Holy Trinity continues to be the ancient Gelasian preface, which is echoed by the other prayers. The new triple series of three readings, however, is a significant enrichment of the lectionary for the feast. The readings from Exodus (A) and Deuteronomy (B) proclaim the transcendence of the only God, the Merciful One, while the reading from Proverbs (C) urges us to listen to the Wisdom of God as a living person. The readings from the Apostle speak of the action of each of the divine Persons in the life of the baptized. The gospels tell of the sending of the Son by the Father (A), the prediction of the proximate coming of the Spirit (C), and the mission which Jesus gave to his apostles of baptizing all nations in the name of the Father and of the Son and of the Holy Spirit (B).

The antiphons in the Liturgy of the Hours are those of the Tridentine Breviary: *Gloria tibi, Trinitas aequalis, una Deitas* ("Glory to you, O Trinity, one God in three equal Persons"). The patristic reading is from a letter of St. Athanasius, the defender of the Nicene dogma.

II. CORPUS CHRISTI

BIBLIOGRAPHY

>   C. Lambot, "L'office de la Fête-Dieu. Aperçus nouveaux sur ses origines," *RBén* 54 (1942) 61–123.
>   C. Lambot and I. Fransen, *L'office de la Fête-Dieu primitive. Textes et mélodies retrouvés* (Maredsous, 1946).
>   F. Callaey, *L'origine della festa del Corpus Domini* (Piccola biblioteca teologica 3; Rovigo: Istituto Padano di arti grafiche, 1958).
>   J. Cottiaux, "L'office liégeois de la Fête-Dieu, sa valeur et son destin," *RHE* 58 (1963) 5–81, 407–59.
>   P. M. Gy, "L'office du Corpus Christi et S. Thomas d'Aquin, état d'une recherche," *Revue des sciences philosophiques et théologiques* 64 (1980) 491–507.

a) *Origin of the feast*—The Solemnity of the Body and Blood of Christ was celebrated for the first time at Liège in 1247 at the insistence of a nun, Juliana of Mont-Cornillon. In a vision she received in 1208, the Lord gave

---

21. Mercenier and Paris, *ibid.* II/2, 361–62.

her to understand (she said) the need of an annual feast to honor the sacrament of the altar. After some initial reserves, the vision was given a favorable hearing by the bishop of Liège and especially by Archdeacon James Pantaleon, who later became Pope Urban IV (1261).

In 1264, impressed by a Eucharistic miracle that took place at Bolsena near Viterbo, where he was in residence, Urban IV promulgated the Bull *Transiturus*, in which he established a new solemnity to be celebrated in honor of the Blessed Sacrament on the Thursday after the octave of Pentecost. Juliana had asked a young religious of Mont-Cornillon to compose an office for the new feast,[22] but the text appended to the papal bull and in use down to our time was quite different. Recent research has tended to confirm the tradition according to which the Mass *Cibavit* and the Office *Sacerdos* were the work of St. Thomas Aquinas.[23]

This was the first time that a pope had used his authority to impose a new feast on the whole Western Church. For this reason it was for a long time referred to as the *nova sollemnitas* or "new solemnity." It was also called "Feast of the Eucharist," "Feast of God," "Feast of the Most Precious Sacrament," and "Solemnity of the Body and Blood of Christ."[24] Pope Urban IV died two months after establishing the new feast, and the Bull *Transiturus* produced little result. Clement V (1311-12) and then John XXII (1317) had to reconfirm it, and only then was the Solemnity of the Body and Blood of Christ universally accepted.

None of the three popes involved in the promulgation refer to a Eucharistic procession. In many places indeed the Eucharist was carried in the palm procession or solemnly transferred from the symbolic tomb of Christ to the sanctuary on Easter morning. A procession of the Blessed Sacrament in our sense appeared sporadically at the end of the Middle Ages (Angers, Cologne), and the practice spread in the course of the fourteenth and fifteenth centuries. It was approved for Rome in the fifteenth century.

b) *Celebration*—The Mass and Office of the Blessed Sacrament are sufficiently well known that there is no need of explaining them here. In 1970 the Mass was given nine readings. The accounts of the offering of Melchizedek (A), the covenant sacrifice at the foot of Mount Sinai (B),

---

22. C. Lambot and I. Fransen, *L'office de la Fête-Dieu primitive. Textes et mélodies retrouvés* (Maredsous, 1946) 39–97.

23. P. M. Gy, "L'office du Corpus Christi et S. Thomas d'Aquin. Etat d'une recherche," *Revue des sciences philosophiques et théologiques* 64 (1980) 491–507. See also idem, "L'office du Corpus Christi et la théologie des accidents eucharistiques," *Revue des sciences philosophiques et théologiques* 66 (1982) 81–86.

24. V. Leroquais, *Les bréviaires manuscrits des bibliothèques publiques de France* (6 vols.; Mâcon: Protat, 1936) 5:70. Note that none of the manuscripts listed speak of the "Body of Christ" alone.

and the eating of the manna in the wilderness (C) were chosen from the Old Testament. The second readings are taken from 1 Corinthians 10 and 11 (A, B) and Hebrews 9 (C). The gospels narrate the miracle of the multiplication of the loaves (C), the discourse of Jesus on the bread of life (A), and the Last Supper (B). Two prefaces are provided: the one for Holy Thursday and another, new composition.

The various aspects of the Eucharistic mystery are expressed with rare felicity in the Liturgy of the Hours. The antiphon for the *Magnificat* in Second Vespers sums up these aspects: "His passion is recalled [the Eucharistic anamnesis refers to the past]; grace fills our hearts [the Eucharist effects a presence]; and we receive a pledge of the glory to come [it offers us the first fruits of future reality]."

III. THE SACRED HEART OF JESUS

BIBLIOGRAPHY

A. Bugnini, "Le messe del SS. Cuore di Gesu," in *Commentationes in Litt. Enc. "Haurietis aquas,"* ed. A. Bea 1 (Rome, 1959) 61–94.
A. Hamon, *Histoire de la dévotion au Sacré-Coeur* 2. *L'aube de la dévotion* (Paris: Beauchesne, 1925).

a) *Origin and evolution of the feast*—In the Middle Ages and even in antiquity, mystics nourished their fervor through contemplation of the open side of Jesus. The feast of the Sacred Heart, however, is not older than the second half of the seventeenth century. It was on October 20, 1672, that a Norman priest, John Eudes, celebrated the Mass of this feast for the first time. A few years later the revelations (1675) which a Visitandine nun, Margaret Mary Alacoque, received from the Lord would help spread the cult.

As far as its formularies were concerned, the spread of the feast of the Sacred Heart was marked by a good deal of disarray. We find that from 1672 to 1840 more than thirty different formularies were used in the dioceses of France and the religious families. Between 1765 and 1970 Rome itself approved four in succession. First, there was the Mass *Miserebor*, granted to Poland and Portugal (1765). Then came the Mass *Egredimini*, which Pius VI granted to Venice, Austria, and Spain (1778). When Pius IX extended the feast of the Sacred Heart to the whole of the Latin Church in 1856, he also published a new Mass, *Miserebitur*, but he allowed some places to keep in their Proper the Mass *Egredimini* and the Office connected with it. In 1929 Pius XI ordered the composition of still another Mass (*Cogitationes*) and Office. Finally, in 1970 the Mass *Cogitationes* was revised and given three series of three readings. To the previous four Roman Masses must be added that of the feast of the Eucharistic Heart of Jesus (*Sciens Jesus*), which was approved in 1921 for all the dioceses that requested it. This feast was abolished in 1960.

The multiplicity of formularies shows how difficult it was to determine the exact object of the feast. For all their diversity they issued essentially from one or other of the two currents of thought that have marked modern devotion to the Sacred Heart and are due respectively to St. John Eudes and St. Margaret Mary: thanksgiving for the inexhaustible riches of Christ (Eph 3:8) and reparative contemplation of the pierced heart (John 19:37). The Mass *Egredimini* (with the preface for Christmas) belonged to the first of these two currents, the Mass *Miserebitur* (with the preface of the Cross) to the other. The spirit of reparation was also dominant in the Mass and Office composed by order of Pius XI.

b) *Celebration*—Since it has nine readings the new Mass *Cogitationes* has been enriched with the most eloquent and evocative texts from the Roman Missal and the French Missals. These include the parable of the sheep lost and found (C), the invitation of Jesus: "Come to me, all who labor" (A), and the account of how the side of the dead Christ was pierced (B). The two opening prayers represent the two currents of Christian devotion to the heart of Jesus: thanksgiving for the wonders of the Father's love for human beings, and reparation to this love that has been rejected. The preface refers to the tradition which since the time of the Fathers has thought of the Church as coming forth from the open side of Jesus as Eve had come from the side of Adam and sees the blood and water flowing from that side as symbols of baptism and the Eucharist.

This last is also the theme which St. Bonaventure develops with moving tenderness in the Office of Readings. The Latin hymn for Morning Prayer, *Iesu, auctor clementiae* ("Jesus, source of mercy"), expresses the same religious outlook. It is made up of various stanzas from the famous *Jubilus* that was for a long time attributed to St. Bernard.[25]

IV. CHRIST, KING OF THE UNIVERSE

a) *Origin and change of focus*—The feast of Christ the King was established in 1925 by Pope Pius XI, who assigned it to the Sunday before the Solemnity of All Saints. The Church had not, of course, waited for this occasion to celebrate the sovereign lordship of Christ; Epiphany, Easter, and Ascension are already feasts of Christ the King. Pius XI's reason for establishing the new feast was, as he explicitly states in the Encyclical

---

25. A. Wilmart provides a critical text in his *Le "Jubilus" dit de saint Bernard* (Rome: Edizioni di storia e letteratura, 1944) (= *EL* 57 [1943]).

Quas primas, that it might be a vehicle for spiritual teaching.[26] Faced with the increasing atheism and secularization of society, he wanted to assert the supreme authority of Christ over human beings and their institutions. Some passages in the Office suggested that the composer still dreamed of a possible Christendom. One stanza of the hymn for Vespers read: "May the rulers of the world publicly honor and extol You; may teachers and judges reverence You, may the laws express Your order and the arts reflect Your beauty," and the next stanza continued: "May kings find renown in their submission and dedication to You."

In 1970 the compilers' aim was to emphasize more the cosmic and eschatological character of Christ's kingship. The feast is now the feast of Christ "King of the Universe" and is assigned to the last Sunday in Ordinary Time. Beyond it we see Advent dawning with its perspective of the Lord's coming in glory. The shift in the theme of the feast is clearly shown by the change in the second part of the opening prayer. The prayer of 1925 asked God to grant that "the family of the nations, torn apart by the wound of sin, may submit to the soothing action of His supreme authority." The modified text asks God to grant that "all creation, freed from servitude, may recognize his power and glorify him for ever" (translation of the Latin text).

b) *Celebration*—As in the case of the other feasts of the Lord, the feast of Christ, King of the Universe, benefits first of all from the larger number of readings. In the gospel there is not only the assertion of kingship by Christ before Pilate (B), but also the announcement of the coming of the Son of man in glory to judge human beings according to their love of the brethren (A) and the vision of the crucified Christ as the crowned king of the Jews (C). The first reading is from Ezekiel (the Shepherd-King), or Daniel (the Son of man to whom dominion, glory and kingship are given), or the second book of Samuel (the anointing of David as king). In the second reading St. Paul extols the victory over death (A) of Christ in whom all things find their complete fulfillment (C), and the seer of the Apocalypse acclaims the One who comes upon the clouds (B). The preface composed in 1925 was an admirable one and has not been altered.

In the Liturgy of the Hours, two of the hymns which V. Genovesi, a Jesuit, composed in 1925 have been retained, although with corrections that are sometimes substantial. Added is a new hymn, *Iesu, rex admirabilis* ("Jesus, wonderful king"), which, like the hymn *Iesu, auctor clementiae,* is taken from the *Jubilus* attributed to St. Bernard. The patristic reading, from Origen, reminds us that the reign of Christ is interior: "There should be in us a kind of spiritual paradise where God may walk and be our sole ruler with his Christ."

---

26. December 11, 1925, in *AAS* 17 (1925) 593–610; text of the Office and Mass, 655–68.

Chapter IV

The Veneration of the Saints

Holiness belongs properly only to God and to his Son, Jesus Christ, who alone is the holy one and the Lord. But God bestows holiness on his people (Exod 19:5-6), and Christ has communicated it to his Church, that is, to each member of his body (1 Pet 2:9). This is why St. Paul can speak of all Christians, those at Rome (Rom 1:7) no less than those at Jerusalem (Rom 15:25), as "saints." But the title "saint" soon came to be attributed in a special way to those of the baptized who had lived out their membership in Christ more fully, namely, to the martyrs. Once the age of persecutions had passed, the title was extended to other followers of Christ in whom the image of the Lord had been seen with special clarity. Christians commemorated the anniversary of their entrance into heaven, invoked their intercession, and offered them as an example to the community. It was in this way that the cult of the saints began and developed. Even though this cult or veneration originated and showed itself among the people, only after being ratified by the Church in each instance did it find liturgical expression.

§1. Origins and Historical Development of the Veneration of the Saints

BIBLIOGRAPHY

S. Boesch Gajano, *Agiografia altomedioevale* (Bologna: Il Mulino, 1976). The work provides an extensive bibliography as a guide for study of the cult of the saints (259–300).

H. Delehaye, *Les origines du culte des martyrs* (Subsidia hagiographica 20; 1st ed., 1912; 2nd rev. ed., Brussels: Bollandistes, 1933).

_____, *Les passions des martyrs et les genres littéraires* (Subsidia hagiographica 13 D; Brussels: Bollandistes, 1921).

_____, *The Legends of the Saints*, trans. Donald Attwater from 3rd ed. of 1927 (New York: Fordham University Press, 1962).

_____, *Sanctus. Essai sur le culte des saints dans l'antiquité* (Subsidia hagiographica 17; Brussels: Bollandistes, 1927).

P.-A. Fevrier, "Le culte des morts dans les communautés chrétiennes durant le IIIe siècle," in *Atti del IX Congreso Internazionale di Archeologia Cristiana, Roma 1975* (Studi di antichità cristiana 32, 1; Vatican City, 1978) 211-74.

A. Grabar, *Martyrium. Recherches sur le culte des reliques et l'art chrétien antique.* 1. *Architecture* (Paris: Collège de France, 1946).

B. de Gaiffier, *Etudes critiques d'hagiographie et d'iconologie* (Subsidia hagiographica 43; Brussels: Bollandistes, 1967).

L. Reekmans, "Les cryptes des martyrs romains. Etat de la question," in *Atti del IX Congreso Internazionale di Archeologia Cristiana, Roma 1975* (Studi di antichità cristiana 37, 1; Vatican City, 1978) 275-302.

V. Saxer, *Morts, martyrs, reliques en Afrique chrétienne aux premiers siècles* (Théologie historique 55; Paris: Beauchesne, 1980).

C. Vogel, "L'environnement cultuel du défunt durant la période paléochrétienne," in *La maladie et la mort du chrétien dans la liturgie* (Conferences Saint-Serge 1974; Bibliotheca EL, Subsidia 1; Rome: Edizioni Liturgiche, 1975).

I. THE CULT OF THE MARTYRS

1. *The Cult of the Dead*

Veneration of the martyrs was one form of the veneration paid to the dead. The latter dated back to prehistorical times and found different expression in various parts of the world. It involved, in the first place, honors paid to the bodies of those who had just died. In Israel the dead were interred, that is, either placed in the earth or laid on a slab in a burial chamber. At Rome the dead were originally buried, but cremation was later permitted. In the first centuries of the Christian era, both practices were followed, as pagan sarcophaguses and the columbaria in cemeteries attest. Tombs often represented the houses in which the dead had once lived.

The members of the family gathered at the tomb on certain days to offer libations or present food to the shade of the deceased and to share a funeral meal in memory of the person, especially on the anniversary of his or her birth. Each year, the last days of February, which until the time of Caesar had been the final month of the year, were devoted especially to a collective commemoration of the deceased members of the clan and to meals for which the living gathered at the tombs of the dead. In the fourth century the feast of the *Cathedra Petri* (Peter's empty chair at the funeral banquet at his tomb) linked the Roman sanctoral, or calendar of saints' feasts, with this ancient tradition.

Christians did not reject any of the family customs connected with death, except those that expressed an idea of survival incompatible with their faith. This faith was given vigorous expression on the walls of cemeteries and in funeral inscriptions: faith in the resurrection and in eternal life in Christ and the certainty that through death Christians reach the goal of the paschal exodus begun in baptism. In their desire to imitate the Lord even in the disposition made of his dead body, Christians from the beginning chose interment: a mortal body would be sown and would rise up a spiritual body (1 Cor 15:44). While not renouncing funeral meals and libations poured on tombs, they also loved to celebrate the Eucharist in cemeteries on the occasion of funerals. Instead of ritual lamentations they sang hymns and psalms of hope.

2. *The Cult of the Witnesses (the Martyrs)*

"Martyr" means "witness." The first of the martyrs was Christ, "the faithful witness" (Rev 1:5). But the Apocalypse gives the same title to Antipas who died for his faith at Pergamum (Rev 2:13). This is to say that Christians who confess their faith in Jesus Christ even to the point of dying for it are bearing witness to the lordship of Christ. More than that: Christ who lives in these Christians bears witness in them to the power of his resurrection. Martyrs are one with the crucified and risen Christ and offer to God the same testimony of fidelity. This was why the community of the brethren, that is, the local Church, paid special homage to their memory.

3. *Forms of the Veneration of the Martyrs*

The cult paid to the martyrs was to some extent the same as that paid to the dead generally. It too was localized at the tomb, but it also had certain differentiating characteristics. First of all, it was veneration paid by a community of believers and not simply by the kindred; those who venerated the martyrs were a family of brothers and sisters in the faith. Secondly, the anniversary celebrated was not the martyr's earthly birthday but the day on which the person died for Christ. This death brought fulfillment and was the person's true *natale:* the day of entry into the heavenly Jerusalem. Finally, martyrs quickly came to be regarded as powerful intercessors with God. Other Christians unhesitatingly prayed to them, as is shown by the earliest graffiti on the Roman *Memoria Apostolorum;* these go back to the sixties of the third century.[1]

One result of the celebration of the martyrs' anniversaries was that each Church kept a list containing the names of these confessors of the

---

1. R. Marichal, "La date des graffiti de la triclia de Saint-Sébastien et leur place dans l'histoire de l'écriture latine," in *Archéologie paléochrétienne et culte chrétien = RevSR* 36 (1962) 111–54.

faith and, as prescribed by Cyprian,[2] the date of their death and the place of their burial. These lists, dating from as early as the middle of the third century, amounted to rough drafts of the first Christian calendars.

Tertullian tells us that the brethren sang at the funerals of the martyrs, and the *Acts of Cyprian* report that the bishop's body was carried "with prayers in great triumph" to the cemetery.[3] The same spirit was displayed on anniversaries: thus when Polycarp was martyred, the faithful of Smyrna resolved to gather each year and remember him "in joy and gladness."[4] The Eucharist celebrated on these anniversary days was especially festive, as the oldest euchological formularies attest.

II. THE CULT OF SAINTS WHO WERE NOT MARTYRS

During the age of persecutions, the veneration shown to the memory of the martyrs was extended to those who did not shed their blood for their faith but did suffer torture, imprisonment, or forced labor in mines. Thus the people gave the honors of the martyrs to Pope Pontian and the priest Hippolytus, who died in prison († 251), and to Pope Cornelius, who died in exile at Civitavecchia († 251). Thus began "a kind of unnoticed erosion of the concept of martyrdom" (H. Delehaye) and what proved to be but a first stage in the extension of the cult of the saints. Once these confessors of the faith were honored as martyrs, ascetics and then bishops soon came to be honored as "confessors."[5]

1. *The Cult of Ascetics and Virgins*

a) *Ascetics*—The end of the age of persecution confronted the most fervent souls with a new problem: How were they to reach the heights of love now that they no longer had the prospect of shedding their blood for Christ? The Fathers of the desert—Anthony († 356) in Egypt, Hilarion († 371) in Palestine, and Basil († 379) in Cappadocia—had already given their answer: there is a substitute for martyrdom, namely, the ascetical life. St. John Chrysostom wrote: "Mortify and crucify your bodies, and you too will receive the crown of the martyrs."[6] A new type of holiness had been born.

---

2. St. Cyprian, *Ep.* 12, 2, ed. L. Bayard, 1 (Collection Budé; Paris: Belles Lettres, 1925) 34.

3. *Acta proconsularia* 5 (CSEL 3:cxiii), trans. in H. Musurillo, *The Acts of the Christian Martyrs* (Oxford: Clarendon Press, 1972) 175.

4. *The Martyrdom of Polycarp* 18, in Musurillo 17.

5. See H. Delehaye, *Sanctus. Essai sur le culte des saints dans l'antiquité* (Subsidia hagiographica 17; Brussels: Bollandistes, 1927) 109–21.

6. St. John Chrysostom, *In Epist. ad Hebraeos homiliae* 2, 3 (PG 63:93).

After death the masters of the ascetical life received the same veneration as was paid to the martyrs. Thus when Hilarion came among Anthony's disciples to celebrate the first anniversary of their master's death,
he saw that they were keeping the location of their father's tomb a secret,
for fear that a rich neighboring landowner might carry the body off to
his village and erect a sanctuary there for it: *ne martyrium fabricaret,* "lest
he build a tomb and sanctuary for the martyr."[7] When Hilarion himself
died, his remains were the object of similar veneration, and the Palestinian
monks celebrated his annual feast amid a throng of pilgrims.

b) *Virgins*—Virginity consecrated to the Lord is a high form of
asceticism. This is why, even before the end of the third century,
Methodius of Olympus could liken the honor of virginity to that of martyrdom: "Have virgins not borne witness, not by enduring bodily agony
for a brief moment, but by persevering without weakening to the end of
a truly olympian, lifelong combat: the struggle to be chaste?"[8]

Next in dignity after virginity comes widowhood, "teacher of faith and
teacher of chastity" (St. Ambrose). This, too, is a form of Christian
asceticism if it is lived in the service of the Church, for then it sparkles
with a radiance that reflects the glory of martyrdom.

But though virgins and other holy women were highly esteemed by
the Church, for a long period they were not honored with an official cult
unless they were also martyrs. Perpetua and Felicity of Carthage and
Felicity of Rome, who were married women, and Agnes of Rome, Agatha
of Catania, and Lucy of Syracuse, who were virgins, were all of them
martyrs. The veneration paid by Gregory of Nyssa to his sister Macrina[9]
or by the monks of Bethlehem to Paula[10] was a private cult rendered to
dead women whom they knew to be friends of God. It was by way of
the foundational legends for titular churches and of the passion stories
of the martyrs that certain Roman virgins and matrons—Pudentiana,
Praxedes, and Sabina—were finally placed in the calendar, and this at
a time when Paris was already honoring Genevieve, and Poitiers the queen
and nun Radegundis as their patron saints (sixth century).

---

7. I refer the reader to the account of Hilarion's pilgrimage in St. Jerome, *Vita Hilarionis*
(PG 23:45), ed. P. de Labriolle (Collection Science et religion 436; Paris: Bloud et Gay, 1907)
59–60.

8. Methodius of Olympus, *Symposium* 7, 3, ed. H. Musurillo and V. Debidour (SC
95; Paris: Cerf, 1963) 186–87. See M. Viller, "Le martyre et l'ascèse," *Revue d'ascétique et
de mystique* 6 (1925) 105–15.

9. St. Gregory of Nyssa, *Vita Macrinae*, ed. P. Maraval (SC 178; Paris: Cerf, 1971).

10. St. Jerome, *Ep.* 108, ed. J. Labourt, *Lettres* 5 (Collection Budé: Paris: Belles Lettres,
1955) 198–201.

2. *The Cult of Bishops*

The great bishops of the early centuries often crowned their steward-ship with martyrdom, as St. Cyprian said when congratulating the Roman Church on the glorious death of Pope Fabian.[11] It was as martyrs that Ignatius of Antioch, Polycarp of Smyrna, Peter of Alexandria, Pothinus of Lyons, and Pontian, Fabian, Cornelius, and Sixtus, all of Rome, were honored with a cult. Others were ranked as confessors of the faith because of the tortures they endured, the responsibilities they accepted in time of persecution, and the demanding missionary tasks they undertook. Such was the reason why Gregory Thaumaturgus († ca. 270) became probably the first bishop to be honored with a cult even though he was not a martyr.

In a period when the most fervent Christians were listening to the call of the desert, it was natural that the Church should choose its leaders from among the ascetics. The monastic background of Basil of Caesarea, Mar-tin of Tours, and Paulinus of Nola gave their episcopates a glamor that played no little part in attracting the crowds to their tombs.

In addition to the calendar in which the anniversaries of its martyrs and even of its confessors were inscribed, each Church had a separate list in which the anniversaries of its bishops were noted down so that they might be remembered in common prayer. The Roman *Depositiones mar-tyrum* (literally: "burials of the martyrs," i.e., anniversary dates) and *Depositiones episcoporum* of 354 are examples of these lists.[12] How did many of the bishops pass from these obituary lists into the calendar? It is hard to say; each case would have to be studied separately. In an age when the term "saint" did not yet have its restricted meaning and when liturgical formularies were still largely improvised, the difference between the two types of anniversaries must have been rather vague in practice. The cult of Pope Sylvester († December 31, 335) provides a choice example of an inadvertent passage from the one category to the other. At the end of the fifth century, Pope Symmachus dedicated the ancient title of Equitius to his illustrious predecessor, who had been a contemporary of Constan-tine; a century later, prayers referring to St. Sylvester were already being given a place in the Verona Sacramentary after the prayers for the dead, and in them the Lord was being asked to grant him the glory of eternal blessedness.[13]

---

11. St. Cyprian, *Ep.* 9, ed. L. Bayard, *Lettres* 1 (Collection Budé; Paris: Belles Lettres, 1925) 22.

12. *LP* 1:10-12.

13. *Le,* nos. 1161-62.

III. THE DEVELOPMENT OF THE CULT OF THE SAINTS

In the early centuries the cult of the saints was carried out at their tombs. This was doubtless not an absolute law, for in the middle of the fourth century we see Rome celebrating the *natale* of the African martyrs Cyprian, Perpetua, and Felicity; homage at the tomb was nonetheless the practice in the majority of cases. Toward the sixth century, however, the cult of the martyrs, while keeping the sacred burial site as its center, began little by little to spread farther afield. On the day of the martyr's *natale*, the main liturgical assembly still took place at the basilica in the cemetery, where the people poured in for the Mass "near the body." At the same time, however, many city churches also celebrated the saint's feast, even though his or her name was not yet in the calendar of other churches.

The Roman sacramentaries of the seventh century are witnesses to an urban cult of the chief martyrs of the apostolic city; in the following century the diffusion of these sacramentaries in Frankish territory brought with it the names and cult of the martyrs of Rome. The same thing happened in the East and in all the other regions of the West. There were many causes of this real revolution in the veneration of the saints.

The most important factor in the extension of a saint's cult was undoubtedly the renown of the person. That is why the entire Church celebrated the Apostles Peter and Paul from as early as the second half of the fourth century. In Augustine's day the feasts of St. John the Baptist, St. Stephen, St. Lawrence, and even of St. Vincent, or of the children of Bethlehem whom Herod massacred, were universally celebrated. Less well-known saints owed the spread of their cult either to the translation and sharing of their relics or to the place given them in various hagiographical documents.

1. *Translation and Sharing of Relics*

The discovery and translation of the relics of saints is a phenomenon that crops up everywhere at the end of the fourth century. St. Ambrose promoted the practice at Milan and Bologna.[14] At Rome, however, it was not until the war between the Goths and Byzantines in the sixth century and, after that, until the end of the eighth century in particular that there was a systematic transfer of the bodies of the martyrs from the suburban cemeteries to the churches of the city in order to prevent their being removed or destroyed. It is obvious, of course, that any basilica possessing the relics of a saint would become a new center for the cult of that saint.

The sharing of relics, a practice long resisted by Rome, was in wide use in other regions. Shortly after the remains of St. Stephen were

---

14. St. Ambrose, *Ep. 22 Dominae sorori* (PL 16:1019-26).

discovered not far from Jerusalem in 415, a parcel of them reached Hippo, where it worked miracles.[15] Any church that in this way came to possess even the least fragment of a saint's body felt obliged to celebrate that saint's *natale*, which, of course, attracted the faithful. Soon it was thought impossible to dedicate a church without placing some relics of martyrs beneath the altar. Rome was more reserved than other Churches to the multiplication of relics of saints' bodies and preferred substitute relics, such as cloths that had touched a martyr's tomb or phials of an oil that had been lit for a night before a tomb.

The diffusion of relics increased the number of places where a saint was venerated, but the cult still remained tied to some visible trace of the saint. It was in the Vatican Basilica that the cult of the saints was finally cut free of any material support. There Pope Gregory III (731–41) had an oratory built in honor of Christ and his Mother, as well as of "all the holy martyrs and confessors and all the just who have reached their consummation, wherever in this world their bodies may rest." He ordered the monks in charge of the basilica to betake themselves to this oratory each evening and recite a short office in honor of all the saints.[16] The feast of All Saints soon came to be celebrated far and wide; in the East it was connected with the Easter solemnities, while in England and the Frankish territories it was assigned to November 1.

2. *Hagiographic Literature*

Along with writings of the saints themselves, hagiographic literature contributed greatly to the spread of their cult. The Acts of the Martyrs, the passion stories, the legends and lives of the saints won popular veneration for various saints down the centuries. All of these writings had for their purpose to rouse admiration and encourage the faithful in fidelity to the Lord. Only a few pursued this aim by means of a scrupulous account of the facts.

The Acts of the Martyrs are the most valuable documents in the hagiographic corpus, but few of them have come down to us in an original and unrevised form. The Acts of Justin at Rome and Cyprian at Carthage are among the few. Next in value are the stories of eyewitnesses, such as the letter of the Christians of Smyrna telling of the martyrdom of Polycarp (156) and the letter of the Churches of Lyons and Vienne describing the final struggle of Pothinus, Blandina, and forty-eight other martyrs of Lyons.[17]

---

15. St. Augustine, *De civ. Dei* XXII, 8 (CCL 48:825-27).

16. *LP* 1:422.

17. For a translation of the Acts of the Martyrs see H. Musurillo, *The Acts of the Christian Martyrs.*

Passion stories are later narratives, the historical value of which it is difficult to appraise. They range from stories based on archives to stories that are pure fiction. In all of them we find the same kind of judges, cross-examinations, responses, and tortures. Sometimes the purpose of these documents was to win renown for a place where a saint was venerated. This was true, for example, of the Roman legends concerning the foundation of the ancient churches or *tituli*.

Lives of the saints made their appearance at a very early date. The oldest is that of St. Cyprian, written by his deacon, Pontius. The ones which achieved the greatest popularity, however, were the lives of the Desert Fathers and the monastic founders; for example, the life of St. Anthony by St. Athanasius and the life of St. Benedict by St. Gregory the Great in the second book of the latter's *Dialogues*. In these lives, and for that matter in the whole body of hagiographic legend, we find the types of holiness that for centuries won the admiration of the Christian people and stimulated their fervor.

We ought not to forget that a number of saints, from Ignatius of Antioch down to Francis de Sales, have left writings which have made them spiritual teachers of others and spread their renown throughout the world.

Finally, it is to be noted that pilgrimages have always played a part in spreading the cult of the saints. After the Holy Land and Rome, other names to conjure with have been Mont-Saint-Michel and Santiago de Compostela, St. Martin of Tours and the Church of the Madeleine at Vézelay.

3. *Theological Reflection*

Even as a conception of holiness based on martyrdom and its substitutes was spreading from the fourth to the sixth centuries, Christian cult was being enriched by a quite different contribution resulting from theological reflection on the mystery of Christ.

This reflection, made necessary by heresy (the heresies of Arius in the fourth century and of Nestorius and Eutyches at the beginning of the fifth), led to the establishment of the feast of Epiphany in the East and of Christmas at Rome. In the Roman calendar for 354, a magnificent symbolic act placed the *natale* of Christ in Bethlehem at the head of the list of the *natalitia* of the martyrs. By the end of the century, East and West were celebrating both solemnities.

But in the circle of light shed by Christmas the New Testament saints soon made their appearance in the company of Christ the Lord: St. John the Baptist, the Precursor whose birth was celebrated six months before the birth of Jesus; then, in the days after Christmas, St. Stephen, St. James and St. John the Evangelist, the children slain by Herod, and, finally, outside the countries directly under Roman obedience, the feast of the Apostles Peter and Paul. Although all these saints had tombs the location of which was well known and which indeed attracted crowds of pilgrims, the Church was unanimous in its desire to honor these individuals as the human beings who had by one or other title been the closest servants of the Word made flesh.

As theological reflection penetrated more deeply into the mystery of the incarnation, it would encounter the Most Holy Mother of God. It did so at Ephesus (431), guided by the acclamations of the people. The cult of Mary will be discussed in the next chapter.

The celebration of all the saints as a body is attributable as much to popular devotion to the martyrs "whose names are known to God alone" as it is to theological reflection. As early as the second half of the fourth century, the calendar of Nicomedia was announcing, on the Friday of the Easter octave, the feast of "all the holy confessors." In Rome, at the beginning of the seventh century, Pope Boniface IV dedicated the Pantheon in honor of "St. Mary and all the holy martyrs," and the anniversary of the dedication was for a long time celebrated on May 13. In the next century a new solemnity made its appearance in England: the feast of All Saints, which was celebrated on November 1.[18] During the ninth century this feast spread throughout the Carolingian Empire. Beginning in the eleventh century, the day after All Saints was dedicated to the commemoration of all the departed faithful. The cult of the saints had originally developed out of the cult of the dead; now it had led back to it again, since there is but a single City of the living.

§2. The Liturgical Expression of Veneration of the Saints

BIBLIOGRAPHY

H. Delehaye, *Commentarius perpetuus in Martyrologium Hieronymianum ad recensionem H. Quentin* (Acta Sanctorum Novembris II, Pars posterior; Brussels: Bollandistes, 1931).

_____, *Martyrologium Romanum ad formam editionis typicae scholiis historicis instructum* (Propylaeum ad Acta Sanctorum Decembris; Brussels: Bollandistes, 1940).

J. Dubois, *Le Martyrologe d'Usuard. Texte et commentaire* (Subsidia hagiographica 40; Brussels: Bollandistes, 1940).

_____, *Edition pratique des martyrologes de Bède, de l'Anonyme lyonnais et de Florus*, in collaboration with G. Renaud (Paris: Institut de recherche et d'histoire des textes, 1976).

---

18. See H. Delehaye, *Martyrologium Romanum ad formam editionis typicae scholiis historicis instructum* (Propylaeum ad Acta Sanctorum Decembris; Brussels: Bollandistes, 1940) 488–89.

R. Aigrain, *L'hagiographie: Ses sources, ses méthodes, son histoire* (Paris: Bloud et Gay, 1953).

P. Delooz, *Sociologie et canonisations* (Liège: Collection scientifique de la Faculte de Droit de l'Université de Liège, 1969).

J. Dubois, *Les Martyrologes du moyen âge latin* (Typologie des sources du moyen âge occidental 26; Turnhout: Brepols, 1978).

V. Grumel, *Traite d'études byzantines* I. *La chronologie* (Bibliothèque byzantin; Paris: Presses Universitaires de France, 1958).

G. Löw, "Canonizzazione," *Enciclopedia Cattolica* 3 (Vatican City, 1950) col. 569-607.

P. Noret, "Ménologes, Synaxaires, Ménées. Essai de clarification d'une terminologie," *Analecta Bollandiana* 86 (1968) 21-24.

H. Quentin, *Les Martyrologes historiques du moyen âge* (Paris: Gabalda, 1908).

A. Vauchez, *La sainteté en Occident aux derniers siècles du moyen âge d'après les procès de canonisation et les documents hagiographiques* (Bibliothèque des Ecoles Françaises d'Athènes et de Rome 241; Rome: Ecole Française de Rome, 1981).

I. ECCLESIAL RECOGNITION OF A CULT

From the beginning, as we have seen, the cult of the martyrs was distinguished by its official character from the veneration paid to the other dead. When Pope Gregory the Great said at the end of the sixth century that the primary concern of officials in Rome was to know the *nomen*, *locus*, and *dies* (name, place, and day) of the martyrs,[19] he was formulating the juridical requirements for a proper liturgical cult: that the name be that of an authentic martyr, a witness to the faith of the Catholic Church, and that those involved should know the place and day for the assembly.

As early as the martyrdom of Polycarp, we see the Christians of Smyrna carefully noting that they had placed the cremated remains of their bishop in a "fitting spot," and recording the day of his martyrdom: "the second day of the first half of the month of Xanthicus (according to the Roman calendar, on February 23)."[20] The orthodoxy of any martyr was carefully examined by both the faithful and the bishops, since, in the well-known words of St. Augustine, *non poena fit martyrium, sed causa* ("it is not the torment but the motive that makes a death a martyrdom").[21]

During the first millennium, on the other hand, the approval of a cult was not expressly formulated in a specific act. The *vindicatio* or acknowledgment of a martyr, to which certain inscriptions in cemeteries supposedly bear witness, seems to have existed only in the imagination

---

19. St. Gregory the Great, *Registrum* Lib. 8, Ep. 28, ed. Ewald and Hartmann (MGH) 2:29.

20. *The Martyrdom of Polycarp* 18 and 21, in Musurillo, *The Acts of the Christian Martyrs* 17 and 19.

21. St. Augustine, *Serm.* 325, 2 (PL 38:1148).

of nineteenth-century archaeologists.[22] It is therefore necessary to advance proofs that a cult actually existed.

1. *The Testimony of the Fathers*

A privileged witness to the cult of a saint is the homily or panegyric which one or other Father pronounced during the celebration of the saint's *natale*, for when St. Augustine at Hippo, St. John Chrysostom at Constantinople, or St. Gregory the Great at Rome addressed the people on the anniversary of a martyr, they did so as bishops and leaders of their communities.[23] While their sermons may subsequently have been incorporated into the Roman Breviary and thereby acquired a new liturgical value, they are already in themselves official documents which authenticate the cult of the saint whose memory they praise.

2. *Calendars*

Every church has a calendar which tells which saints are to be honored in it and on what day. In the same way the churches of antiquity had their calendars. Two of these, dating from the fourth century, deserve special attention because they were the basis of what would subsequently be the Roman sanctoral or calendar of saints' feasts.

The *Almanac of 354*[24] is a splendid manuscript, beautifully written and illustrated by the Greek artist Furius Dionysius Filocalus, who compiled it for the use of a rich Christian named Valentine. Along with a good deal of information regarding the civil order, it contains two lists of anniversaries: one of the burials of bishops (*Depositiones episcoporum*) and the other of the burials of the martyrs (*Depositiones martyrum*). The former gives, in calendar sequence, a list of non-martyr popes, from Lucius († 254) to Sylvester († 335); the list was originally drawn up in 335 but was later continued to 354 in order to bring it up to date.

The *Depositio martyrum* gives first the *natale* of Christ on December 25, and then a list of the martyrs celebrated at Rome, each with the date and place of burial (e.g., *XII Kal. feb. Agnetis in Nomentana*, "January 21. Agnes, cemetery on the Via Nomentana"). The earliest of these martyrs date from the third century (the first martyred pope listed is Callistus, 222); the most recent had died in the persecution of Diocletian, who stopped the killing at Rome in 305. The following are those listed in the

---

22. On approval of a cult see H. Delehaye, *Sanctus* 162–69.

23. H. Delehaye, *Les Passions des martyrs et les genres littéraires* (Subsidia hagiographica 13 D; Brussels: Bollandistes, 1921) 182–235.

24. The text is in *LP* 1:10-12, or in K. Kirch, *Enchiridion fontium historiae ecclesiasticae antiquae* (7th ed.; Freiburg: Herder, 1956) nos. 543–44, or, with an excellent description of the document, in N. M. Denis-Boulet, *The Christian Calendar*, trans. P. Hepburne-Scott (*Twentieth-Century Encyclopedia of Catholicism* 113; New York: Hawthorn, 1960) 51–55.

Almanac who were also in the Roman Calendar until 1969: Christ (December 25), Fabian (January 20), Sebastian (January 20), Agnes (February 21), the Chair of Peter (*Natale Petri de Cathedra*) (February 22), Perpetua and Felicity (March 7), Peter and Paul (June 29), Seven Martyrs (July 10), Abdon and Sennen (July 30), Sixtus, Felicissimus, and Agapitus (August 6), Lawrence (August 10), Pontian and Hippolytus (August 13), Timothy (August 22), Hermes (August 28), Gorgon (September 9), Protus and Hyacinth (September 11), Cyprian (September 14), Callistus (October 14), the Crowned Martyrs (November 8), and Saturninus (November 29).

According to its title the Calendar of Nicomedia, compiled ca. 363, gives "the names of our lords the martyrs and victors, together with the days on which they received their crowns." The Greek text is lost, but we have a Syriac abridgment dating from 411.[25] To the names of the "earlier martyrs" who antedated the persecution of Diocletian this calendar adds those from the great persecution, which we know produced thousands of martyrs in the East until 313, then resumed in 320–21, and flared up for a last time under Emperor Julian (361–63). To the names of the "Western" martyrs, that is, those belonging to the Mediterranean basin, it joins those of the "Eastern" martyrs from Armenia and Mesopotamia.

In particular, we find in this calendar the names of the following: Stephen (December 26), John and James (December 27), Peter and Paul (December 28), Epiphany (January 6), Polycarp (February 23), Perpetua, Saturninus, and ten other confessors (March 7), Commemoration of All Confessors (Friday after Easter), the Maccabees (August 1), Sixtus, bishop of Rome (August 6), and Ignatius of Antioch (October 17). Notable here are the name of Sixtus II, the martyr-pope of the catacombs, and the Antiochene date for the *natale* of St. Ignatius of Antioch, namely, October 17, as well as the existence of an Eastern feast of all saints, five centuries before the Frankish solemnity on November 1.

3. *Martyrologies*

Unlike calendars, martyrologies list the names of a number of saints whose anniversaries fall on the same day, without regard to whether their feast is being celebrated in a given locality. These books do not, therefore, of themselves attest that a saint has a cult in a particular church. The reason why the martyrology is a liturgical book is that it used to be read daily in choir at Prime, thus calling to mind each day the memory of a number of saints to whom the Church often pays no other form of veneration.

---

25. B. Mariani, *Breviarium Syriacum* (Rerum ecclesiasticarum documenta, Series minor, Subsidia studiorum 3; Rome: Herder, 1956).

The *Almanac of 354* was specifically a Roman calendar, but the calendar of Nicomedia was already an embryonic martyrology, since its purpose was to provide a first complete listing of the martyrs of East and West.

The first martyrology properly so called was compiled toward the middle of the fifth century. Its preface pretends that it is the work of St. Jerome, and as a result it has come down to us as the Hieronymian Martyrology.

This martyrology, in its critical edition by H. Quentin (1931), has been the fundamental document for all modern hagiographical study.[26] The manuscripts we have of it (the oldest go back to the eighth century) all depend on a Gaulish recension made at Auxerre in 592. But if we set aside the additions made to the document in Burgundy, it is easy to reconstruct its primitive state and to see that its material came from three main sources: the Roman Calendar of 354 as continued down to 420, the calendar of Nicomedia, and an African calendar of which the calendar of Carthage is a later recension (ca. 530). The Hieronymian Martyrology is usually content to imitate the ancient calendars in giving day, place, and name. Sometimes, however, it adds a short notice regarding the circumstances of a saint's martyrdom.

The historical martyrologies of the eighth to the twelfth centuries attempted to complete the Hieronymian Martyrology in two ways: by telling the story of the martyrs through a short notice on each saint and by adding new names from Scripture, Church history, and the writings of the Fathers, so as to fill in the gaps in the martyrology on certain days. The first author of this new type of martyrology was Venerable Bede († 735), who wrote as a competent historian. In the next century his work was continued at Lyons, where an anonymous cleric compiled a new martyrology in about the year 800; he added new notices to those of Bede (Bibliothèque nationale ms. lat. 3879), and his work was in turn filled out by Florus, a deacon, in about 840.

Up to that point there was no great difficulty since, while the authors thought themselves competent to increase the number of notices in one redaction after another, they did their work conscientiously. Unfortunately, a forger, Ado of Vienne, now took a hand; he presented as the ancient papal martyrology, which he had supposedly discovered in Italy, a "Short Roman Martyrology" which in fact he had made up out of whole cloth. In the process he altered drastically the dates in the earlier martyrologies. For example, he assigned the feast of St. Ignatius of Antioch to February 1 and that of St. Basil to June 14. Despite subtractions and

---

26. See H. Delehaye, *Commentarius perpetuus in Martyrologium hieronymianum ad recensionem H. Quentin* (Acta Sanctorum Novembris II, Pars posterior; Brussels: Bollandistes, 1931) 133.

additions, Ado's Martyrology (compiled ca. 860) was substantially preserved in the Martyrology of Usuard of Saint-Germain (ca. 865); it thus
became for practical purposes the direct ancestor of the Roman Martyrology.[27]

The Roman Martyrology promulgated by Gregory XIII in 1584 was
in fact nothing but a recension of Usuard's Martyrology, which had made
its way into all the Benedictine abbeys and medieval chapter houses and
had eclipsed its predecessors. The authors of the 1584 edition, especially
Cardinal Baronius, realized that their work was imperfect, but they did
not have available at that time the tools of historical criticism, which were
indispensable if the work were to be radically revised. The Roman Martyrology has been frequently reedited since that time, but its historical
value is no greater than that of its sources. These last are clearly inven-
toried in the commentary which the Bollandists published under the direction of H. Delehaye in 1940.[28]

In different forms the Eastern Churches have likewise provided
themselves with comparable guides to the celebration of the feasts of the
saints. The primary book is the Synaxarion, which indicates the place for
the liturgical assembly or synaxis and gives an abridged eulogy of a saint
for each day of the year from the beginning of December to the end of
August. The most important synaxarion is that of Constantinople, which
has been edited by H. Delehaye.[29] It goes back probably to the tenth century. The *Patrologia Orientalis* has published synaxaria of the Coptic,
Ethiopian, Syrian, Armenian, and Gregorian Churches.

4. *Canonizations*

While continuing to perform on their own authority the "elevation"
of holy bodies, the bishops of the eleventh and twelfth centuries began
increasingly to appeal in this matter to the higher authority of the Roman
pontiffs, especially when there was question of placing on the altars individuals who had been dead for only a short time. The first papal approval requested for a cult seems to have been for St. Ulric, bishop of
Augsburg († 973). It was given at the Lateran, during a session of a synod,
by Pope John XV (993). Almost two centuries were to pass before a decretal

---

27. The historical martyrologies have been classified and analyzed by H. Quentin and
edited by J. Dubois; see the bibliography for §2 of this chapter.

28. The most recent official edition of the Roman Martyrology was published in 1922.
The book includes a lengthy letter of Benedict XIV relative to the edition which he had promulgated in 1748 and to a treatise of Baronius, who had been the chief editor of the *editio
princeps* promulgated by Gregory XIII in 1584.

29. There is a good introduction to the Eastern synaxaria, as well as to all problems
of hagiography, in R. Aigrain, *L'hagiographie: Ses sources, ses méthodes, son histoire* (Paris:
Bloud et Gay, 1953); on the East see 69–90.

of Alexander III promulgated the following order: "Do not presume to decree religious veneration for anyone without the consent of the Roman Church."[30] This decretal of 1171 was to become law in the Latin Church. Shortly after the Council of Trent, the task of preparing for the canonization of saints was entrusted to the Congregation of Rites (1588).[31]

In 1534 a preliminary step was introduced into the process of canonization in the form of beatification, which authorizes the public veneration of a servant of God in a specific territory or religious family. Francis de Sales († 1622) was the first person to be beatified (1665).

I shall not go into the procedure for beatification and canonization. Let me at least note, however, that the canonical inquiry focuses essentially on three points: the person's orthodoxy as manifested in any writings he or she may have left; heroic exercise of the evangelical virtues; and miracles obtained through the person's intercession. In the case of a martyr, no miracles are required.

Canonizations are rare in the Orthodox Churches. They are decreed by a synod and promulgated by the patriarch; thus Lydia, the seller of purple goods whom St. Paul baptized at Philippi (Acts 16:6-11), was canonized in 1972. The last canonization undertaken by the Church of Russia was that of St. Seraphin of Sarov, in 1907.

II. THE ROMAN CALENDAR

BIBLIOGRAPHY

Calendarium Romanum ex decreto sacrosancti oecumenici concilii Vaticani II instauratum, auctoritate Pauli PP VI promulgatum (Vatican City, 1969). English translation in *The Sacramentary* and *The Liturgy of the Hours*.

P. Jounel, *Le culte des saints dans les basiliques du Latran et du Vatican au douzième siècle* (Collection de l'Ecole Française de Rome 26; Rome: Ecole Française de Rome, 1977).

_____, "Les développements du sanctoral de Grégoire XIII a Jean XXIII," *LMD* no. 63bis (1960) 74–81.

_____, "Les collectes du sanctoral au Missel romain," in *Lex orandi lex credendi. Miscellanea in onore di P. Cipriano Vagaggini* (Studia Anselmiana 79; Rome: Editrice Anselmiana, 1980) 347–77.

H. Schmidt, *Introductio in liturgiam occidentalem* (Rome: Herder, 1960) 528–685.

Although in the beginning the anniversaries of the saints were celebrated only at their tombs, the formularies used were soon gathered

---

30. *Decretalium* lib. 3, tit. 45, c. I, ed. A. Friedberg, col. 650.

31. P. Delooz and A. Vauchez (see bibliography for §2 of this chapter) have published insightful studies on the sociological aspects of canonizations and on the type of holiness which catches the attention of the Christian people at a given period.

together with those for other celebrations and then arranged according to date in the sacramentaries and lectionaries. In the beginning, too, the temporal and the sanctoral were not kept separate. Starting in the eleventh century, however, the books presented temporal, sanctoral, and commons in that order. That, in fact, is how the first Roman sanctoral came into existence. At the end of the eighth and beginning of the ninth centuries, the Frankish Sacramentary brought together the various local traditions of Rome,[32] for it was now customary for each Church of the West to celebrate all the feasts for which the books contained a formulary. The first Roman calendar was therefore not originally Roman, any more than was the plainchant developed during that same period in the Frankish and Germanic abbeys.

1. *The Roman Calendar of the Twelfth Century*

The end of the twelfth century was a turning point in the history of the Roman Calendar. The immediate spread of a cult of St. Thomas Becket, who had been murdered in his cathedral († 1170), meant that the calendar was now open to contemporary saints. It has retained this openness down to our own time. Until Becket the only saints celebrated were the early martyrs and a few other key figures in the life of the Church, the most recent of these being Gregory the Great. In this older list of saints it was easy to trace the contributions made by succeeding centuries.

The basis for the Roman Calendar was the Roman-Frankish calendar of the eighth and ninth centuries. It contained, along with those saints included in the Gregorian and Gelasian Sacramentaries, the feasts of the Chair of St. Peter, the Conversion of St. Paul, and each of the other apostles. The names of Popes Leo the Great and Gregory the Great and of Augustine and Benedict were soon added, while the later ninth century saw the inclusion of All Saints.

In the eleventh century the veneration paid to saintly popes became more inclusive. All the popes who held office before the Peace of Constantine were now honored as martyrs. The Gregorian Reform could only look with favor on this kind of homage paid to the Roman pontiffs, and a decretal of Gregory VII approved of it.

The twelfth century saw the increasing popularity of the legends of the saints, which formed as it were the catechism of the Middle Ages: the legends of Symphorosa and her sons, of Boniface and Alexis, Thecla, Barbara, Blaise, Pantaleon, Cyprian the sorcerer and Justina the virgin. Another influence, that of the monasteries, also made itself felt at this

---

32. The earliest witness is the Sacramentary of Gellone (last decade of the eighth century): *Liber sacramentorum Gellonensis*, ed. A. Dumas (CCL 159).

time: to the names of Benedict and Scholastica were now added those of the monastic founders (Anthony, Sabas, Hilarion), the patrons of important abbeys (Giles, Denis), and models of the penitential life, such as Mary Magdalene.[33]

2. The Tridentine Calendar (1568)

The calendar for the Breviary and Missal of Pius V contained everything that had been accepted in the twelfth century and to this it added the contributions of the following four centuries. It now included saints whose legends had made them popular, as for example Christopher and Catherine of Alexandria; above all it included the great saints of the thirteenth century: Francis and Dominic, Anthony of Padua, Louis IX, Clare, and Elizabeth of Hungary. In the fifteenth century the names of Thomas Aquinas and Bonaventure were added. The ancient local calendar of Rome continued to provide the basic framework, but it had now adopted a universalist outlook and become an echo of the life of the entire Church. Meanwhile it had also welcomed new forms of devotion, such as the cult of St. Joseph and of the Conception of Mary.

3. The Roman Calendar from 1568 to 1960

Between the end of the sixteenth century and the Second Vatican Council, the calendar experienced what can only be called an excessive growth. The calendar of 1568 contained less than two hundred feasts; by 1900 there were 145 more, 13 being added in the sixteenth century, 49 in the seventeenth, 32 in the eighteenth, 25 in the nineteenth, and 26 between 1900 and 1960. Many of these newer feasts were inevitable, namely, those of the saints who left their mark on the modern age, from Ignatius Loyola, Francis Xavier, Teresa of Avila, and Francis de Sales, to Theresa of the Child Jesus and John Mary Vianney. Other feasts filled gaps, as, for example, those of St. Justin and St. Irenaeus. Still others, especially from the time of Leo XIII on, were meant to emphasize the importance of the great missionaries (Boniface, Augustine of Canterbury, Cyril and Methodius) and of the Eastern doctors of the Church (Cyril of Jerusalem, Cyril of Alexandria, Ephraem, John Damascene). But to these feasts were added those of a large number of obscure saints, mostly Italian (for example, Philip Benizzi, Francis Caracciolo, and Sylvester Gozzolini). As late as 1960 John XXIII enrolled in the calendar the name of St. Gregory Barbarigo, who had been a bishop of Bergamo.[34]

---

33. On the saints of the thirteenth, fourteenth, and fifteenth centuries, see the study of A. Vauchez.

34. P. Jounel, "L'évolution du Missel romain de Pie IX à Jean XXIII," *Notitiae* 14 (1978) 246–58.

4. *The General Roman Calendar of 1969*

On February 14, 1969, Pope Paul VI promulgated a "General Roman Calendar" that had been reformed in accordance with the Constitution on the Liturgy of Vatican II.[35] The main objectives of the reformers had been to assign the celebration of the saint to the anniversary day of their death, in conformity with ancient practice, and to revise the list of saints so as both to weed it out and to enrich it.

The cult of the martyrs had originated in the celebration of their anniversaries, and this rule was observed down to the eleventh century. But back in the ninth century Ado of Vienne had introduced a number of arbitrarily chosen dates into his martyrology, and these gradually made their way into the calendar. Beginning in the seventeenth century the considerations that determined the choice of dates were sometimes rather trivial. At the end of the nineteenth century there was a desire, in particular, to fill in the empty spaces in the weeks of Lent. A return to the sources was obviously needed.

The return to the ancient rule has made it possible for the Roman Church frequently to celebrate Eastern saints on the same day that their feast is observed in their country of origin. Three exceptions have been made to the rule: since the anniversaries of the deaths of St. Benedict, St. Gregory the Great, and St. Thomas Aquinas always fall in Lent, their feasts have been transferred to other days that have long been connected with their memory.

The decision to weed out the list of saints and at the same time to enrich it may seem a contradictory one. To achieve their goal the reformers first reduced to less than 180 the number of saints whom it was proposed to commemorate. The first names to be eliminated were those of personages whose very existence was questionable (John and Paul, Ursula, Catherine, Felix of Valois). Also omitted were the commemorations of the local martyrs of Rome, of whom nothing more is known than the *nomen—locus—dies* which meant so much to Gregory the Great,[36] and of the founders or foundresses of the ancient places of worship within the city (Prisca, Sabina, Chrysogonus). The reformers did, however, keep the names of the principal Roman martyrs (Fabian, Cornelius, Sixtus II, Agnes) and of the patrons of the basilicas that are still visited by pilgrims (Cecilia,

---

35. *Calendarium Romanum* (Vatican City, 1969) (= *EDIL* 91). The calendar is printed at the beginning of the Missal and of the Liturgy of the Hours. On the preparation of the 1969 Calendar see P. Jounel, "L'élaboration du Calendrier romain general," in *Liturgia opera divina e humana. Studi sulla riforma liturgica offerti a S. E. Mons. Annibale Bugnini in occasione del suo 70° compleanno* (Bibliotheca EL, Subsidia 26; Rome: Edizioni Liturgiche, 1982) 671–91.

36. See above, n. 19.

Sebastian, Pancratius, Nereus and Achilles). The calendar thus keeps something of the atmosphere of Rome and antiquity.

As the Council recommended, most of the names eliminated are those of the many saints whose memory is preserved only in a limited territory or in a particular religious family. Their suppression has provided space in which to introduce the names of saints representing the various regions of the world: the martyrs of the United States and Canada, those of Japan and Uganda, St. Peter Chanel, the only saint from Oceania. Just as all the continents now have witnesses in the calendar, so too all the centuries are represented, from the martyrs of the Neronian persecution to St. Maximilian Kolbe.

The saints now inscribed in the Roman Calendar are not all commemorated in the same way. The commemoration of most of them is optional. Thus the Christian people are allowed a legitimate freedom in regard to veneration of the saints.

In keeping with tradition, there is room, alongside the General Roman Calendar, for particular calendars, whether diocesan, regional, or of religious orders and congregations. In addition, on days on which there is no obligatory memorial, it is permitted to celebrate the memory of any saint listed in the Roman Martyrology for that day. For this reason, a revision of the Martyrology of 1584 has now become a necessity.

A renewal of the cult of the saints in the Roman liturgy does not depend solely on the calendar. It also depends on the regulations for the celebration, which have become more flexible, and on the revision of the formularies for Mass and Liturgy of the Hours. The Mass prayers and the hagiographical readings attempt to bring out the spiritual message of each saint.

III. THE LITURGICAL CELEBRATION

1. *The Celebration of the Anniversary in Antiquity*

From the beginning the veneration of the martyrs took the form of a nocturnal vigil celebrated at their tomb on their anniversary. The modest vigil held in time of persecution (such as the one which the priest Pionius and two women celebrated on the feast of St. Polycarp in 250) became, once peace was established, a vast gathering at which the jubilant people filled the cemeterial basilica where the service was held. In fifth-century Egypt Abbot Shenoute wrote that "some of the faithful inside the church sing psalms, read, and celebrate the mystery; outside, others fill the air with the sound of trumpets and flutes."[37] The same could be said of every

---

37. Shenoute, *Oeuvres*, ed. E. Amelineau (Paris: Leroux, 1907) 1:199-200.

region. Reading of the Bible was accompanied by reading of the saint's sufferings in an account sometimes written for this precise purpose. The Eucharist was usually celebrated twice: once beside the tomb at the end of the vigil (*in vigilia*), and again in mid-morning (*in die*).

2. The Formulary for Mass and Liturgy of the Hours

The readings, prayers, and songs for the feasts of the saints show the place which each of these men and women occupies in the Christian mystery. In these texts "the Church proclaims achievement of the paschal mystery in the saints who have suffered and have been glorified with Christ. She proposes them to the faithful as examples who draw all men to the Father through Christ, and through their merits she begs for God's favors."[38]

In the Missal of 1970 each saint's memorial has at least its own opening prayer. The text sometimes echoes the writings of the saint being celebrated (for example, Augustine). In any case, whenever possible, it refers to the way in which the saint lived his or her union with Christ or to the mission which the saint exercised in the Church: the struggles of Athanasius and Hilary for the faith, the love of Francis and Clare for poverty.

It is through listening to the Word of God that we can best enter into the souls of the saints. Sometimes one or other page of the gospel provided them with the light that guided them through life (Athanasius, Thérèse of Lisieux). Others shared in a special way in the trials and joys of Paul; still others were given a mission like that of Isaiah or Jeremiah. The readings for their anniversaries shed a lively light on the character of their mission and the greatness of the grace they received.

Each Common of the saints provides a selection of prayers and readings that help us to realize the meaning of martyrdom, or the mission of a pastor, or the mission of saints who devoted their lives to education or caritative work, or the meaning of virginity and the consecrated life.

In the Liturgy of the Hours, the office of a saint is preceded by a short biographical notice. A passage taken from one of several sources is set before us in the Office of Readings. It may be from something written by the saint (Ignatius of Antioch, Anselm, Teresa of Avila), from the Acts of the saint's martyrdom (Justin, Cyprian), from the testimony of a confidant or companion (as in the case of Jeanne de Chantal and Pierre Chanel), from an ancient life (Cyril and Methodius, Elizabeth of Hungary), or, if all of these are lacking, from a patristic text that is especially appropriate in view of the spiritual character of the saint (Philip Neri) or

---

38. *VSC* 104.

of the saint's mission (Damasus) or even of the legend that has perpetuated the saint's memory (Cecilia).

3. *The Veneration of Relics and Images*

The veneration of a saint's relics or images is not something alien to the liturgy. Christians of the early centuries grasped the connection between the relics of the martyrs and the celebration of the Eucharist. St. Ambrose was therefore happy to be able to place beneath the altar the bodies of those who had shared most closely in the paschal mystery of Christ.[39] The translation of relics and the placing of them beneath or in the altar became one of the most striking rites in the dedication of a church. The Middle Ages went even further in their devotion and did not hesitate to place on the altar reliquaries covered with enamel work and precious stones.

Nor is the function of images or statues of the saints a purely decorative one. They can be the object of special veneration and thus mediate between the visible and the invisible.

The practice of placing a church or altar under the patronage of a saint may be mentioned here with the cult of relics and images. In the fifth century St. Augustine made a distinction: an altar is consecrated to God alone and not to any martyr, but we commemorate the martyr when we offer sacrifice to God.[40] The liturgy for the dedication of an altar or church makes it clear that these are consecrated to the Blessed Trinity even while being placed under the patronage of one or other saint. The dedication to a saint is an invitation to thank the Lord for the miracles of grace that he worked in his servant, while at the same time it reminds the faithful of the intercessory power of the saint who is invoked in this place.

---

39. St. Ambrose, *Ep.* 22, 13 (PL 16:1022).
40. St. Augustine, *Contra Faustum* XX, 21 (CSEL 25:562-63).

Chapter V

The Veneration of Mary

The Council of Ephesus (431) had a decisive impact on the cult of Mary, but the cult was already traditional. The Council itself was held in the Basilica of St. Mary, and some years earlier the feast of Mary Theotokos, "Mary the Mother of God," had been celebrated between Jerusalem and Bethlehem on August 15.[1] This already existing liturgical cult had in turn been preceded by a popular cult, some evidences of which have come down to us.

At Nazareth the words *Chaire Mariam* ("Hail, Mary") are legible on a column of a building discovered in 1960 under the Byzantine Basilica of the Annunciation. The name "Mary" has here been added to the angel's greeting, so that the words are undoubtedly a prayer. Elsewhere a Greek papyrus dating from the third century contains the complete text of the prayer *Sub tuum praesidium* ("In the shelter of your mercy"), with mention of "holy Mary, Mother of God."[2] We ought not be surprised at the antiquity of Christian veneration of Mary, since St. Irenaeus already speaks of her as the new Eve, and the apocryphal narratives trace her history from her birth to her dormition, while a gallery of the cemetery of Priscilla in Rome contains a painting that shows Mary and her child as the fulfillment of Balaam's prophecy.

§1. The Cult of Mary in the East

BIBLIOGRAPHY

D. Baldi, *Enchiridion locorum sanctorum* (2nd ed.; Jerusalem, 1955).

---

1. A. Renoux, *Le Codex arménien Jérusalem 121* (PO 36; Turnhout: Brepols, 1971) 357.
2. E. Mercenier, "La plus ancienne prière à la sainte Vierge," *QL* 25 (1940) 33–36.

130

L. Bouyer, "Le culte de Marie dans la liturgie byzantine," *LMD* no. 38 (1954) 79–94.

B. Capelle, "La fête de la Vierge à Jérusalem au Ve siècle," in his *Travaux liturgiques* 3 (Louvain: Mont César, 1967) 280–391.

I.-H. Dalmais, *Saints et sanctuaires de Terre Sainte* (Paris: Le Centurion, 1968).

_____, "Les Apocryphes de la Dormition et l'ancienne liturgie de Jérusalem," *Bible et Terre Sainte* no. 179 (1976) 11–14.

H. du Manoir, *Maria. Etudes sur la Sainte Vierge* 1 (Paris: Beauchesne, 1949). See: S. Salaville, "Marie dans la liturgie byzantine" (247–326); M. Doumith, "Marie dans la liturgie syro-maronite" (327–40); A. M. Massonat, "Marie dans la liturgie chaldéenne" (341–51); P. Vartan-Tekeyan, "La Mère de Dieu dans la liturgie arménienne" (354–61); G. Nollet, "Le culte de Marie en Ethiopie" (363–413).

E. Mercenier and F. Paris, *La prière des Eglises de rite byzantin* II/1 (Amay, 1939).

I. THE MARIAN FEASTS IN JERUSALEM

The liturgical cult of Mary originated in Jerusalem, with the feast of August 15 as its foundation. Initially celebrated at the Kathisma or place where according to tradition Mary paused to rest before going on to Bethlehem, the feast was transferred, toward the end of the fifth century, to Gethsemane and the basilica where people venerated the tomb of the Virgin. The feast of Mary Theotokos thus became the feast of the Dormition of the Mother of God. At the end of the sixth century, Emperor Maurice ruled that this feast was to be celebrated throughout the empire. According to Georgian sources, a series of celebrations in Mary's honor was held in Jerusalem from August 13 to August 17.[3]

At the beginning of the fifth century, a church was built near the Sheep-Gate, north of the temple, over some ponds which were identified as the Bethzatha where Jesus had cured a sick man (John 5:1-19). A century later, the commemoration of Mary's birth was linked to the spot, and the church was henceforth so designated. This seems to have been the origin of the feast of the Nativity of Mary on September 8.

In the middle of the sixth century, a third basilica was built in honor of Mary (November 20, 543). Archaeologists have recently identified the site as near the square in front of the temple, close to the mosque of Al-Aqsa. This church, the Nea or New St. Mary's, made it possible to celebrate *in situ*, as it were, the Presentation of Mary in the Temple, as described in the Protoevangelium of James. There is every reason to believe that the feast of November 21 developed here.

II. THE SPREAD OF THE MARIAN FEASTS

All the Churches of the East welcomed the feast of the Dormition of

---

3. I. H. Dalmais, "Les Apocryphes de la Dormition et l'ancienne liturgie de Jérusalem," *Bible et Terre Sainte* no. 179 (1976) 13–14.

Mary. In Ethiopia a distinction was made between the death of the holy Mother of God (January 16) and her assumption (August 15). All the Churches, with the exception of the Syro-Nestorian Church, also celebrated the Nativity of Mary and her Entrance into the Temple. The spread of the Marian feasts of Jerusalem was an accomplished fact by the sixth century.

But the cult of Mary did not spring solely from the traditions of the holy city. It also owed its origin to Mary's unique role in the mystery of the incarnation and especially to the feast of Christmas. The Christmas office of the various Churches often speaks of the Virgin Mary. Moreover, in accordance with the Eastern custom whereby relatives and friends visit and congratulate a new mother, there was a commemoration of the Mother of God during the days following the Nativity of the Lord, usually on December 26. The Eastern Syrians call this the feast of the Congratulation of the Mother of God.

Two other feasts of the Lord also involve Mary in a special way: the Annunciation (March 25) and the Meeting of the Lord with aged Simeon (February 2).

In the sixth century the annual basic set of Marian feasts was thus clearly established. Many additions were made to it (Ethiopia has over thirty feasts of Mary), but the basic set has not varied in the course of the centuries.

Finally, it is to be noted that the Marian feasts are only one witness, though the most important one, to the place of Mary in the Eastern liturgies. Eastern devotion to the Theotokos has taken many other forms, from the Ethiopian anaphora of Mary[4] to the Byzantine Akathistos hymn.[5]

§2. The Cult of Mary in the West

I. ORIGINS

BIBLIOGRAPHY

H. Barré, "Antiennes et répons de la Vierge," *Marianum* 29 (1967) 153–254.
B. Botte, "La première fête mariale de la liturgie romaine," *EL* 47 (1933) 425–30.
E. Campana, *Maria nel culto cattolico* (2 vols.; Turin: Marietti, 1933).

---

4. G. Nollet, "Le culte de Marie en Ethiopie," in H. du Manoir, *Maria. Etudes sur la Sainte Vierge* 1 (Paris: Beauchesne, 1949) 376–79.
5. G. C. Meersseman, *Der Hymnus Akathistos im Abendland* (2 vols.; Spicilegium Friburgense 2–3; Freiburg: Universitätsverlag, 1958–60).

B. Capelle, *Travaux liturgiques de doctrine et d'histoire* 3 (Louvain: Mont César, 1967). This volume contains a series of studies of the cult of Mary and of the Assumption in particular (276–455).

_____, "La liturgie mariale en Occident," in H. du Manoir, *Marie. Etudes sur la Sainte Vierge* 1 (Paris: Beauchesne, 1949) 216–45.

G. Frénaud, "Le culte de Notre-Dame dans l'ancienne liturgie latine," in H. du Manoir, *Marie* 6 (Paris: Beauchesne, 1961) 157–211.

G. M. Roschini, "Maria santissima. Il culto in Occidente," in *Bibliotheca Sanctorum* 8 (Rome: Istituto Giovanni XXIII, 1967) col. 889–932.

In the years after the Council of Ephesus, Pope Sixtus III (432–440) dedicated a basilica to the Virgin Mary on the Esquiline hill: *Virgo Maria tibi Xystus nova tecta dicavi* ("I, Sixtus, dedicated a new church to you, O Virgin Mary").[6] This basilica, subsequently called St. Mary Major, has stood there ever since as the first church of the West to be dedicated to Mary. Meanwhile, in the *Communicantes* prayer of the Roman Canon, the Church was venerating the memory "first of all, of the glorious and ever virgin Mary, Mother of God and of our Lord Jesus Christ."

1. The Roman Feast of Mary on January 1

Like the Churches of the East, Rome wished to honor the Virgin Mother of God during the days after Christmas. As a result the *Natale S. Mariae* ("Anniversary of St. Mary") made its appearance on January 1 in the seventh century; it has accurately been called "the first Marian feast of the Roman liturgy."[7] The introduction, in the following decades, of the four feasts of February 2, March 25, August 15, and September 8 caused the feast of January 1 to be somewhat overshadowed, however, especially since January 1 was also the octave of Christmas and the day to which the commemoration of the circumcision of Jesus was attached, and since in numerous Christian circles it became a day of penance in reparation for the pagan festivities in honor of Janus on this day: *Prohibendum ab idolis* ("Keep yourselves from idols"). But the formularies of Mass and office never forgot the Marian dimension of the octave day, as is attested in particular by the antiphons and responses that have been sung down to our own day; for example, at Vespers: *Rubum, quem viderat Moyses incombustum, conservatam agnovimus tuam laudabilem virginitatem: Dei Genetrix, intercede pro nobis* ("Your blessed and fruitful virginity is like the bush, flaming yet unburned, which Moses saw on Sinai. Pray for us, Mother of God").

---

6. *DACL* 19:2093; *LP* 1:235 n. 2.

7. This is the title of an article by B. Botte; see the bibliography for this section.

2. *Mary in the Liturgy of Advent and Christmas*

In the time of St. Leo the Great, there was but a single Eucharistic assembly on Christmas; it was held in the Basilica of St. Peter. One hundred and fifty years later Gregory the Great was celebrating three Masses on Christmas. In the intervening period an oratory commemorating the Christmas crèche had been built near St. Mary Major, and the Mass during the night was celebrated there. Beginning in the twelfth century the daytime station was also moved to St. Mary Major, and the place of Mary in the mystery of Christmas was now expressed by means of the very setting for its celebration.

But on this day Mary was also everywhere expressly presented to the Church for its contemplation; thus the responses in the nocturns sang of her: *Hodie nobis coelorum Rex de Virgine nasci dignatus est* ("Today, for our sake, the King of heaven chose to be born of his virgin mother"); *Beata Dei Genetrix, cuius viscera intacta permanent, hodie genuit Salvatorem saeculi* ("Blessed is Mary, Mother of God, whose womb remains untouched. Today she gave birth to the Savior of the world"). The homage continued at Lauds: for example, the antiphon *Genuit puerpera Regem* ("The Mother gave birth to the King") and, in the hymn *Clausae Parentis viscera Caelestis intrat gratia* ("Heavenly grace enters the chaste Mother").

Nor could the thought of Mary be absent from the Advent season, which is the season of human expectation and had been the season of Mary's expectation. It came to the fore especially in the liturgy of Ember Wednesday and Ember Friday in which the gospels of the annunciation and the visitation were read. In the Middle Ages the gospel *Missus est* ("The angel Gabriel was sent") was solemnly proclaimed in monasteries and followed by a homily on the mystery of the annunciation. The singing of the *Magnificat* was also given an especially solemn form each evening from December 17 to December 23, when it was accompanied by the O-antiphons. One of these sang of Mary: *O coeles pudica sponsa et Domini porta* ("O chaste heavenly spouse and gate of the Lord").[8]

3. *The Four Marian Feasts*

The *Liber Pontificalis* tells us that Pope Sergius I (687–701), who was a Syrian by birth, ordered a procession from St. Hadrian, in the Roman Forum, to St. Mary Major to be held on the four days of "the Annunciation of the Lord, the Dormition and the Nativity of holy Mary, ever virgin Mother of God, and of St. Simeon, the day which the Greeks call the Hypapante or Meeting of the Lord."[9] It is noteworthy that only two of

---

8. R. J. Hesbert, *Corpus antiphonalium Officii* 3 (REDMF 9; Rome: Herder, 1968), no. 4011.

9. *LP* 1:376 and 381.

these feasts had a strictly Marian title. Sergius is not said to have instituted the feasts, but simply to have added a procession during which litanies were sung; in fact each of these feasts had been received at Rome during the course of the seventh century, the first two to have been accepted being February 2 and August 15. Nonetheless, when the pope decided to mark them out by an extraordinary gathering of the people, he gave them a special splendor and established a connection among them. They would henceforth be the four Roman feasts of the Virgin Mary. No others would be added until the fourteenth century.[10]

a) *The Assumption of Mary*—The *Liber Pontificalis* keeps the Greek name "Dormition" for the feast of August 15. The evangeliary of 740 has the title *Solemnitas de pausatione sanctae Mariae* ("Solemnity of the Resting [or: Death] of St. Mary").[11] The title "Assumption" makes its appearance in the Hadrianum, or Gregorian Sacramentary, of the 770's.[12] The title was already in general use at Rome, for we see the same Pope Hadrian giving the Basilica of St. Mary Major an antependium on which this mystery was represented.[13] The ninth century, however, brought a certain reserve, as can be seen from the notice in the Martyrology of Usuard and from the use made in the liturgy of the Pseudo-Hieronymian opusculum *Cogitis me*.[14] These two documents did not deny the bodily assumption of Mary but, given the absence of authentic witnesses, they preferred to remain noncommittal.

The formularies of Mass and office spoke very generally, except for certain antiphons and the prayer *Veneranda* which began the station at the Forum.[15] Pope Pius XII would later cite this prayer in the Bull *Munificentissimus Deus* in which he proclaimed the dogma of the assumption in 1950. Only after this proclamation did the liturgical prayer of the Roman Church give its faith a more explicit form.

Meanwhile, however, this faith found ample expression in popular devotion, and especially in the nocturnal torchlight procession in which the people of Rome accompanied the image of Christ (preserved in the Lateran) first to the Forum and then from there to St. Mary Major, where it was welcomed by the image of Mary *Salus populi Romani* ("Salva-

---

10. A. Chavasse, *Le Sacramentaire Gélasien* (Bibliothèque de théologie; Tournai: Desclée, 1958) 376–402.

11. T. Klauser, *Das römische Capitulare Evangeliorum*. I. *Typen* (LQF 28; Münster: Aschendorff, 1935) 81.

12. *Gr*, p. 262.

13. *LP* 1:500.

14. E. Dekker, *Clavis Patrum Latinorum* (2nd ed.; Steenbrugge: St.-Pieterabdij, 1961) no. 633 (*Ep.* 9).

15. B. Capelle, "L'oraison *Veneranda* à la messe de l'Assomption," in his *Travaux Liturgiques* 3 (Louvain: Mont César, 1967) 387–407.

tion/Health of the Roman People"). The pope then celebrated the early morning Mass. A hymn composed in about the year 1000 gives a poetic and dramatized account of the occasion.[16] The procession would be celebrated down to the sixteenth century, when Pope St. Pius V suppressed it.

The feast of the Assumption remained the most popular of the feasts celebrated in Mary's honor. Many churches were named after it, and many parishes and religious institutes placed under the patronage of Mary assumed into glory.

b) *The Nativity of Mary*—Though a less solemn feast than the Assumption, the Nativity of Mary, like that of John the Baptist, was celebrated with joy by the Christian people: *Cum iucunditate Nativitatem beatae Mariae celebremus* ("Let us joyfully celebrate the birth of blessed Mary"). Both of these births announced that salvation was about to dawn. It was therefore quite natural that in liturgical prayer the birth of Mary be constantly related to her divine motherhood. The antiphons of the office were of Byzantine inspiration, and some were even translated from the Greek. The Mass was of a more general kind, but the reading of the genealogy of Christ in the gospel drew attention to the fact that Mary was very much a part of the people of God.

Although the Romano-German ordo of the mid-tenth century still referred to the procession which Pope Sergius had ordered, this rite left no notable traces outside of monasteries.

c) *The Annunciation and the Purification of Mary*—The two feasts of March 25 and February 2 were originally feasts of the Lord, and in 1969 they became such once again. That is why they are placed among the feasts of the Lord in Ordinary Time. For over a millennium, however, they were celebrated as feasts of Mary: the Annunciation of the Lord had become the Annunciation of the Blessed Virgin Mary, and the Meeting of the Lord had become the feast of the Purification of Mary. At the same time, however, while the office of February 2 lauded Mary as a model of humility and obedience to the Law for accepting the rite of purification, the Mass was focused essentially on the Presentation of the Lord in the Temple.

4. *The Feasts of Mary in Gaul, Spain, and Milan*

Before Frankish Gaul and Visigothic Spain adopted the Roman liturgy (the former at the end of the eighth century, the latter during the eleventh),

---

16. Andrieu, *OR* 5:68-71 and 358-62. See also P. Jounel, *Le culte des saints dans les basiliques du Latran et du Vatican au douzième siècle* (Collection de l'Ecole Française de Rome; Rome: Ecole Française de Rome, 1977) 120-22.

they venerated Mary in accordance with their own traditions. The same was true of Milan.

a) *The feast of Mary in Gaul*—According to Gregory of Tours, in about 550–570 the people of the Auvergne celebrated a feast in honor of Mary in mid-January. The Hieronymian Martyrology announces the *Depositio sanctae Mariae* ("Burial of St. Mary") on January 18,[17] and the liturgical books of the seventh and eighth centuries all have a solemnity of Mary on this day. The reference is undoubtedly to a feast of Mary that had been established in connection with Christmas. Its precise content varies according to the source in question: some announce a *Festivitas sanctae Mariae* ("Feast of St. Mary"), others the Assumption of Mary. The Bobbio Missal even has two Masses, one *In sanctae Mariae solemnitate* ("For the Solemnity of St. Mary"), the other *In adsumptione sanctae Mariae* ("For the Assumption of St. Mary").

We do not know why January 18 was chosen. Perhaps we ought to recall in this context that the Church of Alexandria celebrated the Dormition of Mary on January 16. The most important thing to be noted here, however, is the doctrinal sureness and depth that mark the celebration of the Assumption of Mary in the *Missale Gothicum* (eighth century): "It was right [O Mary] that since you had received [the Son of God] with love when you conceived him by faith, he should in turn receive you with joy on the day of your assumption, so that you, who were a stranger on earth, might not remain shut away beneath a stone."[18]

The Franks did not celebrate any other feast of Mary until they accepted the Roman liturgical books.

b) *The feast of Mary in Spain and at Milan*—In the seventh century, Spain, like Gaul, celebrated only one feast in honor of Mary. This occurred in mid-December during the preparation for the Birth of the Lord. The tenth Council of Toledo (646) assigned the feast to December 18 for all the churches of Spain. The object of the celebration was therefore primarily the mystery of the Annunciation. The Visigothic Orational has thirty-four concluding prayers in connection with the antiphons of the office. The title given to the section is *De festivitate gloriosae sanctae Mariae virginis* ("For the feast of the glorious virgin, St. Mary").[19]

The Church of Milan also celebrated Mary during the days before Christmas. It did so especially on the last Sunday of Advent, when the gospel of the annunciation was read. Soon after the introduction of the

---

17. *Martyrologium Hieronymianum*, ed. H. Quentin, in *Acta Sanctorum Novembris* 2/2:45.

18. *Missale Gothicum*, ed. L. C. Mohlberg (REDMF 5; Rome: Herder, 1961) 30, no. 98.

19. J. Vives, *Oracional Visigótico* (Monumenta Hispaniae Sacra, Ser. liturgica 1; Barcelona, 1946) 67–79.

Roman feasts in the time of Charlemagne, the feast of February 2 was given the name "Purification of Mary."[20]

II. DEVELOPMENT OF THE CULT OF MARY

BIBLIOGRAPHY

In addition to the books of E. Campana and B. Capelle, listed in the previous bibliography, see:

H. Barré, *Prières anciennes de l'Occident à la Mère du Sauveur* (Paris: Lethielleux, 1963).

E. Bishop, "On the Origins of the Feast of the Conception of the Blessed Virgin Mary," in his *Liturgica Historica* (Oxford: Clarendon Press, 1918) 238–59.

B. Capelle, "La fête de la Conception de Marie en Occident," in *L'Immaculée Conception* (Report on the activities of the Seventh National Marian Congress) (Lyons, 1954).

A. Cecchin, "La concezione della Vergine nella liturgia della Chiesa occidentale anteriore al sec. XIII," *Marianum* 5 (1943) 51–114.

W. E. Coleman, *Philippe de Mézières' Campaign for the Feast of Mary's Presentation* (Medieval Latin Texts; Toronto: Institute of Medieval Studies, 1981).

M. Jugie, *"L'Immaculée Conception dans l'Ecriture Sainte et dans la tradition orientale"* (Bibliotheca Immaculatae Conceptionis; Rome, 1952).

V. Leroquais, *Les bréviaires manuscrits des bibliothèques publiques de France* (6 vols.; Mâcon: Protat, 1936). In his introduction the author reproduces the particular calendars of a number of dioceses and religious orders between the thirteenth and the fifteenth centuries.

A. Raes and G. Löw, "Immaculata Concezione. Storia della festa," *Enciclopedia Cattolica* 6 (Vatican City, 1951) col. 1657–62.

G. Löw, "Presentazione di Maria Santissima," *ibid.* 9 (1952) col. 1966–68.

_____, "Rosario. Festa del Rosario," *ibid.* 10 (1953) col. 1351–52.

_____, "Visitazione di Maria Santissima," *ibid.* 12 (1954) col. 1499–1501.

A. Morini, *Origini del culto dell'Addolorata* (Rome, 1893).

J. Polc, *De origine festi Visitationis B. Mariae Virginis* (Corona Lateranensis 9 A; Rome: Lateran University, 1967).

1. *Medieval Development of the Feasts of Mary*

From the seventh to the fourteenth century, the Roman Church felt no need of increasing the number of its Marian feasts and kept to the traditional four. This was the case until 1389 when Pope Urban VI established the feast of the Visitation. A century later, Sixtus IV established the feast of the Conception of Mary (1477).

a) *The Visitation of Mary*—In Byzantium the gospel relating Mary's visit to Elizabeth is read on July 2, the feast of "the Depositing at the

_____

20. P. Borella, "L'anno liturgico ambrosiano," in M. Righetti, *Manuale di storia liturgica* 2 (2nd ed.; Milan: Ancora, 1955) 457–59.

Blachernae of the Holy Robe of the Theotokos." The Franciscans adopted this day as a Marian feast, making it the feast of the Visitation of Mary (1263). It made hardly any headway until Pope Urban VI established it for the entire Church in 1389, in order to secure an end of the Great Schism through the intercession of Mary. The Council of Basel in its final period likewise promoted this feast and provided it with a special Mass (1441).[21] It was accepted only gradually during the fifteenth century by the local Churches and the various religious families (Dominicans 1401, Carthusians 1468, Cistercians 1476, Cluniacs 1480). Sixtus IV (1471-84) had a new Mass composed for it. In the Ambrosian rite the Visitation is celebrated as a feast of the Lord.

b) *The Conception of Mary*—Ever since the eighth century the Byzantine Church has celebrated a feast of the Conception of St. Anne. This feast was brought to England in the middle of the eleventh century, probably by pilgrims to the Holy Land. At the beginning of the following century, it became the feast of the Conception of Mary. Under the influence especially of a treatise by Eadmer, who had been a disciple of St. Anselm,[22] certain circles were already coming to a belief in the immaculate conception of Mary. From England this feast of the Conception of Mary made its way into Normandy, where it won great popularity and became "the feast of the Norman people." The twelfth century saw it continually spreading through Europe. Norman students brought it to Paris, whence it spread in turn, though not without opposition from some theologians. The reader may be familiar with the letter which St. Bernard wrote to the canons of Lyons in an attempt to dissuade them from placing the feast in their calendar (1140).[23]

As the thesis regarding the Immaculate Conception was clarified it won increasing assent. Beginning in the thirteenth century it had the consistent support of the Franciscans, who adopted the feast as early as 1263, celebrating it in their convent in Rome; the popes authorized its celebration in their presence while they were residing in Avignon. A Franciscan pope subsequently established the feast for the diocese of Rome in 1477 (Constitution *Cum praeexcelsa* of Sixtus IV). Meanwhile, the Council of Basel, in its schismatic phase, had defined the Immaculate Conception of Mary (1437). It was only in 1708, however, that Clement XI made the feast obligatory for the entire Roman rite. It officially became the feast

---

21. R. Lippe, *Missale Romanum Mediolani 1474* II. *A Collation with Other Editions Printed before 1570* (HBS 33; London: Henry Bradshaw Society, 1907) 208. Later on, the Mass promulgated by Sixtus IV was used.

22. Eadmer of Canterbury, *Tractatus de Conceptione s. Mariae*, ed. H. Thurston and T. Slater (Freiburg: Herder, 1904).

23. *Ep.* 174, in *Opera omnia*, ed. J. Leclercq and H. Rochais, 7 (Rome: Editiones Cistercienses, 1974) 388-92.

of the Immaculate Conception of Mary only after the dogmatic definition of 1854.

On orders from Sixtus IV, Leonardo Nogaroli, a cleric of the papal
household, composed a Mass which openly professed belief in the Immaculate Conception of Mary.[24] So clearly, in fact, did the opening prayer
of the Mass state the nature and foundation of Mary's privilege that it
inspired the Bull *Ineffabilis Deus* of Pius IX. Meanwhile, in 1570 the
Dominican Pope Pius V preferred to go back to a more general formula-
tion in the Missal which he promulgated. This new and rather colorless
Mass was to be in use until 1863. Pius X then commissioned the Mass
Gaudens gaudebo and the office of the Immaculate Conception, which
he promulgated with some solemnity.[25] The collect of Nogaroli's Mass
is here repeated almost word for word.

c) *Other feasts of Mary*—The end of the Middle Ages brought other
feasts of Mary: the Presentation in the Temple, the Sorrows of Mary, and
Our Lady of the Snow.

The Presentation of Mary in the Temple

The Jerusalem feast of the Entrance of the Blessed Mother of God into
the Temple, which was grafted onto the Dedication of New St. Mary's
(543), spread rapidly throughout the entire East. It celebrated the consecration of Mary to the service of the Lord.

Toward the middle of the fourteenth century, Philippe de Mézières,
a French knight, became an advocate of the feast in the West. This man,
a friend of Petrarch and Froissard, had lived in the East, especially on
Cyprus, and wanted a restoration of unity with the Greeks in order to
open the way to a new crusade. It was in this ecumenical spirit that he
sought the extension to the West of the feast of the Presentation of Mary,
which the Latins on Cyprus were already celebrating. The pope agreed
to the request in 1372. Philippe de Mézières worked upon the kings of
France and England to win their consent for the adoption of the new feast
in their territories.[26]

---

24. R. Lippe, *ibid*. 165–66. Lippe also reproduces the Mass composed by order of the
Council of Basel. The Mass is entitled "Mass Service for the Immaculate Conception of the
Virgin Mary," but the texts are quite general in character.

25. Pius IX, Brief *Quod iampridem* (September 25, 1863), SRC 3119.

26. W. E. Coleman, *Philippe de Mézières' Campaign for the Feast of Mary's Presentation* (Medieval Latin Texts; Toronto: Institute of Medieval Studies, 1981) 1–10. — I may
add that the oldest known image of Mary in Gaul is an engraving on marble that dates from
the fifth century; according to the inscription on it it represents *Maria Virgo minister de
tempulo Gerosale* ("The Virgin Mary serving in the temple at Jerusalem"). It is kept in the
crypt of St. Maximin in Provence; see J. Hubert, *L'Europe des invasions* (L'Univers des formes;
Paris: Gallimard, 1967) 17.

Our Lady of the Snow

The fourteenth century brought the spread of a legend regarding the building of St. Mary Major: its groundplan had supposedly been outlined by a snowfall in the middle of the Roman summer. Rusuti depicted the various phases of the event in the mosaic on the façade of the basilica. The legend ensured the success of the local feast of the Dedication of St. Mary Major (August 5), which, after having been extended to the other churches of Rome, became widely popular, especially in France. St. Pius VI placed it in the universal calendar in 1568.[27]

The Sorrows of Mary

Devotion to the sorrows of the Virgin Mary dates from the twelfth century, when it made its appearance in monastic circles under the influence of St. Anselm and St. Bernard. The Cistercians and then the Servites undertook to propagate it. It became widespread in the fourteenth and especially the fifteenth centuries, particularly in the Rhineland and Flanders, where Confraternities of the Sorrowful Mother sprang up. It was in this context that the first liturgical formularies in her honor were composed. A provincial council of Mainz in 1423 made use of these in establishing a "Feast of the Sorrows of Mary" in reparation for Hussite profanations of her images. In 1494 the feast appeared in Bruges, where the Precious Blood of Christ was venerated; later on it made its way into France. It did not, however, become widespread in France before Benedict XIII included it in the Roman Calendar in 1727 and assigned it to the Friday before Palm Sunday. Some Churches had previously celebrated it during the Easter season.[28] Others, however, celebrated the Joys of the Blessed Virgin during the Easter season, as is still done today at Braga. In some places the feast was entitled "Recollection of the Feasts and Joys of the Blessed Virgin Mary."[29]

d) *Liturgical Devotion to Mary*—The celebration of the Marian feasts did not exhaust medieval Christian devotion to Mary. The people of that time liked to express this love each day, and especially on Saturdays, in many different ways. Some of these belonged to the liturgy, while others were closely allied to it.

The Offices of the Blessed Virgin

In additions to the Marian Books of Hours that were so popular in the fifteenth century, two Offices of the Blessed Virgin Mary demand at-

---

27. The legend is given in M. Th. de Bussière, *Les sept basiliques de Rome* (Paris: Sirou, 1845) 2:59-60.

28. B. Capelle, "La liturgie mariale en Occident," in H. du Manoir, *Maria* 1:229-30.

29. A. P. Frutaz, "La *Recollectio festorum beatae Mariae virginis*," *EL* 70 (1955) 20-40.

tention by reason of their widespread use: the Office of Our Lady on Saturday and the Little Office of the Blessed Virgin.[30]

The Votive Missal compiled by Alcuin contained a Mass of the Blessed Virgin for Saturday.[31] This practice became so popular that Saturday was soon consecrated to Mary and received, in addition to a Mass, a complete office. In the eleventh century this office was in universal use.

In the eleventh and twelfth centuries this Saturday office was assigned for daily use in various religious families: the Cluniacs, Carthusians, Cistercians, and later the Dominicans adopted it in turn, adding it to the office of the day. Since it had only one nocturn it was called the Little Office of the Blessed Virgin. In the modern period many congregations and institutes adopted it as their only Liturgy of the Hours. This remained the case until Vatican Council II.

Prayers Addressed to Mary

First place among the prayers addressed to Mary belongs to the concluding antiphons of the office. They were sung originally at the end of Compline but were later placed also at the end of Lauds and Vespers. Four antiphons: *Alma Redemptoris Mater* ("Loving Mother of the Redeemer"), *Ave Regina coelorum* ("Hail, Queen of heaven"), *Regina coeli* ("Queen of heaven, rejoice"), and *Salve, Regina* ("Hail, [holy] Queen"), were already linked together in a decree of the general chapter of the Franciscans in 1249, but each of the four had a different origin.

The *Alma Redemptoris Mater*, with its rich melody, was probably from the pen of Hermann the Lame (Herimannus Contractus), a monk of Reichenau who died in the middle of the eleventh century. The *Ave Regina coelorum* was originally (twelfth century) connected with the feast of the Assumption, and its full meaning derives from that context.[32] The *Regina coeli*, which appeared in the same period, was sung at Easter Vespers. The most popular of the great antiphons has undoubtedly been the *Salve Regina*. Composed probably in the eleventh century, it spread quickly; Peter the Venerable prescribed its singing at Cluny as early as 1135. Later on, first among the Cistercians and then among the Dominicans, it provided the ending of Compline throughout the year.

The Middle Ages also brought a large number of hymns and sequences in honor of Mary. The most popular were: *Ave, maris stella* ("Hail, Star of the sea") (eighth–ninth century), *O quam glorifica* ("O, how glorious") (ninth century), *Salve, mater misericordiae* ("Hail, Mother of mercy")

---

30. B. Capelle, "La liturgie mariale en Occident," 234–45.

31. J. Deshusses, *Le Sacramentaire Grégorien* 2 (Spicilegium Friburgense 24; Freiburg: Universitätsverlag, 1979) 45.

32. B. Capelle, "*Ave Regina caelorum*," in his *Travaux Liturgiques* 3:302-4.

(fourteenth century?), and *Stabat mater dolorosa* ("At the cross her station keeping") (fourteenth century).

The best loved of all prayers to Mary, however, is the Hail Mary. It
entered the Roman liturgy in the form of an Offertory antiphon for Ember
Wednesday of Advent. The original text, which combined the greetings
of Elizabeth and the angel, began to spread in the tenth century. Only
at the very end of the Middle Ages was the second part, "Holy Mary,
Mother of God . . .," added, and the Hail Mary first appeared in its
definitive form in the Breviary of St. Pius V (1568).

The habit of reciting the Hail Mary in the morning, at noon and in
the evening was promoted by ringing the *Angelus* bell at those three times.
The evening bell, which the Romans still refer to as the *Ave Maria* bell,
is the oldest. The practice of ringing the bell at sunset was already very
widespread when in the thirteenth century, under Franciscan influence,
the faithful were urged to say three Hail Marys when they heard the bell.
This practice spread especially in France; Pope John XXII introduced it
at Rome in 1327. The bell was also rung in the morning at dawn; it seems
that the practice of saying three Hail Marys at this hour was begun at
Parma in 1317. The midday *Angelus* owed its origin to the king of France,
Louis IX, who ordered that the bells be rung at midday in order to remind the people to say three Hail Marys for the peace of the realm; this
decision was ratified by Pope Sixtus IV.[33]

e) *The feasts of St. Joseph and St. Anne*—In their origin the feasts of
St. Joseph and St. Anne are closely connected with the medieval development of the cult of Mary.

The cult of St. Joseph

The earliest mention of a cult of St. Joseph in the West is in the abridged
Martyrology of Rheinau, which was compiled in northern France in about
the year 800. March 19 carries the entry: *Ioseph sponsus Mariae* ("Joseph,
husband of Mary").[34] The mention of Joseph as husband of Mary or as
nutritor Domini ("educator/foster-parent of the Lord") then occurs with
increasing frequency from the ninth to the fourteenth centuries. It was
in the fifteenth century, however, that the cult of St. Joseph took a real
step forward under the influence of St. Bernardine of Siena, Pierre
d'Ailly, and, above all, John Gerson († 1420), who was chancellor of Notre
Dame in Paris and contributed greatly to fostering the desire for a feast
in honor of St. Joseph.

---

33. *Angelus Domini* (a pamphlet published by the Servites of Mary) (Rome: Curia
Generalis Ordinis Servorum Mariae, 1981) 14–16. See below, n. 54, p. 177.
34. A. Hänggi and A. Schönherr, *Sacramentarium Rheinaugense* (Spicilegium Friburgense
15; Freiburg: Universitätsverlag, 1970) 296.

According to Gerson, such a feast was already being celebrated on March 19 by the Augustinians of Milan and, on dates which he says he does not know, in many places in Germany. In France the feast seems to have been celebrated first at Chartres, as a feast of the Espousal (or Marriage) of Mary and Joseph, at the instigation of a canon who was a friend of Gerson. It was this canon who also composed the office for the feast. The feast of March 19 spread rapidly after 1480, when it was approved by Pope Sixtus IV. Gregory XV made it obligatory for the entire Roman rite in 1621.[35]

The cult of St. Anne

The Byzantine calendar lists the commemoration of Sts. Anne and Joachim on September 9, the Conception of St. Anne on December 9, and the Dormition of St. Anne on July 25. The choice of this last date may have been connected with the dedication of the basilica built in St. Anne's honor at Constantinople in about 550. The feast of the mother of Mary reached the West, however, only as a result of the crusades, for in the last years of the eleventh century French knights had built a basilica of St. Anne in Jerusalem near the Probatic Pool. The feast of July 25 was then celebrated in various places in the twelfth and thirteenth centuries, while it reached the height of its popularity in the fourteenth and fifteenth centuries. In 1378 Urban VI authorized its celebration in England. At that time the cult of St. Anne had already been known at Apt (France) for a century. The earliest Roman Missal to contain the feast was the Missal of 1505.[36] It is to be noted, however, that a Vatican Library manuscript of the eleventh century contains five responses and an antiphon for an office designated as "of St. Anne."[37] Pius V removed the name of St. Anne from the Roman Calendar of 1568, but Gregory XIII restored it in 1584.

2. *The Modern Development of Marian Feasts*

The end of the seventeenth century marked the beginning of a new phase in the liturgical cult of Mary, as feasts in her honor began to multiply. Some were motivated by historical events or memories. Others arose

---

35. M. Garrido Bonano,"San José en los calendarios y martirologios hasta el siglo XV inclusive," in *San Giuseppe nei primi quindici secoli della Chiesa. Atti del primo Simposio* (Studi e ricerche su s. Giuseppe, Collana diretta dal Centro Studi san Giuseppe, 1; Rome: Murialdo, 1971) 600–46; Bl. Burkey, "The Feast of St. Joseph, a Franciscan Bequest," *ibid.* 657–80.

36. R. Lippe, *ibid.* 2:216. On 187 Lippe reproduces a Mass in honor of Joachim the patriarch according to a missal of 1530.

37. Bibl. Vatic., ms. Vatic. lat. 651, f° 173ʳ; [G. Tomasi], *Responsorialia et antiphonaria Romanae Ecclesiae*, ed. J. M. Carus (Rome: Typis Vannacci, 1686) (= *Opera omnia*, ed. A. F. Vezzosi, 4:327-28).

at the insistence of religious families which sought to gain from the liturgy an increased renown for their particular forms of devotion to Mary. The best way of appreciating the range of these feasts may be to review them in the order of their inclusion in the Roman Calendar.

Seventeenth Century

Holy Name of Mary (Sunday after the Nativity of Mary)

An Office of the Holy Name of Mary had been granted by Pope Julius II to the diocese of Cuenca in Spain, whence it spread to a good many other areas. The feast was inscribed in the Roman Calendar by Blessed Innocent XI in 1683, in grateful remembrance of the liberation of Vienna by the Polish army of John Sobieski (September 12, 1683). St. Pius X assigned September 12 as the date of the feast.

Our Lady of Mercy (September 24)

The feast is linked to the origins of the Order of Mercedarians, which was founded in the thirteenth century for the ransom of Christians enslaved by the Moors and for the care of the victims of Saracen raids. But the feast itself dates only from the beginning of the seventeenth century, since until that time the Mercedarians had celebrated the Nativity of Mary as their patronal feast. Pope Innocent XII extended the feast to the entire Roman rite in 1696.

Eighteenth Century

Rosary of the Virgin Mary (first Sunday of October)

The feast was initially connected with the Confraternity of the Rosary, an institution inspired by the Dominicans and having for its purpose the propagation of devotion to the rosary. In 1571 Pope St. Pius V established a feast of Our Lady of Victory in thanksgiving for the victory which Don John of Austria had won over the Turks at Lepanto; the victory was attributed to the recitation of the rosary. As early as 1573 the next pope turned this feast into the feast of the Rosary of Mary and made it obligatory for the City of Rome. In 1716 Pope Clement XI extended the feast to the entire Roman rite in thanksgiving for the new victory which Prince Eugene of Savoie-Carignan had won over the Turks at Peterwardein. In 1913 the feast was assigned to October 7 (date of the battle of Lepanto).

Our Lady of Mount Carmel (July 16)

This feast was instituted by the Carmelites in about 1380, in thanksgiving for the cessation of the difficulties their Order had met when it was trying to establish itself in the West after having had to leave the Holy

Land. Pope Benedict XIII entered the feast in the Roman Calendar in 1726 in order to put an end to the historical controversies regarding the origins of the Order. According to Carmelite tradition, the Order would go back to the prophet Elijah.

We may recall in this context that the feast of the Conception of Mary was extended to the entire Roman rite by Clement XI in 1708 and that the feast of the Sorrows of Mary was similarly extended by Benedict XIII in 1727.

Nineteenth Century

Seven Sorrows of the Blessed Virgin (Third Sunday of September)

Devotion to the suffering of Mary took the form initially of contemplation of Mary beneath the cross (*Stabat Mater dolorosa*) but was then extended to embrace all of the sufferings which the Mother of Jesus experienced. At the end of the fifteenth century, the number seven emerged; in the spirit of that age, the seven sorrows were matched by seven joys. In 1668, the Servants of Mary (Servites) were granted permission to celebrate a feast of the Seven Sorrows of Mary on the Sunday following the feast of the Exaltation of the Holy Cross. When Pope Pius VII returned to Rome (1814) after his captivity at Fontainbleu, he extended this feast to the entire Roman rite, as an act of thanksgiving to the Virgin Mary for having safeguarded the Church through the trials of the preceding twenty years. In 1913 the feast was assigned to September 15.

Twentieth Century

The Apparition of the Immaculate Virgin Mary at Lourdes (February 11)

In 1907, on the eve of the fiftieth anniversary of the apparitions of Mary at Lourdes, St. Pius X entered the feast of the Apparition of the Immaculate Virgin Mary in the Roman Calendar. The feast had earlier been granted to the diocese of Tarbes by Pope Leo XIII in 1890.

The Motherhood of Mary (October 11)

This feast was instituted by Pope Pius XI in 1931 as a memorial of the fifteen-hundredth anniversary of the Council of Ephesus. It had already been approved for Portugal in 1751 by Pope Benedict XIV. The date chosen, October 11, was mistakenly thought to have been the date when the Council of Ephesus ended. John XXIII chose this same date for the opening of the Second Vatican Council (1962).

Immaculate Heart of Mary (August 22)

Devotion to the heart of Mary arose in the seventeenth century under the influence of St. John Eudes who won approval for a Mass in honor of the Immaculate Heart as early as 1646. Only during the nineteenth century, however, did the devotion blossom to some extent. In 1807 the Augustinians received permission to celebrate the Most Pure Heart of Mary on the Sunday within the octave of Ascension. In 1855 the Congregation of Rites approved a Mass peculiar to this feast, which Leo XIII subsequently extended to the whole diocese of Rome (1880). After consecrating the world to the Immaculate Heart of Mary in 1942, Pope Pius XII decided to perpetuate the memory of that act by making the feast obligatory throughout the Roman rite (1944).

Queenship of Mary (May 31)

From the early Middle Ages on Christians have greeted Mary as Queen of heaven and earth or, more simply, as "Our Lady." In 1954, the centenary of the proclamation of the Immaculate Conception as a dogma, Pius XII decided to make the title an official one, and he established the feast of Mary our Queen.

This list of the feasts of the Blessed Virgin that were instituted between 1683 and 1954 gives only a limited idea of the number of Marian feasts actually celebrated during the liturgical year in the majority of dioceses and religious congregations down to the reform of St. Pius X (1913) and even beyond that down to the reform of John XXIII.[38] In the Proper for Various Places, the Roman Gradual of 1908 gives melodies for the following feasts: Translation of the Holy House of Loretto (December 10), Expectation of the Childbirth of Mary (December 18), Marriage of Mary and Joseph (January 23), Our Lady of Good Counsel (April 26), Mary Help of Christians (May 24), Most Pure Heart of Mary (third Sunday after Pentecost), Our Lady of Perpetual Help (Sunday before June 24), Motherhood of Mary (second Sunday of October), Purity of Mary (third Sunday of October), Patronage of Mary (second Sunday of November), Manifestation of the Miraculous Medal (November 27).

§3. The Cult of Mary after the Second Vatican Council

BIBLIOGRAPHY

Pope Paul VI, Apostolic Exhortation *Marialis cultus* on Devotion to the Blessed

---

38. *Instructio de calendariis particularibus . . . ad normam et mentem Codicis rubricorum revisendis* 33, in *AAS* 53 (1961) 168–80.

Virgin Mary (February 2, 1974), *AAS* 66 (1974) 113–58, trans. in *The Pope Speaks* 19 (1974) 49–87.

P. Jounel, A. Carideo, E. Manfredini, and F. Brovelli, "Sollennità, feste e memorie della beata vergine Maria," in *Il Messale romano Vaticano II* (Quaderni di Rivista Liturgica, Nuova serie; Turin-Leumann: ElleDiCi, 1981) 2:61–192.

P. Jounel, "Le culte de Marie dans la liturgie romaine renovée," in *La liturgie expression de la foi (Conférences Saint-Serge, XXVe Semaine d'études liturgiques, Paris, 1978)* (Bibliotheca EL, Subsidia 16; Rome: Edizioni Liturgiche, 1979) 159–78.

In its Constitutions on the Liturgy and on the Church the Second Vatican Council taught that in Mary "the Church admires and exalts the most excellent fruit of redemption, and joyfully contemplates, as in a faultless image, that which she herself desires and hopes wholly to be."[39] In order that the cult of Mary might more clearly express this contemplative gaze of the Church and give surer guidance to the people of God in their prayer, it was appropriate (the Council said) that this cult be revised and reduced to its essential forms. The revision affected the calendar of Marian feasts, the readings for the Mass and office of the various feasts, and the prayers which Christians address to God through her intercession. In his Apostolic Exhortation *Marialis cultus* Pope Paul VI himself explained the main lines of this renewal of the liturgical cult paid to Mary. There he makes the point, in particular, that the overall renewal of the liturgy "makes it possible to include, in a more organic and closely knit fashion, the commemoration of Christ's Mother in the annual cycle of the mysteries of her Son."[40]

I. THE CALENDAR OF MARIAN FEASTS

Little has been eliminated from the calendar of Marian feasts, because the liturgical reformers wished to show respect for the variety of ways in which Christians like to express their veneration of the holy Mother of God. The only feasts actually removed from the calendar were the memorials of the Sorrows of Mary in Lent, the Holy Name of Mary, and Our Lady of Mercy. Of the remaining feasts two were turned into feasts primarily of the Lord himself, and the others were reorganized in order to bring out their relative importance.

Three solemnities celebrate the divine Motherhood of Mary, her Immaculate Conception, and her Assumption. The first of these, the Solemnity of Mary Mother of God, represents a restoration of the ancient Roman feast of the *Natale sanctae Mariae* on January 1.

---

39. *VSC* 103.

40. Paul VI, Apostolic Exhortation *Marialis cultus* 2, *AAS* 66 (174) 117; trans. in *The Pope Speaks* 19 (174) 52.

Next in order come the two feasts of the Nativity of Mary and the Visitation. The latter has been transferred to May 31, so that, in accordance with the narrative in St. Luke, it comes between the Annunciation of the Lord and the Nativity of John the Baptist.

There are now four obligatory memorials: the Presentation of Mary in the Temple, Our Lady of Sorrows, the Queenship of Mary, and Our Lady of the Rosary. The memorial of the Queenship of Mary has been transferred from May 31 to August 22, where it functions as a kind of octave day of the Assumption. An optional memorial honors the Immaculate Heart of Mary, and three others highlight the importance of three places of pilgrimage: Our Lady of Mount Carmel (in the Holy Land), the Dedication of St. Mary Major (in Rome), and Our Lady of Lourdes.

II. THE LECTIONARY OF THE MARIAN FEASTS

The principles governing the general revision of the Roman lectionary had to be applied to the readings for the Marian feasts. It was necessary, as far as possible, to avoid repeated use of the same passages, increase the number of pericopes, and make the increased number a matter of something other than what Paul VI called "random choice."[41] As a result, "only those readings have been accepted which can in different ways and degrees be considered Marian, either from the evidence of their content or from the results of careful exegesis, supported by the teachings of the magisterium or by solid tradition."[42] Chapter 8 of the Constitution *Lumen gentium*, which deals with the role of Mary "in the mystery of Christ and the Church," provided a model for such a liturgical reading of Scripture.

We may note, in particular, that this chapter makes no reference to the wisdom literature. Yet in the past this literature almost always supplied the first reading in Marian Masses and the Scripture readings in the Marian offices. On the other hand, the conciliar document emphasizes the passages of the prophets in which Mary, the Mother of the Messiah, appears as the Daughter of Zion, the image of the new Jerusalem, and the perfect exemplar of the poor and humble in Israel. The chapter in *Lumen gentium* also refers several times to the letters of Paul. The woman of whom the Son of God was born (Gal 4:4) was the first among Christians: as one who was predestined to be "holy and spotless" and who shared in the sufferings of the Redeemer, and as the model of the virtues that must shine forth in the lives of the baptized, she in her perfection marked the beginning of the Church.

---

41. *Ibid.* 12, *AAS* 125, *The Pope Speaks* 58.
42. *Ibid.*

All of the biblical texts to which the Council refers in its discussion of Mary occur in the lectionary for one or other of her feasts. The lectionary contains other texts as well, but these have been chosen in accordance with the same approach to the reading of the Old and New Testaments.

III. THE PRAYERS OF THE MARIAN FEASTS

Among the prayers proposed for the feasts of Mary there are, first of all, the prefaces. The medieval preface celebrating the divine motherhood of Mary has been supplemented by four others: a Common preface, which echoes the *Magnificat*; a preface for the Assumption, in which we find the language of the ancient prayer *Veneranda*; a preface for the Immaculate Conception, which is inspired by the conciliar passage on Mary as prefiguration of the Church; and, finally, among the votive Masses, a preface that speaks of Mary as Mother of the Church.

The place of Mary in the annual cycle of the mysteries of her Son emerges most clearly in the prayers of Advent and the Christmas season. Among the prayers from December 17 to December 24, in addition to the preface which speaks of the Virgin Mother who awaited the coming of Christ, we may note the texts for the Mass of the fourth Sunday of Advent, which is a real feast of the Annunciation, and several of the weekday opening prayers (December 17, 19, 20, 23). During the Christmas season, in which the Solemnity of Mary Mother of God occurs, the prayers for the Monday, Tuesday, and Saturday before Epiphany explicitly refer to Mary.

Two prayers, among others, show the new euchological style characteristic of the Marian feasts. On May 31 we ask the Lord: "Keep us open to the working of your Spirit, and with Mary may we praise you for ever." On September 15 we ask that, like Mary, the Church may be "united with Christ in his suffering and death, and so come to share in his rising to new life."

THE LITURGY OF THE HOURS

A. G. Martimort

GENERAL BIBLIOGRAPHY

A. Comprehensive Historical Studies

J. Cardinal Bona, *De divina psalmodia eiusque causis, mysteriis, et disciplinis.* Rome: Typis P. Collinii, 1653; 6th revised and enlarged ed., Paris: Billaine, 1663.

[G. Tomasi], *Responsorialia et antiphonaria Romanae ecclesiae . . . Accedit appendix varia continens monumenta vetera ad antiphonas, responsoria ecclesiasticosque cursus pertinentia* (Rome: Typis Vannacci, 1686. = *Opera omnia,* ed. A. F. Vezzosi, 4 [Rome: Typis Palladis, 1749]).

E. Martène, *Tractatus de antiqua Ecclesiae disciplina in divinis celebrandis officiis* (Lyons: Anisson, 1706). New enlarged edition in *De antiquis ecclesiae ritibus* 3 (Antwerp [= Milan], 1737; repr., Hildesheim: Georg Olms, 1969). See A. G. Martimort, *La documentation liturgique de Dom Eduard Martène* (ST 279; Vatican City, 1978) 449–508.

J. Grancolas, *Commentaire historique sur le bréviaire romain, avec les usages des autres Eglises particulières et principalement de l'Eglise de Paris* (2 vols. Paris: P. Lottin, 1727).

P. Batiffol, *History of the Roman Breviary,* trans. A. M. Y. Baylay (New York: Longmans, Green, 1912).

S. Bäumer, *Geschichte des Breviers* (Freiburg: Herder, 1895). French trans. by R. Biron, *Histoire du bréviaire* (2 vols. Paris: Letouzey, 1905).

V. Leroquais, *Les bréviaires manuscrits des bibliothèques publiques de France* (6 vols. Mâcon: Protat, 1936).

H. Bohatta, *Bibliographie der Breviere 1501–1850* (Leipzig: Hiersemann, 1937, reprinted Stuttgart: Hiersemann, 1983).

A. Baumstark, *Comparative Liturgy,* revised by B. Botte, trans. F. L. Cross (Westminster, Md.: Newman, 1958).

C. Callewaert, *Sacris erudiri. Fragmenta liturgica collecta a monachis S. Petri de Aldenburgo in Steenbrugge ne pereant* (Steenbrugge: St.-Pietersabdij, 1940).

M. Righetti, *Manuale di storia liturgica. 2. L'anno liturgico; Il breviario* (Milan: Ancora, 1947). 2nd, revised and corrected ed., 1955; 3rd, corrected and enlarged ed., 1969.

J. A. Jungmann, *Pastoral Liturgy* (New York: Herder and Herder, 1962) 105–213. Articles published in *ZKT* 1950–56.

J. Pascher, *Das Stundengebet der römischen Kirche* (Munich: Zink, 1954).

153

Brevierstudien. Referate aus der Studientagung von Assisi 14–17 September 1956, ed. J. A. Jungmann (Trier: Paulinus Verlag, 1958).

V. Raffa, *La Liturgia delle Ore* (Bibliotheca di scienze religiose, sezione III, La liturgia 6; Brescia: Morcelliana, 1959).

P. Salmon, *The Breviary through the Centuries*, trans. Sr. Mary David (Collegeville: The Liturgical Press, 1962).

La Maison-Dieu no. 64 (1960): *Priez sans cesse* (main articles by A. Hamman, P. Rouillard, I. H. Dalmais, J. Mateos, and J. Leclercq).

P. Salmon, "La prière des heures," in *L'Eglise en prière* (Tournai: Desclée, 1961) 787–876; 2nd ed. (1962) 787–876; 3rd ed. (1965) 809–902.

Mgr. Cassien and B. Botte, *La prière des heures* (Lex orandi 35; Paris: Cerf, 1963), with contributions from J. Jeremias, K. Hruby, B. Fischer, O. Rousseau, B. Capelle, H. Marot, A. Renoux, A. Kniazeff, J. Mateos, H. Brandreth, M. Thurian, and D. Webb.

P. Salmon, *L'office divin au moyen âge. Histoire de la formation du bréviaire du IXᵉ au XVIᵉ siècle* (Lex orandi 43; Paris: Cerf, 1967).

_____, *Les manuscrits liturgiques latins de la Bibliothèque Vaticane 1. Psautiers, antiphonaires, hymnaires, collectaires, bréviaires* (ST 251; Vatican City: Bibliotheca Apostolica Vaticana, 1968).

P. F. Bradshaw, *Prayer in the Early Church. A Study of the Origin and Early Development of the Divine Office* (Alcuin Club Collections 63; London: SPCK, 1983).

B. Official documents regarding the reform of the office as decreed by Vatican II

Second Vatican Council, *Constitutio de sacra liturgia Sacrosanctum Concilium* (December 4, 1963), in *AAS* 56 (1964) 97–138 (= *EDIL*, nos. 1–131); trans. in A. Flannery, *Vatican Council II. The Conciliar and Postconciliar Documents* (Collegeville: The Liturgical Press, 1975).

Paul VI, *Constitutio apostolica Laudis Canticum* (November 1, 1970), in *AAS* 56 (1964) 527–35 (= *EDIL* nos. 2196–2214). Printed in Volume 1 of the Liturgy of the Hours.

The Liturgy of the Hours according to the Roman Rite, trans. The International Commission on English in the Liturgy (4 vols. New York: Catholic Book Publishing Co., 1975ff.). The Latin original was published by the Vatican Press, 1971–72. The decree of promulgation by the Congregation for Divine Worship was dated April 11, 1971 (= *EDIL* no. 2538).

General Instruction of the Liturgy of the Hours (GILH), printed at the beginning of Volume I of the *Liturgy of the Hours* (= *EDIL* nos. 2253–2537).

Notificatio SCCD de Liturgia Horarum pro quibusdam communitatibus religiosis (August 6, 1972), in *Notitiae* 8 (1972) 254–58 (= *EDIL* nos. 2865–72).

C. Commentaries on these documents, and studies of the present Liturgy of the Hours

E. J. Lengeling, "Liturgia Horarum. Zur Neuordnung des kirchlichen Stundengebets," *Liturgisches Jahrbuch* 20 (1970) 141–60, 231–49.

V. Raffa, *Istruzione generale sulla Liturgia delle Ore. Versione italiana e commento* (Nuova collana liturgica 2; Milan: Edizioni O. R., 1971).

_____, *La nuova Liturgia della Ore. Presentazione storica, teologica e pastorale* (Nuova collana liturgica 3; Milan: Edizioni O. R., 1971). The books of V. Raffa enjoy a special authority, since he was secretary of the commission that compiled the *Liturgy of the Hours*.

A. M. Roguet, *The Liturgy of the Hours. The General Instruction on the Liturgy of the Hours, with a Commentary,* trans. Peter Coughlin and Peter Purdue (Collegeville: The Liturgical Press, 1971).

L. Trimeloni, *La preghiera del popolo di Dio. Tempo di preghiera* (Turin: Marietti, 1971).

Ephemerides liturgicae 85 (1971) 177–232: Liturgia Horarum (articles by C. Braga, V. Raffa, J. Pascher, A. Rose, H. Ashworth); 86 (1972) 5–73: *Liturgia Horarum II* (articles by A. Rose, P. Jounel, V. Raffa, E. Lodi).

La Maison-Dieu no. 105 (1971) 1–179: La liturgie des Heures: Le renouveau de *l'Office divin* (main articles by E. J. Lengeling, J. Leclercq, A. Rose, C. Wiener, G. Raciti, C. de Bourmont).

Seminarium. Commentarii pro seminariis 24 (1972) 1–184: De Liturgia Horarum in *sacerdotali formatione* (articles by G. Card. Garrone, J. Leclercq, S. Mazzarello, V. Raffa, A. G. Martimort, J. Pascher, M. Card. Pellegrino, I. Rogger, W. G. Wheeler, T. Minisci, A. Raes).

Liturgia delle Ore. Documenti ufficiali e studi (Quaderni di Rivista liturgica 14; Turin-Leumann: ElleDiCi, 1972). (Articles by A. Amore, H. Ashworth, B. Baroffio, F. Dell'Oro, A. Dumas, E. J. Lengeling, M. Magrassi, A. G. Martimort, V. Meloni, F. Morlot, J. Pascher, J. Pinell, V. Raffa, P. Visentin).

R. Falsini, *Liturgia delle Ore: Struttura, spirito del nuovo Ufficio* (Milan: Ed. Opera delle Regalita, 1973).

D. de Reynal, *Théologie de la Liturgie des Heures* (Beauchesne Religions; Paris: Beauchesne, 1978).

La Maison-Dieu no. 135 (1978) 4–174: *Prier en Eglise* (main articles by D. de Reynal, P. Jounel, J. Dubois, J. Evenou, J. Gelineau, B. Fischer).

La Maison-Dieu no. 143 (1980) 4–172: *Richesse de la prière des Heures.*

T. Schnitzler, *Was das Stundengebet bedeutet. Hilfe zum geistlichen Neubeginn* (Freiburg: Herder, 1980).

As the week and the year, so the day is sanctified by recurring prayer:

> Christ taught us: "You must pray at all times and not lose heart" (Lk 18:1). The Church has been faithful in obeying this instruction; it never ceases to offer prayer and makes this exhortation its own: "Through him (Jesus) let us offer to God an unceasing sacrifice of praise" (Heb 15:15). The Church fulfills this precept not only by celebrating the eucharist but in other ways also, especially through the liturgy of the hours. By ancient Christian tradition what distinguishes the liturgy of the hours from other liturgical services is that it consecrates to God the whole cycle of the day and the night.[1]

"Liturgy of the Hours" is the name henceforth to be used for this prayer, in preference to "Divine Office" (literally: "divine duty"), which even Vatican II still used. The praise of God is certainly a duty to be carried out; St. Benedict spoke of *Opus Dei,* the "work of God."[2] But the thing that characterizes the Liturgy of the Hours and distinguishes it from other

---

1. *GILH* 10; see *VSC* 84.
2. J. Neufville, "Concordance verbale," in *Régle de saint Benoît* 2 (SC 182; Paris: Cerf, 1972) 790–91.

liturgical actions is that it is distributed throughout the day, thus creating privileged moments which help direct all activities toward the ideal of ceaseless prayer.

With all the greater reason has the term "breviary" been abandoned, although it had become habitual in the Latin Church. A *breviarium* was literally an abridgment and yielded its true meaning only when given its full form, *Breviarium Officii.* In the Middle Ages the *Breviarium* was the name for a book which brought together for convenience in celebration or recitation all the parts which make up the office and which had previously been scattered in several different books.[3] The Eastern Churches give the name *Horologion* to the book which is the basis of their daily office.[4]

---

3. P. Salmon, *The Breviary through the Centuries*, trans. Sr. Mary David (Collegeville: The Liturgical Press, 1962) 26-27.

4. *La prière des Eglises de rite byzantin* I. *La prière des Heures. Horologion* (Chevetogne, 1975), 49-56.

Chapter I

The Hours of Prayer

The Liturgy of the Hours had its origin in the spiritual ideal of ceaseless prayer that is set before us by the New Testament. An effort was made to achieve this ideal by setting aside times for prayer throughout the day. The pattern followed by spiritual-minded groups in the early centuries was based on Jewish usage but also and above all on the example of Jesus himself and of the apostolic community.

§1. Jewish Prayer in the Time of Christ

BIBLIOGRAPHY

A. Hamman, *La prière*. I. *Le Nouveau Testament* (Bibliothèque de théologie; Tournai: Desclée, 1959).

A. Arens, *Die Psalmen im Gottesdienst des Alten Bundes* (2 vols. Trier: Paulinus Verlag, 1961 and 1968).

K. Hruby, "Les heures de prière dans le judaisme à l'époque de Jésus," in Cassien and Botte (see General Bibliography) 59–84.

C. W. Dugmore, *The Influence of the Synagogue upon the Divine Office* (Alcuin Club Collections 45; London: Faith Press, 1964), espec. 59–70.

P. Billerbeck, "Ein Tempelgottesdienst in Jesu Tagen," *Zeitschrift für die neutestamentliche Wissenschaft* 55 (1964) 1–17; "Ein Synagogengottesdienst in Jesu Tagen," *ibid.* 143–61.

H. Haag, "Das liturgische Leben der Qumrangemeinde," *ALW* 10 (1967) 78–109.

J. van Goudoever, "L'arrière-plan liturgique du psautier," *QL* 52 (1971) 79–85.

J. Jeremias, *The Prayers of Jesus*, trans. John Bowden *et al.* (Philadelphia: Fortress, 1978 [1967]) 66–72.

R. T. Beckwith, "The Daily and Weekly Worship of the Primitive Church in Relation to its Jewish Antecedents," *QL* 62 (1981) 5–20, 83–105.

Although the development of Christian public worship was accompanied by a more or less rapid break with the liturgy of the temple and the observances of the old Law, there was nonetheless a continuity in the pattern of prayer. This was doubtless due to the fact that the early communities were made up of Jewish Christians. It was due also, and above all, however, to the fact that the Bible was constantly read and meditated on. Finally, it was in the framework of Jewish prayer life that Christ and the apostles did their praying.

In studying this matter we must avoid proceeding anachronistically and reading back into the age of Jesus regulations and texts that are proper to later Judaism. It is possible, nonetheless, to reach a high degree of certainty about the practices of Jesus' time, especially since these went back to a much earlier period.

Jewish prayer followed two rhythms that differed in origin and kind but nonetheless finally fused into one. One rhythm was based on the prescription in Deuteronomy: morning and evening, "when you lie down and when you rise," all of the faithful were to recite the *Shema*: "Hear, O Israel: The Lord our God is one Lord; and you shall love the Lord your God with all your heart, and with all your soul, and with all your might" (Deut 6:4; see 6:7; 11:19). The commentaries of the rabbis as well as numerous other documents confirm this prescription regarding times for prayer. The choice of times was based initially on the rhythm of human life—retiring and rising—but it was subsequently related by preference to the rhythm of nature: nightfall and dawn. This development may have taken place first in sects and only then been accepted by the teachers of the Mishnah.[1]

But in addition to this first pattern there was a second which involved three times of prayer during the day. It is already attested in the Book of Daniel and therefore in the third century B.C. When Daniel learned of the king's decree forbidding all prayer that was not addressed exclusively to him, "he went into his house where he had windows in his upper chamber open toward Jerusalem; and he got down upon his knees three times a day and prayed and gave thanks before his God, as he had done previously" (Dan 6:11, see 14). The same practice is found in the Book of Judith (9:1; 12:5-6; 13:3). There may be an allusion to it in Ps 55:16-17: "I call upon God; and the Lord will save me. Evening and morning and at noon I utter my complaint and moan, and he will hear my voice." Tractate Berakoth of the Mishnah (middle of the second century A.D.) appoints

---

1. The most important texts may be found in the articles of J. Jeremias and K. Hruby in Mgr. Cassien and B. Botte, *La prière des heures* (Lex orandi 35; Paris: Cerf, 1963) 45–48 and 76–81.

these three times for the saying of the Tephillah ("Prayer") which, in its later form, becomes the prayer of the "Eighteen Blessings."[2]

It is likely that this practice originated in Pharisaic circles; it was connected with the daily liturgy in the temple, although that liturgy had only two parts: morning sacrifice and evening sacrifice (Exod 29:30-42; 1 Chr 16:40; 23:30; 2 Chr 13:11; 2 Kgs 16:15; Ezra 9:4; Dan 9:2l). The evening sacrifice was gradually brought forward to the ninth hour (about 3 p.m.). The offering of sacrifices was accompanied by the singing of psalms by the Levites, with certain psalms being linked especially with particular days.[3] A more or less sizable number of the faithful of Jerusalem used to take part in this liturgy, especially in the afternoon (evening) sacrifice. The somewhat idealized description in Sir 50:1-21 can be checked against Luke 1:10-21 ("The whole multitude of the people were praying outside" while Zechariah was offering the sacrifice of incense) and Acts 3:1 ("Peter and John were going up to the temple at the hour of prayer, the ninth hour").

Outside of Jerusalem and at the same hours, but not every day, devout Jews used to unite themselves in intention with the worship in the temple by gathering in the synagogue. Finally, at the time of the evening sacrifice, those in Jerusalem and elsewhere who were not present at the liturgy would pray privately, as Cornelius the centurion was to do (Acts 10:3-30); they would do so even in the streets and public squares, a practice rendered easier in Jerusalem by the sounding of trumpets in the temple (Sir 50:16; Tamid 7, 3). The "hypocrites" whom Jesus criticizes for loving "to stand and pray in the synagogues and at the street corners, that they may be seen by men" (Matt 6:5), are faulted not because they pray in public but because they pretend to be accidentally caught at the street corner when the time for prayer arrives.

The third time for prayer corresponded to the closing of the temple gates in the evening and thus had a less solid basis than the other two. In any case, the custom of observing three moments of prayer was well established as early as the New Testament period, when the Tephillah was now added by devout Jews to the recitation of the *Shema* morning and evening, while at the time of the afternoon sacrifice they recited the Tephillah alone.

Other moments of prayer were observed on certain fast days or feast days, at least in devout circles; in addition, communities and sects had their own special practices. The most important point to be made,

---

2. There is a study of this prayer in H. L. Strack and P. Billerbeck, *Kommentar zum Neuen Testament aus Talmud and Midrasch* 4 (Munich: Beck, 1928) 208-49. An English translation is given in Lucien Deiss, *Springtime of the Liturgy: Liturgical Texts of the First Four Centuries*, trans. M. J. O'Connell (Collegeville: The Liturgical Press, 1979) 9-14.

3. See below, pp. 191-192.

however, is that the ideal of more frequent prayer and of almost constant meditation on the Law was repeatedly set before the minds of fervent Jews by the psalms, especially Ps 119. The psalms exerted an influence on the spirituality of the people of Israel that extended far beyond the matter of ritual prayer; they were also the object of religious teaching and personal meditation.

It was out of this praying people that Jesus Christ emerged.

§2. The Example of the Prayer of Jesus

BIBLIOGRAPHY

A. Hamman, *La prière*. I. *Le Nouveau Testament* (Bibliothèque de théologie; Tournai: Desclée, 1959) 78–94, 383–404.
J. Jeremias, "La prière quotidienne dans la vie du Seigneur et dans l'Eglise primitive," in Cassien-Botte (see General Bibliography) 43–55.
J. Dupont, "Jésus et la prière liturgique," *LMD* no. 95 (1968) 16–49.
J. Jeremias, *The Prayers of Jesus*, trans. John Bowden *et al.* (Philadelphia: Fortress, 1978 [1967]) 66–81, "Daily Prayer in the Life of Jesus and the Primitive Church." (The essay is described as a completely revised and expanded form of the lecture published in Cassien-Botte.)
―――――――, *New Testament Theology*. 1. *The Proclamation of Jesus*, trans. John Bowden (New York: Scribner's, 1971) 184–203.
GILH 3–4.

Many details in the gospel show us that Jesus was faithful to the religious practices of his fellow Jews. Thus he participated, "as his custom was," in the assemblies in the synagogue (Luke 4:16; see Mark 1:21); when a scribe asked him what is the first of the commandments, he answered by referring to the *Shema* in the form he must have used himself: "Hear, O Israel . . . ." (Mark 12:29-30). He alluded to the prayer of the ninth hour, probably in the parable of the Pharisee and the tax collector (Luke 18:9-14) and more clearly when he criticized the hypocrites who ostentatiously prayed at the street corners (Matt 6:5). He recited the traditional blessings addressed to God at mealtimes, as we are explicitly told in connection with the multiplication of the loaves (Matt 14:19; 15:36, par), the Last Supper (Matt 26:26 par), and the supper at Emmaus (Luke 24:30). He also sang "hymns" with his disciples (Matt 26:30 par).

But, as J. Jeremias remarks, "the prayer life of Jesus went much beyond what was then generally customary."[4] The gospels frequently tell us of occasions when Jesus went apart from the crowd in order to pray. This

---

4. J. Jeremias, in Cassien-Botte 51.

is a point constantly emphasized by Luke, who may be regarded as the evangelist of prayer: the prayer of Jesus, the prayer of Mary, and, later on, the prayer of the Christian community.

Thus at Capernaum, after Jesus had cured Simon Peter's mother-in-law and had seen the entire town gathered at the door of the house, "in the morning, a great while before day, he rose and went out to a lonely place, and there he prayed." Simon, his host, and the other companions set out to look for him (Mark 1:35-36). After the cure of a leper, the people began to speak more and more of him, and great crowds gathered to listen to him and seek healing for their illnesses: "but he withdrew to the wilderness and prayed" (Luke 5:16). Similarly, after the multiplication of the loaves, he sent the crowd away and "went into the hills to pray" (Mark 6:46). On this occasion Matthew adds that he was alone and that it was "the fourth watch of the night" when he rejoined the apostles by walking to them on the water (14:23, 25).

Before the appointment of the Twelve, and as it were by way of preparation for this important choice, Jesus watched and prayed, as Luke tells us: "He went out into the hills to pray; and all night he continued in prayer to God" (6:12). Matthew (9:37-38) has the choice of the Twelve preceded not by prayer on the part of Jesus himself but by an exhortation to the disciples: "Pray . . . the Lord of the harvest to send out laborers into his harvest."

Luke again tells us of Jesus' prayer in connection with the Transfiguration: on that occasion Jesus "took with him Peter and John and James, and went up on the mountain to pray. And as he was praying, the appearance of his countenance was altered" (Luke 9:28-29). The Master's solitude was therefore not always complete, since at times some privileged disciples were witnesses of his prayer. This was also the case (still according to Luke) on the occasion of the confession of faith at Caesarea: "Now it happened that as he was praying (*proseuchomenon*) alone (*kata monas*) the disciples were with him; and he asked them . . . ." (Luke 9:18). Or, again, when Jesus taught his disciples the Our Father: "He was praying in a certain place (*en topō tini proseuchomenon*), and when he ceased, one of his disciples said to him, 'Lord, teach us to pray, as John taught his disciples'" (Luke 11:1).

According, then, to the testimony of Jesus' disciples,

> the work of each day was closely bound up with his prayer, indeed flowed out from it . . . . To the very end of his life, as his passion was approaching [John 12:27ff.], at the last supper [John 17:1-26], in the agony in the garden [Matt 26:36-44 par], and on the cross [Luke 23:34, 46; Matt 27:46; Mark 15:34], the divine teacher showed that prayer was the soul of his Messianic ministry and paschal death.[5]

---

5. *GILH* 4.

Jesus was pointing to his own example when he asked his disciples to watch and pray. Nor was the request simply an urgent appeal to the witnesses of his agony that they should share his painful vigil and forearm themselves against temptation (Mark 14:38; Matt 26:41; Luke 22:40-46). It was also, and even more, an eschatological sign: the waiting for the Master, the Spouse, to come in the night. "Watch at all times, praying that you may have strength to escape all these things that will take place, and to stand before the Son of man" (Luke 21:36; see Mark 13:33). "At all times": the prayer Jesus asks of his followers must be constant and persevering. *Pros to dein pantote proseuchesthai kai mē egkakein*—"They ought always to pray and not lose heart" (Luke 18:1). This would be the ideal of the first Christian community, and Paul would often remind them of it.

§3. The Ideal of the Apostolic Community: Ceaseless Prayer

BIBLIOGRAPHY

L. Cerfaux, "La première communauté chrétienne," *Ephemerides Theologicae Lovanienses* 16 (1939) 5–31 = *Recueil Lucien Cerfaux* 2 (Gembloux: Duculot, 1954) 125–56.

_____, "La prière dans le christianisme primitif," in *La prière* (Problèmes de la vie religieuse aujourd'hui; Paris: Cerf, 1958) 39–49 = *Recueil Lucien Cerfaux* 3 (Gembloux: Duculot, 1962) 253–62.

A. Hamman, *La prière* 1:170-337.

J. Jeremias, *The Prayers of Jesus*, trans. John Bowden *et al.* (Philadelphia: Fortress, 1978 [1967]) 78–81.

After the Savior's ascension and down to the time when the community of disciples was scattered by persecution, the followers of Jesus continued to attend the temple regularly. Thus Luke, who had begun the gospel story with an account of the annunciation to Zechariah in the temple (Luke 1:9-22), ends with a picture of the apostles "continually in the temple praising God" (24:53). Then, in the first of the summaries in the Book of Acts (2:46), he shows the new believers "day by day, attending the temple together." It was in the porches of the temple that the apostles taught and proclaimed the good news that Jesus is the Christ (Acts 5:42; 21:27). Meanwhile, all went to the temple especially for the prayer at the ninth hour; it was on this occasion that Peter and John invoked the name of Jesus to heal the crippled beggar at the Beautiful Gate (Acts 3:1-2).

Although the point is not explicitly stated, there is reason to think that the apostles and their converts were faithful not only to the prayer of the ninth hour but to all three of the moments for daily prayer among the

Jews. The *Didache* (a document not easy to date but which may be very close in time to the first generations of Christians) formally prescribes that the faithful pray three times a day, although it replaces the Jewish formulas with the Our Father.[6] This testimony seems to be indirectly confirmed by the fact that the Synoptic writers cite the *Shema* only in loose and divergent ways (Mark 12:30-33; Matt 2:37; Luke 10:27). This manner of citation would show that by the time these men were writing, the *Shema* was no longer a memorized liturgical text.[7]

Thus, while retaining the times appointed for prayer among the Jews, Christians used these in the new spirit taught by Jesus. But they were not satisfied with these traditional liturgical practices. At Joppa, for example, Peter went up to the roof at about the sixth hour in order to pray (Acts 10:9); this was not one of the usual times for Jews to pray. The vision which Peter received on this occasion played a key role in the acceptance of Gentiles into the Church and, in consequence, made this moment of the day memorable.

On several occasions the Acts of the Apostles mentions prayer at night. In Jerusalem the community prayed through the night for Peter who was in prison (Acts 12:5-12). At Troas the regular liturgy on the day after the sabbath took place in the evening and was prolonged until after midnight, although this may have been because it was Paul's farewell liturgy (Acts 20:7-11). In the prison of Philippi, "about midnight Paul and Silas were praying and singing hymns, and the prisoners were listening to them" (Acts 16:25). Were all of these only vigils on special occasions, or did they represent rather a regular form of fidelity to the example and teaching of Jesus?

These scattered indications do not, however, suffice to make clear the new dimensions of Christian prayer. There were two ideals in particular that this prayer was to meet: it was to be an expression of unanimity and it was to be constant and persevering.

Unanimous: *homothumadon*. This is a word Luke uses often in connection with prayer (Acts 1:14; 2:46; 4:24), and Paul uses it as well (Rom 15:6). Unanimity existed even when the disciples were not assembled (*epi to auto*), for "the company of those who believed were of one heart and soul" (Acts 4:32).

---

6. *La Doctrine des douze Apôtres (Didache)* 8, 2-3, ed. W. Rordorf and A. Tuilier, (SC 248; Paris: Cerf, 1978) 172-75. But J. Daniélou, *The Theology of Jewish Christianity*, trans. John Baker (Chicago: Regnery, 1964) 339-40, disputes the assimilation of the prescription in the *Didache* to classical Jewish practice and connects it rather with the Essene *Manual of Discipline*.

7. J. Jeremias, *The Prayers of Jesus*, trans. John Bowden *et al.* (Philadelphia: Fortress, 1978 [1967]) 80-81. — May we, with J. Jeremias, *ibid.*, hear in Phil 1:3-4 ("I thank my God in all my remembrance of you, always in every prayer of mine for you all making my prayer with joy") the echo of an intercession which replaces or complements a Christian *tephillah*?

Constant, persevering: this is the other characteristic of the prayer practiced by the apostolic community. The little group that gathered after the ascension—Mary, the apostles, and a few of the brethren—remained "in the upper room," where "with one accord they devoted themselves to [literally: were persevering in, *proskarterountes*] prayer" (Acts 1:14). The same perseverance or constancy manifested itself when the community expanded after Pentecost: "they devoted themselves to [were *proskarterountes* in] the apostles' teaching and fellowship, to the breaking of bread and the prayers" (Acts 2:42). Admittedly, the Acts of the Apostles presents a somewhat idealized Church, but the historian of the liturgy must be aware of the importance this ideal had for later Christian generations in their concern for the *vita apostolica* or "apostolic life," that is, for the imitation of the community described in the Acts of the Apostles.

In any case, St. Paul, too, frequently exhorts his readers to persevere (*proskarteroun*) in prayer (Rom 12:12; Col 4:2; Eph 6:18) and thus carries on the teaching of Jesus. What he is speaking of is not simply fidelity to appointed times for prayer; rather, he says, "pray constantly [*adialeiptōs proseuchesthe*]" (1 Thess 5:17), "at all times [*en panti kairō*]" (Eph 6:18). He even seems to allude to vigils: "Pray at all times in the Spirit, with all prayer and supplication. To that end keep alert [*agrupnountes*, keeping awake, keeping watch] with all perseverance, making supplications for all the saints, and also for me" (Eph 6:18-19; see Col 4:2). He says that he himself prays night and day (1 Thess 3:10; 2 Thess 1:11). Whatever be the precise meaning Paul attaches to these various phrases, he sets forth a spiritual program which Christians would henceforth seek to carry out. In their view, the times of prayer would be regarded as only the privileged expression and reminder of a prayer that endeavors to be ceaseless.

§4. The Hours of Christian Prayer and Their Symbolism in the Church of the Third Century

BIBLIOGRAPHY

P. Salmon, "Les origines de la prière des heures d'après le témoignage de Tertullien et de saint Cyprian," in *Mélanges offerts à Mademoiselle Christine Mohrmann* (Utrecht: Spectrum, 1963) 202–10.

A. Hamann, *La prière* II. *Les trois premiers siècles* (Bibliothèque de théologie; Paris: Desclée, 1963).

B. Botte, "Les heures de prière dans la *Tradition apostolique* et les documents dérivés," in Cassien-Botte 101–15.

V. Raffa, "L'orario di preghiera nell'ufficio divino," *QL* 80 (1966) 97–140.

J. Pinell, "El número sagrado de las horas de Oficio," in *Miscellanea liturgica in onore di Sua Eminenza il cardinale Giacomo Lercaro* 2 (Rome: Desclée, 1967) 887–934.

The Church of the first half of the third century was characterized by an intense spiritual fervor. This is evidenced by the advice on prayer that has been preserved in the writings of five Christian authors: Book 7 of the *Stromata* ("Tapestries") of Clement of Alexandria († 211/215), the books *On Prayer* and *On Fasting* of Tertullian, an African († after 220), the *Apostolic Tradition* of Hippolytus of Rome, the treatise *On Prayer* which Origen of Alexandria wrote in 233–34, and, finally, the book *On the Lord's Prayer* which St. Cyprian, bishop of Carthage, composed, probably in 250, in the leisure forced upon him when he went into hiding during a persecution.

All of these teachers emphasize the command given by both the Lord and Paul that Christians must pray uninterruptedly. Thus Clement observes in his hermetic manner: "The gnostic prays throughout life."[8] Tertullian writes: "No precept has been set down regarding times of prayer, except that we are to pray at all times and in all places."[9] Hippolytus, for his part, says: "You cannot be tempted or be lost if you are always mindful of Christ."[10] Origen speaks even more clearly: "The adverse powers insinuate an evil spirit in the souls of those who neglect prayer and do not heed what Paul, following the exhortations of Jesus, asks us to do: pray without ceasing."

All these writers agree, however, that if prayer is to be ceaseless there must be set times for prayer. Origen continues:

> There is only one way of understanding how such a precept can be fulfilled: if the entire life of the saint is a single unbroken prayer and if part of this prayer is prayer in the stricter sense and is made at least (*ouk elatton*) three times a day, as demonstrated by Daniel who prayed three times a day despite the peril threatening him. Or by Peter who went up on the roof at the sixth hour to pray and in a vision saw a cloth, suspended from its four corners, being let down from heaven. This was the second of the three prayers of which David speaks (Ps 54:17-18), the first being: "In the morning you hear my voice, in the morning I make ready for you and abide in watchfulness" (Ps 5:4), and the last of the three being referred to in the words: "My uplifted hands as an evening sacrifice" (Ps 140:2). But even the night we do not allow to pass without prayer, since David says (Ps 118:62): "In the midst of the night I arise and give thanks to you for your just decrees," and Paul, according to Acts, prayed in the night with Silas and praised God, so much so that those in prison listened to him.[11]

---

8. Clement of Alexandria, *Stromata* VII, 40, 3, ed. O. Stählin (GCS 17:30).

9. Tertullian, *De oratione* 24 (CCL 1:272); see *De ieiunio* 170, 3 (CCL 2:1267): "With utter indifference we must pray always and everywhere and at all times."

10. Hippolytus, *Traditio apostolica* 41, ed. B. Botte, *La Tradition apostolique de saint Hippolyte. Essai de reconstitution* (LGF 39; Münster: Aschendorff, 1963) 96–97.

11. Origen, *De oratione* 12 (PG 11:452-53).

Origen is convinced that in adopting this practice he is being faithful to the pattern of prayer which he sees in the Old and New Testaments. At least he is faithful perhaps, without realizing it, to Jewish custom; on the other hand, he does add the typically Christian exhortation to pray during the night.

As a matter of fact, by this time Christians at Alexandria, Carthage, and, perhaps, Rome, had for several decades now been following the practice of praying at the third, sixth, and ninth hours (about 9 a.m., 12 noon, and 3 p.m. by our clocks[12]), but this practice cannot be assimilated to the Jewish horarium. For Clement the threefold division of the day with its three times for prayer symbolizes "the three degrees of the heavenly dwellings."[13] Tertullian, however, is the writer who doubtless gives the decisive reason for this choice of times: "These are the hours that stand out most in human life, since they divide up the day, establish the rhythm of business, and are signaled by the public bells (*publice resonant*)." Moreover, they are not simply "important hours in communal life, distinguishing as they do the parts of the day." They are also "the most important hours in the scriptures," since it was at the third hour that the Spirit was poured out on the assembled apostles for the first time, while the sixth hour was the hour of the vision at Joppa, and the ninth was the hour when Peter cured the paralytic man. While these examples impose no obligation, "it is nonetheless good to set up a kind of program that will urgently remind us of the admonition to pray and be a kind of law compelling us to snatch a moment from business so that we may fulfill this duty."[14]

But for Tertullian and Cyprian, there are, in addition to these three times for prayer, two others which have a different origin and are obligatory rather than optional. Tertullian writes: "I except, of course, the prescribed prayers which, independently of any exhortation, are to be said at dawn and twilight."[15] He does not think it necessary to offer any further justification for these times. Hippolytus, too, includes in the schedule of daily prayer two times which need no justification, but instead of connecting them with dawn and dusk he assigns them to the

---

12. We should bear in mind that in antiquity the twelve hours of daytime were counted from the rising to the setting of the sun; the hours therefore varied in length according to season and matched ours only at the equinoxes.

13. Clement of Alexandria, *Stromata* VII, 40, 4 (Stählin 30–31): "Those who know the blessed trinity of holy abodes are familiar with the distribution of the hours into sets of three that are each to be honored by prayers."

14. Tertullian, *De oratione* 25 (CCL 1:272); *De ieiunio* 10 (CCL 2:1267).

15. Tertullian, *De oratione* 25 (CCL 1:272-73). See *ibid*. 23 (p. 272): "But do any hesitate to prostrate themselves daily before God, at least for the first prayer with which we enter upon the day?" — See St. Cyprian, *De dominica oratione* 35, ed. G. Hartel (CSEL 3/1:292-93).

moments "when the faithful arise from sleep in the morning, before they undertake any work," and "before you take your rest in bed."[16]

Finally, Hippolytus introduces two further times for prayer: "Toward midnight arise, wash your hands, and pray; at cockcrow arise and pray again." Here he goes beyond the ideal of nocturnal prayer as proposed by Origen and makes it more specific. This is the first mention of prayer at cockcrow, but it is a time for prayer that will later be observed in many monastic families.

None of the authors I am citing is thinking of Christians who live withdrawn from the world: ascetics, virgins, or widows. They are thinking of the faithful who are involved in business and must, in Tertullian's expressive phrase, snatch a moment from it in order to pray. They are thinking of married people whose partners, in some cases, do not share their faith. Thus Hippolytus, speaking of prayer at midnight, says: "If your wife is present, pray together; if she is not yet a believer, withdraw to another room, pray, and then return to your bed."[17]

Among these various times for prayer, those not obligatory are presented as a praiseworthy practice that will foster ceaseless prayer. Spiritual writers give these optional times a meaning that links them to the Old and New Testaments and thus, as it were, consecrates them. The example of Daniel praying three times a day is invoked not only by Origen but by Tertullian and Cyprian as well. Origen in fact proposes four times for prayer; Tertullian and Cyprian describe five and, in addition, connect the number three with the Trinity: "that at least three times a day we may adore the Three to whom we are debtors: Father and Son and Holy Spirit."[18] In speaking of three times Tertullian and Cyprian are thinking of the group of three formed by the prayers of the third, sixth, and ninth hours.

In addition, as we saw earlier, Tertullian links these three times to events that occurred in the apostolic community: the coming of the Holy Spirit at the third hour (Acts 2:15); the call of the Gentiles that was revealed to Peter while he prayed at the sixth hour (Acts 10:9); the cure of the paralytic at the Beautiful Gate by Peter and John as they were going up to the temple at the ninth hour (Acts 3:1-2). On this point St. Cyprian simply repeats what Tertullian had already said.

There is a tendency, however, to superimpose on this explanation from the Acts of the Apostles another that is derived from the passion of the Lord. With regard to the ninth hour Tertullian says elsewhere: "Mourn-

---

16. Hippolytus, *Traditio apostolica* 41 (Botte 88 and 92); see the commentary by B. Botte in Cassien-Botte 104–10.

17. Hippolytus, *ibid.* (Botte 92–93).

18. Tertullian, *De oratione* 25 (CCL 1:272); St. Cyprian, *De dominica oratione* 34 (CSEL 3/1:292).

ing at the death of the Lord—a mourning into which the world, covered with darkness from the sixth hour on, was plunged—lasted until the ninth hour. Then the world was filled with light again and we with gladness." This explains why fasting ends at the ninth hour.[19] St. Cyprian recalls the crucifixion of Jesus in connection with the sixth hour, and his death with the ninth.[20] But Hippolytus had already written in detail of these same associations:

> Pray at the third hour and praise God. . . . For at this hour Christ was seen to be nailed to the wood. . . . Pray also at the sixth hour, for when Christ was nailed to the wood of the cross, the day was interrupted and a thick darkness fell. At this hour, therefore, there is to be a mighty prayer in imitation of the voice of him who prayed and who cast darkness on the whole of creation because of the unbelieving Jews. There is also to be intense prayer and great praise at the ninth hour, so as to imitate the way in which the souls of the just praise the God who does not deceive but remembered his holy ones and sent his Word to enlighten them. At this hour Christ's side was pierced and poured out water and blood; he shed his light on the rest of the day and brought it to its evening.[21]

St. Cyprian urges nocturnal prayer in imitation of Christ and of widowed Anna.[22] As we saw above, Origen refers to the example of the psalmist and to that of Paul and Silas in prison. Hippolytus envisages prayer at cockcrow and sees it as filling out the recollection of the passion: "At that hour the children of Israel denied Christ." However, he immediately adds: ". . . whom we acknowledge through faith and in hope of eternal light at the resurrection of the dead, our eyes being always turned to that day." Hippolytus evidently connects the recommended prayer at midnight with eschatological expectation of the Bridegroom, but he also adds an argument, the origin of which is still unclarified:

> The ancients who have passed the tradition on to us have taught us that at this hour all of creation rests for a moment in order to praise the Lord: the stars, the trees, the heavens stop for a moment, and the whole army of angels that serve God praise him at this moment in union with the souls of the just. This is why believers hasten to pray at this hour.[23]

---

19. Tertullian, *De ieiunio* 10, 7 (CCL 2:1268).

20. St. Cyprian, *De dominica oratione* 34 (CSEL 3/1:292): "At the sixth hour the Lord was crucified; at the ninth he washed away our sins with his blood; then, that he might redeem us and give us life, he completed his victory through suffering."

21. Hippolytus, *ibid.* (Botte 90–93). — It is clear that Hippolytus accepts at one and the same time the indications given in Mark 15:25 and in Mark 15:33 (= Matt 27:45; Luke 23:44).

22. St. Cyprian, *De dominica oratione* 29 (CSEL 3/1:288): "If he watched and prayed continually throughout that night, how much more should we spend the night in prayer?" See *ibid.* 36 (p. 293).

23. Hippolytus, *ibid.* (Botte 94–95).

As I said above, in contrast to these various other times of prayer, the obligatory times—morning and evening—receive no justification or explanation from Tertullian and Hippolytus. The reason for the silence is probably that these times of prayer already had a firm place in Christian practice and, in addition, were in continuity with the Jewish tradition. Origen is content simply to refer to the psalms. Yet the rising and setting of the sun awaken so many biblical echoes that these could not but be recalled in connection with the prayer that was to be made at these times. St. Clement of Rome had already seen in the dawn which followed the night an image of the resurrection.[24] St. Cyprian says it in so many words: "We must pray in the morning in order that our prayer may celebrate the resurrection of the Lord." He goes on to say: "So too when the sun sets and day is ending, we must pray again. Christ is the true Sun, the real Day. At the moment when the sun and day of this world disappear, we pray that light may nonetheless be ours. We ask for the coming of Christ and the gracious manifestation of eternal light. . . . Christ is the true Sun, the real Day."[25]

This reminder of Christ the Sun of Justice was certainly opportune at a time when the cult of the sun was developing in the Roman empire, but it is so profoundly tied in with revelation that it remains equally valid at all periods of history: "The true light that enlightens every man was coming into the world" (John 1:9).[26] This theme already inspired the thanksgiving which, according to Hippolytus, the bishop would pronounce at gatherings for the agape when evening had fallen and the deacon brought in a lamp.[27] It would also inspire the fine popular hymn *Phōs hilaron*, which seems to have been composed before the end of the third century.[28]

The agape, with its *lucernarium* or lamplighting service, was not a regular assembly of the community. Tertullian refers to vigils—which must have been equally rare—other than the Easter vigil which, again according to Tertullian, lasted the entire night.[29] Hippolytus gives us to under-

---

24. St. Clement of Rome, *Epistula ad Corinthios* 24 (SC 167:142-43), cited below at n. 17, p. 260.

25. St. Cyprian, *De dominica oratione* 35 (CSEL 3/1:292-93).

26. See F. J. Dölger, *Die Sonne der Gerechtigkeit und der Schwarze* (LQF 2; Münster: Aschendorff, 1919); idem, *Sol salutis. Gebet und Gesang im griechischen Altertum* (LQF 4-5; Münster; Aschendorff, 1920).

27. Hippolytus, *Traditio apostolica* 23 (Botte 64-65). Although this chapter has come down to us only in Ethiopian, B. Botte judges it to have been part of Hippolytus' work (see *ibid.* n. 1).

28. E. Smothers, "Phos hilaron," *RechSR* 19 (1929) 266-83; F. J. Dölger, *Antike und Christentum* 5 (1936) 11-16. A translation of the hymn is given in Lucien Deiss, *Springtime of the Liturgy* 251-52. St. Basil, *De Sancto Spiritu* 73 (SC 17:250), regards the hymn as ancient.

29. Tertullian, *Ad uxorem* II, 4, 2 (CCL 1:388): "spending the night away at the paschal solemnities."

stand that on certain days there might be an instructional discourse (*per verbum catechization*), which was a reason for the faithful to join the assembly.[30] Apart from these limited occasions the only regular gathering was for the Sunday Eucharist. All the times of prayer which the spiritual writers of the third century prescribed or recommended were therefore to be observed either individually or in the family. Nonetheless they did form an invisible community, inasmuch as all of the faithful were betaking themselves to prayer at the same times. The end of persecution and the building of houses of worship would subsequently make it possible to manifest these patterns of prayer in a public way.

The symbolism of the hours as developed by Clement, Origen, Hippolytus, Tertullian, and Cyprian would be adopted and passed on by all the later authors who discussed prayer. It would find its quasi-definitive presentation in John Cassian at the end of the fourth century.[31] Most important, it would in great measure inspire the texts and actions that make of the Liturgy of the Hours a daily commemoration of the economy of salvation.

§5. The Communal Prayer of the Hours after the Peace of Constantine (Fourth–Fifth Centuries)

BIBLIOGRAPHY

V. Raffa, "L'orario di preghiera nell'ufficio divino," *EL* 80 (1966) 97–140. Works listed below in Chapter V, pp. 233–255.

During the fourth century, the peace in which the Church now lived brought a flowering of liturgical life, thanks to the construction of churches, pilgrimages, and, above all, the rapid development of asceticism. The prayer of the hours took on a communal form and was organized almost everywhere in two forms which we now know to have been clearly distinct, thanks to the researches of Anton Baumstark. These two forms were: the prayer of the Christian people assembled around the bishop and

---

30. Hippolytus, *Traditio apostolica* 35 and 41 (Botte 82–83 and 88–89). — Origen seems to have preached almost every day.

31. John Cassian, *De institutis coenobiorum* III, 3 (SC 109:94-103). — For the later tradition see Mary Philomena, "St. Edmund of Abingdon's Meditations before the Canonical Hours," *EL* 78 (1964) 32–57; V. Raffa, "L'orario di preghiera nell'ufficio divino," *EL* 80 (1966) 115–34.

his priests (Baumstark calls this the "cathedral office"), and the prayer of ascetics and monks (the "monastic office").[32]

I. THE LITURGY OF THE HOURS AS CELEBRATED BY THE CHRISTIAN PEOPLE

In about 330–340 Eusebius of Caesarea, commenting on Ps 65, wrote enthusiastically of vv. 8ff. (LXX: 64:9-10): "The fact that at every rising of the sun and every return of evening the Churches of God around the world offer to God 'hymns,' 'praises,' and—literally—'divine pleasures' is no ordinary sign of God's power. The hymns which at dawn and dusk rise up daily everywhere in the Churches are indeed 'pleasures for God.'"[33]

From at least the middle of the fourth century on, testimonies abound which mention or describe these daily assemblies, not only in Palestine, but at Antioch and Constantinople and in Africa.[34] When St. John Chrysostom instructed the newly baptized of Antioch he told them that these gatherings were a necessary part of a Christian's day.[35] The Spanish and Gallican councils of the fifth and sixth centuries frequently regulated the details of the assemblies or recommended that the faithful attend them.[36] And these gatherings were indeed gatherings of the people: the faithful sang "morning psalms" and "evening psalms" which did not vary and which they knew by heart; to these were added, especially in the morn-

---

32. A. Baumstark, *Comparative Liturgy*, ed. B. Botte, trans. F. L. Cross (Westminster, Md.: Newman, 1958) 111ff. — The distinction between the two kinds of office, and the term *Cathedralis ordo*, were in the *Rituale antiquissimum* of Silos; see M. Férotin, *Liber mozarabicus sacramentorum* (Monumenta ecclesiae liturgica 6; Paris: Firmin-Didot, 1912) col. 769–70.

33. Eusebius, *In psalm. 64* (PG 23:639-40).

34. The testimony of Egeria in regard to Jerusalem will be given further on. — For Antioch: St. John Chrysostom, *Homilia 6 in I Tim.* 2 (PG 62:530); see P. Rentinck, *La cura pastorale in Antiochia nel IV° secolo* (Analecta Gregoriana 178; Rome: Gregorian University Press, 1970) 144–46. — For Constantinople: St. John Chrysostom, *Homil. 18 in Acta Apost.* 5 (PG 60:147). — For Africa: St. Augustine, *Conf.* V, 9, 17; *Ep.* 29, 11 (CSEL 34/1:122). — There is a description of these offices in *Constitutiones apostolorum* II, 59 (ed. F. X. Funk 171); VII, 47–48 (Funk 454–58); and VIII, 35–39 (Funk 544–49), but the provenance of these various documents is difficult to pin down. — Ca. 377, St. Epiphanius, *Panarion* 3, 23 (PG 42:829), considers the practice to be already general: "The morning hymns and prayers are celebrated with fervor in holy Church; so too are the evening psalms and prayers."

35. St. John Chrysostom, *Catecheses baptismales* 8, ed. A. Wenger (SC 50:256-57).

36. For Spain see J. Fernandez Alonso, *La cura pastoral en la España romanovisigoda* (Rome: Iglesia Nacional Española, 1955) 341–44. — For Gaul: H. Beck, *The Pastoral Care of Souls in South-East France during the Sixth Century* (Analecta Gregoriana 51; Rome: Gregorian University Press, 1950) 111–23; E. Griffe, *La Gaule chrétienne à l'époque romaine* 3 (Paris: Letouzey, 1965) 194–200.

ing, biblical and even non-biblical canticles; in some Churches there was a sermon almost every day; the ceremony ended with intercessions and a collect pronounced by the bishop or a priest.

In addition to these two daily gatherings for prayer, the faithful might be called more or less frequently to vigils or nocturnal assemblies. For, like Easter, other major feasts could be celebrated in the form of a vigil that included readings, prayers, and songs and ended with Mass: for example, Christmas, Epiphany, and Pentecost. In some Churches there were even vigils every Sunday[37] and sometimes on Friday. The most popular vigils, however, were undoubtedly those of the martyrs, which were celebrated at their tombs.[38] These vigils often followed upon evening prayer, which in this case gave added solemnity to the *lucernarium* or ceremony of lighting the lamps or a large candle.

II. THE LITURGY OF THE HOURS AS CELEBRATED BY ASCETICS AND IN MONASTERIES

Of the numerous Christians who were desirous of living a more perfect life and consecrating themselves to God through asceticism and prayer some remained in the cities. Their organized prayer then had the local church for its venue and a priest for its presiding celebrant. Such people were known in the East as "sons and daughters of the covenant"; in the West they included consecrated virgins and people known as *devoti* ("devout") or *sancti* ("saints" or "holy persons").

Others, however, withdrew into the desert or wilderness and established monasteries in which they set up a place for prayer (an *oratorium* or "oratory"). This second group—but not they alone—obeyed a rule that was sometimes minutely detailed. In Egypt, the most celebrated of these rules was that of St. Pachomius; in the East, that of St. Basil; in the West, the Augustinian *Ordo monasterii* ("Order for a Monastery") and the rules of St. Caesarius, Aurelian, the Master (*Regula Magistri*), St. Benedict, St. Columbanus, St. Isidore, St. Fructuosus, and others.[39]

All of these groups endeavored to observe as fully as possible the precept of ceaseless prayer that is so clearly set down in the New Testament and in the treatises of the early spiritual writers. They implemented it differently, however, depending on the tradition to which they belonged. Cassian, who visited the monasteries of Egypt, Palestine, and the East in about 400, distinguished two main practices. If we are to credit his report,

---

37. See below, p. 267.
38. See above, pp. 127–28.
39. See below, pp. 234ff.

the monks of Egypt had only two daily assemblies—in the morning and in the evening—for prolonged communal prayer; they rejected all the other assigned hours because they wanted to pray ceaselessly rather than inter-mittently.[40] Even if Cassian's description is contradicted on many points by documents we have at our disposal today, it is correct that at least Pachomian monasticism had only these two assemblies for communal prayer in the strict sense.[41]

It can be said that, with the exception noted, all of the monastic families adopted for communal prayer all of the times or hours which we saw recommended to Christians by the spiritual teachers of the third century. In the daytime they observed the third, sixth, and ninth hours, during which they sang or heard proclaimed several psalms which were sometimes followed by readings. They also engaged in prolonged nocturnal prayer, either at midnight (*mesonuktikon*) or at cockcrow; on certain feasts, however, or even every Sunday their vigil might last the entire night (*pan-nuchis*). All these hours were added, of course, to the two hours—the morning and the evening—which the faithful observed in the churches of the towns but which often were differently structured for the monks, especially when the community had no priest. In this case, morning and evening prayer, like the other monastic hours, consisted of a *lectio con-tinua* or continuous reading of psalms and other passages.

In addition, two new times or hours of prayer made their appearance in monastic practice. At the time of retiring there was a prayer which con-sisted chiefly in the recitation of Psalm 91. St. Basil is the first witness to this prayer,[42] but it was soon in use almost everywhere under the name of *completa* or *completorium* (Compline), *apodeipnon* ("after supper"), *sûtâro*. The second time of prayer was not universally accepted: the "first" hour or Prime, which according to Cassian was introduced by the monks of Bethlehem toward the end of the fourth century as a way of keeping lazy monks from returning to bed after prayer at dawn and remaining there until the third hour.[43] Prime was in fact a duplication of the morn-ing office (*matutinum*) and summoned up no echoes of the Bible; it per-sisted down to our time only because it had been adopted by the monastic

---

40. John Cassian, *De institutis coenobiorum* II, ed. and trans. J. C. Guy (SC 109; Paris: Cerf, 1965) 56–89.

41. A. Veilleux, *La liturgie dans le cénobitisme pachômien au IVe siècle* (Studia Ansel-miana 57; Rome: Herder and Pontificio Istituto Anselmiano, 1968) 279–339.

42. St. Basil, *Regulae fusius tractatae*, Qu. 37, no. 5 (PG 31:1016).

43. John Cassian, *De institutis coenobiorum* III, 4–5 (SC 109:102-7). — The interpreta-tion of this passage in Cassian has been the subject of a lively controversy: J. Froger, *Les origines de Prime* (Bibliotheca EL 19; Rome: Ephemerides Liturgicae, 1946); idem, "Note pour rectifier l'interprétation de Cassien," *ALW* 2 (1952) 96–102; J. M. Hanssens, *Aux origines de la prière liturgique. Nature et genèse de l'office des Matines* (Analecta Gregoriana 57; Rome: Pontifical Gregorian University, 1952); V. Raffa, *EL* 67 (1953) 265–68.

lawgivers of Italy and Provence[44] and because in the Carolingian period the "office of chapter" was added on to it.[45]

III. MELDING OF THE TWO RHYTHMS OF PRAYER

It would be a mistake to set up an opposition between the prayer of the ascetics and the prayer of the Christian people. They did indeed have different structures, but they were nonetheless perceived as complementary and they remained complementary. As a result, many monastic rules adopted the morning and evening prayer of the churches, sometimes adding them to a properly monastic service of psalmody, sometimes establishing them as distinct times of prayer (thus in the Augustinian *Ordo monasterii* and the monasteries of Provence there was both a *lucernarium* and a *duodecima* or "twelfth hour"), and sometimes simply taking them as they were from the usage of the churches. So too a vigil of the ecclesial type might be added to the specifically monastic type of vigil on Sundays and feast days.

This fusion of the two rhythms of prayer with their respective geniuses occurred quite naturally in churches frequented by urban ascetics or monks. This was the case at Rome, where urban monasteries grew up alongside the pilgrimage basilicas in the fifth century.[46] It was the case at Caesarea in Cappadocia and in Africa, as is clear if we keep in mind that the rules of St. Basil and the *Ordo monasterii* are addressed to communities of ascetics who prayed together with the faithful.

We have an even better knowledge of the liturgical life of Jerusalem, thanks to the descriptions provided by Egeria. Here the official prayers of the Church and the prayers of the *monazontes* (monks) and *parthenae* (virgins, i.e., nuns) were said in succession in the basilica of the Anastasis. The two types of prayer were easily distinguished, but of course the ascetics took part in the assembly of the people around the bishop, while some of the devout faithful gladly returned for the prayers of the ascetics, at which, in addition, the priests took turns in presiding.[47] Even more in cases where the priests themselves lived a communal life with a bishop such as Augustine or Caesarius of Arles as its center, the faithful were urged to

---

44. Rules of St. Benedict, St. Caesarius, and Aurelian. Prime seems to have been introduced into the Byzantine office in the ninth-tenth centuries: N. Egender in *La prière des Eglises de rite byzantin* I. *La prière des heures* (Chevetogne, 1975) 250–51.

45. See below, p. 251.

46. G. Ferrari, *Early Roman Monasteries. Notes for the History of the Monasteries and Convents at Rome from the V. through the X. Century* (Studi di antichità cristiana 23; Vatican City, 1957) 379–407.

47. *Egeria's Travels* 24–25, trans. John Wilkinson (London: SPCK, 1971) 123–28.

come and join them for the non-obligatory hours of prayer, especially in periods of intense intercession such as Lent or the Rogation Days.

The traditional patrimony of the divine office in the Churches of both East and West originated in this happy meeting of two expressions and two rhythms of the prayer of the hours.

§6. Overloading and Deterioration of the Rhythm of the Hours

In the course of time the ideal embodied in the prayer of the hours was obscured by two almost contradictory tendencies: the tendency to overload the timetable or content of the hours and the tendency to eliminate the reference of the hours to the natural rhythm of day and night.

I. OVERLOADING THE SEQUENCE OF HOURS

Do the times set aside for prayer make it possible to satisfy the precept of ceaseless prayer? Of course not. Yet, as St. Augustine observes, "the words we speak at those moments remind us to renew our fervor; these frequent renewals keep lukewarmness from turning into coldness and prevent the flame of devotion from being extinguished within us."[48] It is impossible to avoid "cares and duties"; even monks must earn their bread. Following the Fathers of the Desert, Eastern Christians therefore sought ways of keeping themselves at prayer while they worked; the "Jesus prayer" was one such means.[49] Certain hermits of the early centuries and, at various periods, even entire monasteries endeavored to practice a *laus perennis* ("perpetual praise"), either by prolonging the prayer of the hours as far as human strength would allow (the *Akoimetae* or "sleepless ones") or by coming in relays into the oratory so that the psalmody would be continuous.[50]

---

48. St. Augustine, *Ep.* 130, 18 (CSEL 44:60-61).

49. On the "Jesus prayer" see, e.g., A Monk of the Eastern Church, *La prière de Jésus* (3rd ed.; Chevetogne, 1959).

50. C. Gindele, "Die gallikanischen *Laus perennis*-Klöster und ihr *Ordo officii*," *RBen* 69 (1959) 32–48; P. Rouillard, "Temps et rythmes de la prière dans le monachisme ancien," *LMD* no. 64 (1960) 32–52; J. Leclercq, "Une parenthèse dans l'histoire de la prière continuelle: La *laus perennis* du haut moyen âge," *ibid.* 90–101; idem, "Prière incessante. A propos de la *laus perennis* du moyen âge," in his *La liturgie et les paradoxes chrétiens* (Lex orandi 36; Paris: Cerf, 1963) 229–42. See also O. Hendricks, "Les premiers monastères internationaux syriens," *OS* 3 (1958) 165–84.

It was doubtless in the same spirit that the monks of Spain increased the number of hours in the office. To the hours of the *ordo cathedralis*—*Matutinum* and *Vesperum*—and to the "canonical" hours of Terce, Sext, None, Compline, and Nocturns the *Rituale antiquissimum* (Silos, ms 7) of the twelfth century adds the following: *Prima et secunda* (First and Second), *Quarta et quinta* (Fourth and Fifth), *Septima et octava* (Seventh and Eighth) (said in sets of two), *Decima, undecima, et duodecima* (Tenth, Eleventh, and Twelfth—a set of three), *Ante completa* (Before Compline), *Post completa* (After Compline), *Ante lectulum* (Before retiring), *Ad medium noctis* (At midnight), and *Ordo peculiaris* [*vigiliae*] (Special service), so as to have twelve daylight hours and twelve nighttime hours.[51]

The same tendency can be seen in the Byzantine Church, in which since the twelfth century the *Horologion* has provided for "Intermediate Hours" (*mesoria*) which come (at least during periods of fast) after the traditional hours of Prime, Terce, Sext, and None. To these are added the office of the *Typika*, the office at table, and, on certain days, "Great Compline."[52]

The Latin Middle Ages were marked by a different kind of overloading, namely, the daily or at least frequent addition of the Little Office of the Blessed Virgin and the Office of the Dead (some monastic orders kept these down to our time) and, on some days, supplementary prayers: the penitential psalms, the gradual psalms, the *psalmi familiares* (psalms for the benefactors and friends), the litanies of the saints, etc.[53]

II. DISAPPEARANCE OF THE SENSE OF THE "TRUTH OF THE HOURS"

The Liturgy of the Hours deteriorated, finally, in a still more important respect. What Vatican II calls the *veritas horarum* ("truth of the hours") was gradually abandoned.

It seems that several causes were at work to alter the timetable for the choral and public recitation of the office. During Lent there was a strict fast until nightfall, that is, until after Vespers; the desire to shorten the

---

51. Text in M. Férotin, *Liber mozarabicus sacramentorum* col. 769-86. See J. Pinell, "Las horas vigiliares del oficio monacal hispánico," *Liturgica* 3 (Scripta et documenta 17; Montserrat: Abadía de Montserrat, 1966) 197-340.

52. All these offices may be found in, e.g., the *Horologion* published in 1917 by the Abbey of Grottaferrata; translation in *La prière des Eglises de rite byzantin* 1. *La prière des Heures* (with introductions by N. Egender, 253, 325-29, 345-49, 423-26).

53. P. Salmon, *Les manuscrits liturgiques latins de la Bibliothèque Vaticane* 4 (ST 267; Vatican City, 1971) xiii; A. le Carou, *Le bréviaire romain et les Frères Mineurs au XIIIᵉ siècle* (Paris: Editions Franciscaines, 1928) 167-70. — See J. Leclercq, "Formes successives de l'office marial," *EL* 72 (1958) 294-301; idem, "Formes anciennes de l'office marial," *EL* 74 (1960) 83-102; G. Dettori, *L'officio dei defunti. Storia, Dissertazione storico-liturgica* (Theses 53; Rome: Lateran University, 1960).

fast inspired a wrong-headed interpretation of the rubric, "Vespers are said before eating," which made it possible to anticipate Vespers as early as before noon. Furthermore, since Mass could be celebrated on the days of Lent only at a late hour (after None), the same desire to shorten the fast led to the celebration of Sext and None being moved forward to the morning.

During the Easter triduum, perhaps in order to facilitate the participation of the people, the office of Tenebrae, which belonged to the end of the night, was anticipated the evening before, thus throwing into disarray the entire sequence of commemorations of the passion; in addition, Tenebrae brought forward with it the office of Lauds, which belonged to the following dawn. Clerics who did not always reside at the church in which they were to fulfill their choir obligations doubtless contributed to the lumping together of the Hours without regard to their meaning; the same defect was to be found, however, in monasteries and convents.

Private recitation was marked by even greater abnormalities. The praiseworthy principle, "The service of God comes first," led devout priests of the nineteenth and first half of the twentieth centuries to read in the early afternoon the Nocturns and Lauds of the following day and to seek the privilege of celebrating Vespers and Compline before noon! Cardinal Richelieu was continually occupied with his duties as prime minister and therefore (it seems) spent the two hours between 11 p.m. and 1 a.m. saying the offices of two successive days, thus leaving himself two days free. More commonly, only too many priests of our century found themselves reciting, late at night, *Jam lucis orto sidere* ("Now that the sun has risen")!

Since at least the end of the fifteenth century, the need, no longer satisfied by the liturgy, of praying in accordance with the rhythm of the passing hours sought expression in other and popular ways, especially in the recitation of the Angelus or Hail Mary, as signaled by the church bells three times a day: at dawn, noon, and twilight.[54]

§7. The "Truth of the Hours" Rediscovered at Vatican II

As early as 1960 the Code of Rubrics published by authority of Pope John XXIII sought to do away with some of the abuses just described. To

---

54. On the Angelus: W. Henry, "Angelus," *DACL* 1/2 (1907) 2068-77; A. Maurin, *Les saluts d'amour* I. *Les troubadours de Notre-Dame* 2 (Montpellier, 1935) 9-13; A. Derey, "L'Angelus office liturgique," *QL* 62 (1981) 155-60. — It is worth noting that Muslims observe five daily times of prayer, which are signaled by a muezzin from atop the minaret of mosques: dawn, noon, mid-afternoon, the moment after sunset, and evening. Is this observance linked to Jewish practice, to the practice of Chaldean Christians, or to that of Oriental sects? It is difficult to determine.

this end it laid down the following principle: "By their very nature the canonical Hours of the Divine Office are ordained to the sanctification of the various hours of the natural day. Hence it is better, whether for really sanctifying the day or for reciting the Hours with spiritual fruit that each canonical Hour be said at a time nearest to the true time for each canonical Hour."[55]

The Second Vatican Council in its Constitution on the Liturgy likewise emphasized the "truth of the hours":

> The divine office, in keeping with ancient Christian tradition, is so devised that the whole course of the day and night is made holy by the praise of God. . . .
> Since the purpose of the office is to sanctify the day, the traditional sequence of the hours is to be restored so that, as far as possible, they may again become also in fact what they have been in name [*ut horis veritas temporis, quantum fieri potest, reddatur*].[56]

But the Council also realized that "account must be taken of the conditions of modern life in which those who are engaged in apostolic work must live."[57] It therefore came to a certain number of decisions which aimed to make the traditional ideal of prayer attainable in modern circumstances. These decisions evidently affect only the Roman Office; they may nevertheless inspire the reform of other liturgical traditions, although in any such reform heed must be given to the special character of each tradition and, in particular, to the nature of monastic life.[58] I shall comment on these decisions further on.[59]

---

55. No. 142; trans. in *The Roman Breviary* (New York: Benziger, 1964) xxviii. Latin text: *AAS* 52 (1960) 622–23.
56. *VSC* 84, 88.
57. *VSC* 88.
58. See *VSC* 3–4.
59. Below, pp. 256ff.

Chapter II

The Liturgy of the Hours
as Prayer of the Church

BIBLIOGRAPHY

Paul VI, Apostolic Constitution *Laudis canticum* (November 1, 1970), in *AAS* 56 (1964) 527–36 (= *EDIL* nos. 2196–2214). Translated in Volume I of the *Liturgy of the Hours*.

GILH 5–33.

J. Pascher, "Thesen über das Gebet im Namen der Kirche," *Liturgisches Jahrbuch* 12 (1962) 58–62.

A. M. Roguet, *The Liturgy of the Hours. The General Instruction with Commentary*, trans. Peter Coughlin and Peter Purdue (Collegeville: The Liturgical Press, 1971) 81–101: "Theology."

V. Raffa, "Teologia dell'ufficio divino," *Rivista liturgica* 52 (1965) 352–80.

_____, *Istruzione generale sulla Liturgia delle Ore. Versione italiana e commento* (Nuova collana liturgica 2; Milan: Edizioni O. R., 1971) 14–58.

_____, *La nuova Liturgia delle Ore. Presentazione storica, teologica e pastorale* (Nuova collana liturgica 3; Milan: Edizioni O. R., 1971) 19–39.

_____, "Preghiera personale e preghiera della Chiesa," *Seminarium* 24 (1972) 33–62.

P. Visentin, "Dimensione orante della Chiesa e Liturgia delle Ore," in *Liturgia delle Ore. Documenti ufficiali e studi* (Quaderni di Rivista liturgica 14; Turin-Leumann: ElleDiCi, 1972) 131–59.

D. de Reynal, "Situation de la prière commune. Perspectives pour la célébration des heures," *LMD* no. 135 (1978) 25–45.

In his Apostolic Constitution *Laudis canticum* Pope Paul VI summarized briefly the history I have just finished sketching:

> The Liturgy of the Hours gradually developed into the prayer of the local church, a prayer offered at regular intervals and in appointed places under the presidency of a priest. It was seen as a kind of necessary complement to the fullness of divine worship that is contained in the eucharistic sacrifice, by means of which that worship might overflow to reach all the hours of daily life.

The pope concluded: "The Office has been drawn up and arranged in such a way that not only clergy but also religious and indeed laity may participate in it, since it is the prayer of the whole people of God." The same assertion is found in the *General Instruction of the Liturgy of the Hours*: "The Church's praise is not to be considered the exclusive possession of clerics and monks either in its origin or by its nature, but belongs to the whole Christian community."[1]

These statements revive ancient tradition that had been lost from sight in the teaching of the rubricists of the preceding century, a teaching still to be found in the Encyclical *Mediator Dei* of Pius XII. According to the rubricists, the Liturgy of the Hours could be celebrated as an act of the Church only by persons deputed for this mission.[2]

§1. The Liturgy of the Hours as Prayer of the Christian People

I. WHY DID THE LITURGY OF THE HOURS CEASE TO BE OF THE PEOPLE?

In the East the Liturgy of the Hours has to a great extent retained its popular character. This is especially true of the Chaldean office.[3]

The Latin Middle Ages, on the other hand, saw the gradual erection of a barrier between the Liturgy of the Hours and the people that finally took material form, in the fourteenth and fifteenth centuries, in the rood-screen that closed off the choir in which canons and clerical monks celebrated the office. Even lay brothers in monasteries were excluded from the celebration.[4]

The rift had several causes. For one thing, the liturgy, being celebrated in Latin, was less and less understood by the faithful, whose languages had moved further and further away from Latin; it was, of course, even more inaccessible in regions in which the people had never spoken Latin. Furthermore, conditions were much less favorable to the office than to the Mass. The Mass not only had an obligatory character which worked

---

1. *GILH* 270.
2. Pius XII, Encyclical *Mediator Dei* (November 20, 1947), nos. 139–40, in *AAS* 39 (1947) 573. See *Codex Iuris Canonici* (1917), can. 1256. A. M. Roguet, *The Liturgy of the Hours. The General Instruction on the Liturgy of the Hours, with a Commentary*, trans. Peter Coughlin and Peter Purdue (Collegeville: The Liturgical Press, 1971) 96, points out that the conciliar Constitution still reflects this outlook to some extent, as compared with *Laudis canticum* and the *GILH*.
3. I. H. Dalmais, *Liturgies d'Orient* (Rites et symboles #10; Paris: Cerf, 1980) 169–70.
4. J. Dubois, "Office des heures et messe dans la tradition monastique," *LMD* no. 135 (1978) 69–71.

in its favor on Sundays; it also had the advantage of a greater sameness, thanks to the chants and prayers of the Ordinary. The office, on the contrary, required that those actively participating in it either know the psalter by heart, as monks did, or possess costly books (which were in any case useless to the illiterate folk who were the vast majority of the Christian people). Finally, the development of the choral liturgy with its splendor and amplitude and the numerous extraneous offices that weighed it down in the Middle Ages prevented the active participation of the people and made it the preserve of specialists: monks, canons, clerics, and holders of benefices.

II. PERSISTENCE OF THE LITURGY OF THE HOURS, AND POPULAR SUBSTITUTES FOR IT

Despite these difficulties and barriers Christians always retained a more or less confused desire for the prayer of the hours and tried to share in it.

They sometimes took actual part in it, with the encouragement of local synods that in some cases even made attendance obligatory on certain feast days.[5] Until the first decades of the twentieth century, all parishes had the celebration of Vespers on Sundays and feast days, as well as the office of Tenebrae during the Easter triduum. The number of the faithful attending these services was sometimes quite large, even though their active participation was reduced to the singing of a few hymns and even though they had received no instruction regarding the texts they were hearing.

So too, lay brothers in monasteries attended the office of the monks on holidays. On the other days they replaced such attendance with the recitation in common of a certain number of Our Fathers at the hours when the monks were singing the psalms in choir. It was doubtless in this way that the rosary originally took shape; the 150 Hail Marys matched the 150 psalms.

Between this prayer of simple folk and the office proper, there was an intermediate form: the "Little Offices" and the "Hours." Eminent persons acquired for this purpose books illuminated by very famous painters; that is why so many Books of Hours have come down to us.[6] But less

---

5. For Normandy see G. Bessin, *Concilia Rothomagensis provinciae* (Rouen: F. Vaultier, 1717) 1:10 (citing canon 15 of a Synod of Rouen of about 878, as reported by Yves of Chartres and the canonical collections); 2:280 (Synodal Constitutions of Avranches, 1550, c. 22); 2:573 (a constitution of Geoffrey, Bishop of Coutances, 1487).

6. See, e.g., V. Leroquais, *Les livres d'heures manuscrits de la Bibliothèque Nationale de Paris* (3 vols.; Mâcon: Protat, 1927); P. Salmon, *Les manuscrits liturgiques latins de la Bibliothèque Vaticane* 4 (ST 267; Vatican City, 1971) xiii–xvii, 135–99.

sumptuous copies must have been quite numerous, and they became even more numerous, of course, after the discovery of printing. These various offices were simplified, unchanging (or close to it), and often translated into the modern languages; down to our own time they were very popular with the faithful and with religious congregations.[7] They enabled many to approach the ideal of prayer represented by the Roman or Benedictine office; on the other hand, they did not provide an adequate spiritual nourishment nor did they bring the user into the great stream of the liturgical year.

III. REDISCOVERY OF THE OFFICE AS PRAYER OF THE CHRISTIAN PEOPLE

Whereas nineteenth-century Catholic opinion seemed to make the office, or "breviary," the exclusive prerogative of priests, the liturgical movement that emanated from various Benedictine abbeys at the beginning of the twentieth century made the prayer of the hours known first to an educated elite and then to groups of young people. Here and there booklets containing Prime and Compline, or Vespers, made their way abroad.

In the Churches springing from the Reformation, the same movement took place earlier and was more widespread, because as early as the sixteenth century these communities had abandoned Latin and had adapted the office in more or less radical ways. Thus in England Cranmer's *Prayer Book* had straightway turned the principal hours—morning and evening—into celebrations involving the people. More recently, the German-speaking Lutherans have also tried to return to this tradition. But it is the monastery of Taizé, a product of the Neuchâtel liturgical movement, that deserves the credit for revealing the prayer of the hours to its countless visitors.[8]

The practical difficulties which kept the faithful away from the Liturgy of the Hours have been removed by the reform that was decreed by

7. See A. Bugnini, *"Parva breviaria fidelium,"* EL 68 (1956) 171–76; H. Schmidt, *Introductio in liturgiam occidentalem* (Rome: Herder, 1960) 469–83.

8. *The Book of Common Prayer* [*of 1662*], *with the Additions and Deviations Proposed in 1928* (Oxford: Oxford University Press, 1928); D. Webb, "Les offices du matin et du soir dans l'Eglise anglicane," in Cassien-Botte 317–81; R. T. Brandreth, "La réforme anglicane de l'office divin," *ibid.* 283–94; W. Gordon Wheeler, "Prayer of the Hours in Anglicanism and the Reformation Churches," *Seminarium* 24 (1972) 154–61; *L'Office divin de chaque jour* (3rd ed.; Neuchâtel: Delachaux et Niestlé, 1961); Community of Taizé, *La louange des jours* (Nouvel office de Taizé, 5th edition completely revised; Taizé, 1971 [there is a translation, by the Taizé Community and Anthony Brown, of an earlier edition: *The Taizé Office* (London: Faith Press, 1966)]; M. Thurian, "L'office quotidien à Taizé," in Cassien-Botte 295–316.

Vatican II in its Constitution on the Liturgy and implemented in the new *Liturgy of the Hours* (promulgated by Pope Paul VI in his Apostolic Constitution *Laudis canticum* of November 1, 1970). The complications and superfluous elements that burdened the old office have been removed; the sequence of parts has been made more evident; it can now be celebrated in the vernacular. As a result, the office is now within the reach of all.

This is why the *General Instruction* describes, and recommends, the Liturgy of the Hours as the prayer of the Christian people. Especially noteworthy from this point of view is chapter I, section IV, "The Participants in the Liturgy of the Hours" (nos. 20–32). The principle which serves as point of departure here is that "the Liturgy of the Hours, like other liturgical actions, is not something private but belongs to the whole body of the Church, which it manifests and influences."[9] Consequently, before specifying those who have a personal mandate from the Church to recite the office, there is need of first emphasizing its communal celebration (nos. 20–27).

The communal celebration of the office has its most perfect form when it is carried out by a local Church "in the presence of its bishop in the company of his priests and ministers, for in the local Church 'the one, holy, catholic and apostolic Church of Christ is truly present and active'" (no. 20). Vatican Council II had several times spoken of the dignity and radical importance of the local Church in terms reminiscent of the Fathers of antiquity.[10] The celebration of the Liturgy of the Hours by a local Church is therefore the model of all such celebrations and provides us with a theological understanding of this Liturgy.

The *General Instruction* then moves on to communities which are less extensive but by reason of their union with the bishop form part of the local Church; the most important of these are the parishes. Hence, "when the people are invited to the liturgy of the hours and come together in unity of heart and voice, they show forth the Church in its celebration of the mystery of Christ" (no. 22). This is why pastors are exhorted to initiate this common prayer, urge it upon the faithful, and prepare them by instruction so that they can fruitfully take part in the principal Hours, especially on Sundays and feast days (no. 23).

The communal celebration of the Hours should logically be a part of all forms of common life, whether stable communities such as residences for priests and religious houses, or temporary communities formed for spiritual exercises, meetings, pastoral congresses, and so on. The *Instruc-*

---

9. *GILH* 20; see *VSC* 26.

10. *VSC* 26, 41, 42, and 84; Dogmatic Constitution *Lumen gentium* on the Church 23; Decree *Christus Dominus* on the Pastoral Office of Bishops in the Church 11; Decree *Apostolicam actuositatem* on the Apostolate of Lay People 10; etc.

tion offers each of these groups reasons why they should give the Liturgy of the Hours a place among them (nos. 25–27). It must be recognized that in many places this exhortation has already produced results. Even the family, "the domestic sanctuary of the Church," is urged to use some parts of the Liturgy of the Hours for its common prayer (no. 27).

The Liturgy of the Hours continues to be a prayer of the Church when it is recited by someone, even a layperson, who cannot take part in a communal celebration. Even when scattered, Christians who unite themselves to this identical prayer being said by many, receive from it "one heart and soul."[11] These statements, which are a logical development of perspectives already opened up by the Council,[12] represent a happy departure from the hitherto traditional view according to which only the office celebrated by those deputed to it is a liturgical action in the strict sense.[13] In order to emphasize even more the radical character of the change, the *Instruction* has also altered its approach to the obligation traditionally imposed on priests, deacons, and monks.

§2. The Liturgy of the Hours Celebrated in the Name of the Christian People

I. COMMISSION GIVEN TO BISHOPS, PRIESTS, AND DEACONS

Sacred ministers have the liturgy of the hours entrusted to them in such a particular way that even when the faithful are not present they are to pray it themselves with the adaptations necessary under these circumstances. The Church commissions them to celebrate the liturgy of the hours so as to ensure at least in their persons the regular carrying out of the duty of the whole community and the unceasing continuance of Christ's prayer in the Church.[14]

This principle of the *General Instruction* represents a propitious doctrinal advance and, in relation to the former legislation, a change of perspective.[15] On the one hand, there is no longer question of the office being obligatory as the result of a benefice. This was the only obligation

---

11. Acts 4:32; *GILH* 32. St. Basil, *Regulae fusius tractatae*, Qu. 37, trans. L. Lebe (Maredsous, 1969) 124, and then St. Benedict, *Regula* 50 (SC 182:608), had already ordered that monks absent from the community should recite the Hours privately.

12. *VSC* 84–85, 98, 100.

13. See above, n. 2, p. 180.

14. *GILH* 28.

15. For a history of the obligation attaching to the office see P. Salmon, *The Breviary through the Centuries*, trans. Sr. Mary David (Collegeville: The Liturgical Press, 1962) 1–27.

recognized in the written law of the Middle Ages: for the holder of a benefice the recitation of the office was an obligation in justice toward those who had supplied the property of which he enjoyed the fruits. On the other hand, the *Instruction* speaks henceforth not of an obligation but of a commission that is entrusted to all in sacred orders. Moreover, the commission does not depend on the sole will of the legislator, as the Code of 1917 (can 135) might suggest, but emanates from the very nature of their mission and the sacramental character impressed upon them. Finally, the principle is nuanced in its application, depending on the relative importance of the various Hours of the office.

1. Basis of the Commission

Those who have received the sacrament of Orders and are appointed to preside over the prayer of the Christian people, must make sure that this prayer continues even if the people are not sharing in it with them. The reason is that they represent the people and therefore Christ as well.

> The bishop represents Christ in an eminent and conspicuous way and is the high priest of his flock; the life in Christ of his faithful people may be said in a sense to derive from him and depend on him. He should, then, be the first of all the members of his Church in offering prayer. His prayer in the recitation of the liturgy of the hours is always made in the name of the Church and on behalf of the Church entrusted to him.
>
> United as they are with the bishop and the whole presbyterium, priests are themselves representative in a special way of Christ the Priest and so share the same responsibility of praying to God for the people entrusted to them and indeed for the whole world.
>
> All these ministers fulfill the ministry of the Good Shepherd who prays for his sheep that they may have life and so be brought into perfect unity.[16]

While intercession for sinners is a duty of the entire Church, it is the duty first and foremost of pastors, who are to follow the example of Moses and, above all, must "continue to offer the prayer and petition which Christ poured out in the days of his earthly life."[17] It would be a mistake to set up an opposition between prayer and action in the lives of priests: "For only the Lord, who said, 'Without me you can do nothing,' can make their work effective and fruitful. That is why the apostles when instituting deacons said, 'We will devote ourselves to prayer and to the ministry of the word.' "[18]

---

16. *GILH* 28; see Vatican II, Decree *Christus Dominus* 15; Decree *Presbyterorum ordinis* on the Ministry and Life of Priests 13.

17. *GILH* 17. See the prayer for the consecration of a bishop: ". . . ministering to you day and night; may he always gain the blessing of your favor . . . ." (*The Rites of the Catholic Church* 2 [New York: Pueblo, 1980] 95). The prayer is from the *Traditio apostolica* of St. Hippolytus.

18. *VSC* 86; see *GILH* 18.

2. The Obligation Attaching to the Various Hours

The obligation flowing from this commission extends in principle to the entire set of Hours: "Hence, bishops and priests and other sacred ministers, who have received from the Church the mandate of celebrating the Liturgy of the Hours, should recite the full sequence of Hours each day, as far as possible at the appropriate times."[19]

The obligation is, however, more or less urgent depending on the relative importance of the various Hours both among themselves and for the sacred ministers who recite them:

> They should, first and foremost, attach due importance to these hours that are, so to speak, the two hinges of the liturgy of the hours, that is, morning prayer and evening prayer, which should not be omitted except for a serious reason.
>
> They should faithfully pray the office of readings, which is above all a liturgical celebration of the word of God. In this way they fulfill daily a duty that is peculiarly their own, that is, of receiving the word of God into their lives, so that they may become more perfect as disciples of the Lord and experience more deeply the unfathomable riches of Christ.[20]
>
> In order to sanctify the whole day more completely, they will also treasure the recitation of daytime prayer and night prayer, to round off the whole *Opus Dei* and to commend themselves to God before retiring.[21]

II. COMMISSION GIVEN TO CANONS, MONKS, AND NUNS

Communities of canons (regular or secular), monks, nuns, and certain other regulars or religious have traditionally, and in virtue of their Rule or Constitutions, celebrated the Liturgy of the Hours in whole or in part. Vatican Council II recalls the principles formulated earlier in canons 413 and 610 of the *Code* of 1917, but it also makes these less rigid, especially as far as the obligation of choir is concerned.[22]

These communities

> represent in a special way the Church at prayer. They are a fuller sign of the Church as it continually praises God with one voice, and they fulfill

---

19. *GILH* 29. — The formula *aliique ministri sacri* ("other sacred ministers") was left deliberately vague. It anticipated the ultimate suppression of the subdiaconate, which in fact was decreed on August 15, 1972, and was meant to leave to the episcopal conferences the decision regarding married deacons (see *ibid*, 30).

20. On this point *GILH* refers to the Dogmatic Constitution *Dei Verbum* on Divine Revelation 25, and to the Decree *Presbyterorum ordinis* 13.

21. *GILH* 29.

22. *VSC* 95; see the Decree *Perfectae Caritatis* on the Up-to-date Renewal of Religious Life 9. — The Roman Pontifical of Clement VIII had the breviary being given to nuns in the ceremony for the consecration of virgins.

the duty of "working," above all by prayer, "to build up and increase the whole Mystical Body of Christ, and for the good of the local Churches."[23] This is especially true of those living the contemplative life.[24]

The extent of the obligation that binds these religious communities, and each of their members, to the celebration of the Liturgy of the Hours is determined henceforth by their particular law and not, as in the past, by the common law of the Church. Those in sacred orders, however, continue to be bound by the prescriptions of the common law.[25]

This much is to be noted, however: When the *General Instruction* states an obligation binding the two groups just discussed, it does so in the broader framework of an exhortation to all Christians and all communities, whether juridically established or simply factual. Moreover, as we shall see further on,[26] the *Instruction* even proposes Hours which are an ideal realizable only by some or only in certain circumstances. The intention of the Church is to place the obligation in its proper perspective: the Christian law is a law of freedom and expresses the interior need of prayer which the Holy Spirit rouses in souls and which is a dynamic and life-giving force.

§3. The Liturgy of the Hours in the Mystery of the Church

It is therefore not enough to see the Liturgy of the Hours as simply a form of prayer proposed to communities and individuals as a model to be followed and as the perfect expression of their personal prayer. Rather the Liturgy of the Hours has an essential role to play in the very mission of the Church; it is one of the Church's primary functions.

The reason is that the Church must be at one and the same time "zealous in action and dedicated to contemplation."[27] Its prayer is "truly the voice of the Bride herself addressed to the bridegroom"[28] in praise, thanksgiving for his redemptive work, and petition for his help in the struggle. This is also why this prayer is so profoundly engaged with the history of salvation. But in its prayer the Church also intercedes for the whole world:

> The ecclesial community thus exercises a truly maternal function in bringing souls to Christ, not only by charity, good example, and works of penance but also by prayer.[29]

---

23. *VSC* 99.
24. *GILH* 24.
25. *GILH* 31.
26. See below, Chapter VI, pp. 256ff.
27. *VSC* 2.
28. *VSC* 84; see *GILH* 15.
29. *GILH* 17.

188 The Liturgy of the Hours

> Those then who take part in the liturgy of the hours bring growth to God's people in a hidden but fruitful apostolate.[30]

The Liturgy of the Hours is not only the "voice of the Bride"; it is also "the very prayer which Christ himself together with his Body addresses to the Father."[31]

> Jesus Christ, High Priest of the New and Eternal Covenant, taking human nature, introduced into this earthly exile that hymn which is sung throughout all ages in the halls of heaven. He attaches to himself the entire community of mankind and has them join him in singing his divine song of praise.[32]

> The excellence of Christian prayer lies in its sharing in the reverent love of the only-begotten Son for the Father and in the prayer that the Son put into words in his earthly life and that still continues without ceasing in the name of the whole human race and for its salvation, throughout the universal Church and in all its members.[33]

There is thus a continuity between the Mass and the Liturgy of the Hours, for the latter "extends to the different hours of the day the praise and thanksgiving, the commemoration of the mysteries of salvation, the petitions and the foretaste of heavenly glory, that are present in the eucharistic mystery, 'the center and apex of the whole life of the Christian community.'"[34]

Not only is the prayer of the Church the prayer of Christ, but Christ himself is present when "the Church prays and sings."[35]

Moreover, it was chiefly through the recital or singing of the psalms that Christian tradition became aware of the Church's prayer as being truly the prayer of Christ himself. St. Augustine often makes this point in his sermons on the psalms; a notable example is this passage from the commentary on Psalm 85 (= Hebrew 86), which is cited in the *General Instruction:*

---

30. *GILH* 18.

31. *VSC* 84.

32. *VSC* 83. — This passage has a long history behind it. Vatican II takes it from the Encyclical *Mediator Dei* of Pius XII (*AAS* 39 [1947] 573), but Pius XII was in turn inspired by a passage in the Bull *Divinam psalmodiam* of Urban VIII (January 25, 1631), which used to be printed at the beginning of the breviary before the reform of 1911: "The divine psalmody of the Spouse as she consoles herself during the absence of her heavenly Bridegroom should itself be without wrinkle or spot. For it is the child of those hymns that are constantly sung before the throne of God and the Lamb. In order that the earthly psalmody may more closely resemble the heavenly, it should as far as possible contain nothing that can disturb or distract the souls of the singers from their fitting attention to God and divine things."

33. *GILH* 7.

34. *GILH* 12.

35. *VSC* 7; see *GILH* 13.

God could give no greater gift to mankind than to give them as their head the Word through whom he created all things, and to unite them to him as his members, so that he might be Son of God and Son of man, one God with the Father, one man with men. So when we speak to God in prayer we do not separate the Son from God, and when the body of the Son prays it does not separate its head from itself, but it is the one savior of his body, our Lord Jesus Christ, the Son of God, who himself prays for us, and prays in us, and is the object of our prayer. He prays for us as our priest, he prays in us as our head, he is the object of our prayer as our God. Let us then hear our voices in his voice, and his voice in ours.[36]

---

36. St. Augustine, *Enarr. in psalmos* 85, 1 (CCL 39:1176), trans. in *GILH* 7.

Chapter III

The Liturgy of the Hours:
Praying the Psalms

It is a tradition shared by the liturgical families[1] that the Liturgy of the Hours should consist principally in praying the psalms. Psalmody has indeed at times been more or less smothered by an exuberant delight in hymns; the chief instance is the office of the western Syrians. Nonetheless the principle enunciated has always been the basis for renewals and reforms. As far as the Roman liturgy is concerned, it was invoked by St. Pius X in his Bull *Divino afflatu* of November 1, 1911; more recently it inspired the reform of 1971.[2]

§1. The Place of the Psalms in Christian Prayer

BIBLIOGRAPHY

B. Fischer, "Le Christ dans les psaumes. La dévotion aux psaumes dans l'Eglise des martyrs," *LMD* no. 27 (1951) 86–113.

F. Vandenbroucke, *Les psaumes, le Christ et nous* (Louvain: Centre liturgique, 1955).

P. Salmon, *The Breviary through the Centuries*, trans. Sr. Mary David (Collegeville: The Liturgical Press, 1962) 42–61: "The Interpretation of the Psalms during the Formative Period of the Office."

---

1. The same can be said of the communities that emerged from the Reformation; see the survey in J. A. Lamb, *The Psalms in Christian Worship* (London: Faith Press, 1962). See G. Scuderi, "L'uso dei salmi nelle Chiese della Riforma," *Rivista liturgica* 63 (1981) 224–39.

2. *VSC* 91; *GILH* 100–9.

B. Fischer, "Les psaumes, prière chrétienne. Témoignage du IIe siècle," in Cassien-Botte 85–99.

A. Rose, "La lecture chrétienne du psautier dans la Liturgie des Heures," *EL* 86 (1972) 5–30.

G. M. Cardinal Garrone, "Prier avec les psaumes," *Seminarium* 24 (1972) 109–20.

I. Saint-Arnaud, "Les psaumes dans la tradition chrétienne," *DBS* 9 (1973) 206–14.

A. Rose, *Les psaumes, voix du Christ et de l'Eglise* (Bible et vie chrétienne, Référence; Paris: Lethielleux, 1981).

I. CONTINUITY OR DISCONTINUITY WITH JEWISH PRAYER?

One might think it evident that in its devotion to the psalms as in other aspects of its prayer the Church simply continued Jewish practice. In fact, however, we have very little information on the place of the psalms in the Jewish liturgy in the time of Christ and the first generations of Christians.[3] They certainly had a role in the liturgy of the temple, where some of them were sung daily: for example, in the morning, Ps 105,[4] which tells of the *magnalia Dei* or "wonderful works of God," and, in the evening, Ps 96, a hymn to the divine king. Other psalms were assigned to one or other day of the week: Ps 24 to the first day; Ps 48 to Monday; Ps 82 to Tuesday; Ps 94 to Wednesday; Ps 81 to Thursday; Ps 93 to the eve of the sabbath; Pss 38 and 91 to the sabbath.[5] In addition, certain psalms were preferred for expressing the meaning of the major feasts, especially Pss 135 and 136 for Passover. Furthermore, the liturgy of the Passover meal included the recitation of the Hallel (Mark 14:26; Matt 26:30).

Scholars have assumed that in the synagogal liturgy the *lectio continua* (continuous reading) of the Torah was accompanied by a similar reading of the psalms,[6] but it is not attested in any document prior to the

---

3. It seems clear that the Book of Psalms was intended chiefly for liturgical use, but we lack the documentation that would enable us to refine this statement; see E. Beaucamp, "Psaumes. II. Le Psautier," *DBS* 9 (1973) 125–206.

4. [The numbering of the psalms in the English Liturgy of the Hours will be used here; it is the numbering of the Hebrew Bible. The Latin Liturgy of the Hours, like the Latin Fathers and the French original of the present book, *L'Eglise en prière*, follows the numbering of the LXX and the Vulgate. — Tr.]

5. It must be noted, however, that in the titles of the Hebrew psalter only Ps 92 is assigned to a specific day of the week; the other indications of special use come from the Septuagint (LXX), except those for Tuesday and Friday, which come from the Mishnah; see E. Beaucamp, *ibid.* 142–43; J. van Goudoever, "L'arrière-plan liturgique du psautier," *QL* 52 (1971) 79–85.

6. For example, A. Arens, *Die Psalmen im Gottesdienst des Alten Bundes. Eine Untersuchung zur Urgeschichte des christlichen Psalmengesanges* (Trierer theologische Studien 11; Trier: Paulinus Verlag) 160ff.; idem, "Hat der Psalter seinen Sitz im Leben in der synagogalen Lesenordnung des Pentateuch?" in *Le Psautier. Etudes presentées aux XIIes journées bibliques* (Louvain, 1962) 107–31.

destruction of the temple. The psalms doubtless also had a place in the instruction given in schools,[7] since they are a kind of primer of the Bible as a whole, and even more in private prayer, but there is hardly any evidence on this last point. In any case, the Jews had an obvious familiarity with the psalms, for Jesus and those with whom he converses cite them frequently and they crop up continually in the preaching of the apostles.

Christian use of the psalms thus goes far beyond Jewish usage (at least as this last is known to us at present), and this in two ways. First, the psalms undergo a "christologization"; this phenomenon already occurs in the New Testament and in the writings of the Fathers of the first centuries. Second, there is the predilection with which the mystics later look to the psalms for an initiation into the prayer of praise, for contemplation of the divine perfections, and for an expression of the sorry state of humanity.

II. THE "CHRISTOLOGIZATION" OF THE PSALMS

Professor Balthasar Fischer has derived from the writings of the second century the principles which guided the early Christians in their devotion to the psalms. According to his analysis, they regarded the psalms as the prayer of Christ himself and as, at the same time, prayers addressed to Christ.

In so doing, these early Christians needed only to follow the direction shown them by the Lord Jesus himself. For, according to the account in Luke 24:44, on Easter evening he explained to his apostles that "everything written about me in the law of Moses and the prophets and the psalms must be fulfilled." This short list already assigns the psalms a special place among the books of the Bible. Moreover, the key to the interpretation of the psalms is provided by the paschal mystery: "Thus it is written, that the Christ should suffer and on the third day rise from the dead, and that repentance and forgiveness of sins should be preached in his name to all nations" (vv. 46-47).

Moreover, the evangelists place verses from Pss 22 and 31 on the lips of Jesus in his final prayer. They see details of the passion prefigured in various psalms, such as 22, 41, and 69. In addition, the psalms often pro-

---

7. J. van Goudoever, *ibid.* 83–84.

vide the apostles with their starting point for proclaiming Jesus Christ in Jerusalem or in the synagogues.[8]

There is thus a homogeneous continuity between the use made of the psalter in the New Testament and the manner in which it is read and commented on by St. Justin, Tertullian, St. Hippolytus, Clement of Alexandria, and, above all, Origen. As B. Fischer accurately observes, "the Church of the martyrs was not satisfied to see in the psalter only a handful of passages that had been given new meaning by the light of Christ; rather the entire psalter was for them a book of prophecies which were fulfilled by Christ."[9] At times they heard in the psalms the voice of Jesus; thus Tertullian writes that "almost all the psalms show us the person of Christ; they make the Son present as he speaks to the Father, that is, Christ as he speaks to God."[10] At other times, they hear the voice of the Father speaking to Christ, as in Ps 89.

Most of the time, however, these early Fathers understood the term *Kyrios* ("Lord"—the translation in the LXX of the name of God that must not be pronounced) as referring to Christ. In their view, this term for God could evoke not only the majesty of the Father but also the glory of the risen Jesus; in this they were once again in tune with the preaching of the apostles (Acts 2:36; 10:36; Rom 10:9; Phil 2:11; Col 2:6; etc.).[11] As a result, the prayers in the psalms became for these Christians prayers addressed to Christ. They also became prayers which speak of Christ, calling to mind his reign (Ps 96, with its characteristic gloss, "God has reigned from the tree"), his role as shepherd (Ps 23), the Eucharist (Ps 34: "Taste and see how good the Lord is").

The psalms are also the voice of the Church, which applies the history of Israel to itself in order to express its suffering in time of persecution, its trust in a divine liberation, its hope.[12] An example of this use of the

---

8. Ps 2 in Acts 4:25-26; Ps 16 in Acts 2:25-28 and 13:35; Ps 69 in Acts 1:20; Ps 109 in Acts 1:20; Ps 110 in Acts 2:34-35; Ps 118 in Acts 4:11. — See J. Dupont, *The Salvation of the Gentiles. Essays on the Acts of the Apostles*, trans. John R. Keating (New York: Paulist, 1979) 103-28 and 146-60. — The Letter to the Hebrews uses successively Pss 2, 97, 104, 45, 102, 110, 8, 22, 95, and 40. — For the place of the psalms in the New Testament as a whole see A. George, "Jésus et les psaumes," in *A la recontre de Dieu. Mémorial A. Gelin* (Le Puy: Mappus, 1961) 297-308; J. Luyten, "Psaumes et paroles de Jésus," *QL* 61 (1980) 241-62; A. Rose, *Les psaumes, voix du Christ et de l'Eglise* (Paris: Lethielleux, 1981) 33-54.

9. B. Fischer, "Le Christ dans les psaumes. La dévotion aux psaumes dans l'Eglise des martyrs," *LMD* no. 27 (1951) 92.

10. *Adversus Praxean* 11, 7 (CCL 2:1172).

11. L. Certaux, "Le titre Kyrios et la dignité royale de Jésus," in *Recueil Lucien Cerfaux* 1 (Gembloux: Duculot, 1954) 3-34; idem, "Kyrios dans les citations pauliniennes de l'Ancien Testament," in *ibid.* 35-64.

12. E. Beaucamp, *ibid.* 166-87, provides a good synthesis of the theology of the psalms as the prayer of God's people in the Old Testament.

psalms may be seen in the prayer of the apostolic community (see Acts 4:25ff.).

For the early period we have only scattered instances of this Christian interpretation of the psalms; these occur here and there in the works of the Apologists. Continuous commentaries on the psalms did exist but they are now lost; we are able to form some idea of them, however, from the fragments of Hippolytus[13] and Origen[14] that have survived. In the fourth century Eusebius of Caesarea and St. Hilary of Poitiers commented on the psalms in this same spirit, and since that time the work has gone on uninterruptedly in the Church.[15] It is one of the glories of St. Augustine that in his *Enarrationes in Psalmos* he has provided us with the most complete method for a Christological interpretation of the psalms and thereby made us aware that the prayer of the Church is one with that of Christ: the prayer of the body and the prayer of the head.[16]

III. THE PSALMS AND THE PRAYER OF HUMAN BEINGS

We must not think that this Christological "rereading" of the psalms excluded every other approach or that it caused Christians to forget the literal meaning of the psalms. On the contrary, as monastic prayer, with its experience in meditation, made clear, the psalter proved to be the best means of initiation into intimacy with God, making audible as it does the voice of the Church and the voice of the faithful soul, the voice of Christ and the voice of the disciple.

---

13. See, above all, P. Nautin, *Le dossier d'Hippolyte et de Méliton* (Patristica 1; Paris: Cerf, 1953) 99–107, 161–84; G. Mercati, *Osservazioni ai proemi del Salterio* (ST 142; Vatican City, 1948).

14. R. Cadiou, *Commentaires inédits des psaumes. Etudes sur les textes d'Origène contenus dans le manuscrit Vindobonensis 8* (Collection d'etudes anciennes; Paris: Belles Lettres, 1936); V. Peri, *Omelie origeniane sui salmi. Contributo all'identificazione des testo latino* (ST 289; Vatican City, 1980). — See R. Devreesse, *Les anciens manuscrits grecques des psaumes* (ST 264; Vatican City, 1970); A. Rose, *ibid*, 73–75, 88.

15. Extensive bibliography covering antiquity, the Middle Ages, and the modern period in L. Jacquet, *Les psaumes et le coeur de l'homme. Etude textuelle, littéraire et doctrinale* 1 (Gembloux: Duculot, 1975) 31–53; the bibliography for antiquity can be completed with the aid of A. Rose, *ibid.* 73–92.

16. The text of the *Enarrationes* is in CCL 38–40 (PL 36–37). In English: *St. Augustine on the Psalms*, trans. and annot. Dame Scholastica Hegbin and Dame Felicitas Corrigan (Ancient Christian Writers 29–30; New York: Newman Press, 1960–61). The two volumes include the sermons on Pss 1–37. There is a complete translation in the old Oxford Library of the Fathers: *Expositions on the Psalms*, trans. by various hands (6 vols.; Oxford: Parker, and London: Rivington, 1847–57; there is also a translation "condensed from the six volumes of the Oxford translation" by A. Cleveland Coxe in Volume 8 of the *Nicene and Post-Nicene Fathers of the Christian Church*, ed. Philip Schaff (New York: Christian Literature Company, 1905). Bibliography in A. Di Bernardino, *Patrologia* 3 (Turin: Marietti, 1978), 376–77.

An especially important testimony to monastic meditation on the psalms comes to us in the letter of St. Athanasius († 373) to Marcellinus.[17] Athanasius was of course loyal to the Christological interpretation of the psalms that had become traditional in Alexandria. At the same time, however (he says), since Christ is the model or "type" of the human race and since the psalter expresses the sentiments of Christ, it provides us with the ideal image of our own spiritual life and tells us how to heal the movements of the soul and resist temptation: "Since Christ is in his person the image of both the earthly and the heavenly human being, anyone who so desires can learn from the psalms to recognize the movements and dispositions of the soul and even find there the means of healing and correcting each movement."[18]

For Athanasius, then, the psalter is as it were a "mirror" in which those who sing the psalms "can look at themselves and observe the movements of their souls." They will feel "that it is they whom the psalter has in view."[19] In our own time we find these formulas echoed in Thomas Merton: "This is the secret of the psalms. Our identity is hidden in them. In them we find ourselves, and God. In these fragments He has revealed not only Himself to us but ourselves in Him."[20]

And in fact the psalms are, and will forever remain, the expression of the prayer of the poor (the *anawim*) and the sinful: "Though the psalms originated very many centuries ago in the East they express accurately the pain and hope, the unhappiness and trust, of people of every age and country."[21] They make no attempt to conceal the harshness of the human condition with its evil impulses, its injustices, its wars and oppression. It is true, on the other hand, that the frequent occurrence in the psalms of bitter curses against enemies and the wicked became a problem once the psalms of the office were sung or recited in the vernacular. A correct view of the history of salvation shows that while such curses occur in the New Testament as well and even in the gospels, they are not directed against any individual. Nonetheless, account must be taken of the possible presence at the office of people who would not realize the true meaning and would be scandalized. The experience of the Anglican Church and other Reformation communities in this area proved helpful in deciding on necessary omissions in the 1971 edition of the *Liturgia Horarum*.[22]

---

17. PG 27:11-45; see M. J. Rondeau, "L'Epître à Marcellinus sur les psaumes," *Vigiliae christianae* 22 (1968) 176–97.

18. St. Athanasius, *ibid*. 13 (PG 27:25).

19. *Ibid*. 12 (PG 27:24).

20. Thomas Merton, *The Sign of Jonas* (London: Hollis & Carter, 1953) 248.

21. *GILH* 107. — See the stimulating book of P. Beauchamp, *Psaumes nuit et jour* (Paris: Editions du Seuil, 1980).

22. *GILH* 131.

The psalter is, above all, a school in which to learn the contemplation of God and his perfections. It teaches us to admire him at work in the splendor of creation; it also teaches us the language of intimacy with him. The Jewish tradition calls the psalms as a whole *tehillim* ("praises") and thus singles out the theme of praise that is typical of the psalter and gives the Christian Liturgy of the Hours its character as a prayer of praise.[23] St. Augustine says of the psalter: "In order that human beings might praise him properly, God first praised himself; and because he deigned thus to praise himself, human beings have been able to learn how to praise him."[24]

§2. The Place of the Psalms in the Liturgy of the Hours

BIBLIOGRAPHY

We lack a work that would compare the distribution of the psalms in the offices of the different Churches and monastic rules. The following are the main references for the Roman and Benedictine traditions:

a) *Historical studies:*

C. Callewaert, *Sacris erudiri* (Steenbrugge: Abbaye Saint-Pierre, 1940) *passim* (a collection of articles published in various periodicals).

J. Pascher, "Das Psalterium der Apostelmatutin," *MTZ* 8 (1957) 1–12.

_____, "Sinnheiten in der Verteilung des Psalters des Breviers: Ein weihnachtlicher und ein österlicher Typus," *ibid.* 189–205.

_____, "Der Psalter für Laudes und Vesper im alten römischen Stundengebet," *ibid.* 255–67.

_____, "Das Psalterium des römischen Breviers. Ein Forschungsbericht," in *Brevierstudien,* ed. J. A. Jungmann (Trier: Paulinus Verlag, 1958) 9–20.

_____, "Zur Frühgeschichte des römischen Wochenpsalteriums," *EL* 79 (1965) 55–58.

_____, "Die Methode der Psalmenauswahl im römischen Stundengebet," *Sitzungsberichte der Bayerischen Akademie der Wissenschaften, Philos.-Hist. Klasse,* 1967, Heft 3.

A. de Vogüé, *La Règle de saint Benoît* 5. *Commentaire historique et critique* (SC 185; Paris: Cerf, 1971) 433–544.

b) *On the distribution of the psalms in the present (Roman and Benedictine) Liturgy of the Hours:*

GILH 126–35.

A. Rose, "La répartition des psaumes dans le cycle liturgique," *LMD* no. 105 (1971) 66–102.

---

23. E. Beaucamp, *ibid.* 126; see *GILH* 103.
24. St. Augustine, *Enarr. in psalmos* 144, 1 (CCL 40:2088).

J. Pascher, "Die Psalmen als Grundlage des Stundengebets," *EL* 85 (1971) 260–80.

_____, "Il nuovo ordinamento della salmodia nella Liturgia romana delle Ore," in *Liturgia delle Ore. Documenti ufficiali e studi* (Quaderni di Rivista Liturgica 14; Turin-Leumann; ElleDiCi, 1972) 161–84.

J. Gibert-Taruel, "La nouvelle distribution du Psautier dans la *Liturgia Horarum*," *EL* 87 (1973) 325–82.

Thesaurus Liturgiae Horarum monasticae (Rome: Sant'Anselmo, 1977) 38–57.

From the time in the fourth century when the prayer of the hours was organized as a communal prayer, the psalms were always the essential element. Morning prayer and evening prayer used selected psalms, "morning psalms" and "evening psalms," which the people must have known by heart. The more or less frequent vigils in what has been known since the work of A. Baumstark as the "cathedral cycle," and especially the vigils celebrated at the martyrs' tombs for their anniversaries, likewise consisted primarily in the singing of either biblical canticles or psalms, for which methods of psalmody that would prevent monotony were used.[25]

As we have seen, however, at the same time that this "cathedral" version of the prayer of the hours was taking a more clearly defined form, another was developing—that of the ascetics and monks—which was often celebrated in the same place of worship. This second type of office was likewise based on the psalms, which were read, or sung, and meditated on, but in this case with the proviso that the entire psalter was to be recited within a certain period of time.

Just as the two cycles of prayer were fused to form a single Liturgy of the Hours, so the two ways of using the psalter came to be used simultaneously: a "continuous reading" (*lectio continua*) and a selection of psalms according to circumstances of time and place.

I. THE CONTINUOUS READING OF THE PSALMS

It seems to have been the Rule of St. Benedict that clearly formulated the principle of a complete recitation of the psalter in the space of a week. After describing in detail the distribution of the psalms that he proposes, Benedict adds: "We urge that if anyone finds this distribution of the psalms unsatisfactory, he should arrange whatever he judges better, provided that the full complement of 150 psalms is by all means carefully maintained every week."[26] In fact, on this point he was simply following a Roman

---

25. Some witnesses: St. Basil, *Ep.* 207, ed. Y. Courtonne, 2 (Collection Budé; Paris: Belles Lettres, 1961) 183–88; *Egeria's Travels* 24–25, trans. John Wilkinson (London: SPCK, 1971) 123–28. — On "cathedral" vigils with biblical canticles see below, p. 209.

26. St. Benedict, *Regula* 18, 22, translated in *The Rule of St. Benedict in Latin and English with Notes*, ed. Timothy Fry (Collegeville: The Liturgical Press, 1981) 215.

usage which despite the vicissitudes of time was continued down to Vatican II. The practice represented a middle way between the exaggerations of certain Egyptian monks who seem to have said the whole psalter daily, and other communities which allowed a longer period for reciting it: the Armenian office distributed the psalms over eight days, the Ambrosian Church over two weeks, and Spain over as much as three weeks. The Chaldeans and the Byzantines use the week as their unit, at least in their present-day practice.[27]

In order to facilitate the practice of the continuous reading of the psalms, the different traditions divided the psalter into sections: the Byzantines call them *kathismata*, the Armenians *canons*, the Chaldeans *hullale* (of nine psalms) and *marmyata* (of three psalms). The ancient Roman and Benedictine offices assigned a group of twelve psalms to each ferial vigil; the resultant groups varied greatly in length, but St. Benedict made them more equal by imitating the Egyptian tradition reported by Cassian[28] and applying the principle that longer psalms were to be divided into sections.[29] The Roman office followed the more austere course and accepted this principle only in 1911, at the reform of St. Pius X; until that time it had made an exception only for Ps 119.

Confronted with these figures, some historians of the liturgy have asked whether the recitation of a given number of psalms was not a purely ascetical exercise. In fact, however, the psalms became the subject of meditation: after the recitation of each the community reflected on it in silence, or else each psalm was interpreted along certain lines with the help of a refrain, a prayer, or a title, as we shall see further on. The continuous reading was not a mere routine, but represented an assertion of fidelity to the entire inspired word. Meditation on the entire psalter, moreover, was not reserved to monks. The *Enarrationes in psalmos* of St. Augustine, many of which were given in the course of the liturgy,[30] make it clear that all the psalms are intended to be the subject of Christian prayer.

Modern life, however, demands a more relaxed rhythm for prayer. In order, therefore, to ensure a more interiorized celebration of the Liturgy

---

27. For further details see the syntheses of A. Baumstark, *Festbrevier und Kirchenjahr der syrischen Jakobiten. Eine liturgiegeschichtliche Vorarbeit* (Studien zur Geschichte und Kultur des Altertums 3, 3-5; Paderborn: Schöningh, 1910) 138–50; idem, *Comparative Liturgy*, ed. B. Botte, trans. F. L. Cross (Westminster, Md.: Newman Press, 1958) 114-15; idem, *Nocturna laus* (LQF 32; Münster: Aschendorff, 1957) 156–66. — For Spain: J. Pinell, "El oficio hispano-visigótico," *Hispania sacra* 10 (1957) 328–427, espec. 419.

28. John Cassian, *De institutis coenobiorum* II, 4; II, 11, 3, ed. J. C. Guy (SC 109:64 and 78).

29. *Regula* 18, 5; 18, 16; 18, 21.

30. On this point see the articles of H. Rondet in *Bulletin de littérature ecclésiastique* from 1960 to 1976.

of the Hours, the Second Vatican Council decided to abandon the weekly cycle for the psalter;[31] in the future the one hundred and fifty psalms are to be distributed over four weeks. Benedictine monasticism has likewise had to envisage other allocations of the psalms (something St. Benedict allowed for) and even their possible distribution over a two-week period.

II. THE USE OF PSALMS IN SPECIFIC CONTEXTS

Except in the *Regula Magistri*,[32] the continuous reading of the psalms was to some extent restricted by the more or less extensive use of some psalms for certain occasions in the various liturgies.

Egeria, for example, was probably accustomed to a more austere psalmody in her own Church and was therefore surprised to find that in Jerusalem "the psalms and antiphons they use are always appropriate, whether at night, in the early morning, at the day prayers at midday or three o'clock, or at Lucernare. Everything is suitable, appropriate, and relevant to what is being done."[33]

Without going so far, most of the liturgies nonetheless granted certain psalms a privileged place in the course of the day, the week, the liturgical year, or the feasts.

a) *In the sequence of Hours* certain psalms have traditionally been regarded as morning psalms (*psalmoi heōthinoi*), e.g., Pss 5, 51, 63 (except in the Syrian world), 67, 100, 143, and, above all, 148–50, or as *ainoi* ("praises"), which gave their name to the office of Lauds in the Roman liturgy. Others have been evening psalms (*psalmoi hesperinoi*), especially Ps 141 ("the lifting up of my hands as an evening sacrifice"). In the course of the day those praying liked to use Ps 119 in the Roman rite and at Milan, or the Gradual Psalms (120-28) in the Rule of St. Benedict. St. Basil and Cassiodorus after him had already prescribed Ps 91 for the moment of retiring.[34] The vigil during the night began quite naturally with Ps 3 and, in Benedictine and Roman usage, Ps 95.

b) As far as the *week* was concerned, the Roman Church—and it alone—retained from Jewish usage only Ps 91 which had been a psalm for the sabbath and was now used on Saturday. The reason for this discontinuity was that the Christian week is something new which derives its character from the death, burial, and resurrection of Christ. On Sunday,

---

31. *VSC* 91.

32. *Regula Magistri* 33, 29, 36; 35, 2; 36, 1; 41, 2; 44, 1, 7, ed. A. de Vogüé 2 (SC 106) 182, 190, 192, 198, 202.

33. *Egeria's Travels* 25, 5 (Wilkinson 126).

34. St. Basil, *Regulae fusius tractatae*, Qu. 37, no. 5 (PG 31:1016); Cassiodorus, *Expos. in psalm. 90* 13 (PL 70:655).

the weekly pasch of Christians, the liturgy therefore decreed that in its prayer of the Hours those psalms were to be sung in which, according to apostolic preaching or the tradition, the paschal mystery of Christ is expressed.

Of these psalms, Ps 93, which glorifies the kingly dignity of the Lord, had an important place in Byzantine spirituality and iconography; in particular it inspired the theme of the *Hetimasia* or "Preparation" (Ps 92:2 LXX: *hetoimos ho thronos sou* and Vg: *parata sedes tua*, "your throne is prepared").[35] Ps 118, so often cited in the New Testament, gave the paschal liturgy of Rome its characteristic note: *Haec est dies quam fecit Dominus; Exultemus, et laetemur in ea* (Ps 117:24 Vg), "This is the day the Lord has made; let us rejoice and be glad in it." Ps 110, which was already regarded as messianic in the time of Jesus and then was given a lengthy commentary in the Letter to the Hebrews, sings of the priesthood and victory of Christ. Finally, Ps 114, which recalls the "wonderful works of God" at the Red Sea and the Jordan, links the pasch of Christ and that of Christians, who have been saved by means of water and have forsaken idols. To this basic heritage that was shared by all the liturgies the Roman Church traditionally added Pss 1, 2, and 3. Ps 2, as I pointed out earlier, had an important place in the apostolic catechesis; in Ps 1 the Fathers saw prefigured the tree of the cross; and in Ps 3 they found the resurrection heralded.

The reform of 1971 endeavored to accentuate the paschal character of the Sunday psalms even further through its selection of psalms for the four Sundays of the cycle.[36] It also introduced an innovation by giving the Friday psalms a penitential character and using them to recall the passion of Christ. In particular it reserved to Fridays Ps 51, which had formerly been recited daily, and Ps 22, the prayer of Christ on the cross.[37]

c) The choice of certain psalms for this or that solemnity in *the course of the liturgical year* made it possible to highlight the Christological interpretation of these psalms. The process is especially clear in the psalms used for Holy Week, Easter, Christmas, and Epiphany in the Roman and Milanese traditions. The Christological interpretation was underscored in particular by the antiphons, which were taken from the psalms themselves. This accounts for the deserved importance of the antiphons in even the individual's celebration of the office.

Fortunately, the shortening of the Office of Readings in the 1971 reform of the Roman office did not cause these traditional riches to be lost. The

35. On the *hetimasia* see K. Künstle, *Ikonographie der christlichen Kunst* I (Freiburg, 1928) 559–60; F. van der Meer, *Maiestas Domini. Théophanies de l'Apocalypse dans l'art chrétien* (Studi di antichità cristiana 13; Vatican City, 1938) 231–45.

36. *GILH* 129.

37. *Ibid.*

reason is that the psalms which no longer kept their place at the tradi- tional hours were transferred to the Daytime Hours of the feast day or, in the case of Christmas, to the days of the octave.[38]

§3. The Delivery of the Psalms

BIBLIOGRAPHY

J. Mateos, "La psalmodie dans le rite byzantin," *POC* 15 (1965) 107–26.
J. Gelineau, "Les psaumes à l'époque patristique," *LMD* no. 135 (1978) 99–116.
GILH 121–25.

I. THE PSALMS ARE POEMS

The psalms are not readings or prose prayers, but poems of praise. They can on occasion be recited as readings, but from their literary genre they are properly called *Tehillim* ("songs of praise") in Hebrew and *psalmoi* ("songs to be sung to the lyre") in Greek. In fact, all the psalms have a musical quality that determines their correct style of delivery. Thus even when a psalm is recited and not sung or is said silently in private, its musical character should govern its use.[39]

This principle is meant, first of all, to determine the way in which the psalms are translated into the various languages. That is, the translator must make clear their poetic character, with their images, their literary devices, and, in a certain measure, their rhythm.[40]

All the more, then,

different psalms may be sung in different ways for a fuller grasp of their spiritual meaning and beauty. The choice of ways is dictated by the literary genre or length of each psalm, by the language used, whether Latin or the vernacular, and especially by the kind of celebration, whether individual, with a group, or with a congregation.[41]

---

38. *GILH* 134. — In addition, "three psalms (78, 105 and 106) are reserved for the seasons of Advent, Christmas, Lent and Easter, as they throw a special light on the history of salva- tion in the Old Testament as the forerunner of its fulfillment in the New" (*GILH* 130).

39. *GILH* 103.

40. On this problem as seen primarily from the standpoint of the French language, see *LMD* no. 118 (1974): *Traduction liturgique du psautier* (articles by C. Wiener, J. Gribo- mont, P. Beauchamp, J. L. Vesco, and D. Rimaud); H. Delhougne, "Le psautier liturgique 77," *LMD* no. 135 (1978) 117–47.

41. *GILH* 121. — On the various literary genres in the psalms, see E. Lepinski, "Psaumes: Formes et genres littéraires," *DBS* 9 (1973) 1–125.

II. METHODS IN THE SINGING OF THE PSALMS

In antiquity different ways of singing the psalms were used in successive periods and even in the same period. The first method, which was practiced in Egyptian monasticism and is still found at times in the East, was to have a soloist read or sing the psalm while the community listened in silence; when the soloist had finished, the monks silently meditated on the psalm and then the presiding monk said a prayer or *collect* in the name of all.

This method was too austere for a congregation of the people, which required an active external participation and some variety in the singing if its interior attention was to be sustained. At times, therefore, the people were asked to sing a response, refrain, or acclamation at the end of the soloist's chant. Sometimes they sang their refrains or alleluias at various points in the chanting of the psalm,[42] thus effectively dividing the latter into stanzas in a way which the Hebrew text itself suggests for some psalms. Sometimes, finally, two choirs sang the psalm, alternating the verses or stanzas. In addition, all could recite together a psalm which was to be delivered without antiphon or response (*in directum* or *directaneus*).

The Roman, Ambrosian, and Benedictine traditions used these various methods; from the Middle Ages on, however, the chief method used was the singing of alternate verses by two groups. Modern translations of the psalms into the vernaculars implicitly urge that the method of delivery be better adapted to the genre of each psalm.

III. THE TRINITARIAN DOXOLOGY

The practice of ending each psalm or group of psalms with the refrain or acclamation, "Glory to the Father . . . ," is attested as early as the end of the fourth century in Provence[43] and was adopted by all the Latin monastic rules.[44] It is also found in the Byzantine *Horologion* and, though less regularly, in other rites. The *General Instruction* of 1971 requires that the practice be continued in the Liturgy of the Hours: The "Glory to the Father" is "the fitting conclusion that tradition recommends, and it gives

---

42. G. Oury, "*Psalmum dicere cum alleluia*," *EL* 79 (1965) 97–108.

43. John Cassian, *De institutis coenobiorum* II, 8 (SC 109:72).

44. *Regula Magistri* 33, 43; St. Benedict, *Regula* 9, 2; 13, 9; 17, 2; 43, 4; 43, 10. — See the apocryphal letter of Jerome to Pope Damasus (probably from the sixth century): P. Hinschius, *Decretales pseudo-Isidorianae* (Leipzig, 1863) 499; P. Blanchard, "La correspondance apocryphe du pape Damase et de saint Jérôme," *EL* 63 (1949) 382. — On this doxology in general, see M. Righetti, *Manuale di storia liturgica* 1 (3rd ed.; Milan: Ancora, 1964) 236–38.

to Old Testament prayer a quality of praise linked to a Christological and Trinitarian interpretation."[45]

§4. Elements Helping Us to Pray the Psalms

In addition to the kind of introduction to the psalms which preachers can supply and which some of the Fathers gave in the form of continuous commentaries, "three elements have greatly contributed to an understanding of the psalms and their use as Christian prayer: the titles, the psalm-prayers and in particular the antiphons."[46]

I. THE TITLES OF THE PSALMS

BIBLIOGRAPHY

P. Salmon, *Les tituli psalmorum des anciens manuscrits latins* (Etudes liturgiques 3; Paris: Cerf, 1959; and Collectanea biblica latina 12; Vatican City, 1959).

_____, "Les tituli psalmorum. Nouvelles series," in *Analecta liturgica* (ST 273; Vatican City, 1974) 9–46.

B. Fischer, "Les titres chrétiens des psaumes dans le nouvel Office divin," *LMD* no. 135 (1978) 149–58.

Medieval manuscripts of the psalter regularly gave each psalm a title which was intended to sum up its contents and guide the rereading of the psalm along Christological or ecclesial lines. Mgr. Salmon's researches have brought to light ten series of such titles, some of them being quite old (Series V may date from the fifth century). Cistercian psalters continued this tradition down to our own time.

In the new *Liturgy of the Hours* (1971) each psalm has two titles. One title sums up its literal meaning and its importance for the human life of the believer; the other consists of a phrase from the New Testament or the Fathers which helps the reader to pray the psalm according to its Christological meaning and, more generally, makes it easier to pray it in the light of New Testament revelation.[47]

---

45. *GILH* 123.
46. *GILH* 110.
47. See *GILH* 111.

II. THE PSALTER COLLECTS

BIBLIOGRAPHY

A. Wilmart and L. Brou, *The Psalter Collects from the V-VI Century Sources (Three Series)* (HBS 83; London: Henry Bradshaw Society, 1949).

J. Mateos, "Une collection de prières entre les marmyata," *OCP* 31 (1965) 53–75.

P. Verbraken, *Oraisons sur les cent cinquante psaumes* (Lex orandi 42; Paris: Cerf, 1967).

J. Pinell, "Le collette salmiche," in *Liturgia delle Ore. Documenti ufficiali e studi* (Turin-Leumann, ElleDiCi, 1972) 269–86.

_____, "Las oraciones del Salterio *per annum* en el nuevo libro de la Liturgia de las Horas," *EL* 86 (1972) 354–89, 417–48 (= Bibliotheca EL, Subsidia 2, 1974).

_____, *Liber orationum psalmographus. Colectas de psalmos del antiguo rito hispánico* (Monumenta Hispaniae sacra, ser. lit., 8; Barcelona–Madrid: Consejo Superior de investigaciones científicas, 1972).

J. M. Canals Casas, *Las colectas de salmos de la serie "Visita nos."* Introducción, *edición crítica e índices* (Bibliotheca Salmanticensis, Estudios 26; Salamanca: Universidad pontificia, 1978).

J. Evenou, "Les oraisons psalmiques. Pour une prière chrétienne des psaumes," *LMD* no. 135 (1978) 158–74.

As we saw earlier, according to Cassian the monks of Egypt prayed silently for a few moments after each psalm, and then the monk whose function it was to end the prayer (*qui orationem collecturus est*, "who was to draw together or 'collect' the prayer") spoke in the name of all;[48] this "collect" seems to have been spoken by a priest.[49] Egeria in turn noted that in Jerusalem each psalm or canticle was followed by a prayer which was said by a priest or a deacon, even in those parts of the office that were meant especially for the *monazontes*.[50] The Council of Agde (506) prescribed that "after the antiphons collects are said by the bishop or the priests."[51] The Chaldean office has maintained the practice of beginning each section (*marmyata*) with a prayer that is a true psalter collect;[52] collections of similar prayers have been found in the ancient Syrian *sacerdotalia*. Among the series of Latin psalm-prayers or psalter collects that have come down to us the more important are those of the Spanish liturgy (published by J. Pinell).

The reform undertaken by Paul VI aimed at reviving this tradition. The *General Instruction* announced the ultimate publication of an appendix to the *Liturgy of the Hours* that would offer collects for each psalm.

---

48. John Cassian, *De institutis coenobiorum* II, 7, 3 (SC 109:70-72).

49. *Ibid.* II, 10, (SC 109:74): "One hears no voice but that of the priest who speaks the concluding prayer."

50. *Egeria's Travels* 24–25 (Wilkinson 123–28).

51. Canon 30, ed. C. Munier (CCL 148:206).

52. J. Mateos, "L'office divin chez les Chaldéens," in Cassien-Botte 273.

These would help persons praying the office to understand the psalms better and especially to pray them in a Christian way. The collects would be optional; if used, then once the psalm was finished and a moment of silence had been observed, the collect would gather up the sentiments of all and round off the psalmody.[53]

III. THE PSALMIC ANTIPHONS

BIBLIOGRAPHY

P. Alfonzo, *L'antifonario dell'ufficio romano* (Subiaco, 1935).

J. M. Hanssens, *Amalarii episcopi opera liturgica omnia* 3 (ST 140; Vatican City, 1950) 110–224: *Tabellae quibus illustratur constitutio antiphonarii ab Amalario compositi.*

P. Blanchard, "Le psautier dans la liturgie," in *Richesses et deficiences des anciens psautiers latins* (Collectanea biblica latina 13; Vatican City, 1959) 231–48.

J. Mateos, "La psalmodie dans le rite byzantin," *POC* 15 (1965) 107–26.

R. J. Hesbert, *Corpus antiphonalium officii* (6 vols.; REDMF 7–12; Rome: Herder, 1963–79), especially volume 3: *Invitatoria et antiphonae. Editio critica.*

Antiphons are refrains meant to be sung before or after a psalm or even between the stanzas of a psalm. The various liturgical traditions show two quite distinct categories of refrains: some are real hymns or poetic compositions and will be described in the next chapter; the others consist of a verse from the psalm itself, the verse being adapted or slightly modified in view of its function as a refrain.

Antiphons of this second kind occur in the Eastern offices.[54] It is above all, however, in the Latin Church and chiefly in the Roman, Ambrosian, and Benedictine offices, that psalmic antiphons acquired a literary and musical form that has made them an important help in praying and understanding the psalms. Rhythm and melody make it easier to memorize the antiphons; these then more readily come to mind throughout the day and give support to personal prayer.

> The antiphons help to bring out the literary genre of the psalm; they highlight some theme that may otherwise not attract the attention it deserves; they suggest an individual tone in a psalm, varying with different contexts: indeed, as long as farfetched accommodated senses are avoided, antiphons are of great value in helping toward an understanding of the typological meaning or the meaning appropriate to the feast.[55]

---

53. *GILH* 112.

54. For example, the Chaldean psalmic refrains (*qanone*) attributed to Mar Aba I; see J. Mateos, *Lelya-Sapra. Essai d'interprétation des matines chaldéennes* (OCA 156; Rome: Pontificio Istituto Orientale, 1959) 315–53.

55. *GILH* 113.

This is the case especially with the Ambrosian antiphons for Holy Week and with the Roman antiphons for Christmas, Epiphany, the sacred triduum, and Ascension.

During various attempts at reforming the office, in particular that of Quiñones in the sixteenth century, the question was raised whether it was really appropriate to keep the antiphons, especially in private recitation. The question showed a failure to understand the important role of the antiphons in praying the psalms more fully and deeply, a role of which the *Instruction* of 1971 has now reminded us. It is true, nonetheless, that the antiphons do find their full meaning in the communal and sung celebration of the Liturgy of the Hours; private celebration retains only a kind of echo of that primary celebration. Moreover, in view of the extraordinary quality of the Gregorian musical repertory, it is not surprising that the establishment of a modern repertory which satisfies the same demands should still be only in the experimental stage.

Chapter IV

The Other Elements in the Liturgy of the Hours

Although the psalms are the most characteristic component of the Liturgy of the Hours, other elements have also traditionally been part of it. Some—the biblical canticles and the hymns—function as a prolongation of the psalmody. Others belong to a quite different literary genre; these include, on the one hand, the readings (though these are not found as universally in the various forms the office has taken), and, on the other, the prayers that begin or end the hours.

§1. The Biblical Canticles

BIBLIOGRAPHY

F. Cabrol, "Cantiques," *DACL* 2 (1909) 1975-94.

W. S. Porter, "*Cantica mozarabici officii,*" *EL* 49 (1935) 126-45.

W. M. Whitehill, "A Catalogue of Mozarabic Liturgical Manuscripts Containing the Psalter and *Liber Canticorum,*" *JLW* 14 (1938) 95-122.

H. Schneider, *Die altlateinischen biblischen Cantica* (TA 29-30; Beuron, 1938).

O. Rousseau, "La plus ancienne liste des cantiques liturgiques tirés de l'Ecriture," *RechSR* 35 (1948) 120-29.

H. Schneider, "Die biblischen Oden," *Biblica* 30 (1949) 28-65, 239-72, 433-52, 479-500.

J. Pinell, "Los cánticos del oficio en el antiguo rito hispánico," *HBS* 27 (1970) 5-50.

M. Kochammer, *Die monastischen Cantica im Mittelalter und ihre altenglischen interlinear Versionen. Studien und Textausgabe* (Münchener Universitätsschriften 6; Munich: Fink, 1976).

J. Pinell, "Las oraciones *de cantico* del antiguo rito hispánico," *Didaskalia* 8 (1978) 193-329.

GILH 136-39.

The Greek manuscript of the Bible that is known as the Codex Alexandrinus (London, British Library, Royal 1 D V. VIII), which dates from the fifth century, already adds the following canticles after the psalter: Exod 15:1-12 (Canticle of Moses); Deut 32 (second Canticle of Moses); 1 Sam 2:1-10 (Canticle of Hannah); Isa 26:9-20 ("My soul yearns for thee in the night"); Jonah 2:3-10 (Canticle of Jonah); Hab 3:2-19 (Complaint of Habakkuk); Isa 30:10-20 (Canticle of Hezekiah); the apocryphal Prayer of Manasseh; Dan 3:26-57 (Prayer of Azariah); Dan 3:57-88 (Canticle of the Three Young Men); Luke 1:46-55 (Canticle of the Virgin Mary); Luke 2:29-32 (Canticle of Simeon); Luke 1:69-78 (Canticle of Zechariah). The collection ends with the *Doxa en hupsistois Theō* ("Glory to God in the highest").

The Codex Alexandrinus is not an isolated witness. H. Schneider has collected a good number of others from the fourth to the sixth century, showing how widely used most of these canticles were in vigils, the daytime hours, and even the Mass. Moreover, the list is a good deal longer in Benedictine usage, in the Spanish liturgy (W. Porter has counted 122), and, in the twentieth century, in the Roman office.

I. CANTICLES FROM THE OLD TESTAMENT

a) *In morning prayer*—These canticles have always had a privileged place in morning prayer (*orthros, sapra, matutinum,* or Lauds). In the Byzantine *orthros* nine canticles, called "odes," were originally sung each day; they included most of those given in the Codex Alexandrinus: the two Canticles of Moses and the Canticles of Hannah, Habakkuk, Isa 26, Jonah, Azariah, and the Three Young Men. This group made up the first eight odes; the ninth combined the Canticles of Mary and Zechariah. Eventually, however, the hymns which accompanied them supplanted the first eight, so that in practice they are now sung only during Lent.

In their morning office the Syrians, Chaldeans, and Maronites use one or other of these canticles, depending on the day; in addition they use almost daily the Canticle of the Three Young Men, the *Magnificat,* and the Glory to God.

The early Roman Church preferred to distribute the Old Testament canticles throughout the week, one per day. Instead of Isa 26, however, it chose Isa 12:1-6 ("With joy you will draw water from the wells of salvation") and, in place of Jonah, the Canticle of Hezekiah (Isa 38:10-20). St. Benedict accepted this kind of distribution: "On other days . . . a Canticle from the Prophets is said, according to the practice of the Roman Church."[1] The Ambrosian tradition reserved the canticle from Dan 3:57-88

---

1. *Regula* 13, 10; translated in *The Rule of St. Benedict in Latin and English with Notes,* ed. Timothy Fry (Collegeville: The Liturgical Press, 1981) 209.

for Sunday Lauds, and, from Advent to Epiphany, the one from Deuteronomy; Dan 3:52-57 was sung every night.

In Visigothic Spain, Lauds always included a canticle that varied from day to day. At times, it was one of the gospel canticles, but usually one of the many Old Testament canticles available in that rite. On Sundays and feast days the canticle in Dan 3:52-57 was added.

When the Roman Breviary was reformed in 1911 under St. Pius X, the Roman Church introduced a second series of canticles for Lauds and reserved the traditional series for penitential seasons; the reason for this change was that several of the traditional canticles were very long. The new Liturgy of the Hours has chosen instead to abridge the traditional canticles, sometimes to the detriment of their meaning as expressions of the economy of salvation. Moreover, in order to ensure variety throughout the four-week cycle, it has added two more series to the one introduced in 1911. On the other hand, however, it has continued to give the Canticle from Daniel the privileged place which it has on Sundays in all the rites.

b) *In vigils*—Alongside the great Easter Vigil which served as a model for feast-day vigils and consisted principally in readings (though at Rome three of the readings were followed by a canticle[2]), there was another type of vigil known as the "cathedral" vigil. This type of vigil, so named because it was celebrated with the participation of the people, was held on Sundays in some Churches and included the singing of three canticles. It is still found in the Ambrosian liturgy and still recognizable in the Chaldean office.[3] St. Benedict added it to his monastic vigil, where it constitutes the third nocturn; in this way the Benedictine office too added to the selection of Old Testament canticles. Finally, the new Roman Liturgy of the Hours proposes these same canticles for the vigil on Sundays and solemnities which it suggests as a way of extending the Office of Readings.[4]

II. GOSPEL CANTICLES

The three gospel canticles—the *Benedictus*, the *Magnificat*, and the *Nunc dimittis*—are found in almost all the liturgies. In Eastern offices and in Spain they were generally not separated from the Old Testament canticles which they followed in the celebration or with which they were in-

---

2. At least in the liturgy of the Gelasian Sacramentary: *Ge* nos. 435, 438, 440.

3. J. Mateos, "Les différentes espèces de vigiles dans le rite chaldéen," *OCP* 27 (1961) 46–63; idem, "La vigile cathédrale chez Egérie," *ibid*. 302–12. — A group of three canticles is found in the *Ordo peculiaris vigiliae* and the *Ordo ad nocturnos* of the Spanish monastic office; see J. Pinell, *Las horas vigiliares del oficio monacal hispánico* (Montserrat: Abadía de Montserrat, 1966) 89–93, 110, 114–15.

4. *GILH* 73.

terchangeable. The Roman liturgy and the Benedictine office, on the other hand, made a sharp distinction between the two groups and gave the gospel canticles a place of honor at the high point of the celebration, after the Old Testament psalms and the readings. The Canticle of Zechariah ("When the day-star from on high shall visit us, to shine on those who dwell in darkness and the shadow of death") was used in Lauds; the Canticle of the Virgin Mary in Vespers; and the Canticle of Simeon in Compline.[5] Since these are passages from the gospel, they received the same signs of esteem as were given to the proclamation of the gospel: they were sung standing, after the Sign of the Cross.[6]

To these three canticles some Churches added the gospel of the Beatitudes (Matt 5:3-12). Thus the Syrians sing it in the morning office; the Byzantines use it as one of the antiphons before Sunday Mass. But in its literary genre the passage on the Beatitudes is not a canticle; much less can it be appropriately used as a hymn, since hymns are nonbiblical compositions.

III. OTHER NEW TESTAMENT CANTICLES

In the early liturgical tradition no other New Testament passage was used as a canticle, except for Rev 15:3-4, "Great and wonderful . . ." which was treated as a hymn in the office of the monks of Provence.[7] The introduction into the 1971 Liturgy of the Hours of nine further New Testament canticles to be used in Vespers was, therefore, a happy innovation and a response to the desire expressed by a number of the Fathers at Vatican II.

Some of these new canticles bring together acclamations from the Apocalypse (Rev 4-5; 11-12; 15; 19) and are an echo of the heavenly liturgy. Three are Christological hymns from the letters of St. Paul (Eph 1:3-10; Phil 2:6-11; Col 1:11-20). One, which is assigned to the Sundays of Lent, is taken from the First Letter of St. Peter (1 Pet 2:21-24). Finally, the short passage from 1 Tim 3:16 is in the office for Epiphany and Transfiguration.

The contemplation of Christ the Redeemer, which these canticles mediate, helps better to express the thanksgiving that is a fundamental theme of Vespers.[8] The Ambrosian liturgy has adopted these same can-

---

5. In the Byzantine liturgy the canticle of Simeon is sung in Vespers because, as we have seen, the *Magnificat* is sung in the morning, along with the *Benedictus.*

6. *GILH* 138. — In the Rule of St. Benedict and in the early Roman texts, these antiphons are often called "gospel" without qualification.

7. St. Caesarius of Arles, *Recapitulatio* 69, ed. G. Morin, *S. Caesarii Regula sanctarum virginum* (Florilegium patristicum 34; Bonn: Hanstein, 1938) 24; Aurelian, *Regula monachos* (PL 68:394). G. Tomasi, *Opera omnia,* ed. A. Vezzosi, 2:404.

8. *GILH* 137.

ticles as a way of celebrating on certain days the commemoration of baptism with which it ends Vespers.

§2. Hymnography

BIBLIOGRAPHY

A. Baumstark, *Comparative Liturgy*, ed. B. Botte, trans. F. L. Cross (Westminster, Md.: Newman, 1958) 92–110.

G. Del Ton, G. Schirò, and A. Raes, "Innografia," *Enciclopedia cattolica* 7 (1951) 28–39.

J. P. Foucher, *Poésie liturgique. Orient, Occident* (Paris: Mame, 1963).

By "hymnography" is usually meant the collection of chants or songs that are neither canonical psalms nor biblical canticles, but enter into the celebration of the liturgy, especially the Liturgy of the Hours (hymns, troparia, antiphons, responses, etc.). The distinction is often imperceptible between psalms proper and hymns, since hymns have for the most part been composed to prolong or accompany the psalms. That is why in the oldest manuscripts of the psalter the biblical canticles are often followed by a nonbiblical song or even by a complete collection of hymns intended usually for use immediately after the psalms. Troparia or antiphons were likewise composed as accompaniments or refrains for the psalms, although sometimes even these songs have an autonomous function. In any case, the dividing line between the two genres is not easy to pin down, since responses may be psalmic or at least biblical, and have often been explained as a development of responsorial psalmody.

The introduction of hymns met with resistance here and there. Some anchorites thought them inappropriate to the austerity of the contemplative life, especially because they were set to music.[9] The Council of Braga in 561 rejected all poetic songs that were not biblical.[10] Only at a late date did the Roman Church accept the use of hymns which was already widespread throughout the West; they did not become part of the office in the Basilica of St. Peter until the twelfth century. The short-lived Breviary reform attempted by Cardinal Quiñones in 1535 sought to return

---

9. See, e.g., the reactions of an Abbot Sylvanus of Palestine as reported in the *Plérophories de Jean Rufus*, ed. F. Nau (PO 8; Turnhout: Brepols, 1912) 179–80, or those of the monk Pembo as reported *ibid* and by Evergetinos, *Synagoge* 2, 11 (Venice, 1783; repr., Athens, 1900) 371. — See J. Grosdidier de Matons, "Kontakion et canon. Piété populaire et liturgie officielle à Byzance," *Augustinianum* 20 (1980) 191–93.

10. Canon 12: "We have likewise determined that, as the sacred canons prescribe, no poetic composition is to be sung in the Church apart from the psalms or canonical scriptures of the New and Old Testaments." Document in J. Vives, *Concilios visigóticos e hispano-romanos* (España cristiana, Textos 1; Barcelona-Madrid: Consejo Superior de investigaciones científicas, 1963) 73.

to the strict norms of the Council of Braga. But all these forms of resistance could not stem a tide that had been on the rise since the very beginnings of Christianity and that had an acknowledged pastoral importance. It is a fact, on the other hand, that these poetic compositions call for artistic and, above all, doctrinal discernment and that, especially in the East, their exuberance has at times reduced psalmody to a secondary role.

I. THE BEGINNINGS OF HYMNOGRAPHY

It can be maintained that the letters of Paul already contain echos of hymns sung at Christian assemblies.[11] Eusebius of Caesarea speaks of "all the psalms and hymns written from the beginning by faithful brethren, which sing of Christ as the Word of God and address Him as God."[12] Bardesanes of Mesopotamia (154–222) seems to have composed 150 psalms,[13] while Nepos, an Egyptian bishop, wrote hymns that were "still a source of comfort to many of our fellow-Christians" in the time of Dionysius of Alexandria (middle of the third century).[14]

Of the psalms known as *idiotikoi*, that is, composed by private individuals, hardly any but the *Odes of Solomon* have survived,[15] because this literature was soon ruled out on account of the doctrinal errors that too often marred it. As for the hymns of the pre-Nicene period with their very free poetic structure and their closeness to the biblical psalms and canticles, it seems possible to identify a few, namely, *Phōs hilaron* ("Joyous light"), *Doxa en hupsistois Theō* ("Glory to God in the highest") and *Soi prepei ainos* (*Te decet laus*, "It is fitting that we praise you"), which are still being sung today in the various languages.[16]

---

11. Eph 5:14; 1 Tim 3:16; perhaps 2 Tim 2:11.

12. *Historia ecclesiastica* V, 28, 5, trans. G. A. Williamson, *Eusebius: The History of the Church from Christ to Constantine* (Baltimore: Penguin, 1965) 236.

13. I. Ortiz de Urbina, *Patrologia syriaca* (Rome: Pontificio Istituto Orientale, 1958) 40.

14. Dionysius, cited by Eusebius, *ibid.* VII, 24, 4 (Williamson 307).

15. *The Odes of Solomon*, ed. and trans. James Hamilton Charlesworth (Oxford: Clarendon Press, 1973).

16. The *Phōs hilaron* was regarded as already old by St. Basil, *De Sancto Spiritu* 29, 73 (SC 17:250). — See E. Smothers, *"Phōs hilaron," RechSR* 19 (1929) 266–83. — The *Doxa en hupsistois Theō* is found, as we saw earlier, in the *Codex Alexandrinus* of the Bible; see B. Capelle, "Le texte du *Gloria in excelsis Deo," RHE* 44 (1949) 439–57 (= Capelle, *Travaux liturgiques* 2:176-91); it is also found, along with the *Soi prepei ainos*, in the liturgical anthology in the *Constitutiones apostolicae* VII, 47–48 (ed. Funk 454-58). — The Latin *Te Deum* is of much later origin: A. Baumstark, *"Te Deum* und eine Gruppe griechischer Abendhymnen," *OC* 34 (1937) 1-26. — Translations of the *Phōs hilaron* ("Joyous light") and the *Doxa en hupsistois Theō* ("Glory to God in the highest heaven") are given in L. Deiss, *Springtime of the Liturgy,* trans. M. J. O'Connell (Collegeville: The Liturgical Press, 1979) 251-52; the version of the *Doxa en hupsistois Theō* in the *Apostolic Constitutions* is translated *ibid.* 220-21, and the *Soi prepei ainos* (*Te decet laus,* "To you praise") on 221, where it forms the middle section of an evening prayer.

II. HYMNS IN THE PROPER SENSE

1. The Eastern Tradition

BIBLIOGRAPHY

I. H. Dalmais, "L'apport des Eglises syriennes à l'hymnographie chrétienne," *OC* 2 (1957) 243–60.

E. Wellesz, *A History of Byzantine Music and Hymnography* (2nd ed.; Oxford: Clarendon Press, 1961).

I. H. Dalmais, "L'hymnographie syrienne," *LMD* no. 92 (1967) 63–72.

Romanos Melodus, *Hymnes* ed. with Introduction, Critical Text, Translation, and Notes by J. Grosdidier de Matons (5 vols.; SC 99, 110, 114, 128, 283; Paris: Cerf, 1964ff.).

Ephraem of Nisibis, *Hymnes sur le Paradis*, ed. F. Graffin (SC 137; Paris: Cerf, 1968.

J. Grosdidier de Matons, *Romanos le Mélode et les origines de la poésie religieuse à Byzance* (Paris: Beauchesne, 1977).

D. Webb, "L'expression de la foi dans les hymnes de l'office quotidien nestorien," in *La liturgie expression de la foi*. Conferences Saint-Serge, 25ᵉ Semaine d'études liturgiques. Paris, 1978 (Bibliotheca EL, Subsidia 16; Rome: Edizioni liturgiche, 1979) 315–37.

J. Grosdidier de Matons, "Kontakion et canon. Piété populaire et liturgie officielle à Byzance," in *Ecclesia orans. Mèlanges. . . . A. G. Hamman* (Rome: Augustinianum, 1980) 191–203 = *Augustinianum* 20 (1980).

The real father of Christian hymnography was undoubtedly St. Ephraem (306–73). In order to offset the success which the canticles of Bardesanes enjoyed and to win the victory for Nicene orthodoxy, Ephraem composed metrical homilies (*memrê*), using the same rhythms as Bardesanes, with each verse having the same number of syllables and a set number of accents. They became extremely popular, for, when divided into stanzas, they allowed the congregation to participate by singing a refrain (*madrocho*); sometimes they took the form of acrostic poems (*sôghîtê*).

Ephraem's work[17] was continued among the Syrians by James of Sarug and among the Nestorians by Narsai of Nisibis. But his influence was also felt in the Greek-speaking Churches and even in the West. Romanos Melodus, who was of Syrian origin, transposed Ephraem's method into Greek and won a place in the Byzantine liturgy for the genre known as the kontakion, a hymn composed of stanzas (*kôla*) having the same number of syllables or at least the same rhythm; all the stanzas were sung according to the same *hirmos* (model stanza), with a refrain being sung by the congregation. Each hymn was preceded by a prooemium that served as a prelude, and each ended with a prayer. Romanos' work was later

---

17. Critical edition with German translation by E. Beck in CSCO 154–55, 169–70, 174–75, 186–87, 198–99, 212–13, 218–19, 223–24, 240–41, 246–47, 248–49 (series not yet completed).

replaced by that of Andrew of Crete († 740) and St. John Damascene († 749), who worked in the genres of troparion and canon (see further on). But the Byzantine liturgy has retained the kontakion with its stanzas after the sixth ode of the festal *orthros*; the well-known Akathistos hymn is a kontakion.

The Chaldean festal office gives a great deal of space to hymns in the course of the night office (in the form of *madrochê*) and in the prayer at dawn ("hymns of the light"). The Armenian repertory is especially rich, due in great part to the work of Narses the Kindly (twelfth century).

2. The Latin Tradition

BIBLIOGRAPHY

G. Tomasi, *Hymnarium*, in *Opera omnia*, ed. A. Vezzosi 2 (Rome: Typis Palladis, 1747) 351–434.

G. Dreves and Cl. Blume, *Analecta hymnica medii aevi* (Leipzig: Reisland, 1886–1922). 55 vols., plus 3 vols. of Indexes by M. Lütolf (Bern: Francke, 1978).

U. Chevalier, *Repertorium hymnologicum. Catalogue des chants, hymnes, proses, séquences, tropes en usage dans l'Eglise latine depuis les origines jusqu'à nos jours* (6 vols.; Subsidia hagiographica 4; Brussels: Bollandistes, 1892–1921). Reprinted 1959.

Cl. Blume, *Der Cursus sancti Benedicti Nursini und die liturgischen Hymnen des 6. bis 9. Jhr. in ihrer Beziehung zu den Sonntags- und Ferialhymnen unseres Breviers* (Hymnologische Beiträge 3; Leipzig: Reisland, 1906).

A. Wilmart, "Le psautier de la Reine, n. 11," *RBen* 28 (1911) 341–76.

J. Mearns, *Early Latin Hymnaries. An Index of Hymns in the Hymnaries before 1100* (Cambridge: Cambridge University Press, 1913).

U. Chevalier, *Poésie liturgique des Eglises de France aux XVIIᵉ et XVIIIᵉ siècles* (Paris: Picard, 1913).

J. Perez de Urbel, "Origen de los himnos mozárabes," *Bulletin hispanique* 28 (1926) 5–21, 113–39, 209–45, 305–20.

P. Paris, *Les hymnes de la liturgie romaine* (Paris: Beauchesne, 1954).

W. Bulst, *Hymni latini antiquissimi LXXV, psalmi 3* (Heidelberg: Kerle, 1956).

H. Gneuss, *Hymnar und Hymnen im englischen Mittelalter* (Beiträge der Anglia 12; Tübingen: Niemeyer, 1968).

A. G. Martimort, "La place des hymnes à l'office dans les liturgies d'Occident," in *Studi ambrosiani in onore di Mons. Pietro Borella* (Archivio ambrosiano 43; Milan, 1982) 138–53.

During his exile in Asia Minor (356–59) St. Hilary of Poitiers became familiar with Syriac and Greek hymns and was inspired by these to compose Latin hymns based on a periodically recurring accent.[18] These, however, had no lasting success. St. Ambrose became the real founder of Latin hymnody. His intention was to defend the faith of his flock from

18. Until the promised edition by J. Fontaine appears, the reader will find these hymns in W. Bulst, *Hymni latini antiquissimi LXXV, psalmi 3* (Heidelberg: Kerle, 1956) 31–35, and CSEL 65:209ff.

e attraction exerted by Arian congregations. To this end, while remain-
ıg faithful to the laws of Latin prosody, he composed hymns that were
ıopular in style, using a stanza consisting of four iambic dimeters. The
ınthusiasm which these hymns aroused is attested by St. Augustine[19] and
ɔy St. Ambrose himself.[20] Their adoption by St. Benedict and later by
the Roman Church assured them a permanent place in the repertory of
the Latin Church.[21]

Various hymns of Prudentius (fifth century) and Sedulius (fifth century), using the same meter as those of Ambrose, likewise gained a permanent place in the liturgical repertory. Other poets went back to less
popular classical meters or even abandoned metrical rhythm entirely and
opted for an accentual rhythm. The result of this labor was that all the
Hours of the office were provided with hymns that changed according
to day, season, and feast. The sixteenth century Renaissance caused a profound crisis in Latin hymnody, in part because of an excessive concern
with prosody, in part because a profane humanism made its way into
hymns. The result was a series of reforms, the most recent being that of
1971.[22]

3. The Present Liturgy of the Hours

The reform of 1971 emphasized the proper role of hymns in the Liturgy
of the Hours, placing them at the beginning of each office where they serve
as a kind of overture.

> A very ancient tradition gives hymns the place in the office that they
> still retain. By their mystical and poetic character they are specifically
> designed for God's praise. But they also are an element for the people; in
> fact more often than the other parts of the office the hymns bring out the
> proper theme of individual hours or feasts and incline and draw the spirit
> to a devout celebration. The beauty of their language often adds to this
> power. Furthermore, in the office hymns are the main poetic element created
> by the Church.[23]

A high standard is thus set for hymns, from the viewpoints of doctrine, literary and musical value, and popular character. The ideal is still

---

19. *Confessiones* IX, 6, 7; X, 49–50.

20. St. Ambrose, *Sermo contra Auxentium* 34 (PL 16:1017).

21. Among the hymns attributed to St. Ambrose, a dozen or so are doubtless his; three
are authenticated by the testimony of St. Augustine; see A. Rimoldi, "Gli studi di Mons.
Luigi Biraghi su sant'Ambrogio," in *Ricerche storiche sulla Chiesa ambrosiana* IV (Archivio
ambrosiano 27; Milan, 1974) 216–29.

22. *VSC* 93; [A. Lentini], *Hymni instaurandi breviarii Romani* (Vatican City, 1968);
A. Lentini, *Te decet hymnus. L'innario della "Liturgia Horarum"* (Vatican City: Vatican
City Press, 1984).

23. *GILH* 173.

that of St. Ambrose, but it must be admitted that the ideal has not always been reached in the hymns of the Latin repertory. Moreover, once the Liturgy of the Hours came to be celebrated in the vernaculars, it became clear that the poetic quality of the finest traditional hymns would be difficult to reproduce in translations. The need therefore is gradually to build up a repertory in each area.

> For vernacular celebration, the conferences of bishops may adapt the Latin hymns to suit the character of their own language and introduce fresh compositions, provided these are in complete harmony with the spirit of the hour, season, or feast. Great care must be taken not to allow popular songs that have no artistic merit and are not in keeping with the dignity of the liturgy.[24]

This passage is an appeal to poets and musicians, but it requires that the latter have a familiarity with liturgical prayer and the kind of spiritual experience which will make it possible for their work to be no longer simply the voice of an individual but the voice of the Church. This is why the episcopal conferences have the final say, since they must guarantee the doctrinal correctness and liturgical appropriateness of new compositions.[25]

The *Instruction* also notes that "a hymn follows the traditional rule by ending with a doxology, usually addressed to the same divine Person as the hymn itself."[26]

III. TROPARIA, ANTIPHONS, RESPONSES

The various liturgies have developed, even more than hymns, other and more concise literary and musical genres which may either serve as refrains for the psalms or be performed independently of any connection with the psalmody. Troparia, antiphons, and responses are some of the names given to them in the different rites or according to their structure and function.

1. Eastern Troparia

BIBLIOGRAPHY

E. Wellesz, *A History of Byzantine Music and Hymnography* (2nd ed.; Oxford: Clarendon Press, 1961) 170–245.

---

24. *GILH* 178.
25. There are helpful assessments for the French-speaking world a decade after the Constitution *Laudis canticum*, in Y. Calais, "Les hymnes de l'office en français," *LMD* no. 143 (1980) 47–60; M. Coste, "L'hymne et sa fonction dans l'office," *ibid*. 61–78; J. Gelineau, "La création des chants liturgiques dans les milieux monastiques depuis le Concile," *LMD* no. 145 (1981) 49–65. — For other languages see *LMD* no. 151 (1982) 47–82.
26. *GILH* 174.

O. Heiming, *Syrische Eniânê und griechische Kanones* (LQF 26; Münster: Aschendorff, 1932).

Troparia seem originally to have been refrains for use during the singing of a psalm or at least toward the end of it.[27] They were initially simple
phrases in free prose with a certain degree of accentual rhythm, and in
this form are found in almost all Eastern offices. The Syrian Church may
have originated their use.[28]

Gradually, however, the troparia became full-blown poetic stanzas,
introduced by Andrew of Crete and John Damascene into the Byzantine
liturgy where they became immensely popular and numerous. They give
the office of the day its special coloration, but they inevitably tend to over-
whelm the psalmody which they are meant to accompany. The most
typical instance, from this point of view, is the odes of the Byzantine *orthros*: the troparia, which were meant to serve as refrains for the biblical
canticles, ended by completely replacing them (except during Lent); a set
of troparia is known as a canon.

Other troparia are independent of any psalmody and have for their
purpose to express the meaning of the day or Hour; this is especially the
case with the *Apolytikon* and the act of devotion to Mary. More specifically, each Hour of the Byzantine office has a variable Marian troparion,
known as the *Theotokion*, which is often a distant echo of the enthusiasm
that greeted the definition issued by the Council of Ephesus.

2. Antiphons of the Latin Liturgies

BIBLIOGRAPHY

H. Leclercq, "Antienne (liturgie)," *DACL* 1 (1907) 2282–2319.

Amalarius, *Liber de ordine antiphonarii* 8–80, in *Amalarii episcopi opera liturgica
omnia*, ed. J. M. Hanssens, 3 (ST 140; Vatican City, 1950) 37–109, and
Tabellae . . . . 110–224.

A. Baumstark, *Comparative Liturgy*, ed. B. Botte, trans. F. L. Cross (Westminster,
Md.: Newman, 1958) 97–102.

J. Lemarié, "Les antiennes *Veterem hominem* du jour octave de l'Epiphanie et les
antiennes d'origine grecque de l'Epiphanie," *EL* 72 (1958) 3–38.

L. Brou and J. Vives, *Antifonario visigótico mozárabe de la catedral de León*
(2 vols.; Monumenta Hispaniae sacra, ser. lit., 5; Barcelona–Madrid: Consejo
Superior de investigaciones científicas, 1959).

R. J. Hesbert, *Corpus antiphonalium officii* 3. *Invitatoria et antiphonae* (REDMF 9;
Rome: Herder, 1968).

---

27. J. Mateos, "La psalmodie dans le rite byzantin," *POC* 15 (1965) 107–26.

28. Severus, Patriarch of Antioch (512–19), provided his Church with a complete collection of responses, the Book of the *Ma'nyoto*: see J. Puyade, "Composition interne de l'office syrien," *OS* 3 (1958) 34–42.

U. Franca, *Le antifone bibliche dopo Pentecoste. Studio codicologico storico testuale con appendice musicale* (Studia Anselmiana 73, Analecta liturgica 4; Rome: Ed. Anselmiana, 1977).

I spoke earlier of the psalmic antiphons and their important function in the Liturgy of the Hours in most rites, but especially those of the West. These same rites also have other types of antiphons that are closer in genre to the Eastern troparia and are more fully developed than the psalmic antiphons. We may distinguish three main categories.

First, there are biblical antiphons which are taken from the Old Testament or the gospel and, in the medieval Roman antiphonary, were intended primarily for the *Magnificat* and *Benedictus* on Sundays. The antiphon in First Vespers of Sunday announced the book of the Bible which was to be read at the vigil for that week; the antiphons of Lauds and Second Vespers echoed the gospel of the day. All were especially remarkable for both text and melody.

Next, there are hagiographical antiphons, which accompany the psalms and canticles of the feasts in the sanctoral. They give varied expression to the ideal of Christian holiness. The liturgical reform has, however, had to eliminate a good many of them because they were too closely dependent on legendary occurrences.

Some series of antiphons were translated from Greek troparies and possess a genuine literary and spiritual beauty. This is especially the case with the antiphons for January 1, the Baptism of Christ, the Nativity of Mary, and other feasts.

Finally, there are antiphons intended to be sung alone and not as an accompaniment to a psalm. This is the case with the Marian antiphons of Compline as well as various antiphons in the Ambrosian office.

3. Responses of the Latin Liturgies

BIBLIOGRAPHY

P. Alfonzo, *I responsori biblici dell'Ufficio romano* (Lateranum, nov. ser., II, 1; Rome: Pontifical Lateran University, 1936).

Amalarius. See preceding bibliography.

A. Baumstark, *Comparative Liturgy*, ed. B. Botte, trans. F. L. Cross (Westminster, Md.: Newman, 1958) 98–102.

R. Le Roulx, "Les répons *de psalmis* pour les matines de l'Epiphanie à la Septuagésime," *Etudes grégoriennes* 6 (1963) 39–148.

G. Gindele, "Zum Ausdruck 'Responsorium' im *Ordo officii* der Benediktiner- und Magisterregel," *Erbe und Auftrag* 39 (1963) 139–43.

R. J. Hesbert, *Corpus antiphonalium officii* 4. *Responsoria, versus, hymni et varia* (REDMF 10; Rome: Herder, 1970).

Whatever their precise origin may have been and whatever the original manner of executing them, the responses of the Latin liturgical repertories are now lyrical compositions with a finale that serves as a refrain which is repeated after one or two verses. They can be performed as processional songs, as prolongations of hymns (in the Ambrosian office), and, above all, as responses to readings with which they are in some way connected. This last is how they are thought of in the Rule of St. Benedict.[29]

The Roman office has always had a very varied repertory of responses. The biblical readings from the Old Testament were often followed by a cento, or patchwork, of texts selected to form a prayer ("My sin is greater than the sands of the sea. . . .") or a song ("Hills of Gilboa, may neither dew nor rain fall upon you . . . ."). After the New Testament readings, verses from the psalms were preferred. On the feasts of the saints the responses repeated passages from the biographies. Some responses were translations of Greek troparia.

The short readings in Lauds and Vespers were accompanied by short, often psalmic responses. In the Little Hours, Benedictine usage, followed by the Roman office, reduced the response to the short reading to a simple verse.

The reform of the Liturgy of the Hours lays special emphasis on the response to the biblical reading. The text of the response is taken from the traditional repertory or is newly composed with the help especially of eighteenth-century Breviaries. According to the *General Instruction*, the response is intended "to throw new light on the passage just read, put it in the context of the history of salvation, lead from the Old Testament to the New, turn what has been read into prayer and contemplation, or provide pleasant variety by its poetic beauty" (no. 169). The responses after the second reading are generally not so directly connected with the passage and are meant to leave "a greater freedom in meditation" (no. 170). The short responses and verses which follow the short readings are offered "as a kind of acclamation, enabling God's word to enter more deeply into the mind and heart of the one listening or reading" (no. 172).

§3. The Readings

The 1971 Liturgy of the Hours keeps, while revising, the traditional Roman practice of making room in its celebration of the office for biblical, patristic, and hagiographical readings.

---

29. *Regula* 9–11; 12, 4; 13, 11; 15, 1–4.

I. BIBLICAL READINGS

BIBLIOGRAPHY

Andrieu, *OR* 2:469-526 (= *OR* 13A, 13B, 13C, 13D); *OR* 3:25-41 (= *OR* 14).

A. Baumstark, *Comparative Liturgy*, ed. B. Botte, trans. F. L. Cross (Westminster, Md.: Newman, 1958) 111-29.

H. Marot, "La place des lectures bibliques et patristiques dans l'Office latin," in Cassien-Botte 149-66.

A. Renoux, "Liturgie de Jérusalem et lectionnaire arménien, vigiles et année liturgique," *ibid.* 167-200.

A. Kniazeff, "La lecture de l'Ancien et du Nouveau Testament dans le rite byzantin," *ibid.* 201-52.

R. Zerfass, *Die Schriftlesung im Kathedraloffizium Jerusalems* (LQF 48; Münster: Aschendorff, 1968).

E. J. Lengeling, "Liturgia Horarum. Die Lesungen und Responsorien im neuen Stundengebet," *Liturgisches Jahrbuch* 20 (1970) 231-49.

A. Rose, "La répartition des lectures bibliques dans le livre de la Liturgie des Heures," *EL* 85 (1971) 281-305.

C. Wiener, "Le lectionnaire biblique de l'office," *LMD* no. 105 (1971) 103-16.

J. Pascher, "Die Schriftlesung im Stundengebet Pauls VI," *Seminarium* 24 (1972) 86-106.

E. J. Lengeling, "Le letture bibliche e i loro responsori nella nuova Liturgia delle Ore," in *Liturgia delle Ore. Documenti ufficiali e studi* (Turin-Leumann: ElleDiCi, 1972) 185-219. An expansion of the article listed above.

"Lectiones biblicae Liturgiae Horarum iuxta cyclum duorum annorum," *Notitiae* 12 (1976) 238-48, 324-56, 378-402.

U. Zanetti, "Premières recherches sur les lectionnaires coptes," *EL* 98 (1984) 3-34.

The researches of recent historians, and those of R. Zerfass in particular, have shown that in the traditions both of the various Eastern Churches and of their monasteries readings from the Bible had no place in the daily Liturgy of the Hours, which was focused entirely on praise and prayer. The reading of the gospel in the dawn office on Sunday is a practice that originated in Jerusalem and had for its purpose to celebrate the resurrection of Christ on the anniversary day and at the anniversary hour.[30] The presence of several Old Testament readings in Vespers (*megaloi hesperinoi*, "Great Vespers") on the eve of certain feasts is a holdover from a cathedral vigil that in turn imitated the Easter Vigil. In practice it is only in Lent that the Byzantine office contains readings from Scripture: primarily in Vespers that include a liturgy of the presanctified, and secondarily in one or other Hour during the day. These readings are doubtless an echo of prebaptismal catechesis.

In the Syrian office a gospel passage is read in Vespers and in the morning office of feasts, and sometimes during night prayer as well. In

---

30. See below, n. 52, p. 269.

the Vespers of feasts the Maronites even anticipate the readings of the next morning's Mass. The present Coptic and Ethiopian office is the only one that has gospel pericopes in all the Hours of all seasons and Old Testament readings in morning prayer during Lent. But is this practice an ancient one? Scholars no longer credit Cassian's description of the prayer of the Egyptian monks; it seems rather that originally these monks read Sacred Scripture privately and not in the course of their communal office.[31]

The ideal proposed by Cassian as being that of the Egyptian monks was that psalmody should always be followed by the reading of the Old and New Testament.[32] This ideal was not followed completely by all the Churches (the Ambrosian office has no Scripture reading in Lauds nor regularly in Vespers), but it did become part of most of the Western monastic rules.

The Rule of St. Benedict, following the Rule of the Master, distinguishes long and short readings. During the night office in winter, the first six psalms are followed by a Scripture passage that is divided into three lessons, between which three responses are sung; the next six psalms are followed, during the week, by a reading from the Apostle which is recited from memory. In summer this program is abbreviated due to the shortness of the night. On Sunday, however, the first six psalms are followed by four lessons; the next six by another four; and the canticles by still another four, this time from the New Testament. The usage would eventually prevail of assigning to the second group of four lessons the patristic reading recommended by St. Benedict. In all the other Hours the psalms are followed by a short reading that is recited from memory; in morning prayer this reading is from the Apostle during the week and from the Apocalypse on Sundays.[33]

At Rome, the night office regularly had three readings from the Old Testament in keeping with an annual sequence that according to *Ordo Romanus* 14 (dating perhaps from the sixth century) made it possible in the Basilica of St. Peter to read all of the books while also taking the variety of liturgical seasons into account. In *Ordo* 13, which dates from the eighth century and describes the practice at the Lateran Basilica, Acts, the Letters, and the Apocalypse were henceforth part of this annual cycle; previously they had doubtless been read only at Mass or possibly in

---

31. R. Zerfass, *Die Schriftlesung im Kathedraloffizium Jerusalems* (LQF 48; Münster: Aschendorff, 1968) 52 and, especially, A. Veilleux, *La liturgie dans le cénobitisme pachomien au IVe siècle* (Studia Anselmiana 57; Rome: Herder, 1968) 262–69, 279–87, 337. But on 308 Veilleux expresses the opinion that the Pachomian monks at their "synaxes" used to recite not the psalms exclusively but passages from the Scriptures generally.

32. John Cassian, *De institutis coenobiorum* II, 6 (SC 109:68-70).

33. On all this see A. de Vogüé, *La Règle de saint Benoît* 5 (SC 185; Paris: Cerf, 1971) 434–98.

the third nocturn of Sundays and feasts. All these pericopes were evidently quite lengthy; the medieval abridgement (*Breviarium*) of them reduced them to a few verses, so that only the incipits of some books were read, while others were no longer read at all.

This distribution lasted down to our own time despite its very unsatisfactory character. In keeping with the requirement set down by Vatican II,[34] a two-year cycle was planned for the Scripture readings in the Office of Readings; it would, as far as possible, retain the traditional place of certain books in the liturgical year and would present the history of salvation in the course of each year. It is desirable that such a plan be followed. However, the material difficulties of publication made it necessary to provide a one-year cycle, and this is the only one that is printed in its totality in the *Liturgy of the Hours*. The need of a two-year cycle will eventually be met by a supplementary volume that will give a second annual cycle of Scripture readings with their responses and corresponding patristic readings.

In each of the other Hours the Roman office, like the Benedictine, follows the psalms with a reading that is reduced to a few verses. Far from rendering the reading negligible, this brevity makes it possible to "set[ting] forth some passage of Sacred Scripture in a striking way, or highlight[ing] some shorter sentence that may receive less attention in the continuous cycle of Scripture readings."[35] It would therefore be a mistake to think of these readings as a new form of continuous reading. Furthermore, in keeping with tradition the gospels are excluded from these short readings, since a certain amplitude and solemnity should mark the reading of the gospel.[36]

II. READINGS FROM THE FATHERS AND ECCLESIASTICAL WRITERS

BIBLIOGRAPHY

a) Historical Studies

H. Rahner, *"Zur Reform der Väterlesungen des Breviers,"* in *Brevierstudien,* ed. J. A. Jungmann (Trier: Paulinus Verlag, 1958) 42–56.

H. Marot, "La place des lectures bibliques et patristiques dans l'Office latin," in Cassien-Botte 155–65.

R. Grégoire, "Les homéliaires liturgiques des Eglises d'Orient," *Melto. Recherches orientales* 4 (Kaslik, Lebanon, 1968) 37–53.

---

34. *VSC* 92a.
35. *GILH* 45.
36. See *GILH* 158a.

_____, *Homéliaires liturgiques médiévaux. Analyse des manuscrits* (Biblioteca Studi medievali 12; Spoleto: Centro italiano di studi sull'alto medioevo, 1980). Revision of an earlier edition in REDMF 6 (Rome: Herder, 1966).

R. Etaix, "Quelques homéliaires de la région catalane," *Recherches augustiniennes* 16 (1981) 333–98. Etaix has published numerous studies of manuscript patristic lectionaries.

b) The Patristic Readings in the New Liturgy of the Hours

H. Ashworth, "Il lezionario patristico del nuovo Ufficio divino," in *Liturgia delle Ore. Documenti ufficiali e studi* (Turin-Leumann: ElleDiCi, 1971) 221–27.

G. Raciti, "Les textes de la tradition chrétienne à l'Office de lecture," *LMD* no. 105 (1971) 117–33.

M. Card. Pellegrino, "Temi di spiritualità nelle nuove lezioni patristiche," *Seminarium* 24 (1972) 122–39.

"Index lectionum patristicarum Liturgiae Horarum," *Notitiae* 10 (1974) 253–76.

H. Ashworth, "A Proposed Monastic Lectionary. References and Themes," *EL* 91 (1977) 74–92, 171–89, 246–70, 382–413, 499–514; 92 (1978) 88–110.

R. Kaczynski, "Vom Lesen der Väter," in *Gott feiern (Festgabe Th. Schnitzler)*, ed. J. G. Plöger (Freiburg: Herder, 1980) 423–35.

M. L. Guillaume, "Richesse spirituelle de l'office. Les secondes lectures," *LMD* no. 143 (1980) 125–35.

Readings from the commentaries and homilies of the Fathers were part of the ancient Syrian festal office, where they were given metrical form or even put into verse (*memrê*), after the manner of the didactic hymns of St. Ephraem. In fact, collections still exist which show by their organization that they were intended for liturgical use.[37] This practice, however, did not become permanent. In the Greek tradition the *orthros* used to have patristic readings. This usage is now found only here and there in Lent, but in the eleventh century the Typikon of Evergetis shows that it was a regular practice.[38]

It was perhaps St. Benedict who took the initiative in the Latin Church and introduced into the night office readings from commentaries on Scripture, that is, from "explanations of Scripture by reputable and orthodox catholic Fathers."[39] At about the same period it was also customary at St. Peter's in Rome that "treatises of St. Jerome, St. Ambrose, and the other Fathers should be read as the ritual requires."[40] These readings doubtless had their place in the second nocturn, that is, after the second series

_____

37. A. Baumstark, *Festbrevier und Kirchenjahr der syrischen Jakobiten. Eine liturgiegeschichtliche Vorarbeit* (Studien zur Geschichte und Kultur des Altertums 3, 3–5; Paderborn: Schöningh, 1910) 53–62; J. Puyade, "Composition interne de l'office syrien," *OS* 3 (1958) 46–49; R. Grégoire, "Les homéliaires liturgiques des Eglises d'Orient," *Melto* 4 (1968) 48–53.

38. A. Baumstark, *Comparative Liturgy*, ed. B. Botte, trans. F. L. Cross (Westminster, Md.: Newman, 1958) 28; R. Grégoire, *ibid.* 40–46.

39. *Regula* 9, 8, trans. *The Rule of St. Benedict*, ed. Timothy Fry, 205.

40. *OR* 14, no. 10, redaction V (Andrieu, *OR* 3:41; see 3:29-30). In the eighth century, *OR* 13A, nos. 13–20, 22 (Andrieu 2:486-88).

of psalms in the vigils of festal offices. Moreover, when the Letters of St. Paul became part of the set of readings for the first nocturn,[41] room was made available in the third nocturn for homilies on the gospel of the Sunday or feast. Later on, finally, the office for each day of Lent had a homily on the gospel in place of the biblical reading.

In order to facilitate the selection from these commentaries and to have the text readily available, collections of sermons and then collections of homilies, or homiliaries, were compiled. The best known are those of Agimond for the Roman Basilica of Sts. Philip and James (beginning of the eighth century), Alain of Farfa (ca. 760–70), Egino of Verona (796–99), and of the Vatican Basilica (second half of the tenth century); all of these were tributary to the early usage at St. Peter's in Rome.[42] Finally, the homiliary which Paul the Deacon (end of the eighth century) compiled by order of Charlemagne became for practical purposes that of the Latin Church throughout the Middle Ages.[43]

These readings, however, underwent the same shortening as the biblical pericopes, leaving only the beginning of each sermon or homily and thus often omitting the most interesting passages. The reform of Pius V brought some rather profound changes in the patristic lectionary of the Roman Breviary, especially the introduction of passages from the Greek Fathers; this reform nonetheless left the defects almost untouched.[44] That is why Vatican Council II called for a complete overhaul of the patristic lectionary.[45]

To begin with, the repertory in the 1971 Liturgy of the Hours was considerably enlarged because there is a patristic reading every day (except on the saints' feasts which have a hagiographical reading) and because the selection is no longer limited to the Fathers but is meant to offer the best spiritual passages from Christian writers of every age. The task of expansion was a difficult one because it was necessary to avoid allegorical or excessively artificial commentaries on Scripture, as well as didactic passages that are not suited for liturgical prayer.

In addition, the anthology offered in the 1971 edition is open-ended. The *General Instruction* (no. 161) announced that a second lectionary

---

41. *OR* 13, no. 22 (Andrieu 2:488). In fact, not until the reforms of St. Pius V and Paul V did the distribution of the readings uniformly follow this rule.

42. A description of these various collections is given in R. Grégoire, *Homéliaires liturgiques médiévaux. Analyse des manuscrits* (Biblioteca Studi medievali 12; Spoleto: Centro italiano di studi sull'alto medioevo, 1980).

43. *Ibid.* 423–78.

44. One of these defects was the large number of erroneous attributions (the *False Decretals*, Pseudo-Augustine, Pseudo-Chrysostom, etc.). See S. Bäumer, *Histoire du bréviaire* (Paris: Letouzey, 1912) 2:452–60.

45. *VSC* 92b.

would be compiled; this would correspond to the second cycle of biblical readings. Furthermore, "conferences of bishops may prepare additional texts, adapted to the traditions and mentality of their own region" (no. 162). Finally, on weekdays in Ordinary Time and even, if it seems opportune, on weekdays of the major liturgical seasons, "the choice is open for a semicontinuous reading of the work of a Father of the Church, in harmony with the biblical and liturgical context" (no. 250).

This last-named condition is necessary in view of the biblical structure of the liturgy and the liturgical year. There are other criteria, too, that limit the choice of texts. Since the office is the prayer of the Church and is celebrated in the Church's name, the texts must be taken exclusively "from the works of Catholic writers, outstanding for their teaching and holiness of life" (no. 162). No works of noncatholic writers may be read, however estimable these may be in their way; nor are the works of writers still living to be read,[46] except, of course, for the acts of the ecclesiastical magisterium.

The presence, in the office, of readings from these witnesses to the Church's universal tradition helps those celebrating this liturgy to enter into "the contemplation of the word of God [which has been carried on] over the centuries by the Bride of the incarnate Word: the Church, 'possessing the counsel and spirit of its Bridegroom and God,' is always seeking to attain a more profound understanding of the sacred Scriptures."[47] These writings help Christians to advance in the spirit of the economy of salvation and of the liturgical seasons and feasts, and give them access to the treasures which are the spiritual patrimony of the Church.[48]

III. HAGIOGRAPHICAL READINGS

BIBLIOGRAPHY

V. Leroquais, *Les Bréviaires manuscrits des bibliothèques publiques de France* 1 (Mâcon: Protat, 1934) xlviii–lii.

B. de Gaiffier, "La lecture des Actes des Martyrs dans la prière liturgique en Occident," *Analecta Bollandiana* 72 (1954) 134–66.

A. Amore, "Le letture agiografiche nella Liturgia delle Ore," in *Liturgia delle Ore. Documenti ufficiali e studi* (Turin-Leumann: ElleDiCi, 1972) 229–40.

P. Jounel, "Les lectures du Sanctoral," *EL* 86 (1972) 31–40.

---

46. Congregation of the Doctrine of the Faith, July 9, 1972; see *Notitiae* 8 (1972) 229.
47. *GILH* 164.
48. See *GILH* 165.

In the East hagiography does not seem to have found a place in the liturgy of Mass or office in the form of readings from the Acts of the martyrs or the lives of the saints. At most, the Byzantine *orthros* makes room after the sixth ode for the Synaxarion, a kind of historical martyrology.

In the Latin Church, however, and specifically in the Church of Africa as early as the time of St. Augustine, readings from the passions of the martyrs did find a reception at liturgical assemblies, doubtless during the vigils of their feasts, which were attended by the people.[49] The same practice can also be seen later on in the lectionaries of Spain, Gaul, and Milan, in which hagiographical readings were given on certain occasions for Mass and sometimes for the office.[50] The monastic Rules of southern France prescribed such readings during the vigils of the feasts of the martyrs.[51]

Rome, on the other hand, remained long opposed to their introduction into the liturgy; the document known as the *Decretum Gelasianum* ("Decree of Gelasian") rejects them in the name of "ancient custom."[52] *Ordines Romani* 13 and 14 in their original redaction still made no mention of them; there is question of them only in the later Frankish adaptation of these *Ordines*, while *Ordo* 12 attributes their introduction into the liturgy at St. Peter's to Pope Hadrian I (772–95).[53] In the Romano-Frankish office the *Passiones* or *Legendae* became all-absorbing, supplying as many as six and at times nine lessons; at the end of the twelfth century John Beleth rebelled and expressed the desire that no more than six lessons should ever be allowed to this kind of literature. Finally, the Breviary of St. Pius V limited them to the three lessons of the second nocturn of the saints.

But there was a deeper problem that needed solving. The "Roman *Legendarium*" (or collection of readings from the lives of saints and passions of martyrs) was made up of texts that in some cases dated from as far back as the sixth century. These gave a sometimes moving testimony to the Christian ideals of virginity, religious life, and holiness of the peri-

---

49. See the detailed information in V. Saxer, *Morts, martyrs, reliques en Afrique chrétienne aux premiers siècles* (Théologie historique 55; Paris: Beauchesne, 1980) 200–8, 224–27, 315–21.

50. In the Lectionary of Luxeuil the *Passio s. Iuliani* is mentioned for vigils; in the Spanish liturgical books a reading from passions is often assigned to *Matutinum*, although the more usual place for such readings in these two liturgies seems to have been the Mass.

51. St. Caesarius of Arles, *Recapitulatio huius regulae* 69, ed. G. Morin, *S. Caesarii Regula sanctarum virginum* (Bonn: Hanstein, 1933) 25; Aurelian, *Regula ad monachos* (PL 68:396); St. Ferreolus of Uzès, *Regula ad monachos* 18 (PL 66:965).

52. A. Thiel, *Epistolae Romanorum Pontificum* I (Braunsberg: Peter, 1868) 458–59; there is a better text in E. von Dobschütz, *Das Decretum Gelasianum de libris recipiendis et non recipiendis* (TU 38/4; Leipzig, 1912). See DS 353.

53. Andrieu, *OR* 2:454, 466; *OR* 3:29, 30, 41.

ods when they were composed, but they gave little thought to historical accuracy and showed a delight in miracles and wonders. Cardinal Sirleto's sixteenth-century revision of the Roman lectionary was inadequate, and there were periodic calls for a reform. Vatican II decreed that "the accounts of the martyrdom or lives of the saints are to be made historically accurate."[54]

The 1971 *Liturgy of the Hours* adopted a radical solution: it deliberately abandoned the genre of biography. Instead, a short historical note, a kind of private instruction that is not part of the celebration, is prefixed to the offices of the saints. The readings themselves, however, are henceforth "either texts from a Father of the Church or other Church writer which refer specifically to the saint who is being commemorated or are rightly applied to him or her, or texts from his or her own writings." Only rarely has it been possible to offer "an account of his or her life."[55]

§4. Intercessions and Presidential Prayers

Like the Mass, the celebration of the office has traditionally included intercessions or prayers of petition for the general intentions of the Church and the world. The Lord's Prayer has also been almost always included. Finally, in all the Churches of East and West, the office has included presidential prayers of bishops or priests; if no bishop or priest is present, monastic tradition allows another member of the community to read these prayers.

I. THE INTERCESSIONS

BIBLIOGRAPHY

B. Fischer, "*Litania ad Laudes et Vesperas.* Ein Vorschlag zur Neugestaltung der Ferialpreces in Laudes und Vesper des römischen Breviers," *Liturgisches Jahrbuch* 1 (1951) 55–74.

A. Baumstark, *Comparative Liturgy*, ed. B. Botte, trans. F. L. Cross (Westminster, Md.: Newman, 1958) 70–78.

B. Fischer, "Die Anliegen des Volkes im kirchlichen Stundengebet," in *Brevierstudien*, ed. J. A. Jungmann (Trier: Paulinus Verlag, 1958) 57–70.

F. Morlot, "Les *Preces* des Laudes et des Vêpres," *LMD* no. 96 (1968) 57–89.

GILH 179–93.

M. C. de Bourmont, "Fonction et expression des prières d'intercession," *LMD* no. 105 (1971) 134–49.

---

54. *VSC* 92c.
55. *GILH* 166; see 167–68.

V. Raffa, "Le intercessioni di Lodi e di Vespri," *EL* 86 (1972) 41–60.

F. Morlot, "Le *preces* delle Lodi e dei Vespri," in *Liturgia delle Ore. Documenti ufficiali e studi* (Turin-Leumann: ElleDiCi, 1972) 141–49.

J. Evenou, "Les prières d'intercession," *LMD* no. 143 (1980) 107–23.

B. Fischer, "La prière du prêtre comme ministère pastoral," *Bulletin de Saint-Sulpice* 8 (1982) 121–29.

The fourth-century documents that describe the morning and evening prayer of the Christian people at Jerusalem, in Syria, or at Constantinople speak of intercessory prayers that were a kind of culmination of these offices.[56] These prayers underwent a variety of developments in the East. The Byzantine liturgy includes a number of diaconal litanies, long (ectenies) or short (synaptes), in the Hours of the cathedral office, that is, *orthros* and Vespers. In the Little Hours, it simply has the *Kyrie eleison* repeated many times over. The Chaldean office likewise has a diaconal litany or supplication (*karozuta*) at the end of Vespers (*ramcho*), the night office (*lelya*), and the vigil of feasts; oddly enough, it does not have one at the end of morning prayer (*sapra*).[57] In the Syrian liturgy the classic diaconal litany (*karouzoutho*) is indeed found, but another form of intercessory prayer, the *sedro*, has also been developed; it is a prayer said by a priest but according to A. Baumstark it evolved out of the diaconal litany.[58]

In Gaul the intercessory prayers took the form of a series of psalm verses (of which the ferial prayers of the early Roman office are a legacy). These were the *capitella de psalmis* ("little sections from the psalms") which the Council of Agde recommended in 506.[59] In Spain, at least in offices in tradition B, there was a diaconal exhortation, called a *supplicatio*, to which the people responded, after a moment of silence, with *Kyrie eleison*.[60]

The Rule of the Master ends the Hours with a prayer of petition called *rogus Dei* ("prayer, or petition, to God"). Was this a litany, or a prayer

---

56. The most important texts are in V. Raffa, "Le intercessioni di Lodi e di Vespri," *EL* 86 (1972) 49–57; see J. A. Jungmann, *Pastoral Liturgy* (New York: Herder and Herder, 1962) 180–91.

57. The litany for Vespers is translated in *LMD* no. 64 (1960) 84–87; the litanies of the *Lelya* and of the festal vigil are in J. Mateos, *Lelya-Sapra. Essai d'interprétation des Matines chaldéennes* (OCA 156; Rome: Pontificio Istituto Orientale, 1959) 52–53 and 65.

58. A. Baumstark, *Festbrevier und Kirchenjahr der syrischen Jakobiten* 86–87; *Comparative Liturgy* 71–72. — On the *Sedrê* see the text below at n. 74.

59. Canon 30: "At the end of the morning or evening *missae* [groups of psalms], after the hymns, the *capitella de psalmis* are to be said." Text in *Concilia Galliae a. 314—a. 506*, ed. C. Munier (CCL 148:206).

60. J. Pinell, "Una exhortación diaconal en el antiguo rito hispánico: La 'supplicatio,'" *Analecta sacra Tarraconensia* 36 (1964) 3–25.

said silently?[61] St. Benedict prescribes a *letania* before the *missae* ("dismissals") in *Matutinum* and Vespers; nocturnal vigils likewise end with a *supplicatio litaniae, id est Quirie eleison* (a "litany, that is, 'Lord, have mercy' "); for the Little Hours Benedict speaks simply of *Quirie eleison.*[62] At the end of Lauds, the Ambrosian office had twelve *Kyries*, which were probably the remnant of a more developed prayer.

This universal and popular tradition had been gradually abandoned in the Roman office, as it had also been in the Mass. The intercessions were restored in the Mass by order of Vatican II, and the 1971 *Liturgia Horarum* reintroduced them into the evening office. At the same time, "since there is also a tradition of morning prayer that recommends the whole day to God, there are invocations at Morning Prayer for the purpose of consecrating the day to God" (*General Instruction* 181). Evening intercessions and morning invocation have, therefore, different purposes. They are nonetheless symmetrical as far as the place they occupy in these principal Hours is concerned. They are similar in style, taking the form either of a litany with an answering refrain or Kyrie, or of alternating verses as in the ancient *capitella de psalmis*. The regulations governing these prayers are detailed in the *General Instruction;* episcopal conferences are free to adapt the formularies offered in the Latin edition and to approve new ones.[63]

II. THE RECITATION OF THE OUR FATHER

BIBLIOGRAPHY

J. A. Jungmann, "The Lord's Prayer in the Roman Breviary," in his *Pastoral Liturgy* (New York: Herder and Herder, 1962) 191–200.

The *Didache*, as we saw earlier, urged the recitation of the Our Father three times a day.[64] It can be said that the Lord's Prayer has a place in the offices of all the rites, but this place has varied greatly. In the Rule of St. Benedict, the Our Father is said in a low voice in the Little Hours, but proclaimed aloud or sung by the abbot at the end of *Matutinum* and Vespers so that the commitment undertaken in this prayer may create a

---

61. *Regula Magistri* 33, 30, ed. A. de Vogüé 2 (SC 106; Paris: Cerf, 1964) 182–83 and note 30. Other references are given in the verbal concordance in 3 (SC 107; Paris: Cerf, 1965) 396.

62. *Regula* 9, 10; 12, 4; 13, 11; 13, 14; 17, 4–10; passages quoted in the text are translated in *The Rule of St. Benedict*, ed. Timothy Fry, 204 and 213.

63. *GILH* 179–93.

64. See above, n. 6, p. 163.

readiness to forgive if there are any "thorns of contention."⁶⁵ In Spain the Our Father was proclaimed by the priest at the end of these same two Hours.⁶⁶

In twelfth-century Rome, the custom was still followed in the Lateran Basilica of ending Vespers with the Our Father, but the prayer was said silently.⁶⁷ The Breviary of St. Pius V had the Our Father during the *preces*; as in the Benedictine office it was also said aloud at Lauds and Vespers. The *preces*, however, ended up being used very rarely. The Our Father became in turn a simple prelude and a hasty conclusion of the Hours; it was said in a low voice and was almost not a part of the office.

The reform of 1971 restored the Lord's Prayer to a place of honor. It is said or sung at the end of the intercessions in Vespers and the invocations in Lauds; moreover, it is prolonged, as at Mass, by a formula which is spoken by the presiding celebrant and takes the form of the prayer of the Hour or day. Thus, since we now say the Our Father at Mass, Lauds, and Vespers, we have restored the tradition reflected in the *Didache*.⁶⁸

III. THE PRESIDENTIAL PRAYERS

In the time of Egeria, the prayer of the Hours in Jerusalem was marked, even at the daily vigils, by the presence of "two or three presbyters and deacons each day by rota, who are there with the monazontes and say the prayers between all the hymns and antiphons."⁶⁹ The reference is to the psalm prayers or psalter collects that were discussed earlier. The custom of psalm prayers was almost universal in antiquity and has partially survived in the Ambrosian office and the office of the Eastern Syrians.⁷⁰

Another form of presidential prayer is the closing prayer, which puts a kind of seal on the celebration. This too is attested for Jerusalem in the time of Egeria. It does not have a place in the Rule of St. Benedict, for which the Our Father is the real concluding prayer. Nor was it used by the community at the Lateran; it is likely that Rome was as strict as Jerusalem in reserving to those in priestly orders the right to pronounce such

---

65. St. Benedict, *Regula* 13, 12–14, trans. in *The Rule of St. Benedict* 209.

66. Council of Gerona (517), can. 10: "We have decided that every day after the morning office and Vespers a priest should recite the Our Father" (J. Vives, *Concilios visigóticos e hispano-romanos* 41).

67. Bernhard, *Ordo officiorum ecclesiae Lateranensis*, ed. L. Fischer (Munich: Daterer, 1916), *passim* (see the *Sachregister* 181).

68. *GILH* 194–96.

69. *Egeria's Travels* 24, 1 (Wilkinson 123).

70. In the Ambrosian liturgy the offices of Lauds and Vespers have several presidential prayers, often connected with the canticles and psalms. — On the psalter collects see above, pp. 204–5.

a prayer, inasmuch as the sacramentaries do have the needed formularies for morning and evening, while the eighth-century Gelasian Sacramentaries also have them for the other Hours.[71] In the Spanish liturgy each office ended with a prayer called the *Completuria* ("concluding [prayer]"), which preceded the Our Father and the final blessing.[72] The office to which the Antiphonary of Bangor bears witness had presidential prayers in all its component parts.

In the medieval Latin office, both Roman and monastic, there was general use of a concluding collect reserved to the celebrant. These prayers were assembled in a book called a collectary; later on they became part of the breviary.

The 1971 Liturgy of the Hours distinguishes two types of celebration. On the one hand, there are festal and Sunday celebrations, along with those of the special seasons of the liturgical year. In these, the collect or opening prayer of the Mass is repeated in the office. On the other hand, there are the weekday celebrations in Ordinary Time. In these the prayers, which vary over the course of the four-week cycle, express the spirituality proper to each Hour. If a priest or deacon is present, it is for him to say these prayers, in accordance with tradition.[73]

In the East the prayers said by a priest take very different forms. They are very frequent, but are often said in a low voice while the choir sings hymns or psalms. In the Byzantine office these prayers consist either of numerous "apologies," or of prayers attributed to venerable authors (St. Basil, St. Eustratus, etc.), or of morning or evening prayers. Only in the Little Hours is the role of the priest sometimes limited to saying a short collect. The Syrian (and Maronite) office has a type of prayer that is peculiar to it: the *sedro*. This has three parts: a prooemium, devoted chiefly to praise; the prayer proper (*sedro*); and a prayer of incensation (*'etro*), since the *sedro* is usually accompanied by an incensation.[74]

The dismissal prayer, usually consisting of a blessing, must be included among the presidential prayers. It is attested for Jerusalem by Egeria,[75]

---

71. *Le,* nos. 587–93; *Ge,* nos 516–40, 646–51, 1576–94; *Gr,* nos. 935–79, 70, 389, 398, 405, 412, 420, 427, 433, 438, 577, 598, 774; *Gell,* nos. 2101–75; Sacramentary of Angoulême, nos. 1873–1906.

72. J. Vives, *Oracional visigótico* (Monumenta Hispaniae sacra, ser. lit. l; Barcelona-Madrid: Consejo Superior de investigaciones científicas, 1946) xvi; J. Pinell, "El oficio hispano-visigótico," *Hispania sacra* 10 (1957) 401–5, 409.

73. *GILH* 197–200, 256. — A. Dumas, "Le orazioni dell'ufficio feriale nel tempo *per annum,*" in *Liturgia delle Ore. Documenti ufficiali e studi* (Turin-Leumann: ElleDiCi, 1972) 251–68.

74. A. Baumstark, *Festbrevier und Kirchenjahr der syrischen Jakobiten,* 85–91.

75. *Egeria's Travels* 24, 1–7 (at dawn and the sixth and ninth hours, and at the end of the *Lucernarium*).

for Gaul by the Council of Agde in 506,[76] for the Spanish liturgy, where it is paired with the *Completuria*,[77] and for the Syrian office, where it is known as the *houttomo*.[78] The Rule of St. Benedict indicates a blessing at the end of Compline: "a blessing and the dismissal," and at the end of Sunday vigils: "after a final blessing." For Vespers and the Little Hours it indicates only *missas*, "the dismissal," or *fiant missae*.[79]

Down to our time the Roman liturgy had no other form of dismissal except the acclamation: *Benedicamus Domino*, "Let us bless the Lord." The bishop, however, did give his blessing at the end of Lauds and Vespers. Henceforth in the same Hours the celebrant (bishop, priest, or deacon) gives the blessing as at Mass, and this is followed by the diaconal proclamation "Go in peace." If no one in sacred orders is present, another form of dismissal is proposed.[80]

---

76. Canon 30: "After a collect, the bishop dismisses the people in the evening with a blessing" (CCL 148:206).

77. J. Vives, *ibid.* xvi–xvii.

78. A. Baumstark, *ibid.* 86–87, 119, 135, 137, 152, 156; A. Raes, "Les deux composantes de l'office divin syrien," *OC* 1 (1956) 72–73.

79. *Regula* 11, 10; 17, 2, 5, 8, 10; passages quoted are translated in *The Rule of St. Benedict* 207 and 213.

80. *GILH* 54.

Chapter V

The Varied Forms of the Liturgy of the Hours

In a work such as the present one, it is not possible to describe in detail all the varied forms taken by the Liturgy of the Hours in the different cathedral and monastic traditions. Each has its own spiritual genius; each developed in a particular cultural milieu. Moreover, an authentic knowledge of these forms of prayer can be acquired only from within, that is, by participating in them. It will profit the reader, nonetheless, if I provide here a brief overview that will help them, if they wish, to pursue the matter further.

The previous chapters will have already shown how much light the comparative method sheds on our own Roman tradition. Today there is a further consideration: the celebration of the Liturgy of the Hours in the various modern languages is calling for an effort at adaptation and creation, and in this context the patrimony of these other traditions can often enrich our own, as has happened in other periods of liturgical history.

§1. In the East

BIBLIOGRAPHY (for a quick survey)

A. Raes, *Introductio in liturgiam orientalem* (Rome: Pontificio Istituto Orientale, 1947) 178–206: "De Officio Vespertino."

J. M. Hanssens, *Aux origines de la prière liturgique. Nature et genèse de l'office des Matines* (Analecta Gregoriana 57; Rome: Gregorian University, 1952).

A. Baumstark, *Comparative Liturgy*, ed. B. Botte, trans. F. L. Cross (Westminster, Md.: Newman, 1958).

J. P. Foucher, *Poésie liturgique. Orient, Occident* (Paris: Mame. 1963).

La prière des heures, ed. Mgr. Cassien and B. Botte (Lex orandi 35; Paris: Cerf, 1963).

A. Raes, "L'office divin du prêtre de rite oriental," *Seminarium* 24 (1972) 175–84.

I. H. Dalmais, *Les liturgies d'Orient* (Rites et symboles 10; Paris: Cerf, 1980).

————, *La prière des liturgies orientales. Textes choisis et présentés* (Prière de tous les temps 24; Chambray: C. L. D., 1981).

I. EGYPT AND ETHIOPIA

BIBLIOGRAPHY

a) Coptic Office

O. H. E. Burmester, "The Canonical Hours of the Coptic Church," *OCP* 2 (1936) 78–100.

————, "The Greek Kirugmata: Versicles and Responses and Hymns in the Coptic Liturgy," *ibid.* 363–94.

M. Brogi, *La santa salmodia annuale delle Chiesa copta* (Cairo: Edizioni del Centro francescano di studi orientali cristiani, 1962).

A. Veilleux, *La liturgie dans le cénobitisme pachômien du IVe siècle* (Studia Anselmiana 57; Rome: Herder 1968).

H. Quecke, *Untersuchungen zum koptischen Stundengebet* (Publications de l'Institut orientaliste de Louvain, 3; Louvain, 1970).

O. H. E. Burmester, *The Horologion of the Egyptian Church* (Studia orientalia cristiana egyptiaca; Cairo: Edizioni del Centro francescano di studi orientali cristiani, 1973).

b) Ethiopian Office

A. Van Lantschoot, *Horologion aethiopicum iuxta recensionem Alexandrinam copticam* (Vatican City, 1940). Latin translation made in behalf of the Congregation for the Eastern Churches.

R. Taft, "Praise in the Desert: The Coptic Monastic Office," *Worship* 55 (1982) 513–36.

B. Vélat, *Etudes sur le Me 'erâf, commun de l'office éthiopien. Introduction, traduction française, commentaire liturgique et musicale* (PO 33; Paris: Firmin-Didot, 1966). Idem, *Texte éthiopien avec variantes* (PO 34, 1–2; 1966).

R. Izarn, "Sur l'office divin éthiopien," *RechSR* 56 (1968) 283–88.

As far back as the third century, as we saw earlier, Clement of Alexandria and Origen were urging the Christians of Egypt to use the prayer of the hours as a way of attaining to the ideal of ceaseless prayer. It was also in Egypt that monasticism first flowered. John Cassian made known to the Latin world the monastic Liturgy of the Hours, or at least what he conceived it to be, for in fact the office of the Pachomian tradition seems to us today quite different from Cassian's description of it.[1]

---

1. A. Veilleux, *La liturgie dans le cénobitisme pachômien au IVe siècle* (Studia Anselmiana 57; Rome: Herder, 1968) 315, pulls together the elements of the office that are attested in the authentic Pachomian documents.

Moreover, there was a great deal of divergence within Egyptian monastic usage.[2]

The Coptic tradition has remained faithful to the austerity of the anchorites. Thus the daily office demands the recitation of about seventy-five psalms, always the same ones, with some even being repeated in different Hours. Morning prayer has an invitatory with Ps 51; then twelve psalms (1–6, 10–13, 15–16, 19), followed by morning psalms (25, 27, 63, 67, 70, 113, 143); there is neither biblical canticle nor Pss 148–50.

Terce, Sext, None, Vespers, and Compline likewise have a dozen psalms each. Between Compline and the midnight office there is an "Office of the veil" (or "of the indulgence") in which eighteen psalms already recited are repeated. In each of these Hours, the psalmody is preceded by preludes and followed by a reading from the gospel, a troparion, a *Theotokion* (song to Mary), the Our Father, many *Kyrie eleisons*, and a short prayer of dismissal. In addition, the morning Hour includes the recitation of the *Gloria in excelsis*.

The midnight office is divided into three nocturns, each containing psalms (Ps 119, the psalms of Vespers, and the psalms of Compline), a gospel, a troparion, a *Theotokion*, Kyries, and the Our Father. The gospels do not form a continuous reading, but are chosen in each case to fit the meaning of each Hour.

The Ethiopian office has an almost identical distribution of psalms, but, in keeping with its own special genius, it gives more space to lyrical elements, especially to songs to the Blessed Virgin. There is no "Office of the veil"; the midnight office ends with the Canticle of Moses, Ps 136, and the Canticle of the Three Young Men. The Ethiopians have, in addition, an office "at cockcrow," which begins with Pss 148–50 and includes the three gospel canticles as well as the Canticle of Hezekiah.

II. THE EASTERN SYRIANS

BIBLIOGRAPHY

A. J. Maclean, *East Syrian Daily Office* (London: Rivington, 1894).

J. Mateos, *Lelya-Sapra. Essai d'interprétation des Matines chaldéennes* (OCA 156; Rome: Pontificio Istituto Orientale, 1959).

_____, "Un office de minuit chez les Chaldéens?" *OCP* 25 (1959) 101–13.

---

2. Doubt has been cast on the authenticity of the *De virginitate* that is attributed to St. Athanasius (*Clavis Patrum Graecorum* no. 2248), so that we cannot rely on its description of the office; see J. Mateos, "Office de minuit et office du matin chez saint Athanase," *OCP* 28 (1962) 173–80, with the correction in his "L'office monastique à la fin du IVe siècle," *OC* 47 (1963) 71, n. 52.

_____, "Matines chaldéennes, maronites et syriennes," *OCP* 26 (1960) 51–73.

_____, "L'office paroissial du matin et du soir dans le rite chaldéen," *LMD* no. 64 (1960) 65–89.

_____, "Les différentes espèces de vigiles dans le rite chaldéen," *OCP* 27 (1961) 46–63.

_____, "L'office divin chez les Chaldéens," in Cassien-Botte 253–81.

S. H. Jammo, "L'office du soir chaldéen au temps de Gabriel Qatraya," *OS* 12 (1967) 187–210.

H. Husmann, *Die Melodien des chaldäischen Breviers Commune nach den Traditionen Vorderasiens und der Malabarküste* (OCA 178; Rome: Pontificio Istituto Orientale, 1967).

The Chaldean office is perhaps even more austere and closer to its origins. At the same time, however, as I. H. Dalmais observes, "it is worth noting that the nocturnal office despite its length has continued to be esteemed in this Church, not only by the monks but also by the laity who form veritable confraternities and claim the name of 'deacons' for themselves."[3] The nocturnal office (*Lelya*) includes three sections (*hullalê*) of psalms, with the entire psalter being recited in the course of the six weeknights (Sunday follows a different cycle). To the psalms are added hymns but no readings. On Sunday this nocturnal office is followed by a second (*Shahra*, vigil) which doubtless is descended from an ancient cathedral vigil.

Morning prayer (*Sapra*) is celebrated after *Lelya*. It comprises a fixed set of psalms, namely, the morning psalms (100, 91, 104 in part, 113, 93, 148–50, 117), followed by hymns, and includes an incensation ceremony and a ceremony celebrating the light. The evening office (*Ramcho*) also has an incensation rite, the evening psalms (141, 142, an octonary [section of eight verses] from 119, and 117), and the repeated singing of an acclamation (*Laku mara*) during which at one time the lamps used to be lighted.

The other traditional Hours were doubtless said daily in the past. At present only Compline and the equivalent of Terce and Sext are recited on the weekdays of Lent.[4] None also existed in the time of Pseudo-George of Arbela (tenth century).[5]

III. PALESTINE, ANTIOCH, AND CAPPADOCIA IN THE FOURTH AND FIFTH CENTURIES

BIBLIOGRAPHY

J. Mateos, "La vigile cathédrale chez Egérie," *OCP* 27 (1961) 281–312.

---

3. I. H. Dalmais, *Les liturgies d'Orient* (Rites et symboles 10; Paris: Cerf, 1980) 169–70.

4. J. Mateos, "L'office divin chez les Chaldéens," in Cassien-Botte 257–60.

5. *Anonymi auctoris Expositio officiorum Ecclesiae Georgio Arbelensi vulgo adscripta*, trans. R. H. Connolly (CSCO 71; Louvain, 1954) 107, lines 15–18 (Syriac text, CSCO 64:133).

_____, "L'office monastique à la fin du IVe siècle," *OC* 47 (1963) 53–88.

A. Renoux, "Liturgie de Jérusalem et lectionnaires arméniens. Vigiles et année liturgique," in Cassien-Botte 167–99.

R. Zerfass, *Die Schriftlesung im Kathedraloffizium Jerusalems* (LQF 48; Münster: Aschendorff, 1968).

J. Mateos, "Quelques anciens documents sur l'office du soir," *OCP* 35 (1969) 347–74.

P. Rentinck, *La cura pastorale in Antiochia nel IV secolo* (Analecta Gregoriana 178; Rome: Gregorian University, 1970) 144–46.

Cassian's description of the office in the "monasteries of Palestine, Mesopotamia, and the entire East" at the beginning of the fourth century[6] is a little less inaccurate than the one he gives of the office of the Egyptian monks. In addition, we have direct and more reliable documents on the celebration of the Hours in Cappadocia in the time of St. Basil,[7] at Jerusalem when Egeria made her pilgrimage there,[8] and at Antioch before John Chrysostom went on to be archbishop of Constantinople.[9]

St. Basil organized both the popular liturgy of his Church of Caesarea and that of the ascetics who lived around him; his letters and his monastic Rules made rather widely known the principles he followed in this organization. Jerusalem, a pilgrimage city, was also a model for the entire Christian world; later on, the organization of the liturgy in the monastery of St. Sabas would become the norm for many Churches in the Byzantine world. Antioch, for its part, exerted an influence both in Greek-speaking milieus and in the Syriac-speaking East.

These various spiritual centers followed an almost identical path in harmonizing the "cathedral" liturgy, with its daily morning and evening prayers, and the spiritual tradition of Christian asceticism. Morning prayer, which was characterized by Pss 51 and 148–50, might follow immediately upon a vigil that was celebrated at cockcrow, or it might be separated from a vigil by a time of rest; Basil, in particular, instituted a *mesonuk-tikon*, a vigil in the middle of the night. During the day there were prayers at the third,[10] sixth, and ninth hours. Evening prayer was celebrated as it was everywhere else; at Jerusalem it included the *luknikon* (lucernarium or lamplighting ceremony). Finally, Basil introduced still another

---

6. John Cassian, *De institutis coenobiorum* III, 1–6, ed. J.-C. Guy (SC 109; Paris: Cerf, 1965) 92–109.

7. St. Basil, *Ep.* 207, ed. Y. Courtonne, 2 (Collection Budé; Paris: Belles Lettres, 1961) 185–87; *Regulae fusius tractatae*, Qu. 37, 3–5 (PG 31:1013-16), trans. L. Lèbe (Maredsous, 1939) 121–25.

8. *Egeria's Travels* 24–25 (Wilkinson 123–28).

9. Main sources: *Homil. 14 in 1 Tim.* 3–4 (PG 62:575-77) and *Homil. 68(69) in Matt.* 3–4 (PG 58:644-46).

10. If we judge by Egeria's description, the Church of Jerusalem seems to have celebrated Sext and None but not Terce.

time of prayer at the beginning of night: "To ensure a peaceful and dreamless sleep, they shall say Ps 91 at this moment."

All these assemblies for prayer were filled with the varied singing of the psalms by alternating choirs and with supplications; despite Cassian's assertion, there seems to have been no place for readings.

IV. THE BYZANTINE OFFICE

BIBLIOGRAPHY

N. Borgia, *Horologion diurno delle Chiese di rito bizantino* (OCA 56; Rome: Pontificio Istituto Orientale, 1929).

J. Leroy, "Le cursus canonique chez saint Théodore Studite," *EL* 68 (1954) 5–19.

M. Black, *A Christian Palestinian Syriac Horologion* (Cambridge: Cambridge University Press, 1954).

J. Mateos, "Quelques problèmes de l'Orthros byzantin," *POC* 11 (1961) 17–35, 201–20.

—————, "L'office monastique à la fin du IVe siècle. Antioche, Palestine, Cappadoce," *OC* 47 (1963) 53–88.

V. Janeras, "La partie vespérale de la liturgie byzantine des présanctifiés," *OCP* 30 (1964) 193–222.

J. Mateos, "Un Horologion inédit de Saint-Sabas, le codex Sinaïtique grec 833 (IXe siècle)," in *Mélanges Eugène Tisserant* 3. *Orient chrétien*, Part II (ST 233; Vatican City, 1964) 47–76.

—————, "Prières initiales fixes des offices syrien, maronite et byzantin," *OS* 11 (1966) 489–98.

M. Arranz, "Les prières sacerdotales des Vêpres byzantins," *OCP* 37 (1971) 85–124.

—————, "Les prières presbytérales des Matines byzantins," *OCP* 37 (1971) 406–36; 38 (1972) 64–114.

—————, "Les prières presbytérales des petites Heures dans l'ancien euchologe byzantin," *OCP* 39 (1972) 29–82.

—————, "Les prières presbytérales de la Pannychis de l'ancien euchologe byzantin," *OCP* 40 (1974) 314–43; 41 (1975) 119–39.

La prière des Eglises de rite byzantin 1. *La prière des heures. Horologion* (Chevetogne, 1975), with introduction by N. Egender. 3. *Dimanche selon les huit tons. Octōechos* (Chevetogne, 1972).

M. Arranz, "L'office de la veillée nocturne dans l'Eglise grecque et dans l'Eglise russe," *OCP* 42 (1976) 117–55, 402–25.

—————, "Les prières de la Tritoektî de l'ancien euchologe byzantin," *OCP* 43 (1977) 70–93, 335–54.

—————, "L'office de l'asmatikos hesperinos (Vêpres chantées) de l'ancien euchologe byzantin," *OCP* 44 (1978) 107–30, 391–419.

—————, "La Liturgie des Heures selon l'ancien euchologe byzantin," in *Eulogia. Miscellanea liturgica in onore di P. Burkhard Neunheuser* (Studia Anselmiana 68, Analecta liturgica 1; Rome, 1979) 1–20.

—————, "L'office de l'asmatikos Orthros (matines chantées) de l'ancien euchologe byzantin," *OCP* 47 (1981) 122–37.

—————, "Office. II. En Orient," *Dictionnaire de spiritualité* 11 (1982) 707–20.

Western readers have been given access to the present-day Byzantine office through excellent translations and numerous works of popularization. This office came into existence as a result of the meeting of several traditions: some of these were "cathedral" traditions: those of the Church of Jerusalem and of Hagia Sophia in Constantinople; others were monastic: the Palestinian monastic tradition of the Laura of St. Sabas, and the Constantinopolitan tradition of Studios, which was the work of Theodore (who intended to follow St. Basil). The occupation of Constantinople by the Latins (1204) destroyed the cathedral office and its repertory of songs; very little was left of it, probably the morning and evening prayers which are now said in a low voice by the celebrant while the psalms are being sung in Orthros and Vespers. From that point on, the monastic office according to the usage of St. Sabas was celebrated almost everywhere.

This office contains all the Hours: office for the middle of the night (*mesonuktikon*), Prime, Terce, Sext, None, and Compline, to which are added, as I indicated above, some intermediate Hours. Of the prolonged vigils for great feasts a vestige remains in "Great Compline" (*mega apodeipnon*). The cathedral Hours of morning and evening have undergone extensive development. *Orthros*, which in fact combines two offices, is an Hour in which hymnography has been given free rein; on Sundays this office contains the Hierosolymitan commemoration of the resurrection. Vespers, or *hesperinos*, includes a celebration of the light; on days of strict fast, the liturgy of the presanctified with its readings becomes part of Vespers.

The traditional psalms are prescribed for morning and evening, and sections of the psalter at all the Hours; the abundance of troparia, however, too easily serves as an invitation to shorten the psalmody; the biblical canticles have even disappeared completely from *Orthros*, except during Lent, being replaced by the poetic canon that should have simply accompanied the canticles. Since the *Horologion*, which gives the structure and unvarying parts of the office, is a relatively small book, a whole library of other books is needed for the songs of each day in Ordinary Time (the *Paraklitikē*), in Lent (the *Triodion*), and in the Easter season (the *Pentekostarion*), which intermingle with those of celebrations that have a fixed date (the *Menaia*), that is, chiefly those of the saints, and this even during Holy Week. In order to get one's bearings in this maze one needs still another book, the *Typikon*, which resembles the Ordinals of the medieval Latin liturgy.

V. THE ARMENIAN OFFICE

BIBLIOGRAPHY

F. C. Conybeare, *Rituale Armenorum, Being the Administration of the Sacraments and the Breviary Rites of the Armenian Church* (Oxford: Clarendon Press, 1905) 447–88.

A. Raes, "Les anciennes Matines byzantines et arméniennes," *OCP* 19 (1953) 205–10.

A. Renoux, "Liturgie de Jérusalem et lectionnaires arméniens. Vigiles et année liturgique," in Cassien-Botte 167–99.

The Armenian office, like the other parts of this liturgy, depended originally on the ancient usage of Jerusalem, but it also benefited by contributions from the tradition of Constantinople. In fact, it still retains elements of the latter which ultimately disappeared from the Byzantine liturgy, to the point where the Greek original is now lost.[11] Its own creativity is to be seen above all in a large number of hymns which are valuable both for their doctrinal wealth and for their poetic quality; they are the work above all of Gregory of Narek (tenth century) and Narses the Kindly (twelfth century).

VI. THE WESTERN SYRIANS AND MARONITES

BIBLIOGRAPHY

a) Syrian Office

A. Baumstark, "Das syrisch-antiochenische Ferialbrevier," *Der Katholik*, 3. Folge, 26 (1902) 416–27.

_____, *Festbrevier und Kirchenjahr der syrischen Jakobiten. Eine liturgiegeschichtliche Vorarbeit* (Studien zur Geschichte und Kultur des Altertums 3/3-5; Paderborn: Schöningh, 1910).

A. Raes, "Les deux composantes de l'office divin syrien," *OS* 1 (1956) 66–75.

F[rère] A[lphonse] [= Ch. de Champeaux de la Boulaye], *Commun du bréviaire de la liturgie syrienne* (mimeographed, 1957); *Office syrien, Ramchê propres* (mimeographed, n. d.).

J. Puyade, "Composition interne de l'office divin syrien," *OS* 2 (1957) 77–92; 3 (1958) 25–62.

_____, "Les Heures canoniales syriennes et leur composition," *OS* 3 (1958) 401–28.

O. Hendricks, "La vie quotidienne du moine syrien," *OS* 5 (1960) 293–330.

J. Mateos, "Les Matines chaldéennes, maronites et syriennes," *OCP* 26 (1960) 51–73.

---

11. One example is the group of antiphons studied by J. Lemarié, "Les antiennes *Veterem hominem* du jour octave de l'Epiphanie et les antiennes d'origine grecque de l'Epiphanie," *EL* 72 (1958) 3–38.

_____, "Sedrê et prières connexes dans quelques anciennes collections," *OCP* 28 (1962) 239–87.

_____, "L'invitatoire du nocturne chez les Syriens et les Maronites," *OS* 11 (1966) 353–66.

_____, "Prières initiales fixes des offices syrien, maronite et byzantin," *OS* ll (1966) 489–98.

A. Cody, "L'eucharistie et les heures canoniales chez les Syriens jacobites. Une description des cérémonies," *OS* 12 (1967) 66–81, 115–86.

J. Mateos, "Trois recueils anciens de Prooemia syriens," *OCP* 33 (1967) 457–82.

J. Tabet, "Le témoignage de Sévère d'Antioche sur la vigile cathédrale," *Melto* 4, no. 2 (1968) 5–12.

_____, "Le témoignage de Bar Hebraeus sur la vigile cathédrale," *Melto* 5, no. 1 (1969) 113–21.

J. Mateos, "Les strophes de la nuit dans l'invitatoire du nocturne syrien," in *Mémorial Mgr. Gabriel Khouri-Sarkis* (Louvain: Imprimerie Orientaliste, 1969) 71–81.

b) Maronite Office

J. Mateos, "Les Matines chaldéennes, maronites et syrienne," *OCP* 26 (1960) 51–73.

P. E. Gamayel, "La structure des Vêpres maronites," *OS* 9 (1964) 105–34.

J. Mateos, "L'invitatoire du nocturne chez les Syriens et les Maronites," *OS* 11 (1966) 353–66.

_____, "Prières initiales fixes des offices syrien, maronite et byzantin," *OS* 11 (1966) 489–98.

_____, "Le *Gloria in excelsis* du début des offices maronites," *OS* 12 (1967) 117–21.

M. Breydi, *Kult, Dichtung und Musik im Wochenbrevier der Syro-Maroniten* (2 vols.; Kobayath, Lebanon, 1970–71).

J. Tabet, *L'office commun maronite. Etude du Lilyo et du Safro* (Bibliothèque de l'Université du Saint-Esprit; Kaslik, Lebanon, 1972).

E. Khalife-Hachem, "Office maronite du grand dimanche de la Résurrection," *Parole de l'Orient* 6–7 (1975–76) 281–308.

The Western Syrians use, as required, either a "Weekday Breviary" or a "Festal Breviary." The former has only a one-week cycle, for which it provides all the texts. The second adds the texts required for the celebration of feasts and Sundays. Vespers (*ramsho*) includes the same psalms as are used by the Eastern Syrians (141, 142, an octonary from 119, and 117), some songs, and the priestly prayer of incensation with its three parts. On feastdays all this is preceded by a variable psalm and followed by a proclamation of the gospel and a litany.

Prayer during the night (*Lilyo*) opens with an invitatory made up of psalms (134, 119:169–76, and 117). The main part is divided into several vigils, each comprising songs, *sedrê*, and petitions, but no psalms. It ends with the *Magnificat* which is followed by a Marian song, Pss 133, 148–50, 117, and the *Gloria in excelsis* or, in other words, by a part of the traditional morning office. The morning office (*Sapro*) has, however, its independent existence and includes psalms (51, 63, 103, and 148–50 again), songs, and one or more *sedrê*. A festal morning office also includes a canticle (Isa 42:10-13 and 45:8), the *Magnificat*, the Beatitudes, and a reading from the gospel. Terce, Sext, and None have no psalms, but only hymns, a *sedro*, and petitions. Compline (*Sûtôro*) includes Pss 4, 91, and 119.

The present-day Syrian office thus emphasizes hymnography and leaves a very limited place to psalmody. The hymns come from two sources: songs composed in Greek, especially by Severus of Antioch, and then translated into Syriac, and songs written in Syriac and borrowed from Edessa or even Nisibis.

The Maronite office has approximately the same structure as the Syrian, except that the current psalmody kept its place for a longer time in the monastic celebration of the office.[12] In morning prayer (*Safro*) a hymn of St. Ephraem is sung (*Nuhro*); the Beatitudes are not included. In Vespers and in morning prayer on feast days there are readings taken from the Mass, with which the office is to be joined.

§2. In the West

Until the seventh century the "cathedral" prayer, that is, the morning and evening prayer, of the Churches of the West is known to us only through references made to it by the Fathers in their preaching, by hagiographical narratives, and, above all, by various conciliar decrees, notably Canon 30, already mentioned several times, of the Council of Agde (506) over which St. Caesarius presided.

> Since it is fitting that all alike follow the organization of the [prayer of the] Church, we must see to it that after the antiphons, in accordance with universal usage, the collects are said in order by the bishops or priests; that the morning and evening songs (*hymnos*) are sung every day; that at the end of the morning and evening assemblies the songs (*hymnos*) are followed by *Capitella de psalmis*; and that in the evening the bishop, after the collect, dismisses the people with a blessing.[13]

By the year 506 Latin monasticism had already had a long experience of the Liturgy of the Hours. The *Ordo monasterii* was doubtless compiled in the entourage of St. Augustine; at that same period—the first decades of the fifth century—Cassian set down his ideal of monastic prayer. In

---

12. P. E. Gemayel, "La structure des Vêpres maronites," *OS* 9 (1964) 110-12.

13. Text in CCL 148:206. — It should be noted, moreover, that the lucernarium is mentioned as early as canon 9 of the First Council of Toledo (397-400); see J. Vives, *Concilios visigóticos e hispano-romanos* (España cristiana, Textos 1; Barcelona-Madrid: Consejo Superior de investigaciones científicas, 1963) 22.

the course of the sixth and seventh centuries the usages followed in Gallic, Italian, Celtic, and Spanish monasteries would be codified in Rules.

I. THE PRAYER OF THE HOURS IN THE MONASTIC RULES

BIBLIOGRAPHY

O. Heiming, "Zum monastischen Offizium von Kassianus bis Kolumbanus," *ALW* 7 (1961) 89–156.

La Règle du Maître, edited with introduction, text, translation and notes by A. de Vogüé (SC 105–6; Paris: Cerf, 1964). *Concordance verbale* by J. M. Clément, J. Neufville, and D. Demeslay (SC 107 in 3 vols.; Paris: Cerf, 1965).

J. Pinell, "Las horas vigiliares del oficio monacal hispánico," *Liturgica* 3 (Scripta et documenta 17; Montserrat: Abadía de Montserrat, 1966) 197–340.

L. Verheijen, *La Règle de saint Augustin* (2 vols.; Paris: Etudes Augustiniennes, 1967).

J. M. Clément, *Lexique des anciennes Règles monastiques occidentales* (Instrumenta patristica 7; 2 vols.; Steenbrugge: St-Pietersabdij, 1978).

La Règle de saint Benoît. Vols. 1–2: Critical text by J. Neufville; introduction, translation and notes by A. de Vogüé (SC 181–82; Paris: Cerf, 1972). Vol. 3: *Etude de la tradition manuscrite* by J. Neufville (SC 183; 1972). Vols. 4–6: *Commentaire historique et critique* by A. de Vogüé (SC 184–86; 1971).

RB 1980. The Rule of St. Benedict in Latin and English with Notes, ed. Timothy Fry (Collegeville: The Liturgical Press, 1981).

The prayer of the hours that is described in the *Ordo monasterii*[14] was perhaps practiced in the area of Rome;[15] in any case, it was certainly practiced in Spain, since the *Ordo officii Escorialensis* is an adaptation of it to Visigothic usage.[16] The liturgy of the monks of Lérins was codified by St. Caesarius of Arles in his two Rules, especially in the *Recapitulatio* of the Rule for Virgins that dates from 534,[17] and by St. Aurelian, Caesarius' successor in the see of Arles (546–51), in his *Regula ad monachos*.[18] St. Columban († 615) likewise gave his monks directives for the office

---

14. Critical edition of the text in L. Verheijen, *La Règle de saint Augustin* (Paris: Editions Augustiniennes, 1967) 1:148–52; commentary and attribution, 2:205–13.

15. Compare the description of the office containing the *cautio* (promise) sworn by the bishops who were in dependence on the pope: *Liber diurnus*, ed. H. Foerster (Bern: Francke, 1958) 245 (earlier ed. by T. von Sickel [Vienna, 1889, or repr.: Aalen: Scientia Verlag, 1966] 77–78).

16. Text in Verheijen, *ibid.*, 1:140–42; commentary, 2:209–11; see J. Pinell, "Las horas vigiliares del oficio monacal hispánico," *Liturgica* 3 (Scripta et documenta 17; Montserrat: Abadía de Montserrat, 1966) 43–48.

17. St. Caesarius, *Regula monachorum*, in *S. Caesarii opera omnia*, ed. G. Morin, 2 (Maredsous, 1942) 149–55 (= PL 67:1099-1104); idem, *Statuta sanctarum virginum*, in *ibid.* 101–29 (= PL 67:1105-24).

18. PL 68:393-96.

along with their Rule.[19] In the Spanish world of the seventh century, two other monastic legislators set down their organization of prayer: St. Isidore of Seville († 636)[20] and, later, St. Fructuosus of Braga († 665).[21] Finally, three Rules were written in Italy as early as the sixth century: the *Regula Pauli et Stephani*,[22] the *Regula Magistri* (this is at least the most likely origin),[23] and the Rule of St. Benedict which was destined soon to replace all the others one by one.

The Rule of St. Fructuosus represents a further development that will be discussed below. The others as a group clearly diverge from Eastern practice by the very limited room they give to hymns and by the linear structure of the Hours: psalms, readings, prayers. The essential role belongs to psalmody, which is at times very prolonged; St. Columban even has the entire psalter being recited in two days. The psalms are always grouped in threes, sixes, twelves, or even larger units, but some of them are removed from the *psalterium currens* because they have a special place: in the morning office, in the *lucernarium*, or as preludes to some offices.

These organizations of the prayer of the hours represent varying solutions to the problem of combining the cycles of monastic Hours and cathedral Hours: at times, a *lucernarium* and a *duodecima* coexist in the evening; the characteristic components of cathedral morning prayer are either tied to the nocturnal office or are repeated. Another characteristic of these monastic schemes is the varying length of the nocturnal office depending on the season, with either the number of psalms or the length of the readings being changed. Different kinds of psalmody help prevent monotony: sometimes the psalms are sung or recited *in directum* (by one individual or by all the monks together, and without any refrain); sometimes they are sung responsorially, antiphonally, or with alleluias. St. Basil had already made use of such variety at Caesarea. In general, these Rules allow for readings in all the Hours; between supper and the prayer for

---

19. *Regula monachorum* 8: *De cursu,* and *Regula coenobialis* 9, in *Opera,* ed. G. S. Walker (Scriptores Latini Hiberniae 2; Dublin, 1957) 128–32 and 158. — Little has survived of the Celtic office except the Antiphonary of Bangor (end of seventh century), ed. F. E. Warren (HBS 4 and 10; London: Henry Bradshaw Society, 1893–95); ed. E. Franceschini (Testi e documenti di storia e letteratura latina medioevale 4; Padua: Editrice Gregoriana, 1941); and in PL 72:583–606. — See M. Curran, *The Antiphonary of Bangor and the Early Irish Monastic Liturgy* (Dublin: Irish Academic Press, 1984).

20. *Regula monachorum* 6 (PL 83:875-77); see *De origine officiorum* 4–10, 13, 17, 19–22 (PL 83:741-60). — J. Pinell, *ibid.* 42–48.

21. *Regula Complutensis* 2–3 (PL 87:1099-1101); see J. Pinell, *ibid.,* 52–55, and idem, "San Fructuoso de Braga y su influjo en la formación del oficio monacal hispánico," *Bracara Augusta* 22 (1968) 127–46.

22. *Regula Pauli et Stephani* 10–15, ed. J. Vilanova (Scripta et documenta 11; Montserrat: Abadía de Montserrat, 1959) (= PL 66:949ff.).

23. This is the conclusion reached by A. de Vogüé; see *La Règle du Maître,* ed. with introduction, text, translation, and notes by A. de Vogüé, 1 (SC 105; Paris: Cerf, 1964) 225–33.

retiring or Compline there is a longer period for reading or spiritual conversation. The Rules from Provence, the Rule of the Master, and the Rule of St. Benedict adopt the additional Hour of Prime advocated by Cassian.

As seen in the context of these many Rules the Rule of St. Benedict is an effort to achieve a balanced synthesis of the various Western cathedral and monastic traditions, together with some borrowings from the East. During the day there are four Hours with the same structure: a hymn, three psalms, a short reading, a verse, an Our Father, a Kyrie, and a dismissal. The Hour of retiring, Compline, follows an almost identical order, except for the place of the hymn.

The nocturnal office, which Benedict calls a "vigil," is celebrated toward the end of night. It begins with Pss 3 and 95 and an "Ambrosian" hymn. It then has twelve psalms which are separated into two series by an Old Testament reading with its response and are followed by a chapter from the New Testament. The difference in the overall length of the office from season to season is obtained by shortening the readings. On Sunday the daily vigil is supplemented by a vigil of the cathedral type, with three canticles, readings, the *Te Deum*, a gospel (which must originally have been the gospel of the resurrection), and the *Te decet laus*.

The *Matutina Sollemnitas* ("Morning Solemnity," i.e., Lauds), which is of the cathedral type, includes Pss 67 and 51, two morning psalms which vary according to the day, an Old Testament canticle, Pss 148–50, a short reading with its response, an "Ambrosian" hymn, gospel canticle, litany, and Our Father. The "evening synaxis," or Vespers, belongs rather to the monastic tradition: four psalms from the series 110–147, short reading followed by its response, "Ambrosian" hymn, gospel canticle, litany, Our Father, and blessing.

St. Benedict is the only one to break up psalms that are excessively long; in this he was following the practice of the Egyptian monks as reported by Cassian.[24] He also gives the abbot the freedom to adopt a quite different distribution of the psalms, the only condition being that the entire psalter is to be recited in the course of a week. Abbots have not availed themselves of this permission, and the office of St. Benedict has been celebrated for fourteen centuries now with no change except the shortening of the readings in the Middle Ages. The reform of the Roman office under the egis of Vatican II has brought in its train various attempts to reform the Benedictine office within the limits set down in the *Thesaurus liturgiae Horarum monasticae* which the Abbot Primate published in 1977.[25]

---

24. John Cassian, *De institutis coenobiorum* II, 11, ed. J.-C. Guy (SC 109) 76–78.

25. On the reform of the lectionary see H. Ashworth, "A Proposed Monastic Lectionary. References and Themes," *EL* 91 (1977) 74–92, 171–89, 246–70, 382–413, 499–514; 92 (1978) 88–110.

II. THE PRAYER OF THE HOURS IN THE SPANISH LITURGY

BIBLIOGRAPHY

The Spanish office has been the object of a great deal of research over the last thirty years, especially by Dom Jorge Pinell or at his instigation. There is a quite complete bibliography of this work in *Estudios sobre la liturgia mozárabe* (Publicaciones del Instituto provincial de investigaciones y estudios Toledanos III, 1; Toledo: Disputación provincial, 1965). Only a few items are listed here:

F. de Lorenzana, *Breviarium gothicum secundum regulam beatissimi Isidori* (Madrid, 1776 (= PL 86).

J. M. Martín Patino, "El Breviarium mozárabe de Ortiz, su valor documental para la historia del oficio catedralicio hispánico," *Miscellanea Comillas* 40 (1963) 3–93.

J. Pinell, "El Matutinarium en la liturgia hispana," *Hispania sacra* 9 (1956) 61–85.

―――――――, "El Oficio hispano-visigótico," *Hispania sacra* 10 (1957) 385–427.

Antifonario de León, ed. facsimile (Monumenta Hispaniae sacra, ser. lit., 5/2; Barcelona-Madrid: Consejo Superior de investigaciones científicas, 1953). *Texto y indices*, ed. L. Brou and J. Vives (Monumenta Hispaniae sacra, ser. lit., 5/1; 1959). See *Archivos Leoneses* 8 (1954); the entire volume is concerned with this manuscript.

J. Pinell, "Las horas vigiliares del oficio monacal hispánico," *Liturgica* 3 (Scripta et documenta 17; Montserrat: Abadía de Montserrat, 1966) 197–340.

―――――――, "Primeros vestigios del lucernario en España," *ibid.* 21–49.

―――――――, *Liber orationum psalmographus. Colectas de salmos del antiguo rito hispánico* (Monumenta Hispaniae sacra, ser. lit. 9; Barcelona-Madrid: Consejo Superior de investigaciones científicas, 1972).

The Spanish liturgy maintained down to the eleventh century the distinction between "the cathedral order, which includes the morning office and the evening office or Compline" and that which monks were obliged to add to this ("the office to be attentively celebrated by monks").[26] During that period this monastic supplement comprised twelve Hours and thus added to the cycle of Hours in the Rule of St. Fructuosus, who himself had already increased the number of intermediate Hours during the day and the number of nocturnal Hours. But in 1056 the Council of Compostella obliged all bishops and priests to recite a sizable part of this sequence of Hours: "He is daily to celebrate all the Hours: the first, third, sixth, and evening Hours, Compline, the midnight and nocturnal Hours, and the morning Hour."[27]

On the other hand, the Visigothic Church constantly sought to unify the liturgical celebration as a whole. Thus the Fourth Council of Toledo

---

26. Silos, ms. 7, f° 31, ed. M. Férotin, *Liber mozarabicus sacramentorum* (Paris: Firmin-Didot, 1912) 770; J. Pinell, "Las horas vigiliares," 246. As a matter of fact, Compline is not found in the manuscripts of the *ordo cathedralis*: J. Pinell, "El oficio hispano-visigótico," *Hispania sacra* 10 (1957) 405–7.

27. Canon 1, in Mansi 19:855; cited by M. Férotin, *ibid.* 769; J. Pinell, *ibid.* 247.

(633) asked for "one manner of celebration of Mass, one manner of celebration of the morning and evening offices."[28] Despite these efforts two traditions continued to co-exist: the one proper to the Church of Toledo and represented by the printed breviary of Ortiz and Lorenzana (tradition B) and the more widespread one found in the majority of manuscripts (tradition A).

If we are to judge by the various documents of these two traditions—documents which date from a time not long before the Roman office prevailed (tenth–eleventh centuries)—the Spanish office was heir to the fruits of an intense spiritual and musical activity carried on over many centuries. Psalmody was accompanied by prayers and by songs which were both numerous and highly developed: antiphons, responses, *alleluiaticum* (an antiphon containing one or more alleluias), etc. The readings were rather lengthy. In every Hour the psalmody was followed by a hymn. In Vespers there was an offering of light, but the evening psalm came to be reduced to an antiphon (the *vespertinum*).

The morning office comprised three "canonical" psalms (3, 51, 57), a *missa* or further group of three (variable) psalms with their antiphons, prayers, and closing response, a canticle, the morning psalm (or the Canticle of the Three Young Men), and finally Pss 148–50. The nocturnal, or monastic, office was double. The *Ad nocturnos* was composed of "canonical psalms," then three *missae* of psalms (each *missa* always containing three psalms with their antiphons, prayers, and closing response), a *missa* of canticles, and two readings (Old and New Testaments). The *Post nocturnos*, in which a dozen psalms were recited, came from the Rule of St. Fructuosus and represented a supplement.

III. THE AMBROSIAN OFFICE

BIBLIOGRAPHY

E. Cattaneo, *Il breviario ambrosiano. Note storiche ed illustrative* (Milan: Ambrosius, 1943).
P. Borella, "Il breviario ambrosiano," in M. Righetti, *Manuale di storia liturgica* 2 (2nd ed.; Milan: Ancora, 1955) 675–715.
_____, *Il rito ambrosiano* (Biblioteca di scienze religiose III, 10; Brescia: Morcelliana, 1964) 225–71.

The history of the Ambrosian office is difficult to reconstruct because of a lack of early documents and because of the tribulations which the Church of Milan suffered especially during the Lombard occupation. We

---

28. Canon 2, in J. Vives, *Concilios visigóticos e hispano-romanos* 188.

do, however, have manuscripts from the eleventh and twelfth centuries—
especially the *Manuale* of Valtravaglia[29] and the *Ordo et caeremoniae* of
Beroldus[30]—which give a detailed description of the liturgy. Into this we
can fit the fragmentary earlier documents and show that despite various
reforms this liturgy has retained its original character down into the twentieth century. I shall here provide only a quick survey showing the varied
influences exerted upon this liturgy by the Eastern liturgies, the monasteries
of Provence and even Celtic usages, and, finally, the Roman office.

Vespers begins with a *lucernarium* that is notable for the singing of
an appropriate response and ends with a procession to the baptistry to
the singing of antiphons and responses (fortunately, this commemoration
of baptism has now been restored to its place). On major feasts and at
certain important moments of the liturgical year Vespers becomes a kind
of vigil, with readings and sometimes the celebration of the Eucharist. The
prolonged vigils that at one time were held at the tombs of the martyrs
and of certain saints have left their trace in First Vespers.

In the morning office (*Matutinum*) the nocturnal part, *Ad galli can-
tum* ("At cockcrow"), which was of monastic origin, was not separated
from Lauds, which was the cathedral part. It began with a hymn of
St. Ambrose; this was followed by the canticle *Benedictus es*. From Monday to Friday, in a two-week cycle, the psalmody covered the first 109
psalms of the psalter; these were divided into "decuries" or groups of ten
(Pss 110–18 and 120–47 were assigned to Vespers, somewhat as in Roman usage). Saturday was given a certain solemnity, as in the East, by
the singing of the canticle of the Exodus and Ps 119. Finally, on Sunday
instead of psalms there are simply three canticles, as in the ancient cathedral
vigil.

The reading, which is reduced to a passage from the Bible or to a
homily, is divided into three lessons, with a response after each of the
first two. The singing of Zechariah's *Benedictus* marks the passage from
nocturn to Lauds. This last begins on Sundays with two canticles (the Canticle of the Exodus and the Canticle of the Three Young Men) and during
the week with Ps 51; then come Pss 148–50, 117, a variable psalm sung
in directum, a hymn, a supplication (twelve Kyries), and the baptismal
station as in Vespers. On days of greater solemnity an *antiphona ad crucem* ("antiphon at the cross") seems to be an echo of the rites at the Holy
Sepulcher in Jerusalem. The Little Hours may be a borrowing from the
Roman office.

---

29. *Manuale Ambrosianum*, ed. M. Magistretti (2 vols.; Monumenta veteris Liturgiae
Ambrosianae 2; Milan: Hoepli, 1905).

30. *Beroldus sive ecclesiae Ambrosianae Mediolanensis kalendarium et ordines saec.
XII*, ed. M. Magistretti (Milan: Giovanola, 1894).

The Church of Milan is proud that it possesses the hymns composed by St. Ambrose, and it has therefore been reluctant to increase the repertory; besides, antiphons or responses supply variety. On the other hand, the Milanese office is richly endowed with prayers; thus in Vespers and Lauds several prayers provide opportunity for meditating on each of the canticles and on the spirit of the day.

The reform of the Ambrosian office in the spirit of Vatican II has been brought to completion with the publication of *Liturgia delle Ore secondo il rito della santa Chiesa ambrosiana* in five volumes (Milan: Centro ambrosiano di documentazione, 1983–84). Its primary aims are to make the office less burdensome by a better distribution of the psalms, to emphasize more the commemoration of baptism and the intercessions, and to revise the euchological repertory.

§3. The Roman Office from the Sixth to the Twentieth Century

I. THE ROMAN OFFICE BEFORE THE CAROLINGIAN ERA

BIBLIOGRAPHY

C. Callewaert, *Sacris erudiri* (Steenbrugge: St-Pietersabdij, 1940) 53–167.

Andrieu, *OR* 2:451-66 (*OR* 12); 2:469-88 (*OR* 13A); 3:265-73 (*OR* 23); 3:298 (Appendix to *OR* 24); 3:309-29 (*OR* 26); 3:333-72 (*OR* 27). The other *ordines* used by the old historians are not witnesses to Roman usage.

Amalarius, *Liber de ordine antiphonarii*, in *Amalarii episcopi opera omnia liturgica*, ed. J. M. Hanssens 3 (ST 140; Vatican City, 1950) 5–224.

Antiphonary of St. Peter's (Bibl. Vatic., Archivio di San Pietro, B 79), dating from the twelfth century and published in G. Tomasi, *Opera omnia*, ed. A. Vezzosi, 4 (Rome: Typis Palladis, 1749) 1–170, and in *Monumenta musica medii aevi* 1 (Kassel, 1956).

C. Gindele, "Zur Geschichte von Form und Abhängigkeit bei römischem und monastischem Brevier," *RBen* 65 (1955) 192–207.

_____, "Die römische und monastische Überlieferung im Ordo officii der Regel St. Benedikt," *Studia Anselmiana* 42 (1957) 171–222.

If we compare the organization of the Roman office, as known to us from documents of the eighth and ninth centuries or even later, with that found in the Rule of St. Benedict, it becomes clear that St. Benedict made this Roman organization the basis of his own but also that, finding it too burdensome, he meant to make it less so. It follows from this that by the time of St. Benedict the Roman office already possessed its essential traits. It represented essentially a monastic office, doubtless that of the monks who provided the services in the great urban basilicas and the sanctuaries of the martyrs.[31]

It is also a fact that this office was an austere one. Hymns, as we saw earlier, were introduced only at a very late period. Morning prayer, or Lauds, had seven psalms (every day Pss 51 [replaced on Sunday by Ps 93], 63, 66, 148-50, as well as a variable psalm from the group of morning psalms: 100, 5, 43, 65, 90, 143, 92), a biblical canticle, a reading, the gospel canticle *Benedictus,* and the litany.

The daytime Hours: Prime, Terce, Sext, and None, uniformly used octonaries from Ps 119.[32] Compline, which likewise did not vary, used Pss 4, 31 (verses 1-6), 91, and 134. The rest of the psalter was read weekly in the form of two series: Pss 1-109 in the nocturnal office, and Pss 110-147 in Vespers. With the exception of Ps 119, no psalm or canticle, however long, was divided. Thus the nocturnal office during the week had twelve psalms in accordance with the Egyptian tradition and three readings; on Sunday it had twenty-four psalms divided into three series with three groups of readings. Astonishingly enough, Vespers retained nothing from the cathedral office except the brief echo in the verse *Dirigatur.* It had five psalms,[33] a reading, the gospel canticle *Magnificat,* and the litany.

Despite its being so burdensome, this distribution of the psalms was maintained until 1911, with one exception: the nocturnal office for Sunday was reduced by six psalms which were redistributed, being added to Prime on weekdays in the Breviary of St. Pius V. Moreover, the office I have been describing had doublets being constantly added to it. Amalarius in his day was already saying that on Christmas and feast days the nocturnal office was a double one: a festal office, comprising only nine selected psalms and nine readings, preceded the regular office. Later on, the shorter festal office became the only office in such cases. It thus became possible to make the office less burdensome by multiplying feasts, but at the cost of losing sight of the psalter as a whole. This gave rise to a malaise that was dissipated only by the decrees of St. Pius X.

---

31. On the Roman monasteries see G. Ferrari, *Early Roman Monasteries. Notes for the History of the Monasteries and Convents at Rome from the V. through the X. Century* (Studi di antichità cristiana 23; Vatican City, 1957).

32. In Prime the first four octonaries were preceded by Ps 118 on Sundays and by Ps 54 on weekdays.

33. But there may have been a period when Roman Vespers contained six psalms; see J. Pascher, "Der Psalter für Laudes und Vesper im alten römischen Stundengebet," *MTZ* 8 (1957) 258-62. This hypothesis is rejected by J. Claire in *Etudes grégoriennes* 15 (1975) 134, note.

II. THE ROMAN OFFICE IN THE FRANKISH EMPIRE (EIGHTH-TENTH CENTURIES)

BIBLIOGRAPHY

Amalarius. See preceding bibliography.
Antiphonary of Compiègne, Bibl. Nat., ms. lat. 17436 (written between 860 and 880), edited by the Maurists in *PL* 78:725-850.
V. Raffa, "L'ufficio divino dei tempi dei Carolingi e il Breviario di Innocenzo III confrontati con la Liturgia delle Ore di Paolo VI," *EL* 85 (1971) 206-59.

The spread of the Roman liturgy in the Frankish lands, even well before any interventions of the Carolingians, carried with it beyond the Alps the Roman form of the office; the process paralleled the spread of the Benedictine organization of the office which gradually replaced all the other monastic forms of the office. The Roman office benefited by the reform of the clergy that took shape in the institution of canons under the patronage of St. Chrodegang, bishop of Metz († 766). It also benefited from initiatives that were taken by Pepin the Short and Charlemagne and were approved by the Council of Aix in 816 in its *Institutio canonicorum.*[34] Paul Warnefried (Paul the Deacon), a monk of Monte Cassino, compiled a lectionary.[35] The antiphonary was enriched with antiphons and responses as well as with a new manner of singing. The hymns of the Benedictine repertory were taken over and others were composed.

This was also the period that saw the institution of the *officium capituli,* "the office of chapter," as described by St. Chrodegang: the monks and canons gathered daily in the chapter room to hear the reading of the martyrology and necrology, to receive their work assignments, and to listen to a passage from the Rule or the Fathers, with possibly a commentary on it by the abbot.[36] This office regularly followed the Hour of Prime.

However, at the same time that feasts of the saints were multiplying and causing the ever more frequent omission of parts of the psalter, other offices and prayers were burdening the Roman office with doublets and supplements: Office of the Blessed Virgin, Office of the Dead, penitential psalms, gradual psalms, etc. A person or group might even have to recite three Vespers or three night offices in a row. This abuse persisted here and there down to our own time.

A shortening was finally introduced, but it affected solely the readings; only the opening sections of these were read. This practice was given official recognition through the acceptance of breviaries.

---

34. Published by A. Werminghoff in *Concilia aevi Karolini* II/1 (MGH) 312-421.
35. See above, n. 43, p. 224.
36. C. Morgand, "La discipline pénitentielle et l'*officium capituli,*" *RBén* 72 (1962) 22-60.

III. THE OFFICE OF THE ROMAN CURIA
AND OF THE FRANCISCANS (THIRTEENTH CENTURY)

BIBLIOGRAPHY

A. Le Carou, *Le bréviaire romain et les Frères Mineurs au XIIIe siècle* (Paris: Editions franciscaines, 1928).
G. Abate, "Il primitivo breviario francescano (1224–1227)," *Miscellanea franciscana* 60 (1960) 47–240.
S. J. P. van Dijk, "An Official Copy of the Franciscan 'Regula Breviary,'" *Scriptorium* 16 (1962) 68–76.
_____, *Sources of the Modern Roman Liturgy* (Leiden: Brill, 1963).
V. Raffa. See preceding bibliography.

Contrary to an assertion often made, there was no reform of the office during the pontificate of St. Gregory VII (1073–85); the synodal decree found in the collections of canons simply recalled the traditional structure of the office, though by this very act it doubtless made that structure more venerable.[37] The thirteenth century, on the other hand, felt a keen need to codify the usages found in rubrics and ordinals.[38] In this context, the Roman Curia, separated by its travels and enterprises from the community of canons at the Lateran, compiled a breviary for its own use. This breviary, which had been given its first form under Innocent III and was revised under Honorius III, was adopted, with some minor changes, by the Franciscan Order under the leadership of its Minister-General, Haymo of Faversham († 1244).

The number of psalms in the night office of Sunday was reduced to eighteen, but the other six were added to Prime of the same day. The *officium capituli* was also made part of Prime, while the *Quicumque* creed was added to it on Sundays. The Hour of Compline was preceded by a reading and a penitential act. The lectionary canonized the abridgments which disfigured it in the breviaries already in widespread use; it also included hagiographical readings that could lay little claim to historical authenticity. The intercessions were turned into prayers of a penitential character. The prayer of the day in Lauds and Vespers was followed by commemorations and intercessions in which free rein was given to devotion. Meanwhile the calendar was becoming overloaded with ever new feasts of the saints.

---

37. *Decr.* III, *De consecratione*, Dist. 5, c. 15, ed. A. Friedberg 1:1415-16.
38. The *Ordo* of a church or monastery is the book that describes the liturgical celebrations throughout the year, including the incipits of the parts that are sung. The Benedictines of Solesmes have published a provisional inventory in *Le Graduel romain. Edition critique* II. *Les sources* (Solesmes, 1957) 189-96.

This neatly codified office, so convenient to use because it required but a single book, became widespread and, for better or for worse, rendered increasingly uniform the practice of the prayer of the hours.

IV. VICISSITUDES AND REFORMS OF THE ROMAN OFFICE (FIFTEENTH-TWENTIETH CENTURIES)

BIBLIOGRAPHY

S. Bäumer, *Histoire du bréviaire*, trans. from the German by R. Biron (Paris: Letouzey, 1905) 2:87-424 (detailed history of the various actual or projected reforms of the breviary from the sixteenth to the twentieth centuries).

P. Battifol, *History of the Roman Breviary*, trans. A. M. Y. Baylay (New York: Longmans, Green, 1912) 177-330.

L. K. Mohlberg, *Radulph de Rivo, der letzte Vertreter der altrömischen Liturgie* (Université de Louvain, Recueil de travaux 29 and 42; Louvain, 1911-15). Vol. 1: *Studien*; Vol. II: *Texte*.

J. W. Legg, *Breviarium Romanum a Francisco cardinali Quignonio editum et recognitum iuxta editionem Venetiis a. D. 1535 impressum* (Cambridge: Cambridge University Press, 1888).

—————, *The Second Recension of the Quignon Breviary, Following an Edition Printed at Antwerp in 1537* (HBS 35 and 42; London: Henry Bradshaw Society, 1908-11).

J. A. Jungmann, "Why Was the Reform Breviary of Cardinal Quiñones a Failure?" in his *Pastoral Liturgy* (New York: Herder and Herder, 1962) 200-14.

H. Jedin, "Das Konzil von Trient und die Reform der liturgischen Bücher," *EL* 59 (1945) 5-38.

G. Mercati, *Opuscoli inediti del beato card. Giuseppe Tomasi tratti in luce* (ST 15; Rome, 1905; repr.: Vatican City, 1976).

S. Sólymos, D. Söveges, and A. Häussling, "Einführung und Geschichte des Maurinerbreviers in der ungarischen Benediktiner-Kongregation," *ALW* 8 (1963) 79-84.

P. Piacenza, *In Constitutionem Divino Afflatu . . . commentarium* (Rome: Desclée, 1912).

By the end of the fourteenth century demands were being made for a reform of the breviary. Thus Raoul de Rivo, dean of Tongres († 1403), called for the abrogation of the "novelties" propagated by the Franciscans and a return to the ancient Roman tradition; such a return did, in fact, become a preoccupation of most of the later popes. The humanists, on the other hand, were soon leveling sharp criticism of a different kind at the Roman office and creating dissatisfaction with it. As a result, Zacharias Ferreri, with the encouragement of Leo X, undertook to revise the hymns so that they might please Latin ears. The result was a pastiche interspersed with mythological echoes in bad taste (1525); fortunately, the revision had little success.

Clement VII showed a better grasp of the situation when he called for a simplification of the office, a return to the Fathers of the Church, and a greater concern for historical accuracy. He put the work in the hands of Cardinal Quiñones, whose titular church was Holy Cross in Jerusalem. Quiñones' breviary was published in 1535 but enjoyed only a brief success, for the office was artificial, rigid, and monotonous, and was intended solely for private recitation. The psalms were distributed in an arbitrary manner and without regard for traditional usage. Only in the second edition and in response to criticism did the compiler reintroduce some patristic readings; the readings from Scripture, on the other hand, were abundant, almost to excess. The chief merit of this new breviary was its hagiographical readings, which had been purified of many legendary elements.

The stern rejection which Quiñones' breviary met with, especially in Spain, deterred the authorities from seeking to reform the breviary by altering its structures. Attention was henceforth directed solely to the elimination of added offices, the simplification of the calendar, which had too many saints' feasts, and, above all, the removal of legendary or apocryphal elements from the hagiographical readings. The task was a difficult one, however, since there were too many particular interests and divergent mentalities to be placated. Paul IV (1555–59) made the attempt but failed.

St. Pius V, following the urgent wishes of the Council of Trent, was apparently successful at last, thanks to the collaboration of Guglielmo Sirleto and his commission, for the new breviary published in 1568 did contain some of the desired improvements; in addition, it suppressed all local usages that had not been in place for more than two hundred years. Unfortunately, the new book did not bring about a change in mentalities. Thus under all the successors of St. Pius V down to Leo XIII († 1903) inclusive the calendar once again became increasingly overloaded. One reason for this was that it was the only way in which those using the breviary could avoid the lengthy Sunday and ferial offices; the offices of the saints were much shorter. Benedict XIV tried unsuccessfully to get a new revision under way.

The most promising attempts at reform during the seventeenth and eighteenth centuries were made in France. First, there was the Paris breviary of François de Harlay in 1680 and the Cluny breviary in 1686; then, in 1736, the breviary of Charles de Vintimille, another archbishop of Paris, which was adopted by most of the dioceses of France down to the middle of the nineteenth century; finally, the breviaries of the Benedictine Congregations of Saint-Vanne (1771) and Saint-Maur (1787). These various reforms were certainly open to criticism on many points; in particular, the decision to eliminate all nonbiblical responses and antiphons stripped the office of much of its lyrical element. They did not, however, deserve the passionate opposition which they met in the nineteenth century due to the hostility of Dom Prosper Guéranger. In any case, St. Pius X was inspired by these breviaries in his reform of the psalter.

The coming of St. Pius X marked the beginning of a new era for the Roman office. In his Apostolic Constitution *Divino afflatu* of November 1, 1911, he definitively set aside the old arrangement of the psalms (which in any case was not observed) and established a new and less burdensome one that at last ensured the reading of the entire psalter in the space of a week. The pope intended an even more radical reform, the first elements of which were published in the Brief *Abhinc duos annos* of October 23, 1913, but the war of 1915 halted the project. Only after the Second World War was the business of breviary reform taken up again under Pius XII (1939–58), who created a special commission for the purpose. The latter produced in succession: a new Latin translation of the psalter (March 25, 1945); a decree simplifying the rubrics (March 23, 1955); and, finally, in the pontificate of John XXIII, a new Code of Rubrics that was introduced by the Motu Proprio *Rubricarum instructum* of July 25, 1960. In this document the pope made it known that all the bishops of the world had been polled,[39] and he stated that the coming Council would decide on the fundamental principles which would govern a general reform of the liturgy.

As far as the office was concerned, these "more important principles" were set down by Vatican II in chapter 5 of its Constitution on the Liturgy (December 4, 1963) and applied in the *General Instruction* and the 1971 *Liturgy of the Hours*.

---

39. The results were collated in *Memoria sulla riforma liturgica. Supplemento IV* and published (Vatican City, 1957) for the use of the historical section of the SCR (*S. hist.* n. 97).

Chapter VI

Structure and Spirituality of Each Hour

GENERAL BIBLIOGRAPHY

GILH, Chapter 2, nos. 34–99, and the commentaries on it.

One of the important lessons that has been taught us by the history of the Liturgy of the Hours and that is now recorded in the conciliar Constitution on the Liturgy and in the *General Instruction* is that there is a hierarchical order among the Hours, whereas in the past the tendency, both in practice and in the handling of moral cases, was to regard the daily office as a uniform whole. Each Hour has its own special character, its unique spirituality; some Hours, moreover, are more important than others. In addition, provision is now made for different ways of celebrating the office, depending on the communities or individuals involved and depending also on spiritual possibilities and attractions. This accounts for the recurrence in the *General Instruction* of phrases such as *de more* ("normally"), *pro opportunitate* (usually just "may [be used, etc.]" in English; sense: "according as is spiritually or pastorally advisable"), and *laudabiliter* ("laudably").

§1. Introduction to the Entire Office

BIBLIOGRAPHY

J. Pascher, "Das Invitatorium," *Liturgisches Jahrbuch* 10 (1960) 149–58.

In almost all the forms of the office that were reviewed in the previous chapter, the first Hour begins with an introduction that usually takes the form of an invitatory, that is, an exhortation to praise God. This is given a certain solemnity and is made up of one or several psalms with variable refrains. Thus in the Syriac liturgies (Syrian, Chaldean, Mesopotamian, and Maronite) Pss 134, 117, and verses 169–76 of 119 are sung, together with some very beautiful stanzas.[1]

The Spanish office likewise has an antiphon and one or several psalms depending on the day.[2] In the Ambrosian liturgy we may regard as an invitatory the ornate and festive singing of the Canticle of the Three Young Men, *Benedictus es* (or its variant, *Et benedictum*), which has its own refrain.[3] The monastic tradition set down in the Rule of the Master and the Rule of St. Benedict uses the verse "Lord, open my lips, and my mouth will proclaim your praise" to break the great silence imposed during the night.[4] To this St. Benedict adds Ps 3, "O Lord, how many are my foes" and Ps 95, which is sung with a refrain. The Roman office likewise uses the verse "Lord, open my lips," and Ps 95, which is sung with a refrain and an ornate melody.

Ps 95 is especially appropriate, since it urges the reader to sing the praises of God, to hear his voice today, and to look forward to "the rest of the Lord"; these are formulas whose wealth of meaning has been revealed to us in the New Testament.[5] Nonetheless the *General Instruction* allows that Pss 100, 67, or 24 may be used instead (*pro opportunitate*, that is, if it promises to be more profitable).[6] The antiphon which serves as a refrain varies with the variety of liturgical days, since it announces the theme of the day.

When the Office of Readings is celebrated as the first Hour, whether at night or in the very early morning, the invitatory keeps its traditional place at the beginning of it. Apart from choral celebration, however, the Office of Readings is no longer a nocturnal office. If, then, the first Hour actually celebrated is Morning Prayer (Lauds), the invitatory comes at the start of this Hour, so as truly to mark the beginning of a day of prayer.[7]

---

1. J. Mateos, "L'invitatoire du nocturne chez les Syriens et les Maronites," *OS* 11 (1966) 353–66; idem, "Les strophes de la nuit dans l'Invitatoire du nocturne syrien," in *Mémorial Mgr. Gabriel Khouri-Sarkis* (Louvain: Imprimerie Orientaliste, 1969) 71–81.

2. Details in J. Pinell, "Las horas vigiliares del oficio monacal hispánico," *Liturgica* 3 (Scripta et documenta 17; Montserrat: Abadía de Montserrat, 1966) 265–66.

3. It is the melody that signals the invitatory role of the canticle, for the latter comes not at the very beginning of the nocturn, but after the hymn and response and before the psalms.

4. *Regula Magistri* 30, 14–22 (SC 106:164–65); St. Benedict, *Regula* 9 (SC 182:510), and A. de Vogüé's commentary (SC 185:435).

5. 1 Cor 10:1-12; Heb 3:7–4:16.

6. *GILH* 34.

7. *GILH* 35.

§2. Morning Prayer and Vespers: The Morning and Evening Offices

I. "THE TWO HINGES ON WHICH THE DAILY OFFICE TURNS"

BIBLIOGRAPHY

V. Raffa, "Lodi e Vespro, cardine delle preghiera oraria ecclesiale," *Rivista liturgica* 55 (1968) 488–511.

As we saw a moment ago, the Constitution on the Liturgy strongly emphasizes the importance of Morning and Evening Prayer, or Lauds and Vespers: "By the venerable tradition of the universal Church, Lauds as morning prayer, and Vespers as evening prayer, are the two hinges on which the daily office turns. They must be considered as the chief hours and are to be celebrated as such."[8] Furthermore, "their public or communal celebration should be encouraged, especially in the case of those who live in community [a desire already fulfilled in many places]. Indeed, the recitation of these hours should be recommended also to individual members of the faithful unable to take part in a celebration in common."[9]

In Jewish practice, it will be recalled, these two times of prayer were singled out from the others by the offering of sacrifices in the temple. As early as the end of the second century, Tertullian was speaking of them as obligatory for Christians (*legitimae orationes*).[10] Starting in the fourth century all the Churches of East and West organized the communal celebration of these Hours,[11] and over the centuries councils and liturgical commentaries have ceaselessly urged their practice.[12] Finally, it has always been the custom to celebrate them with a certain solemnity. Besides, these two Hours have their place in the natural rhythm of human life. Thus St. Ambrose writes: "Either going to the church or applying ourselves to prayer in our own homes, we daily begin the day with God and we end it with him. Let every day of our earthly life, and the entire course of each day, find in him its beginning and its end."[13]

---

8. *VSC* 89, cited in *GILH* 37; see *VSC* 100.
9. *GILH* 40.
10. See above, n. 15, p. 166.
11. See above, pp. 171–72.
12. Texts cited by V. Raffa, "Lodi e Vespro cardine della preghiera liturgica," *Rivista liturgica* 55 (1968) 498–503; idem, "L'orario di preghiera nell'ufficio divino," *EL* 80 (1966) 123–25.
13. St. Ambrose, *De Abraham* II, 5, 22 (PL 14:465).

II. MORNING PRAYER OR LAUDS

BIBLIOGRAPHY

C. Callewaert, "Laudes matutinae in officio Romano ante Regulam s. Benedicti," *Collationes Brugenses* 28 (1928) 63–72, 153–66, 245–51, 327–38. = *Sacris eruditi* (Steenbrugge: St.-Pietersabdij, 1940) 53–89.

J. Pinell, "El *matutinarium* en la liturgia hispana," *Hispania sacra* 9 (1956) 61–85.

J. Pascher, "Der Psalter für Laudes und Vesper im alten römischen Stundengebet," *MTZ* 8 (1957) 255–67.

J. Jungmann, "Die vormonastische Morgenhore," in *Brevierstudien*, ed. J. A. Jungmann (Trier: Paulinus Verlag, 1958) 21–41.

J. Mateos, *Lelya-Sapra, Essai d'interprétation des Matines chaldéennes* (OCA 156; Rome: Pontificio Istituto Orientale, 1959).

_____, "Quelques problèmes de l'orthros byzantine," *POC* 11 (1961) 17–35, 201–25.

_____, "Quelques aspects théologiques de l'office du matin," *Revue du clergé africain* 20 (1965) 335–49.

1. Symbolism of the Hour

Morning Prayer is, first of all, the prayer of Christians as they begin their day. Here is how St. Basil of Caesarea describes it.

> We offer praise in the morning for several reasons: in order to conse-crate to God the first movements of our souls and minds; in order to avoid undertaking anything at all before having rejoiced at the thought of God, in accordance with what is written: "I remembered God and took my delight in him" (Ps 76:4); and in order that our bodies too may not set to work before we have done what is written: "I will direct my prayer to you, O Lord; in the morning you will hear my voice, in the morning I will stand before you and see you" (Ps 5:4-5).[14]

It is, in addition, the prayer said at the moment of dawn (*orthros*) when the sun is about to rise. This accounts for the Christological symbolism attached to this Hour, for Christ is presented to us in the gospel as the "rising Sun who comes to visit us" (Luke 1:28) and thus fulfills the prophecy of Mal 4:2 ("for you . . . the sun of righteousness shall rise") and as "the true light that enlightens every man [by] coming into the world" (John 1:9). Here, for example, is how Clement of Alexandria writes on this subject:

> The break of dawn is a time for prayer because the dawn signals the birth of day and because from that point on the light advances which first "shone in the darkness" (John 1:5), while for those who have been living

---

14. St. Basil, *Regulae fusius tractatae*, Qu. 37, 3 (PG 31:1014); see trans. by L. Lèbe (Maredsous, 1969) 123.

in ignorance, the daylight of knowledge of the truth shines forth like the sun.[15]

Because this prayer is both a prayer upon rising and a prayer at dawn, the thought of Christ's resurrection is associated with it. St. Cyprian writes: "We must pray in order thereby to celebrate the resurrection of the Lord."[16] St. Clement of Rome had already suggested this symbolism to some extent:

> Observe, beloved, how the Master is constantly keeping before us that resurrection to come of which he has given us the first fruits in the Lord Jesus Christ by raising him from the dead. Consider, beloved, the resurrection that takes place at fixed intervals. Day and night have their resurrection: night lies down to rest and day rises up; day departs, night comes.[17]

In commenting on Lauds, the medieval liturgists all emphasized the commemoration of Christ's resurrection.[18] The Eastern Churches added prayers or hymns which call to mind the eschatological Day, the morning that will have no evening but will continue in unending light.[19]

2. Structure of Morning Prayer

a) In all the liturgies without exception, morning prayer has for its primary characteristic the praise of God (therefore "Lauds"); the classic expression of this focus was the daily presence of Pss 148, 149, and 150.[20] In the Roman rite the need of making the office less burdensome and of varying its texts led the reformers of 1911 and 1971 to retain only one psalm of praise but at the same time to enrich the repertory so that there might be a different psalm of praise each day of the psalter cycle.

b) Another characteristic which lends this Hour its meaning is the selection of one or more psalms which evoke the thought of morning. In this context Pss 63 and 51 become traditional. Ps 63, "God, you are my God; I keep watch for you from break of dawn" (Vg; LXX: *soi orthrizō*), is com-

---

15. *Stromata* VII 7, 43, ed. Stählin (GCS) 3:32-33 (= PG 9:462-63).

16. See this citation above, at n. 25, p. 169.

17. St. Clement of Rome, *Ep. ad Corinthios* 24. trans. A. Jaubert (SC 167) 142-43.

18. For example, St. Isidore, *De ecclesiasticis officiis* I, 23 (PL 83:760); Pseudo-Alcuin, *De divinis officiis* 46 (PL 101:1276); Praepositinus (Prévostin) of Cremona, *Tractatus de officiis* 4, 95, ed. J. Corbett (Publications in Medieval Studies 21; Notre Dame: University of Notre Dame Press, 1969) 257.

19. J. Mateos, "Quelques aspects théologiques de l'office du matin," *Revue du clergé africain* 20 (1965) 342-44.

20. According to R. T. Beckwith, "The Daily and Weekly Worship of the Primitive Church in Relation to its Jewish Antecedents," in *Influences juives sur le culte chrétien* (Textes et études liturgiques 4; Louvain: Mont César, 1981) 109, this practice was connected with that mentioned by Rabbi José in the Babylonian Talmud (*Shabbat* 118b) of saying Pss 148-50 daily; but there is no indisputable testimony to this practice prior to the dispersion of the Jews. Beckwith's study also appeared in QL 62 (1981) 5-20, 83-105.

mented on along these lines by the Fathers and by St. John Chrysostom in particular.[21] Ps 51 was chosen less for its penitential meaning than as an expression of praise: "And my mouth shall proclaim your praise." Some liturgies, especially the Latin, extended the repertory of morning psalms to include Pss 67, 100, 5, 43, 65, 90, 143, and 9 among others. From this traditional repertory, found especially in the Spanish liturgy, the 1971 reformers took the psalms which begin Lauds each day of the four-week cycle. On Sunday, Ps 93, "The Lord reigns," commemorates the victory of the glorious Christ; it is one of the psalms which the Eastern liturgies like to use for expressing the paschal mystery. The same is even more true of Ps 118.

c) A third element universally found in the morning prayer of praise is the canticles. In the Byzantine liturgy, we may recall, eight Old Testament canticles and the three gospel canticles, grouped to form nine "odes," used to be sung daily; subsequently, however, they were sacrificed to the hymns which had as their original purpose to serve as refrains for the canticles. The Roman liturgy kept the gospel canticle *Benedictus* as a daily part of Lauds ("The dawn from on high shall break upon us, to shine on those who dwell in darkness and the shadow of death"), but it distributed the Old Testament canticles among the various days of the week. In the reform of 1911, a second series of nine Old Testament canticles was added, and in 1971 their number was increased to twenty-six, with the two canticles of the Three Young Men (the *Benedicite* and the *Benedictus es*) being reserved to Sundays.

d) A last characteristic of Lauds is the prayer which forms its conclusion. It is in part a litany with diaconal intentions and stereotyped responses that facilitate participation by the congregation; this is followed by the Lord's Prayer, which is recited with a certain solemnity; the celebrant, finally, says a prayer or collect. These various components were already noted in the testimonies from the end of the fourth century and are common to all the Churches. The reform of 1971 therefore endeavored to restore them to their due place, assigning them as their focus the consecration of the day and its labors. The celebrant's closing prayer picks up one or other of the general themes of this morning Hour, unless there is a proper prayer for the day or feast.

The practice of having a reading from Scripture in Lauds has not been as widespread as is sometimes claimed. Such a reading does, however, exist in the Benedictine and Roman traditions in the form of a short reading or "little chapter," which consists of only a few lines; meditation on the reading is prolonged with the aid of a response. The *General Instruction*, however, allows for a longer reading and even for a homily which

---

21. St. John Chrysostom, *In psalm. 140* 1 (PG 55:427-28).

comments on it.[22] Such a choice can only be something of an exception, since the liturgical day already has a cycle of continuous readings in the Office of Readings and another at Mass.

In older practice the hymn was sung after the short reading; it has now been moved to the beginning of the celebration. This change has been made because "the purpose of the hymn is to provide a setting for the Hour or the feast, and, especially in celebrations with a congregation, to form a simple and pleasant introduction to prayer."[23]

Finally, when morning or evening prayer take its recommended public or at least communal form and when someone—priest or deacon—in sacred orders presides, he dismisses the congregation in the same manner as at Mass. When no such person is presiding, the formula formerly used at the end of Prime is used here as well: "May the Lord bless us . . . ."[24]

III. EVENING PRAYER OR VESPERS

BIBLIOGRAPHY

C. Callewaert, "Vesperae antiquae in officio praesertim Romano," *Collationes Brugenses* 29 (1929) 217–37, 310–27 = *Sacris erudiri* (Steenbrugge: St.-Pietersabdij, 1940) 91–117.

F. Dölger, "Lumen Christi. Untersuchungen zum abendlichen Licht-Segen," in his *Antike und Christentum* 5 (Münster: Aschendorff, 1936) 1–43.

A. Raes, *Introductio in liturgiam orientalem* (Rome: Pontificio Istituto Orientale, 1947) 181–206.

J. Pinell, "Vestigis del lucernari a Occident," *Liturgica* 1. *Cardinali I. Schuster in memoriam* (Scripta et documenta 7; Montserrat: Abadía de Montserrat, 1956) 91–149.

J. Pascher, "Der Psalter für Laudes und Vesper im alten römischen Stundengebet," *MTZ* 8 (1957) 255–67.

J. Mateos, "L'office du soir," *Revue du clergé africain* 19 (1964) 3–25.

P. Borella, "La Costituzione liturgica del Concilio e il canto dei Vespri domenicali," *Ambrosius* 60 (1964) 59–84.

P. E. Gamayel, "La structure des vêpres maronites," *OS* 9 (1964) 105–34.

V. Janeras, "La partie vespérale de la liturgie byzantine des présanctifiés," *OCP* 30 (1964) 193–222.

J. Bernal, "Primeros vestigios del lucernario en España," *Liturgica* 3 (Scripta et documenta 17; Montserrat: Abadía de Montserrat, 1966) 21–50.

S. H. Jammo, "L'office du soir au temps de Gabriel Qatraya," *OS* 12 (1967) 187–210.

J. Mateos, "Quelques anciens documents sur l'office du soir," *OCP* 35 (1969) 347–74.

G. Winkler, "Über die Kathedralvesper in den verschiedenen Riten des Ostens und Westens," *ALW* 16 (1974) 53–102.

---

22. *GILH* 46–48.
23. *GILH* 42.
24. *GILH* 54.

1. *Symbolism of the Hour*

This is first and foremost the hour when almost all human beings cease their work, even though, unlike the ancients, they no longer depend on the light of the sun. St. Basil orders that "at the end of the day we are to thank God for the benefits we have received from him and the good actions we have been fortunate enough to do." He adds to this thanksgiving a penitential act which later became linked to Compline.[25]

Evening is also the hour when, generally speaking, people light their lamps. As early as the beginning of the third century, Hippolytus suggested that on days when the Christian community gathered with the bishop for an agape, there should be an act of thanksgiving for light: the daylight that has been given to us, the evening light which "we do not lack," but above all the "incorruptible light" revealed to us through Jesus Christ.[26] Here, then, an action of everyday life links us to the theme of Christ as the true light. We find it in St. Cyprian[27] and in the splendid hymn *Phōs hilaron* ("Joyous light") which is attested from before the fourth century and which in the East has always been the climactic moment in the celebration of Vespers.[28]

As morning calls to mind the resurrection of Christ, so evening prayer recalls his passion. As a result, Ps 141 has been universally adopted as an evening psalm ("Let my prayer be counted as incense before thee, and the lifting up of my hands as an evening sacrifice!").[29] But the evening sacrifice in the temple was only a shadow of the "true evening sacrifice" of Christ. John Cassian commented that this evening sacrifice of Christ could be understood

> either as the sacrifice which Christ taught his apostles in the evening at the Supper when he instituted the most holy mysteries of the Church, or as the sacrifice which he himself offered to the Father on the next day as an evening sacrifice—that is, a sacrifice at the end of the ages—by lifting up his hands for the salvation of the whole world.

Cassian immediately added: "His action of extending his hands on the cross is rightly called a 'lifting up'[30] for all of us were lying in hell and he raised

---

25. St. Basil, *Regulae fusius tractatae*, Qu. 37, 3 (PG 31:1014), trans. L. Lèbe (Maredsous, 1969) 124–25.

26. Hippolytus of Rome, *Traditio apostolica* 25, ed. B. Botte (LQF 39) 64–65.

27. See the citation above, at n. 25, p. 169.

28. Cited in *GILH* 39; see above, n. 16, p. 212.

29. See the references given by J. Pinell, "El número sagrado de las horas de oficio," in *Miscellanea liturgica . . . Lercaro* 2 (Rome: Desclée, 1967) 910–11.

30. The phrase "lifting up of my hands"—*mas'at happay, eparsis tōn cheirōn mou, elevatio manuum mearum*—reminded the Fathers of Christ on the cross.

us up to heaven in accordance with the promise he had made: 'When I am lifted up from the earth, I will draw everything to myself.' "[31]

Finally, Vespers also has an eschatological perspective: in order to direct our hope to the light that will never be dimmed, "we pray fervently that the light may return to us; we pray for the coming of Christ that will bring us the blessing of eternal life."[32]

2. Structure of Vespers in the 1971 Liturgy of the Hours

The traditional Roman office retained only two elements from evening prayer as celebrated in the cathedral office, and these two were reduced to a vestigial state: the verse *Dirigatur* ("Let my prayer, O Lord, come like incense before You"), which recalled Ps 141, and the litany in the ferial *preces*. The incensation, which might have suggested the "evening sacrifice," had turned into an incensation of the altar, clergy, and people, and sometimes lasted throughout the singing of the *Magnificat* (it even lasted so long as to make necessary an extended polyphonic singing of this canticle or else organ interludes).[33] The litany, which was made up of psalm verses (*capitella*), was said only on fast days. For the psalmody Pss 110-17 and 120-47 were used, these being distributed through the week and providing a quasi-monastic continuous reading of the psalter.

As a result of the 1971 reform Vespers, like Morning Prayer, now begins with a hymn, and for the same reason. For psalmody there are two psalms and a canticle, but the psalms no longer constitute a simple continuous reading; rather they are "suited to the hour and to celebration with a congregation."[34] The canticle is a passage from the New Testament letters or the Apocalypse. I pointed out earlier the significance of this innovation: it emphasizes the element of thanksgiving and promotes meditation on the mystery of redemption. In Lauds the Old Testament canticle is placed among the psalms; in Vespers the New Testament canticle comes after the psalms, thus preserving the traditional order for the presentation of scriptural passages in the liturgy. For the same reason, the short reading that follows the psalmody is likewise to be taken from the New Testament. After this reading the gospel canticle *Magnificat* is sung.

As in Lauds, the short reading is followed by a short response. Provision is made in certain cases, especially a celebration with a congregation, for replacing the short reading with a longer one and for a possible

---

31. John Cassian, *De institutis coenobiorum* III, 3, 9-10, trans. J.-C. Guy, SC 109:101-03.
32. St. Cyprian, *De oratione dominica* 35 (CSEL 3:293).
33. It is regrettable that *GILH* 261 still permits this kind of incensation both at the *Magnificat* in Vespers and at the *Benedictus* in Lauds.
34. *GILH* 43.

commentary on it in the form of a homily.[35] Again as in Lauds, the gospel canticle is followed by a litany, the Our Father, the concluding prayer, and, if a priest or deacon has been presiding, the rites of dismissal. The litany consists of general intercessory prayers, though in a different form than at Mass.

3. Characteristic Elements of Vespers in Other Liturgies

In a good many liturgical families Vespers has continued to be more recognizably an ecclesial evening prayer. This is due especially to the use of psalms traditionally regarded as evening psalms. These include: Ps 141, which is attested everywhere in antiquity and is still sung daily by the Chaldeans, Syrians, Maronites, Byzantines, and Armenians; Ps 142 ("I cry with my voice to the Lord"); and Ps 117 ("Praise the Lord, all nations!"). The Byzantines add Ps 104 ("Bless the Lord, O my soul!") and Ps 130 ("Out of the depths I cry to thee, O Lord!"). The Chaldeans and Syrians sing an octonary of Ps 119: "Thy word is a lamp to my feet and a light to my path." The distribution of psalms in the new Liturgy of the Hours has as far as possible taken these traditional choices into account.

In antiquity the *lucernarium*, or ritual of lamplighting, existed in almost all the Churches. The Roman Church retained it only for the Easter Vigil, where it is followed by the singing of the *Exsultet*. It seems that in Africa the *lucernarium* was also the first act of all nocturnal vigils. It has persisted in the Ambrosian rite at the beginning of Vespers, where it is accompanied by an appropriate song in the form of responses, and in the Byzantine rite, where it follows the psalmody and is as it were the high point of the celebration. The *Phōs hilaron* is sung at this point, and on Sundays there is a procession.

The rite of incensation was never as universally practiced, and in addition it took on different meanings in different liturgies. For the Syrians it has more of a penitential character; elsewhere it is part of the *lucernarium*. In the Byzantine liturgy it acquires its fullest significance in Vespers of the Presanctified, where it is accompanied by the singing of the *Kateuthunthetō* ("Let my prayer rise up like incense").

The Ambrosian liturgy has fortunately continued to give Vespers a baptismal aspect, thanks to the procession to the baptistery which daily concluded this Hour. The procession was accompanied by the singing of *psallendae* (a *psallenda* consists of antiphon, doxology, antiphon), *Responsoria in baptisterio* ("Responsories in the baptistery"), and prayers. The reform of 1983 has sought to highlight this baptismal commemoration even more, while also making it possible in private recitation of

---

35. *GILH* 46–48.

the office.[36] As everyone knows, during Easter week in Rome there used to be regular processions of the neophytes to the baptistery.[37]

A final point to be mentioned is the connection which various liturgies make, on certain days, between Vespers and some other liturgical celebration. This is the case, for example, in Great Vespers among the Byzantines and in Milan: on the eve of certain feasts, Vespers is structured as a vigil with readings, and it ends with the Eucharistic sacrifice. On days of strict fast in the East, Vespers is joined to a liturgy of the Presanctified with its readings.

§3. Vigils and the Office of Readings

BIBLIOGRAPHY

J. M. Hanssens, *Aux origines de la prière liturgique. Nature et genèse de l'office des Matines* (Analecta Gregoriana 57; Rome: Pontifical Gregorian University, 1952).

C. Marcora, *La vigilia nella liturgia. Ricerche sulle origini e sui primi sviluppi (sec. 1–6)* (Archivio ambrosiano 6; Milan, 1954).

A. Baumstark, *Nocturna laus. Typen frühchristlicher Vigilienfeier und ihr Fortleben vor allem im römischen und monastischen Ritus*, ed. O. Heiming (LQF 32; Münster: Aschendorff, 1957).

P. Borella, "Struttura dell'antica vigilia," *Ambrosius* 33 (1957) 179–87.

J. Mateos, "Un office de minuit chez les Chaldèens," *OCP* 25 (1959) 101–13.

_____, *Lelya-Sapra, Essai d'interprétation des Matines chaldéennes* (OCA 156; Rome: Pontificio Istituto Orientale, 1959).

H. Goltzen, "Nocturna laus. Aus Arbeiten zur Geschichte der Vigil," *Jahrbuch für Liturgie und Hymnologie* 5 (1960) 79–88.

J. Mateos, "Les matines chaldéennes, maronites et syriennes," *OCP* 26 (1960) 51–73.

_____, "Les différentes espèces de vigiles dans le rite chaldéen," *OCP* 27 (1961) 46–63.

_____, "La vigile cathédrale chez Egérie" *OCP* 27 (1961) 281–312.

_____, "Office de minuit et office du matin chez saint Athanase," *OCP* 28 (1962) 173–80.

A. Renoux, "Liturgie de Jérusalem et lectionnaires arméniens. Vigiles et année liturgique," in Cassien-Botte 167–99.

J. Pinell, "Las horas vigiliares del oficio monacal hispánico," *Liturgica* 3 (Scripta et documenta 17; Montserrat: Abadía de Montserrat, 1966) 197–340.

---

36. In the new Roman Liturgy of the Hours, the thought of baptism occurs frequently in the invocations of Lauds and the intercessions of Vespers; see V. Raffa, "Der Taufgedanke in den Preces des Laudes und der Vesper im Stundengebet," in *Zeichen des Glaubens. Studien zu Taufe und Firmung, Balthasar Fischer zum 60. Geburtstag* (Zürich: Benziger, and Freiburg: Herder, 1972) 505–19.

37. See above, p. 58.

I. FROM NOCTURNAL PRAYER TO OFFICE OF READINGS

We will recall that nocturnal prayer has always had an important place in Christian spirituality and liturgy. It both expresses and arouses an expectation of the Lord who has come, is risen, and will come again. This prayer has taken different forms, as can be seen from the diversity of terms for it. At the same time, this varying terminology has also given rise to confusion. Thus, whereas the word *matutinum* ("morning [office]") evidently refers to a morning or dawn office (as in the Rule of St. Benedict), in the Roman books it has been mistakenly placed at the beginning of the night office, which comprises one or more "nocturns."

The chief vigil for the Church, and the one most fervently celebrated, has always been the Easter Vigil. In the beginning, this vigil occupied the entire night (it was a *pannuchis*); it was spent in meditation on the Scriptures and was crowned by the celebration of baptism and the Eucharist. In imitation of the Easter Vigil, various Churches developed the practice of beginning certain solemnities—the Nativity of Christ and Pentecost foremost among them—with a vigil.[38] In like manner, the anniversaries of saints, when celebrated at their tombs, and pilgrimages were traditionally marked by vigils, traces of which can still be seen in popular custom and the liturgies.[39] In antiquity many Churches celebrated a vigil—though not so prolonged a one—for Sundays; it was a vigil of the "cathedral" type, meant for popular participation and having the bishop as its presiding celebrant; the liturgy of Jerusalem supplied the model for this kind of vigil.[40]

But the Fathers and spiritual writers, as we have seen, exhorted Christians, especially those leading a contemplative life, to engage in daily nocturnal prayer. This in turn was given an organized form in monasticism. Sometimes it has been prayer in the middle of the night (*mesonuktikon*), sometimes prayer toward the end of night, at the hour of cockcrow. The Roman office and the Benedictine office preferred this second time, which is often alluded to in the hymn.

II. THE ROMAN OFFICE OF READINGS

The Second Vatican Council wished to continue and support this ideal: "The hour called Matins . . . should retain the character of nocturnal

---

38. See *GILH* 71; see also the calendar of vigils at Tours, a work attributed to Bishop St. Perpetuus (490) by Gregory of Tours, *Historia Francorum* X, 31, ed. W. Arndt and B. Krusch (MGH, Script. Rer. Meroving. 1; 1884), Part I, pp. 444–45.

39. See above, pp. 127–28 and 172.

40. *Egeria's Travels* 24 (Wilkinson 123–25).

when recited in choir."[41] The *General Instruction* goes further: "All who maintain the character of the office of readings as a night office, therefore, are to be commended."[42] This character is then underscored by the inclusion of the traditional series of hymns.[43]

Many, however, are unable to put this ideal into practice. But, even when removed from its vigil setting and recited at some other time of the day, this office retains its spiritual importance because of the prolonged readings it has traditionally included in Benedictine and Roman usage. Vatican II even asked that it "be made up of fewer psalms and longer readings."[44]

Yet, even though the readings are the distinguishing part of this office, to the point where it is called *Officium lectionis* ("Office of Reading") or in English, and more accurately, "Office of Readings," it continues to be a real prayer by reason of its psalms, hymn, collect, and other formulas. For "prayer should accompany 'the reading of sacred Scripture so that there may be a conversation between God and his people.' "[45] The reading done here is not an intellectual examination of a document but a meditation on the Bible (thus filling out the cycle provided in daily Mass) and on the finest passages from the spiritual writers.

The office therefore begins, like the other Hours, with the invocation *Deus in adiutorium* ("God, come to my assistance") and the *Gloria Patri*, unless it is celebrated at the beginning of the day and is therefore preceded by the invitatory. The hymn for this Hour corresponds to the feast or season; in Ordinary Time, depending on the hour of the day when this office is celebrated, a nocturnal hymn or a daytime hymn will be chosen.

The psalmody henceforth consists of three psalms or parts of psalms from the current week and day, except on solemnities and feasts which have psalms and antiphons of their own (or from the Commons of the Saints). Between psalmody and readings the practice of reciting a verse has been kept, for experience has shown its value in providing "a transition in the prayer from psalmody to listening."[46]

There are always two readings, each followed by a response; one reading is from Scripture, according to a one-year or two-year cycle (but solemnities and feasts have a reading proper to them), the other is from tradition.

---

41. *VSC* 89c.

42. *GILH* 72.

43. *GILH* 58.

44. *VSC* 89c.

45. *GILH* 56, citing St. Ambrose, *De officiis ministrorum* I, 20, 88 (PL 16:50).

46. *GILH* 63. — On the role of the verse see Amalarius, *Liber de ordine antiphonarii* I, 6: " 'Verse' is the name given to the song by which the mind is turned (*revertitur*) to another thought . . .; with the sweetness of its melody it eases the mind's turning from one affection to another."

In a seasonal office this second reading is a commentary on the Scripture passage or a meditation suited to the season or the mystery of the day. Under certain conditions the one praying the Hour is allowed to choose a different reading, according to norms set forth earlier in this book.[47] In celebrations of the saints, the second reading is hagiographical;[48] in seasons which do not allow the celebration of saints' feasts this reading may be added to the two readings of the day.[49]

On Sundays outside of Lent, on days in the octaves of Easter and Christmas, and on solemnities and feasts, the second reading and its response are followed by the hymn *Te Deum*, unless the vigil is being prolonged in the way I shall describe in a moment. The Office of Readings ends with the prayer from the office of the day and, at least in a communal celebration, with the acclamation, "Let us praise the Lord—and give him thanks."[50]

III. THE FESTAL VIGIL

The Office of Readings has been made fairly short, primarily in view of the time available to those engaged in apostolic work. On the other hand, provision has also been made so that those who desire and are able to continue an ancient tradition may celebrate this office as a prolonged nocturnal vigil. The elements added in this case are those of the "cathedral" vigils celebrated on Sundays in the early Church.[51]

Thus, after the regular Office of Readings and before the *Te Deum*, the celebrant adds three canticles as indicated in the appendix to the *Liturgy of the Hours*. We saw earlier that these canticles have traditionally been sung at this point in the Chaldean liturgy, the Ambrosian liturgy, and the Benedictine office.

On Sundays the canticles are followed by a proclamation of the gospel of the resurrection, in keeping with a tradition that goes back to the Jerusalem liturgy and with the practice in the Byzantine *orthros*. This gospel highlights in a solemn way the paschal character of Sunday.[52]

---

47. See above, pp. 224–25.
48. See above, pp. 226–227.
49. *GILH* 239.
50. *GILH* 68–69.
51. *GILH* 70–73.
52. It is also prescribed by St. Caesarius, *Regula ad monachos* 21 (PL 67:1102) and *Regula sanctarum virginum. Recapitulatio* 69 (Florilegium patristicum 34; Bonn: Hanstein, 1933) 24. It is probably this gospel, and not the gospel of the Mass, that St. Benedict is thinking of in his *Regula* 11. — On the reading of the gospel of the resurrection: A. Kniazeff, in Cassien-Botte 209–10; R. Zerfass, *Die Schriftlesung im Kathedraloffizium Jerusalems* (LQF 48; Münster: Aschendorff, 1968) 115–18; D. de Reynal, *Théologie de la Liturgie des Heures* (Paris: Beauchesne, 1978) 117–18.

During Lent, however, the reformers preferred gospel passages that proclaim both the passion and the resurrection. On solemnities which do not fall on Sundays, a gospel passage appropriate to the solemnity is read. The gospel may then be the subject of a homily. Finally, the *Te Deum* is sung and the concluding prayer said.

§4. Terce, Sext, and None, or Daytime Prayer

BIBLIOGRAPHY

> P. Borella, "L'ufficiatura meridiana nell'antico rito ambrosiano," *Ambrosius* 34 (1958) 99–105.
>
> P. Salmon, "Les origines de la prière des heures d'après le témoignage de Tertullien et de saint Cyprien," in *Mélanges offerts à Mademoiselle Christine Mohrmann* (Utrecht: Spectrum, 1963) 202–10.
>
> Mary Philomena, "St. Edmund of Abingdon's Meditations before the Canonical Hours," *EL* 78 (1964) 33–57.
>
> V. Raffa, "L'orario di preghiera nell'ufficio divino. Profilo storico e prospettive postconciliari," *EL* 80 (1966) 97–140.

The Hour of Prime was a doublet, and Vatican II was therefore correct in removing it from the Roman office.[53] The Hours of Terce, Sext, and None, on the other hand, possess a historical and spiritual importance, as we saw earlier,[54] for they are intended to help the Christian realize the ideal of ceaseless prayer and to be ever mindful of the Lord's passion and the first steps taken in spreading the gospel. For this reason the Council retained these Hours:[55] "The liturgical practice of saying these three hours is to be retained, without prejudice to particular law, by those who live the contemplative life. It is recommended also for all, especially those who take part in retreats or pastoral meetings."[56]

Outside of the circumstances mentioned, it is permitted to choose from among these three Hours the one that best corresponds to the time of day when it is being said. The purpose of saying at least one of these Hours is to maintain the tradition of praying in the course of the day's work. That is what the compilers of the Liturgy of the Hours and of the *General Instruction* had in mind when they designated this Hour *Hora media*. A translation of *Hora media* as "Middle Hour" might misleadingly suggest an office said at noon; the English "Daytime Hour" captures the true meaning.

---

53. *VSC* 89d.
54. See above, pp. 166–168.
55. *VSC* 89e.
56. *GILH* 76.

Each of these three Hours has the same unaltered structure:[57] after the introductory verse and *Gloria Patri,* there is a hymn, three psalms or parts of psalms, a short reading followed by a verse which serves as response, a prayer, and, at least in a communal celebration, the acclamation "Let us praise the Lord . . . ." The hymn and, on weekdays of Ordinary Time, the prayer recall the symbolism of the Hour and the memories it evokes of the events of salvation.

In order to allow both for those who celebrate only one of these three Hours and those who celebrate all three, a distinction is made between a current psalmody which is used for one of the three, and a complementary psalmody which is used for the other two. Almost every day the current psalmody includes an octonary from Ps 119, in keeping with ancient Roman tradition, and two other psalms or parts of psalms. Sundays and certain solemnities have proper or appropriate psalms; on Friday of the third week Ps 22, the psalm *par excellence* of the passion, is recited. On solemnities which are celebrated on a weekday and have no proper psalms of their own, the Gradual Psalms are used.

The Gradual Psalms (120–28), which are regularly found in these Hours in the Benedictine tradition, also supply the complementary psalmody. They are easily memorized and can be said even in the midst of work. The Ambrosian *Liturgia delle Ore* of 1983–84 continues the custom of using octonaries from Ps 119 for these Hours, in keeping with the tradition of Rome and Milan.

§5. Night Prayer, or Compline

BIBLIOGRAPHY

A. Raes, "Les Complies dans les rites orientaux," *OCP* 17 (1951) 133–45.
V. Raffa, "Alcuni problemi relativi a Compieta," *EL* 82 (1968) 315–34.

"Night prayer is the last prayer of the day, said before retiring, even if that is after midnight."[58] Night Prayer, or Compline, used to begin with a short reading, thus recalling its monastic origin in the reading for which the monks gathered in the cloister after the evening meal. It was understandable that the reform of 1971 should eliminate this vestigial organ.

Compline now begins, as do the other Hours, with the verse "God, come to my assistance . . ." and the *Gloria Patri.* In the Roman breviary the initial short reading used to be followed by the *Confiteor;* after the

---

57. *GILH* 78–83.
58. *GILH* 84.

beginning of this Hour in the reformed office "it is a laudable practice to have next an examination of conscience; in a celebration in common this takes place in silence or as part of a penitential rite based on the formularies in the Roman Missal."[59] Next comes an appropriate hymn and the psalms. After First Vespers for Sunday the psalms are 4 and 134, and after Second Vespers, 91; all three are traditional in this context, especially Ps 91, which St. Basil prescribed long ago. On the other days of the week the same psalms may be used, especially if one wishes to recite Night Prayer from memory, but other psalms are also provided which chiefly express trust in God.

After the psalms there is a short reading which in turn is followed by the beautiful and traditional Roman responsory: "Into your hands, Lord . . . ." The gospel canticle *Nunc dimittis* with its antiphon is now said "as a climax to the whole hour," followed by the appropriate final prayer and the blessing *Noctem quietam* ("May the all-powerful Lord grant us a restful night and a peaceful death. Amen").[60]

The Cistercians popularized the custom of greeting the Blessed Virgin at the end of Compline; for this purpose they sang each day the *Salve Regina* ("Hail, holy Queen"), which was the work either of Adhémar, bishop of Puy in Velay (end of the eleventh century), or of Herimannus Contractus († 1054), a monk of Reichenau. In the thirteenth century this practice was widely adopted: the breviary of the Roman Curia added the *Regina caeli* ("Queen of heaven rejoice"—which in the twelfth century was already being sung at Easter Vespers in the Basilica of St. Peter), the *Alma Redemptoris* ("Loving mother of the Redeemer"), and the *Ave Regina caelorum* ("Hail, Queen of angels"). In France the antiphon *Inviolata* was often sung. The *Liturgia Horarum* of 1971 added the *Sub tuum* ("In the shelter of your mercy"), an ancient antiphon that has always been popular. But the episcopal conferences can approve other antiphons as well.[61]

---

59. *GILH* 86.
60. *GILH* 89-91.
61. *GILH* 92. — On the Marian antiphons see especially M. Righetti, *Manuale di storia liturgica* 2 (2nd ed.; Milan: Ancora, 1955) 629-32 (with bibliography). See also above, "Prayers Addressed to Mary," pp. 142-143.

Conclusion

Spiritual Conditions Needed
for the Celebration of the Hours

BIBLIOGRAPHY

Paul VI, Apostolic Constitution *Laudis canticum* (November 1, 1970). Translated at the beginning of *The Liturgy of the Hours*, Volume 1.
GILH 19, 105–8, 201–3, and *passim*.
A. M. Roguet, *The Liturgy of the Hours. The General Instruction on the Liturgy of the Hours with a Commentary*, trans. Peter Coughlan and Peter Purdue (Collegeville: The Liturgical Press, 1971) 126–41.
J. Leclercq, "L'ascèse de la prière," *Seminarium* 24 (1972) 13–23.
M. Magrassi, "La spiritualità dell'Ufficio divino," in *Liturgia delle Ore. Documenti ufficiali e studi* (Quaderni di Rivista liturgica 14; Turin-Leumann: ElleDiCi, 1972) 363–404.
Soeur Marie du Saint-Esprit, "Prière personnelle, prière commune, prière de l'Eglise," *LMD* no. 135 (1978) 9–24.

When seen as part of this long history of the Liturgy of the Hours, the reform of 1971 evidently had for its purpose not to make Christians pray less but, on the contrary, to make the entire people of God pray better. As Paul VI wrote in his Apostolic Constitution *Laudis canticum*, "it is supremely to be hoped that the [now reformed] Liturgy of the Hours may pervade and permeate the whole of Christian prayer, giving it life, direction and expression and effectively nourishing the spiritual life of the people of God."

What the celebration of this liturgy requires more than anything else, therefore, is an effort at interiorization: the important thing is not the quantity of the prayer but its quality. The prayer of the hours must become personal prayer. The conciliar Constitution on the liturgy and the *General Instruction* several times repeat St. Benedict's watchword: "Mind and voice must be in harmony."

If this effort is to succeed, the celebration, whether public or private, must be peaceful and uncomplicated, and at certain moments during it there must be the "sacred silence" that allows the participants to meditate on and taste what has been read, sung, or recited.[1] Furthermore, while our daily tasks and concerns have some place in our prayer (the liturgy allows for their expression, especially in the intercessions), the office requires that there be a break with our routines, a pulling back, a recollection or gathering up of ourselves.

On the other hand, the concern for spontaneity and sincerity that is a distinguishing mark of our age seems at times to be accompanied by the tendency to oppose personal prayer, in which Christians express themselves as they are and in their everyday milieu, and the Liturgy of the Hours, which they regard as something presented to them ready-made because of its biblical content and its structure inherited from long centuries of ecclesial life. Would they not prefer to use the book of the Liturgy of the Hours simply as a collection of material from which they can derive elements for their own prayer as suggested to them by their state of soul at any given moment?

Christians must therefore come to understand in a concrete way the true nature of all liturgy and realize that it requires them to move beyond themselves in three ways.

a) The Liturgy of the Hours obliges them, first of all, to rise above personal taste and make their own the prayer of the Church. Even when they celebrate this liturgy by themselves, it remains the voice of the Church, the *Catholica*: "Everyone shares in this prayer, which is proper to the one body as it offers prayers that give expression to the voice of the beloved spouse of Christ, to the hopes and desires of the whole Christian people, to supplications and petitions for the needs of all mankind" (*Laudis canticum*). The *General Instruction* allows a certain flexibility in order to make it easier to adapt to this prayer and to bring into it certain important events or moments in the life of communities and individuals.[2] Nonetheless, the basic attitude of Christians who celebrate the Liturgy of the Hours must be a desire to be one in heart and soul with all of their brothers and sisters, scattered though these may be, and to receive each day the ever-new spiritual message the Spirit is communicating to them through the prayer of the Church.

b) We have seen throughout this study that the Liturgy of the Hours is a prayer of constant meditation on the economy of salvation. This historical dimension means that we cannot limit our vision to the present moment. Those who pray with the Church must open themselves to

---

1. *GILH* 201–3.
2. *GILH* 241–52.

contemplation of the deeds God accomplished in his people of the old covenant; they must repeatedly travel for themselves the road followed by Jesus Christ from Christmas to Easter; with the Apostles and saints they must even relive all the ages of Church history.

> These liturgical actions are part of the history of the Church: they bring about a deeper and deeper penetration of human history by the mystery of Christ. Christ is not just a figure from the past, the historical founder of the Church and the person who instituted the sacraments; nor is it sufficient to say that he is with us, accompanying us and sustaining us on our journey: he stands at the end of our journey; he calls us and draws us to him, he is our hope and our future.[3]

c) The history of salvation is, of course, filled with the struggles of God's people, their sufferings, their cries for help; and in its prayer the Church constantly asks God to grant us his light and strength and his vision of the "land of the living." Nonetheless the prayer of the hours is first and foremost a prayer of praise and thanksgiving, a prayer of spontaneous wonder at the greatness of God, his work of creation, his mercy, his providential care. For this reason, "to the different hours of the day the liturgy of the hours extends the praise and thanksgiving, the memorial of the mysteries of salvation, the petitions and the foretaste of heavenly glory that are present in the eucharistic mystery, 'the center and high point in the whole life of the Christian community.' "[4]

---

3. A. M. Roguet, *The Liturgy of the Hours. The General Instruction on the Liturgy of the Hours with a Commentary,* trans. Peter Coughlan and Peter Purdue (Collegeville: The Liturgical Press, 1971) 89.

4. *GILH* 12. — *GILH* 93–99 shows how in particular cases the Mass may be organically linked with one or other Hour of the office.

Index

The following pages list the people, places, and events about which a pertinent statement is made in this book. By no means should this index be considered a complete listing of the scores of people, places, and events recorded in this book.